Shojo Beat

BABY & Me

Vol. 12

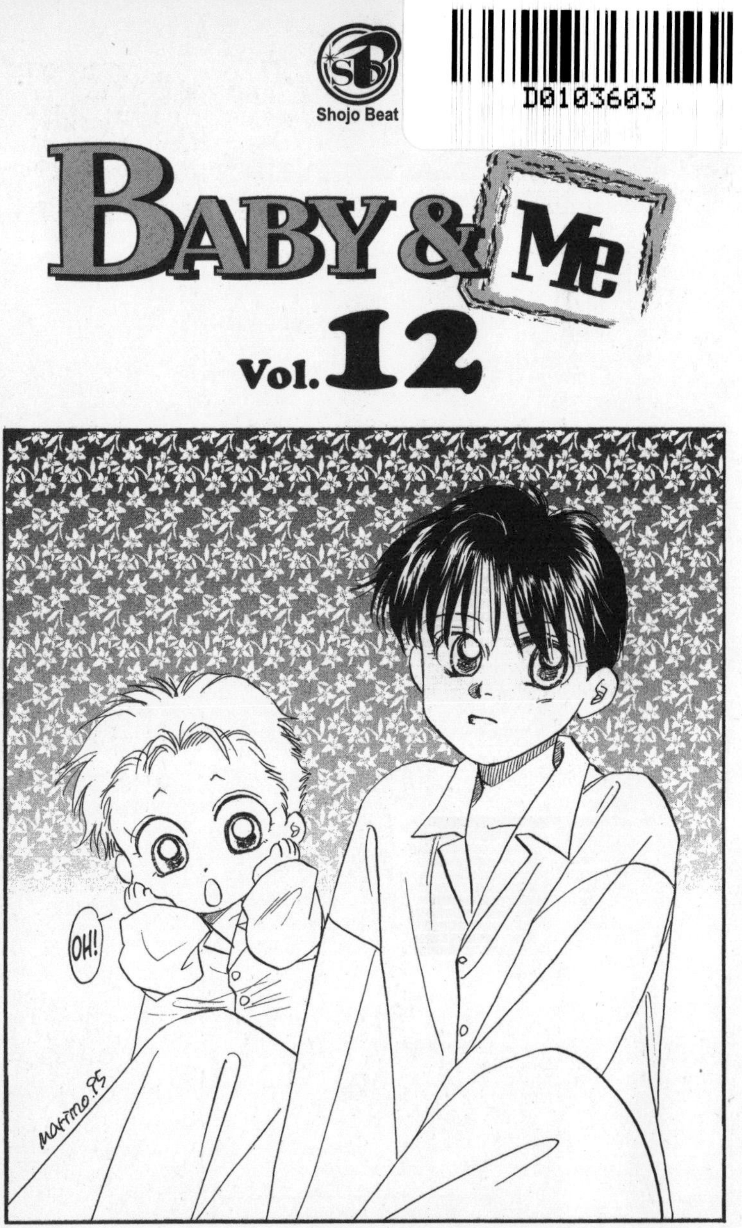
OH!

Story & Art by Marimo Ragawa

BABY & ME, Vol. 12
The Shojo Beat Manga Edition

STORY & ART BY
MARIMO RAGAWA

English Adaptation/Lance Caselman
Translation/JN Productions
Touch-up Art & Lettering/Vanessa Satone
Design/Yuki Ameda
Editor/Shaenon K. Garrity

Editor in Chief, Books/Alvin Lu
Editor in Chief, Magazines/Marc Weidenbaum
VP, Publishing Licensing/Rika Inouye
VP, Sales & Product Marketing/Gonzalo Ferreyra
VP, Creative/Linda Espinosa
Publisher/Hyoe Narita

Printed in Canada

Published by VIZ Media, LLC
P.O. Box 77010
San Francisco, CA 94107

Shojo Beat Manga Edition
10 9 8 7 6 5 4 3 2 1
First printing, February 2009

PARENTAL ADVISORY
BABY & ME is rated T for Teen and is recommended for ages 13 and up. This volume contains adult situations.
ratings.viz.com

store.viz.com

Creator: Marimo Ragawa

SBM Title: *Baby & Me*

Date of Birth: September 21

Blood Type: B

Major Works: *Time Limit,
Baby & Me, N.Y. N.Y.,* and
Shanimuni-Go (Desperately—Go)

Marimo Ragawa first started submitting manga to a comic magazine when she was 12 years old. She kept up her submissions for four years, but to no avail. She decided to submit her work to the magazine *Hana to Yume*, where she received Top Prize in the Monthly Manga Contest as well as an honorable mention (Kasaku) in the magazine's Big Challenge contest. Her first manga was titled *Time Limit*. *Baby & Me* was honored with a Shogakukan Manga Award in 1995 and was spun off into an anime.

Ragawa's work showcases some very cute and expressive line work along with an incredible ability to depict complex emotions and relationships. Some of her other works include *N.Y. N.Y.* and the tennis manga *Shanimuni-Go*.

Ragawa has two brothers and two sisters.

BABY & ME Table of Contents

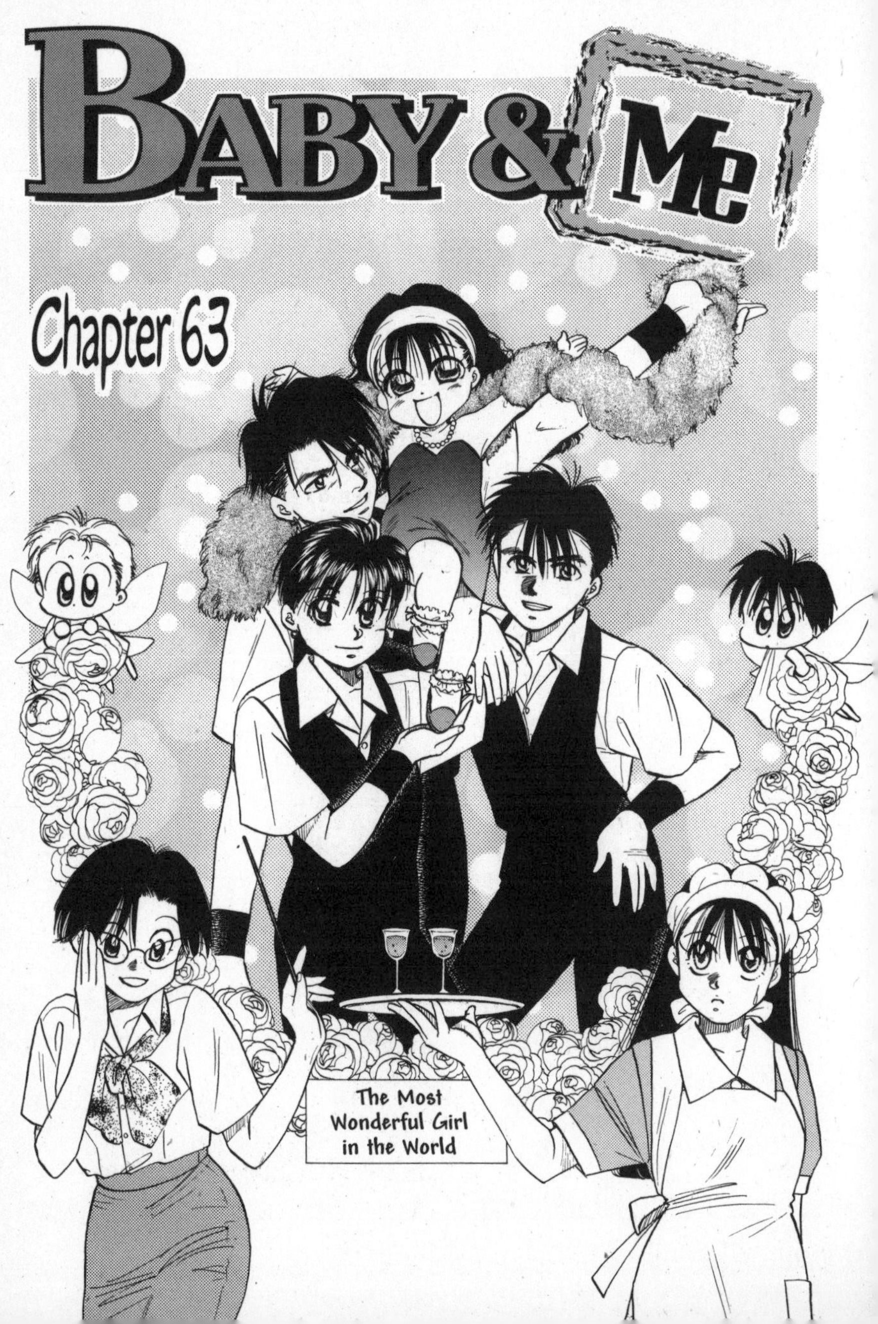
BABY & ME
Chapter 63
The Most Wonderful Girl in the World

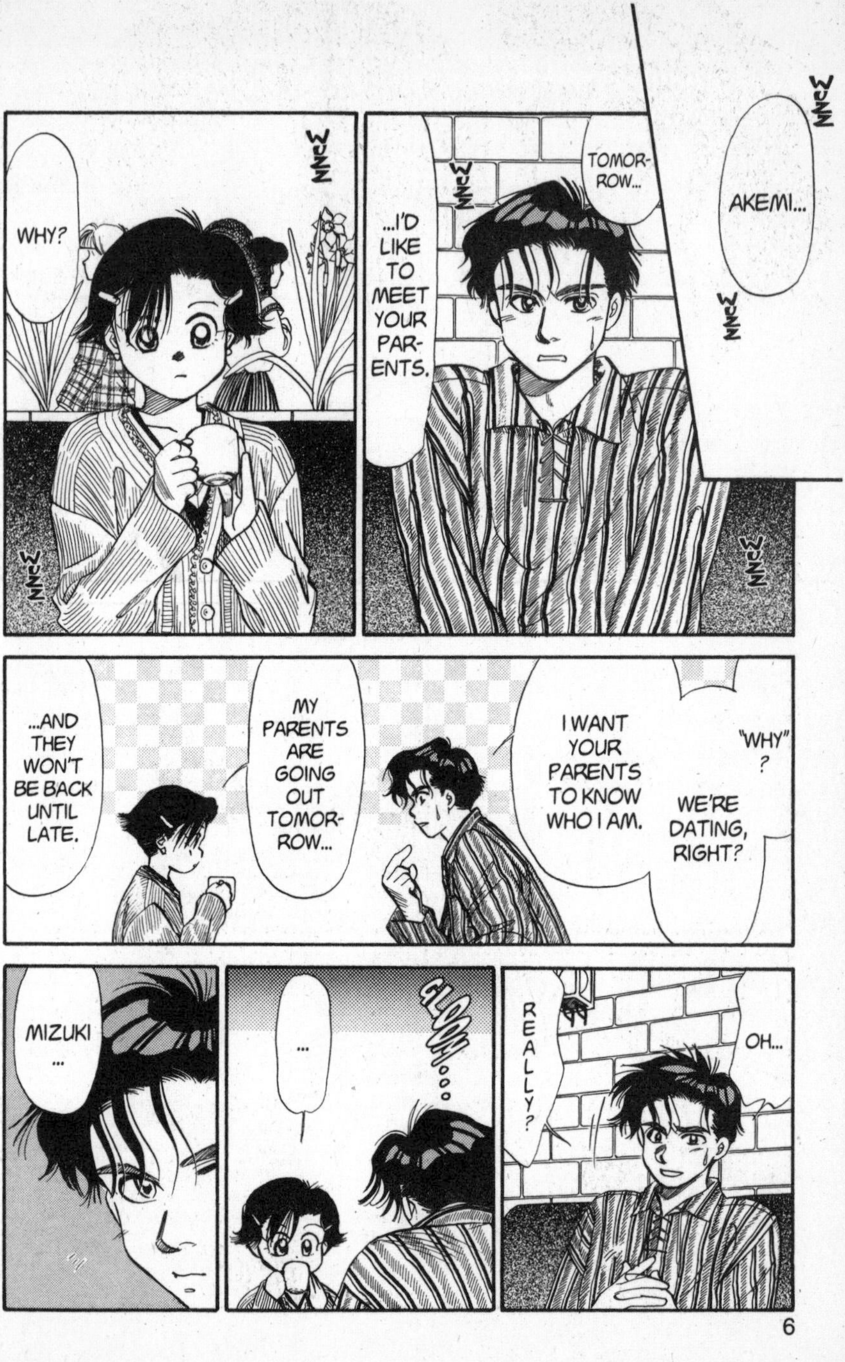
WUZN
AKEMI...
WUZN
TOMOR-ROW...
WUZN
...I'D LIKE TO MEET YOUR PAR-ENTS.
WUZN
WUZN
WHY?
WUZN
"WHY"?
WE'RE DATING, RIGHT?
I WANT YOUR PARENTS TO KNOW WHO I AM.
MY PARENTS ARE GOING OUT TOMOR-ROW...
...AND THEY WON'T BE BACK UNTIL LATE.
OH...
REALLY?
GLOOM ooo
...
MIZUKI ...

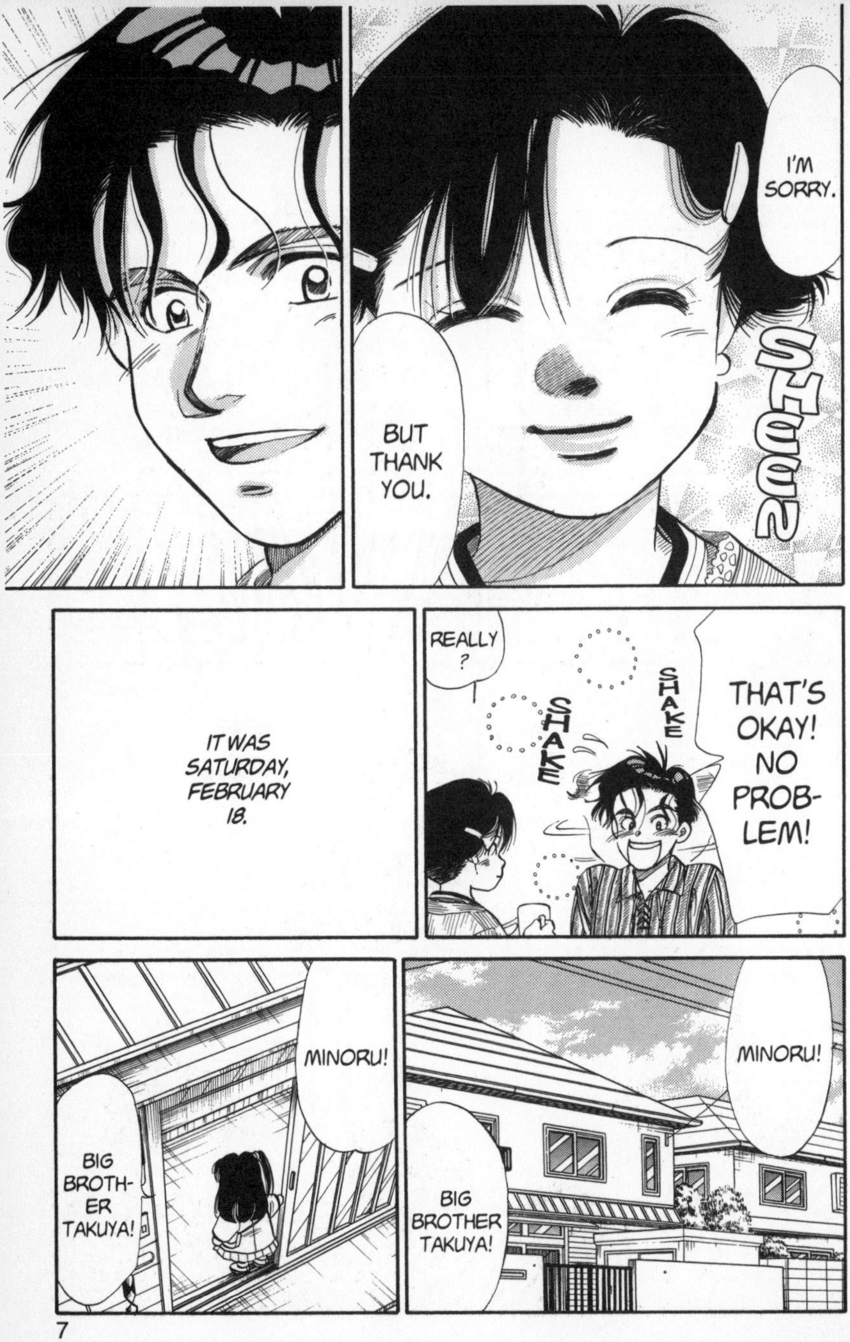
I'M SORRY.
SHEEN
BUT THANK YOU.
THAT'S OKAY! NO PROB-LEM!
SHAKE
SHAKE
REALLY?
IT WAS SATURDAY, FEBRUARY 18.
MINORU!
BIG BROTHER TAKUYA!
MINORU!
BIG BROTH-ER TAKUYA!

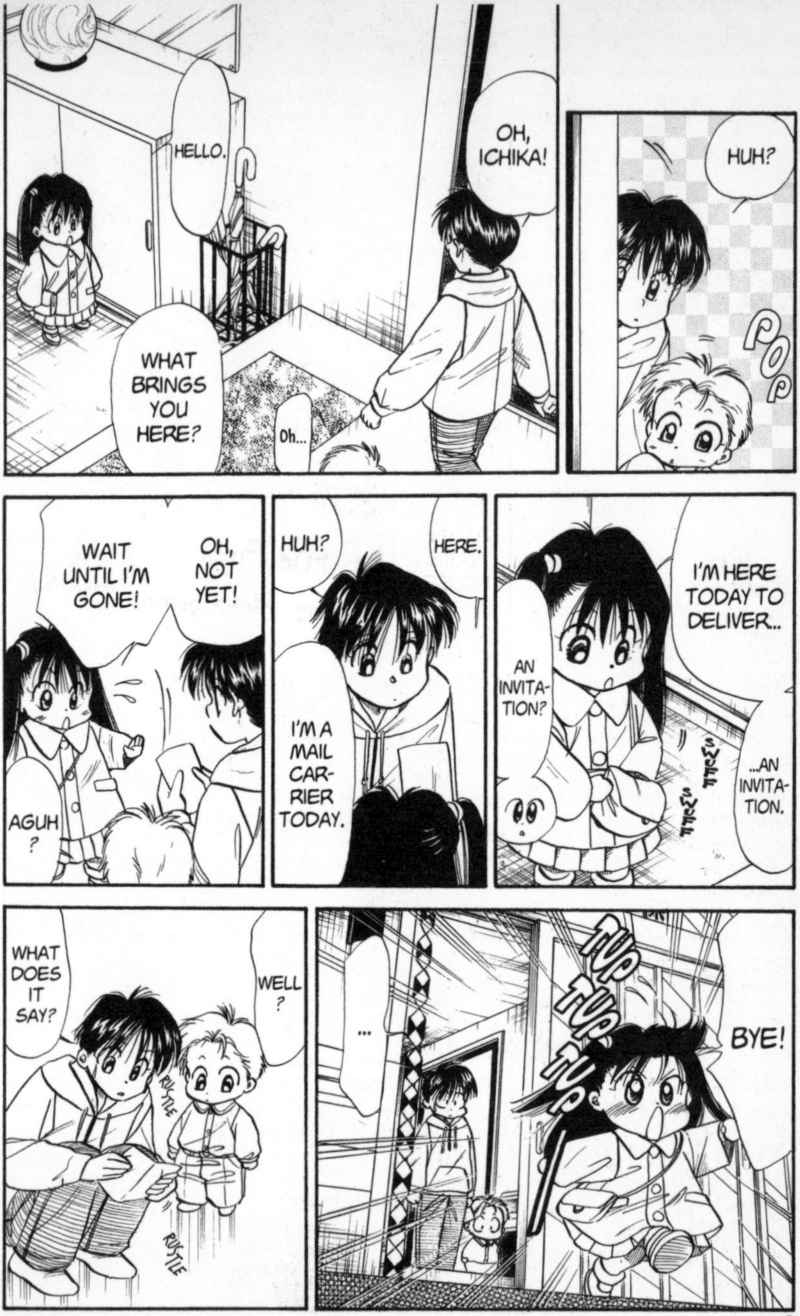
HUH?
POP
OH, ICHIKA!
HELLO.
WHAT BRINGS YOU HERE?
Oh...
I'M HERE TODAY TO DELIVER...
AN INVITATION?
SWUFF
SWUFF
...AN INVITATION.
HERE.
HUH?
I'M A MAIL CARRIER TODAY.
OH, NOT YET!
WAIT UNTIL I'M GONE!
AGUH?
BYE!
TUP TUP TUP TUP
...
WELL?
WHAT DOES IT SAY?
RUSTLE
RUSTLE

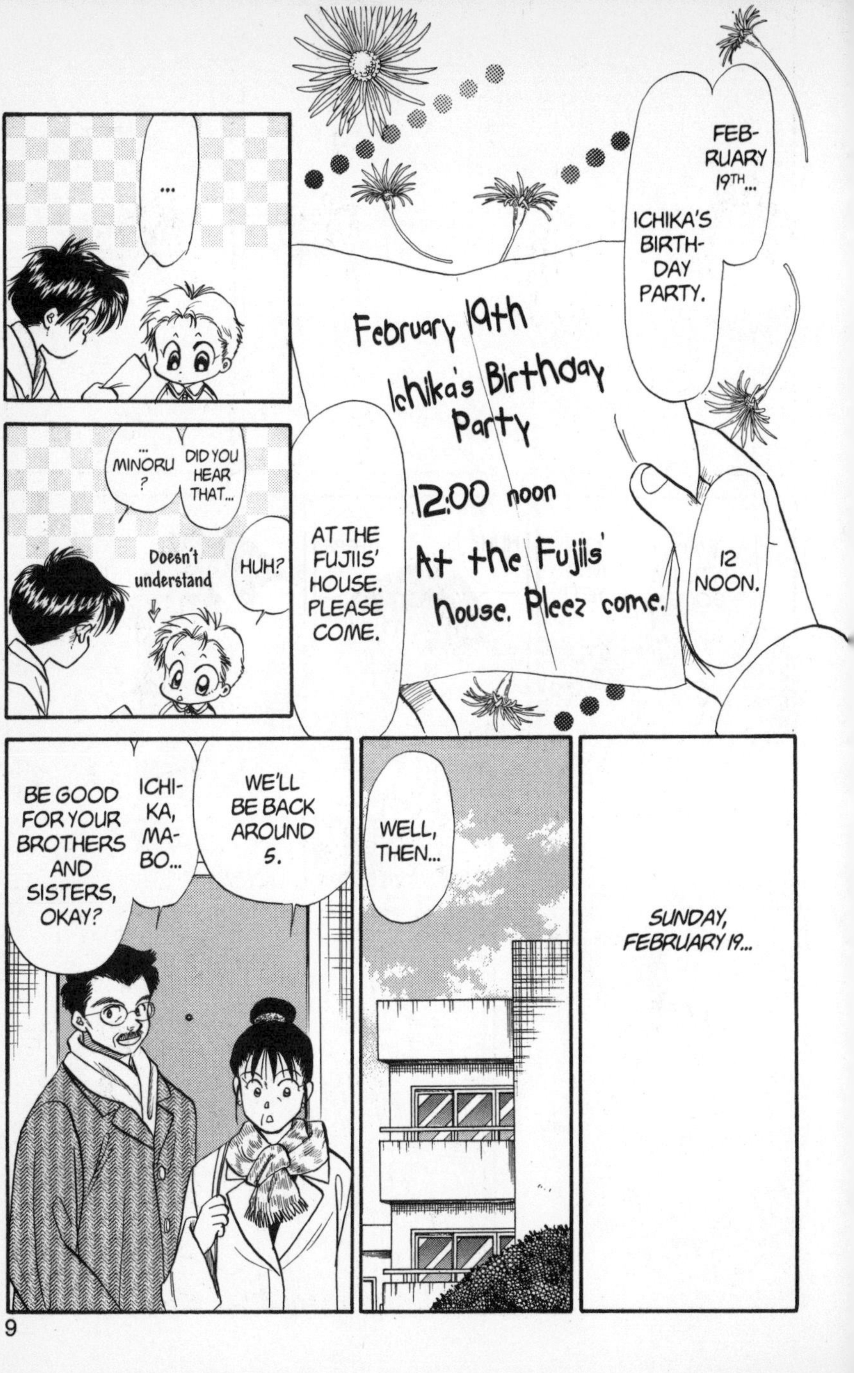
FEBRUARY 19TH...
ICHIKA'S BIRTHDAY PARTY.
February 19th
Ichika's Birthday Party
12:00 noon
At the Fujiis' house. Pleez come.
12 NOON.
AT THE FUJIIS' HOUSE. PLEASE COME.
...
DID YOU HEAR THAT...
... MINORU ?
HUH?
Doesn't understand
SUNDAY, FEBRUARY 19...
WELL, THEN...
WE'LL BE BACK AROUND 5.
ICHIKA, MABO...
BE GOOD FOR YOUR BROTHERS AND SISTERS, OKAY?

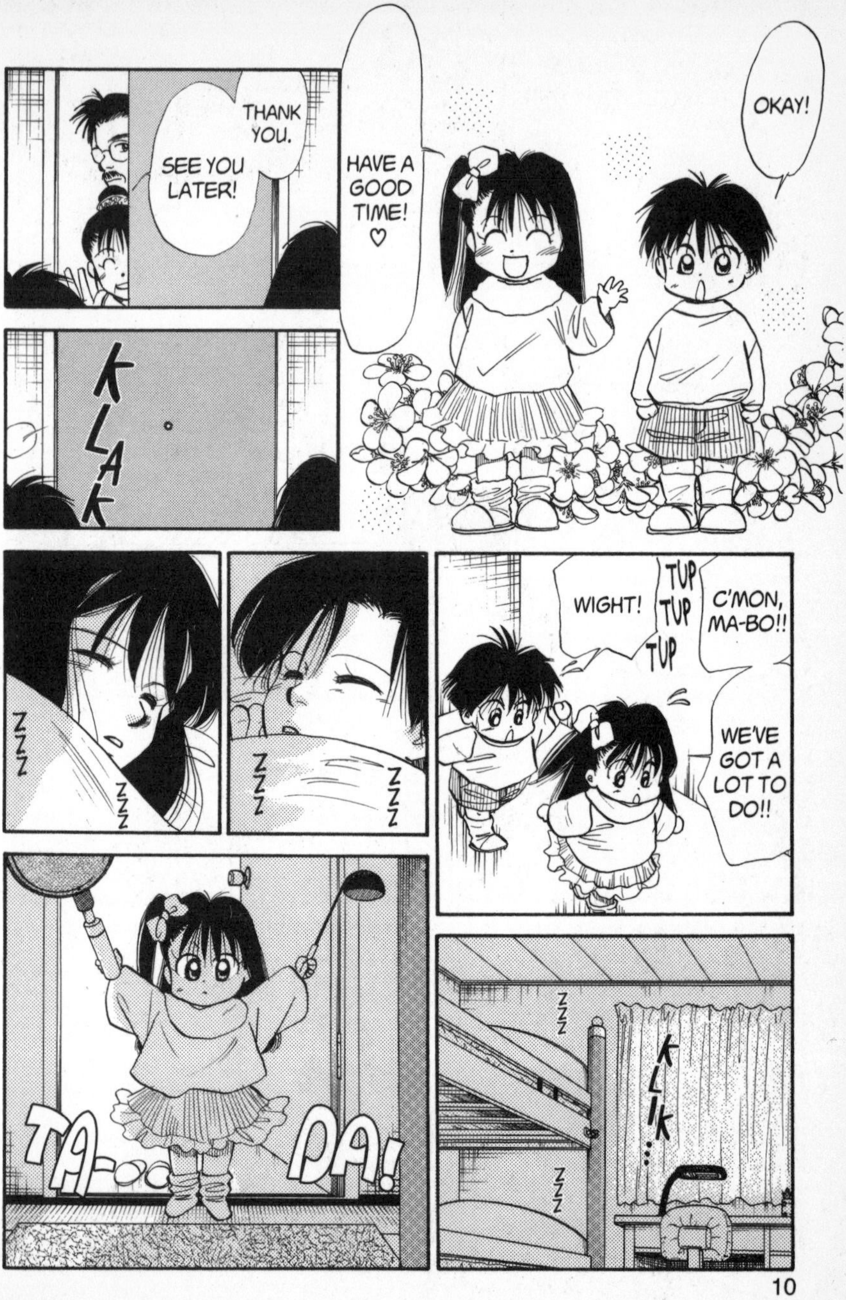

OKAY!
HAVE A GOOD TIME! ♡
THANK YOU.
SEE YOU LATER!
KLAK
C'MON, MA-BO!!
TUP TUP TUP
WIGHT!
WE'VE GOT A LOT TO DO!!
ZZZ
ZZZ
ZZZ
ZZZ
ZZZ
KLIK...
ZZZ
TA-DA!

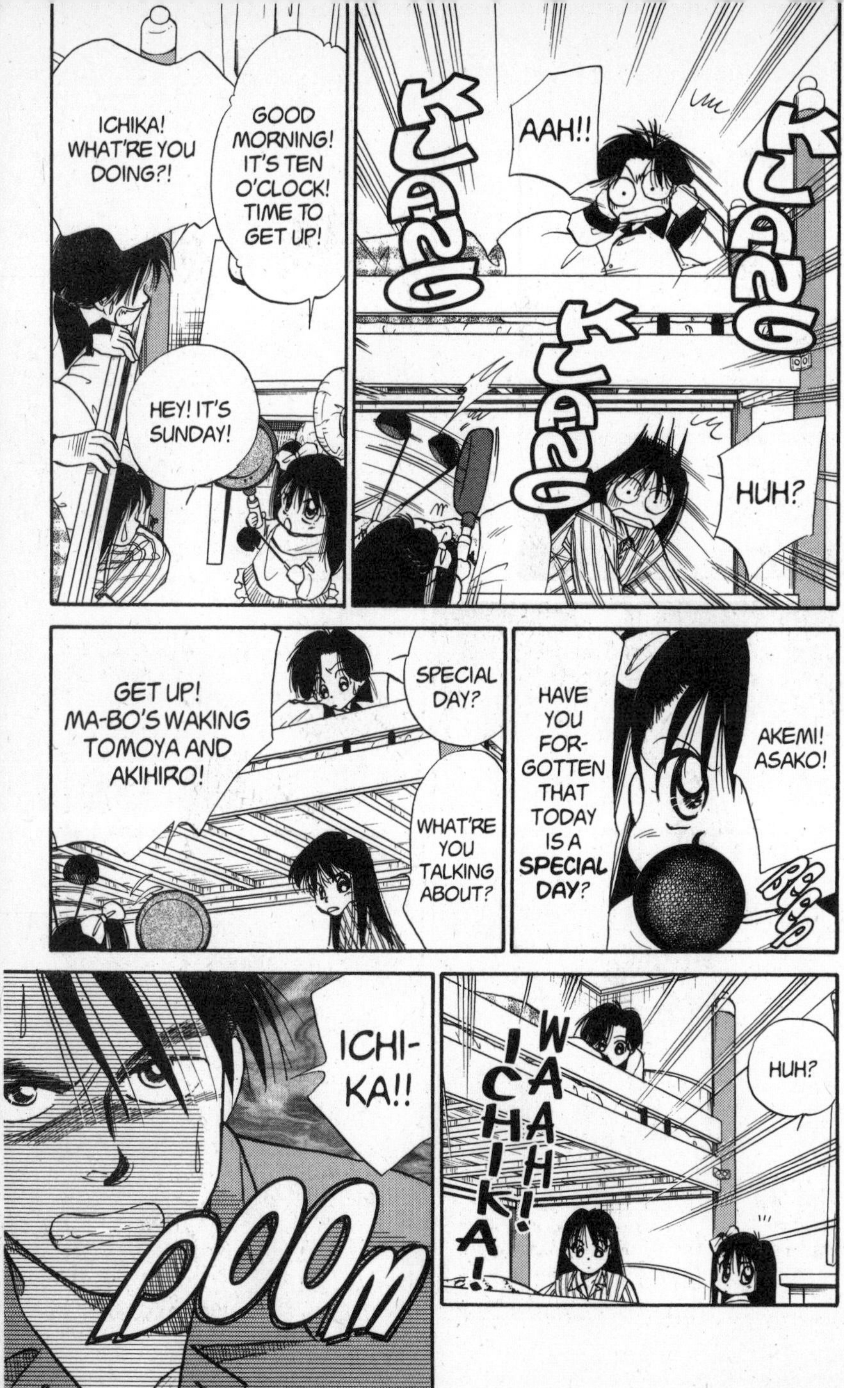
KLANG
AAH!!
KLANG
KLANG
HUH?
GOOD MORNING! IT'S TEN O'CLOCK! TIME TO GET UP!
ICHIKA! WHAT'RE YOU DOING?!
HEY! IT'S SUNDAY!
AKEMI! ASAKO!
HAVE YOU FOR-GOTTEN THAT TODAY IS A SPECIAL DAY?
SPECIAL DAY?
WHAT'RE YOU TALKING ABOUT?
GET UP! MA-BO'S WAKING TOMOYA AND AKIHIRO!
HUH?
WAAH!
ICHIKA!
ICHI-KA!!
DOOM

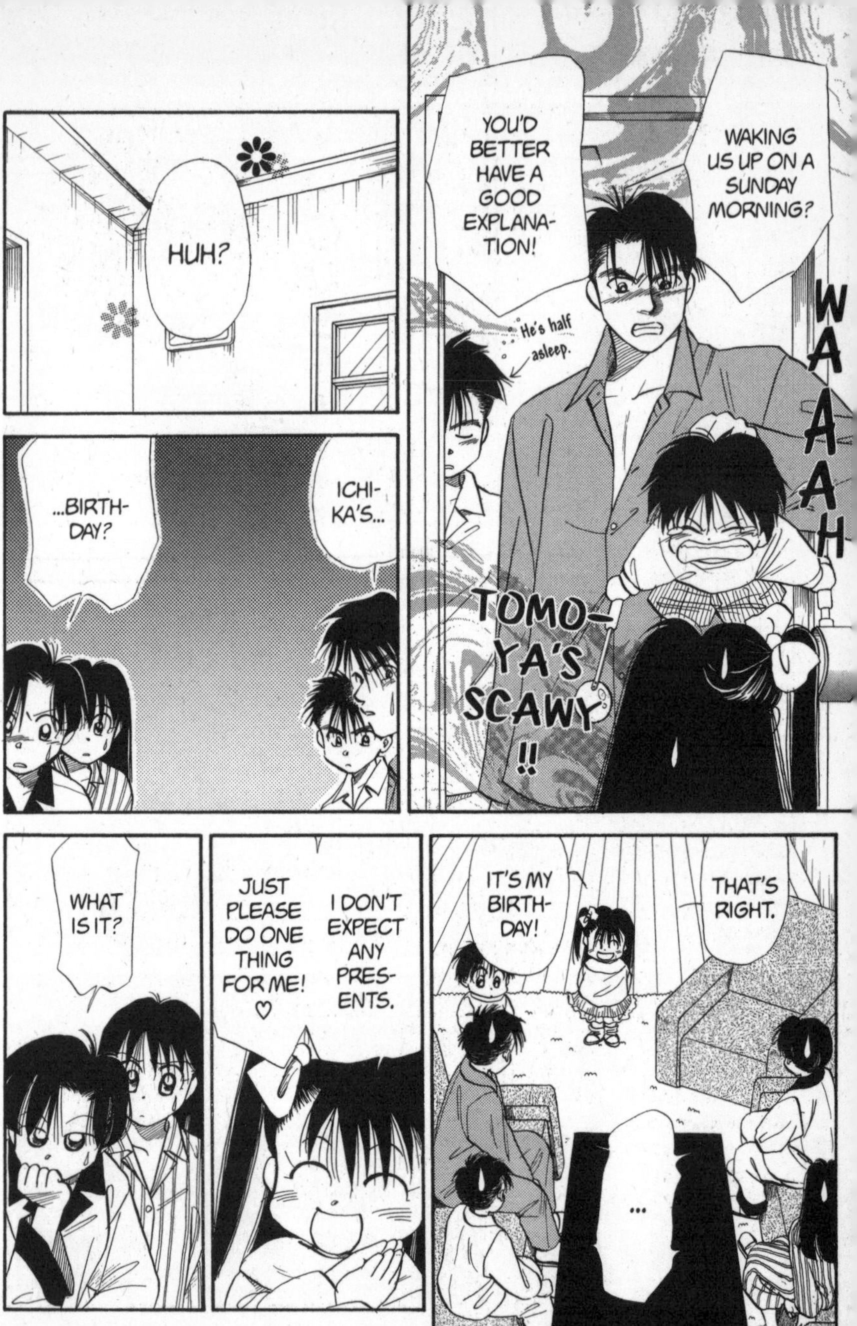
WAKING US UP ON A SUNDAY MORNING?
YOU'D BETTER HAVE A GOOD EXPLANATION!
WAAAAH
He's half asleep.
TOMOYA'S SCAWY!!
HUH?
ICHIKA'S...
...BIRTHDAY?
THAT'S RIGHT.
IT'S MY BIRTHDAY!
...
I DON'T EXPECT ANY PRESENTS.
JUST PLEASE DO ONE THING FOR ME! ♡
WHAT IS IT?

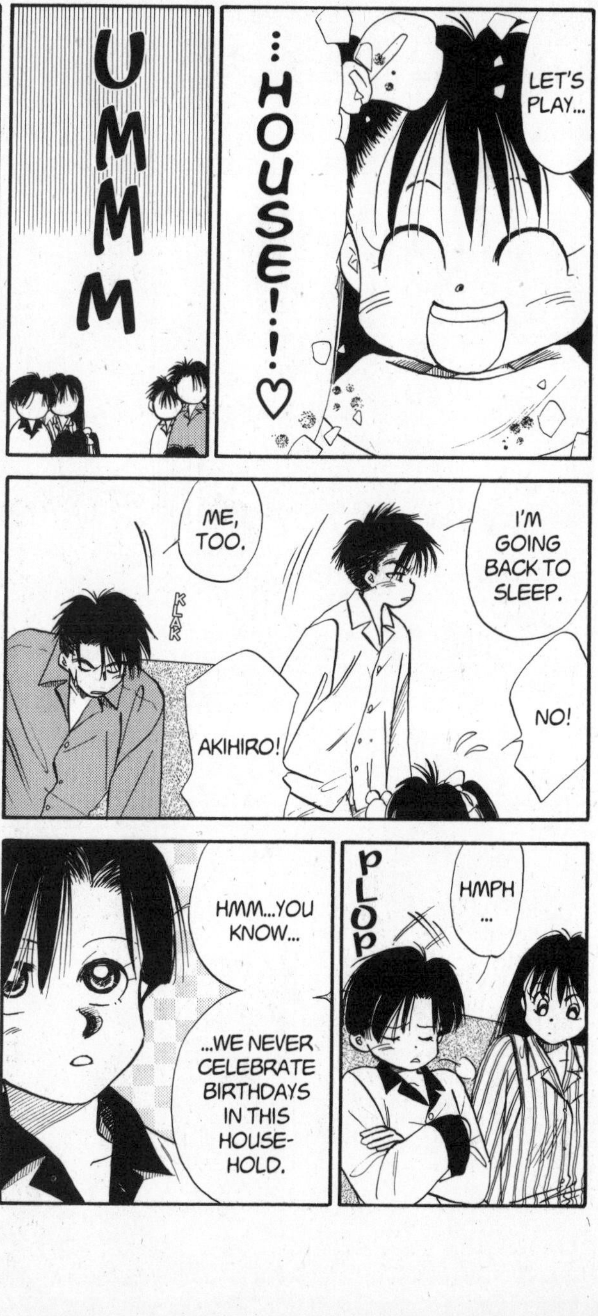
LET'S PLAY...
...HOUSE!! ♥
UMMM
I'M GOING BACK TO SLEEP.
ME, TOO.
NO!
KLAK
AKIHIRO!
PLOP
HMPH...
HMM...YOU KNOW...
...WE NEVER CELEBRATE BIRTHDAYS IN THIS HOUSE-HOLD.

Author's Note Part 1

How are you? Ragawa here.

This is volume 12 of Baby & Me!

Oh, I hate it. I'm writing this at 6:00 A.M. I just finished coloring the front page and drawing the title page illustration. I need to get this note and "Marimo Ragawa's Let Me Draw What I Want" done today because my editor is coming over tonight to pick up the manuscript! Aah! And I have to go see a doctor in the morning too. But I guess complaining won't help.

Last time, when I wrote about cocktails, I mentioned this thing that looks like a straw that they stick in the glass, and how you can suck it or scoop your drink with it. The other day, my sister told me that it lets air in and makes it easier to drink your cocktail. I don't care. I still enjoy drinking my cocktail through it. What's wrong with that?

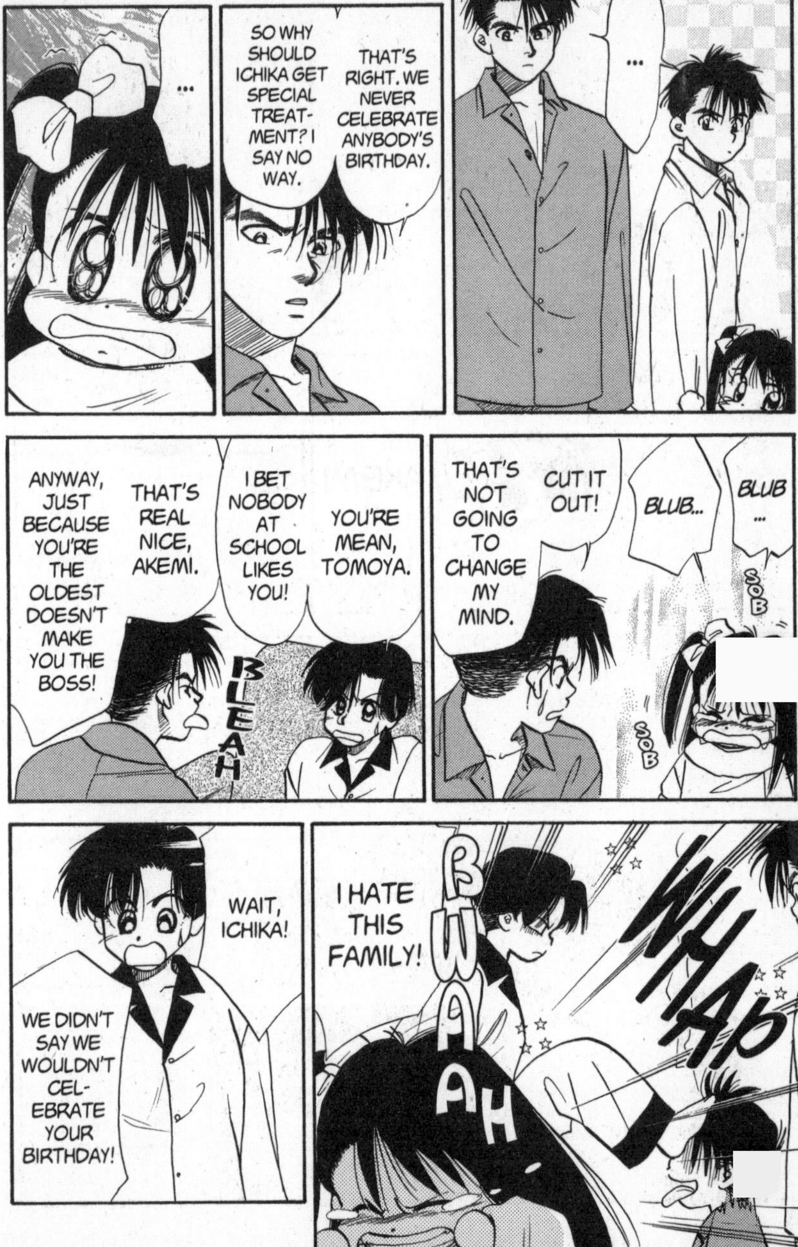
...
THAT'S RIGHT. WE NEVER CELEBRATE ANYBODY'S BIRTHDAY.
SO WHY SHOULD ICHIKA GET SPECIAL TREATMENT? I SAY NO WAY.
...
BLUB ...
BLUB...
SOB
SOB
CUT IT OUT!
THAT'S NOT GOING TO CHANGE MY MIND.
YOU'RE MEAN, TOMOYA.
I BET NOBODY AT SCHOOL LIKES YOU!
THAT'S REAL NICE, AKEMI.
ANYWAY, JUST BECAUSE YOU'RE THE OLDEST DOESN'T MAKE YOU THE BOSS!
BLEAH
WHAP
BWAAAH
I HATE THIS FAMILY!
WAIT, ICHIKA!
WE DIDN'T SAY WE WOULDN'T CEL-EBRATE YOUR BIRTHDAY!

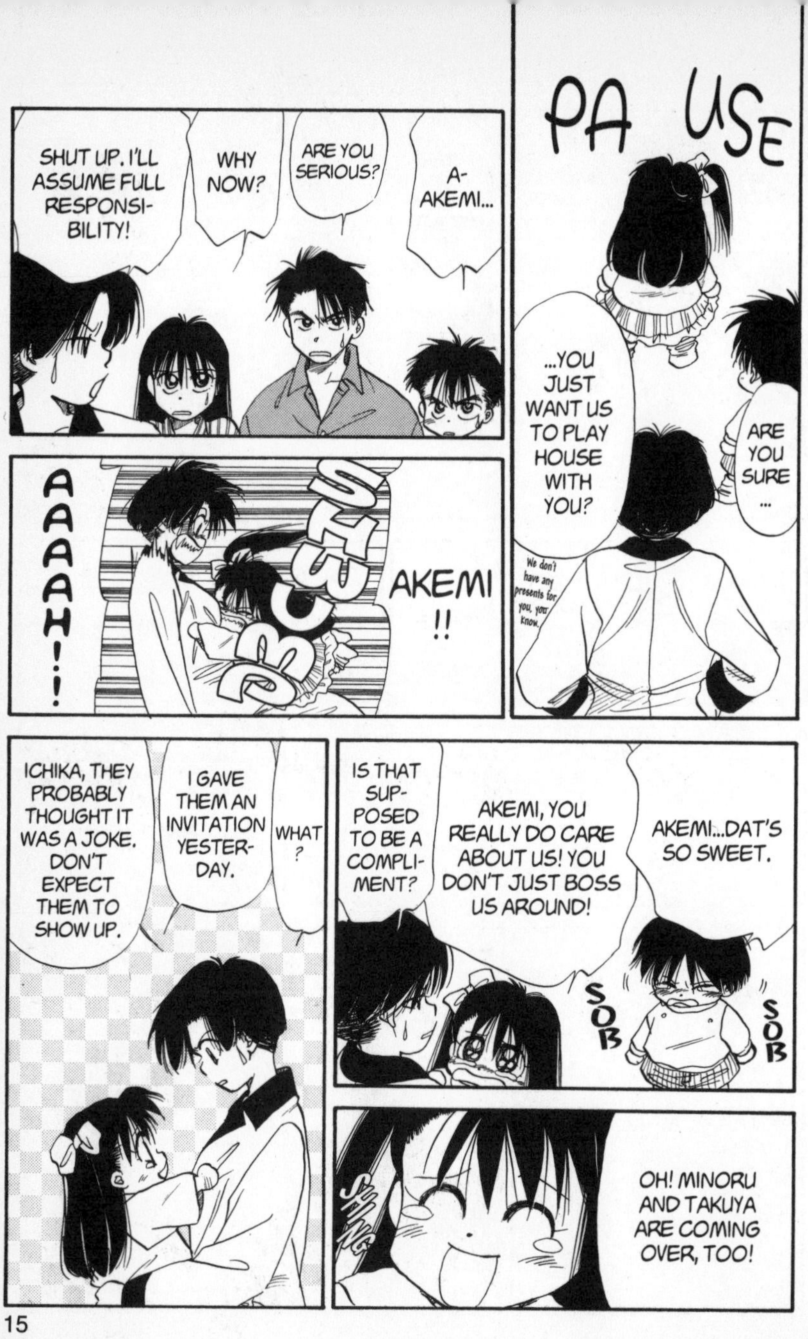
PAUSE
ARE YOU SURE...
...YOU JUST WANT US TO PLAY HOUSE WITH YOU?
We don't have any presents for you, you know.
A- AKEMI...
ARE YOU SERIOUS?
WHY NOW?
SHUT UP. I'LL ASSUME FULL RESPONSIBILITY!
AKEMI!!
SHWUMP
AAAAH!!
AKEMI...DAT'S SO SWEET.
SOB SOB
AKEMI, YOU REALLY DO CARE ABOUT US! YOU DON'T JUST BOSS US AROUND!
IS THAT SUPPOSED TO BE A COMPLIMENT?
OH! MINORU AND TAKUYA ARE COMING OVER, TOO!
SHING
WHAT?
I GAVE THEM AN INVITATION YESTERDAY.
ICHIKA, THEY PROBABLY THOUGHT IT WAS A JOKE. DON'T EXPECT THEM TO SHOW UP.

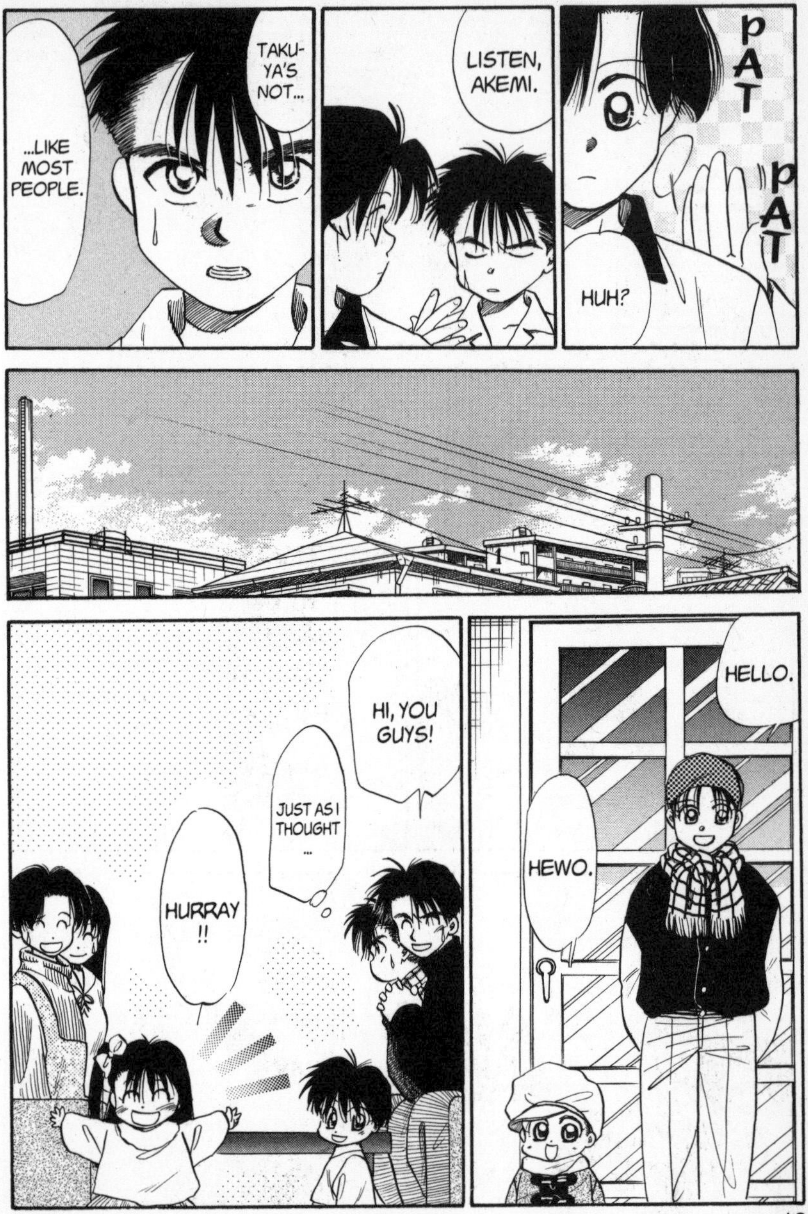
pAT pAT
HUH?
LISTEN, AKEMI.
TAKU-YA'S NOT...
...LIKE MOST PEOPLE.
HELLO.
HEWO.
HI, YOU GUYS!
JUST AS I THOUGHT ...
HURRAY !!

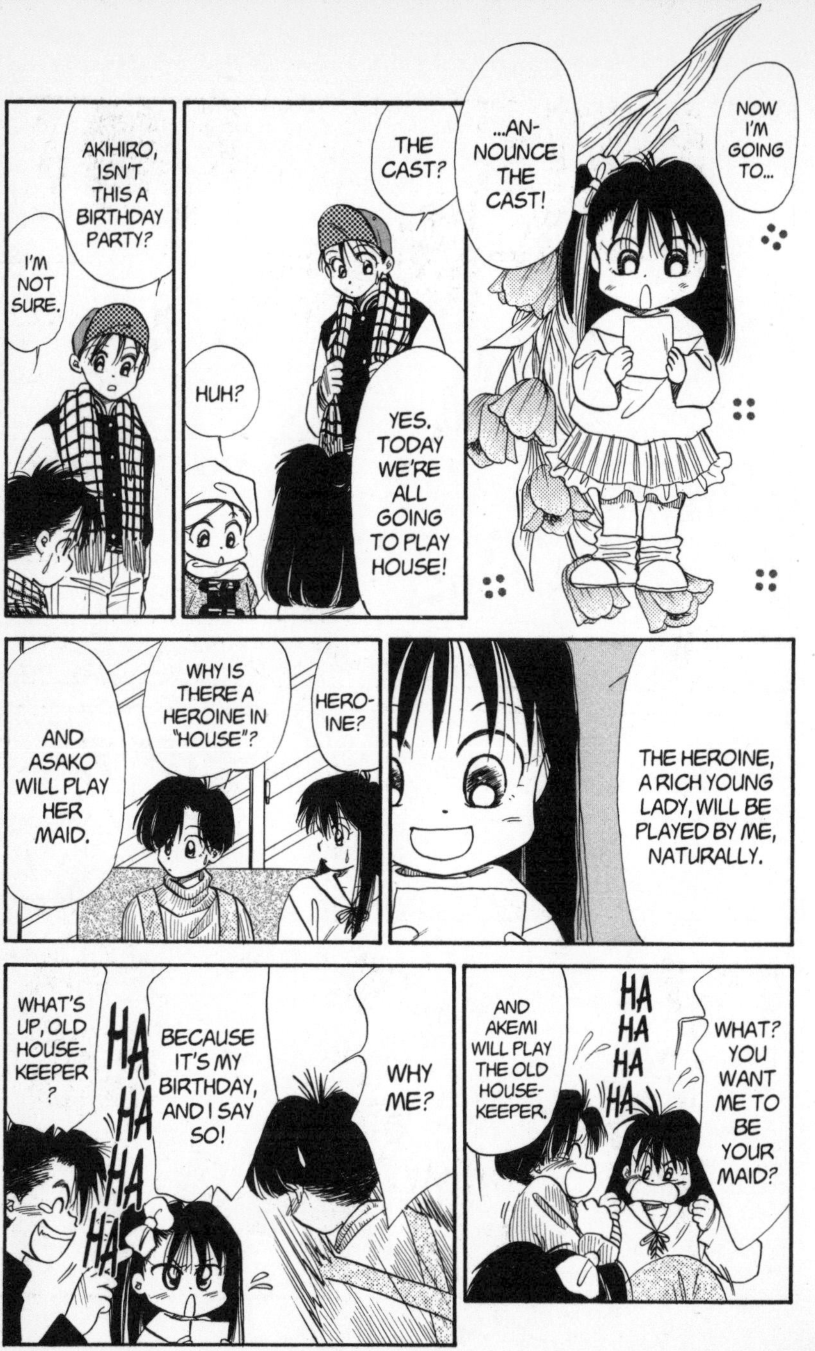
NOW I'M GOING TO...
...AN-NOUNCE THE CAST!
THE CAST?
YES. TODAY WE'RE ALL GOING TO PLAY HOUSE!
HUH?
AKIHIRO, ISN'T THIS A BIRTHDAY PARTY?
I'M NOT SURE.
THE HEROINE, A RICH YOUNG LADY, WILL BE PLAYED BY ME, NATURALLY.
HERO-INE?
WHY IS THERE A HEROINE IN "HOUSE"?
AND ASAKO WILL PLAY HER MAID.
WHAT? YOU WANT ME TO BE YOUR MAID?
HA HA HA HA
AND AKEMI WILL PLAY THE OLD HOUSE-KEEPER.
WHY ME?
BECAUSE IT'S MY BIRTHDAY, AND I SAY SO!
HA HA HA HA HA
WHAT'S UP, OLD HOUSE-KEEPER?

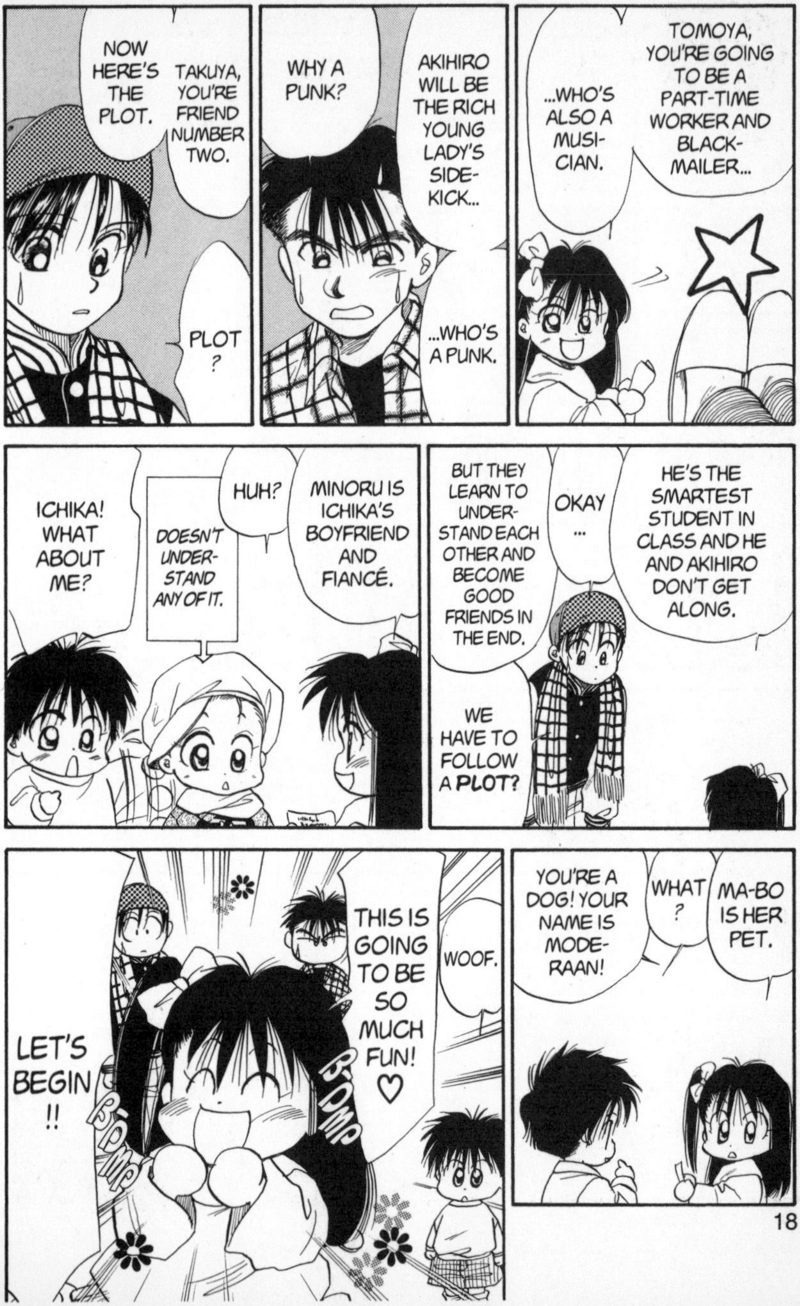
TOMOYA, YOU'RE GOING TO BE A PART-TIME WORKER AND BLACK-MAILER...
...WHO'S ALSO A MUSI-CIAN.
AKIHIRO WILL BE THE RICH YOUNG LADY'S SIDE-KICK...
...WHO'S A PUNK.
WHY A PUNK?
TAKUYA, YOU'RE FRIEND NUMBER TWO.
NOW HERE'S THE PLOT.
PLOT?
HE'S THE SMARTEST STUDENT IN CLASS AND HE AND AKIHIRO DON'T GET ALONG.
OKAY...
BUT THEY LEARN TO UNDER-STAND EACH OTHER AND BECOME GOOD FRIENDS IN THE END.
WE HAVE TO FOLLOW A PLOT?
MINORU IS ICHIKA'S BOYFRIEND AND FIANCÉ.
HUH?
DOESN'T UNDER-STAND ANY OF IT.
ICHIKA! WHAT ABOUT ME?
MA-BO IS HER PET.
WHAT?
YOU'RE A DOG! YOUR NAME IS MODE-RAAN!
THIS IS GOING TO BE SO MUCH FUN! ♡
WOOF.
BOMP
BOMP
BOMP
LET'S BEGIN!!

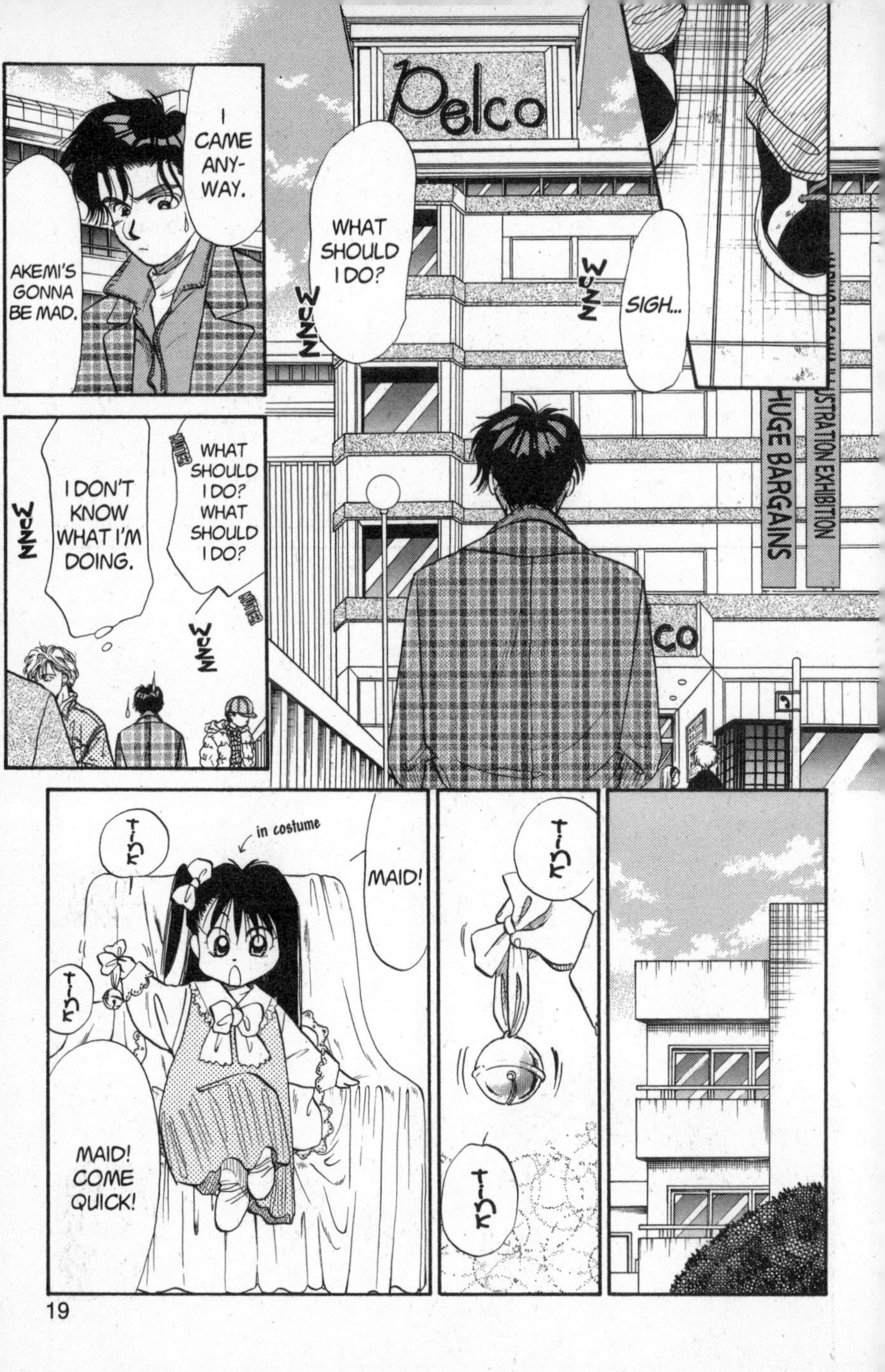
Pelco
SIGH...
WUZZ
WHAT SHOULD I DO?
WUZZ
USTRATION EXHIBITION
HUGE BARGAINS
CO
I CAME ANYWAY.
AKEMI'S GONNA BE MAD.
MUTTER
WHAT SHOULD I DO? WHAT SHOULD I DO?
MUTTER
WUZZ
I DON'T KNOW WHAT I'M DOING.
WUZZ
tink
tink
MAID!
tink
in costume
tink
MAID! COME QUICK!

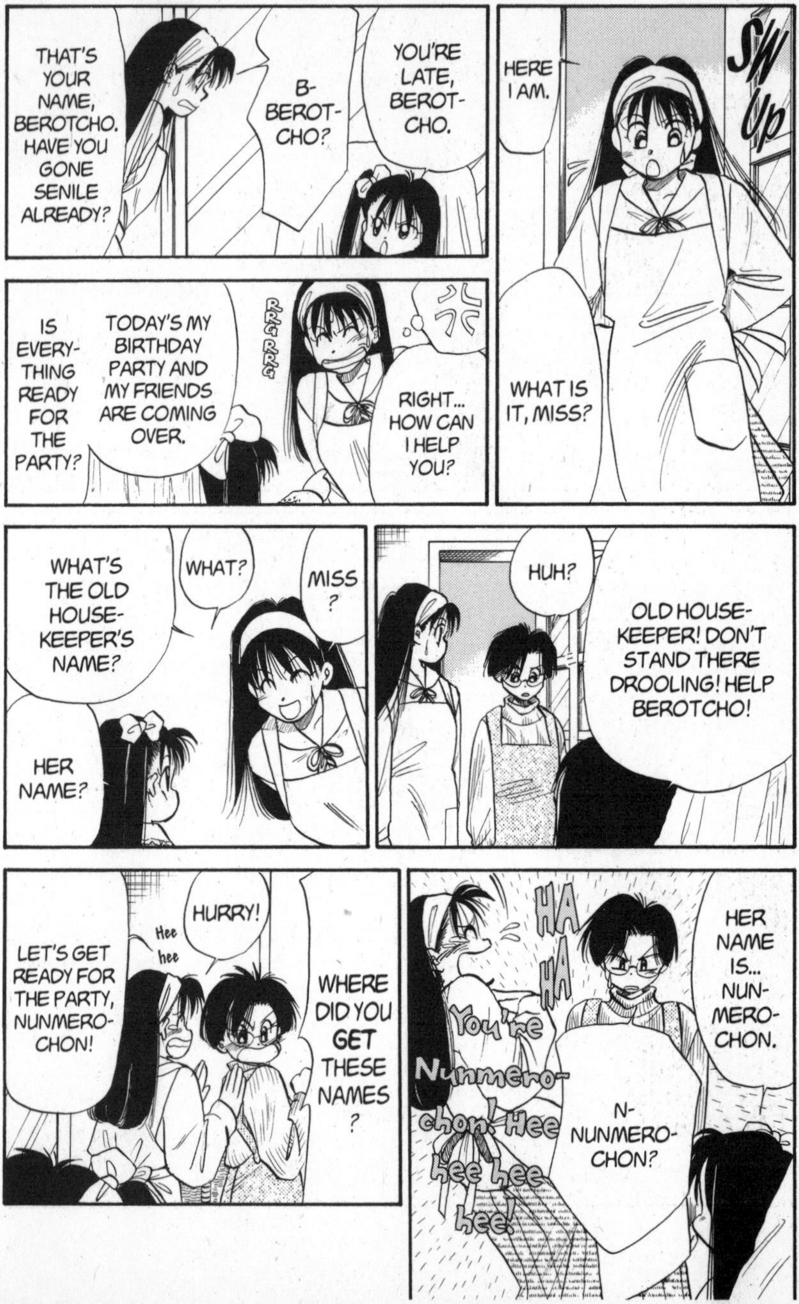
SW Up
HERE I AM.
WHAT IS IT, MISS?
YOU'RE LATE, BEROTCHO.
B-BEROTCHO?
THAT'S YOUR NAME, BEROTCHO. HAVE YOU GONE SENILE ALREADY?
RIGHT... HOW CAN I HELP YOU?
RRG RRG
TODAY'S MY BIRTHDAY PARTY AND MY FRIENDS ARE COMING OVER.
IS EVERYTHING READY FOR THE PARTY?
OLD HOUSEKEEPER! DON'T STAND THERE DROOLING! HELP BEROTCHO!
HUH?
MISS?
WHAT?
WHAT'S THE OLD HOUSEKEEPER'S NAME?
HER NAME?
HER NAME IS... NUNMEROCHON.
HA HA
N-NUNMEROCHON?
You're Nunmerochon! Hee hee hee hee!
WHERE DID YOU GET THESE NAMES?
HURRY!
Hee hee
LET'S GET READY FOR THE PARTY, NUNMEROCHON!

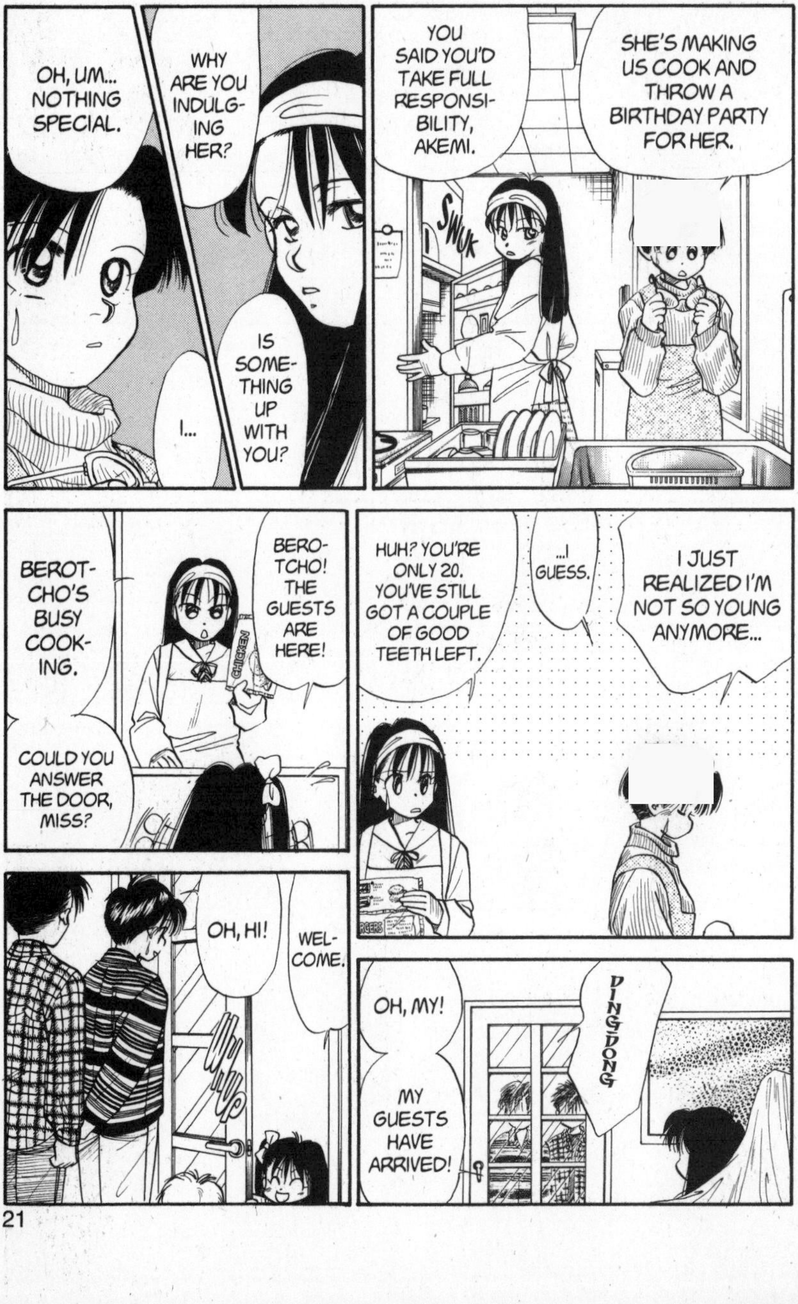

SHE'S MAKING US COOK AND THROW A BIRTHDAY PARTY FOR HER.
YOU SAID YOU'D TAKE FULL RESPONSI-BILITY, AKEMI.
SWUK
WHY ARE YOU INDULG-ING HER?
IS SOME-THING UP WITH YOU?
I...
OH, UM... NOTHING SPECIAL.
I JUST REALIZED I'M NOT SO YOUNG ANYMORE...
...I GUESS.
HUH? YOU'RE ONLY 20. YOU'VE STILL GOT A COUPLE OF GOOD TEETH LEFT.
DINGDONG
OH, MY!
MY GUESTS HAVE ARRIVED!
BERO-TCHO! THE GUESTS ARE HERE!
CHICKEN
BEROT-CHO'S BUSY COOK-ING.
COULD YOU ANSWER THE DOOR, MISS?
WEL-COME.
OH, HI!

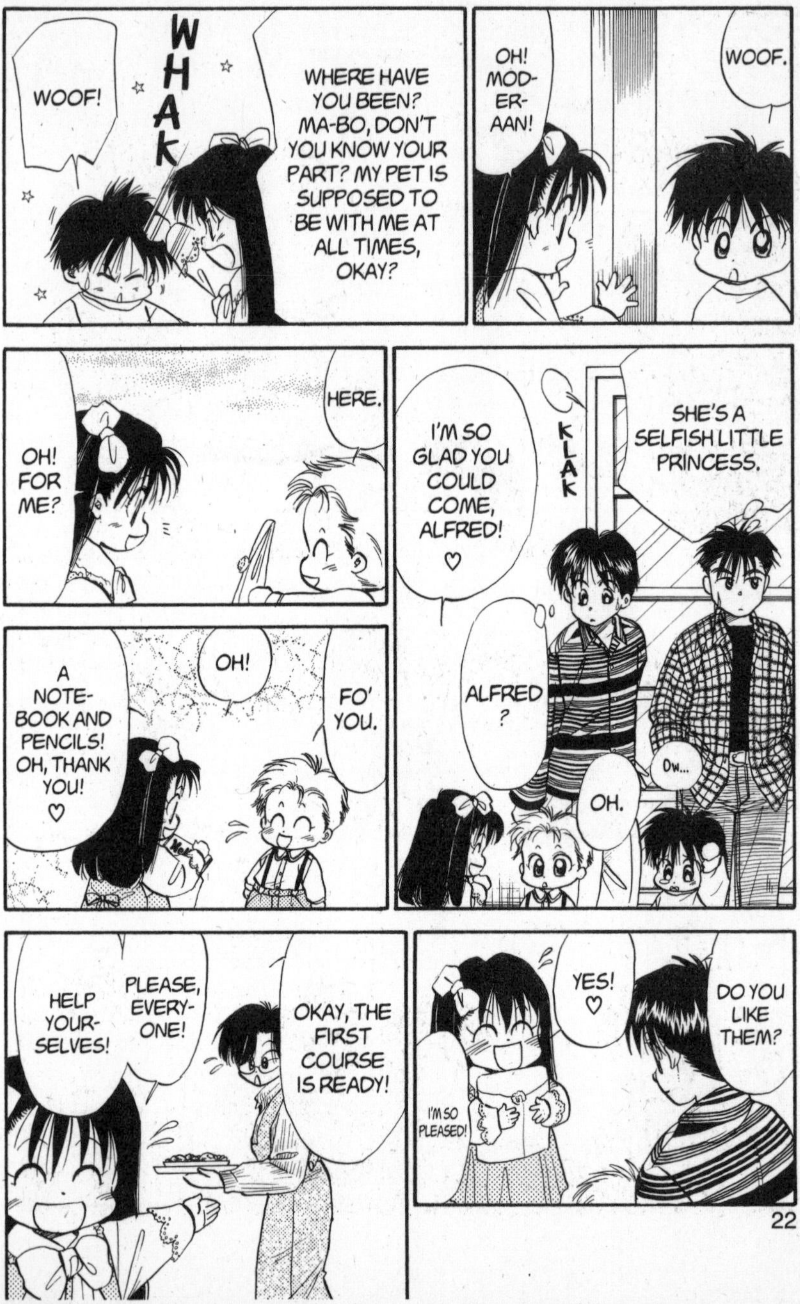
WOOF.
OH! MOD-ER-AAN!
WHERE HAVE YOU BEEN? MA-BO, DON'T YOU KNOW YOUR PART? MY PET IS SUPPOSED TO BE WITH ME AT ALL TIMES, OKAY?
WHAK
WOOF!
SHE'S A SELFISH LITTLE PRINCESS.
KLAK
I'M SO GLAD YOU COULD COME, ALFRED! ♡
ALFRED?
Ow...
OH.
HERE.
OH! FOR ME?
FO' YOU.
OH!
A NOTE-BOOK AND PENCILS! OH, THANK YOU! ♡
DO YOU LIKE THEM?
YES! ♡
I'M SO PLEASED!
OKAY, THE FIRST COURSE IS READY!
PLEASE, EVERY-ONE!
HELP YOUR-SELVES!

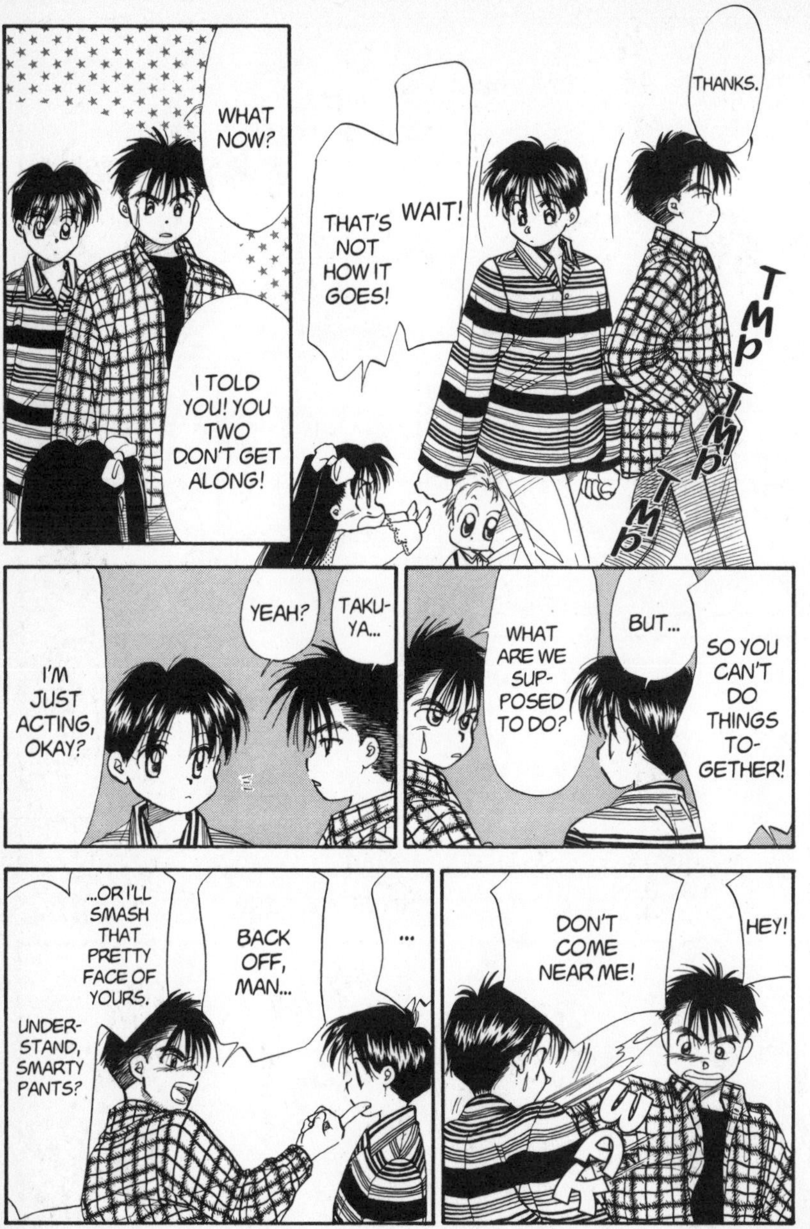
THANKS.
TMP TMP TMP
WAIT!
THAT'S NOT HOW IT GOES!
WHAT NOW?
I TOLD YOU! YOU TWO DON'T GET ALONG!
SO YOU CAN'T DO THINGS TO-GETHER!
BUT...
WHAT ARE WE SUP-POSED TO DO?
TAKU-YA...
YEAH?
I'M JUST ACTING, OKAY?
HEY!
DON'T COME NEAR ME!
WAK
...
BACK OFF, MAN...
...OR I'LL SMASH THAT PRETTY FACE OF YOURS.
UNDER-STAND, SMARTY PANTS?

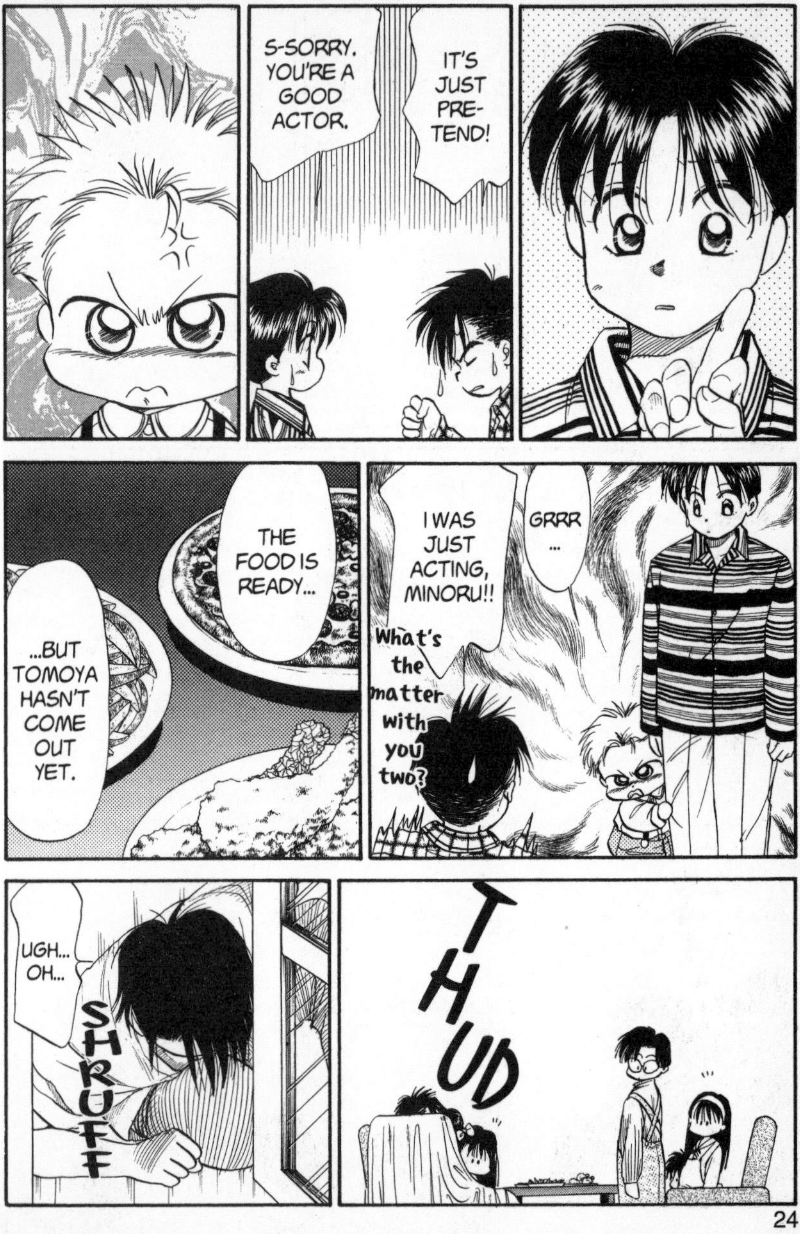
IT'S JUST PRE-TEND!
S-SORRY. YOU'RE A GOOD ACTOR.
GRRR ...
I WAS JUST ACTING, MINORU!!
What's the matter with you two?
THE FOOD IS READY...
...BUT TOMOYA HASN'T COME OUT YET.
THUD
UGH... OH...
SHRUFF

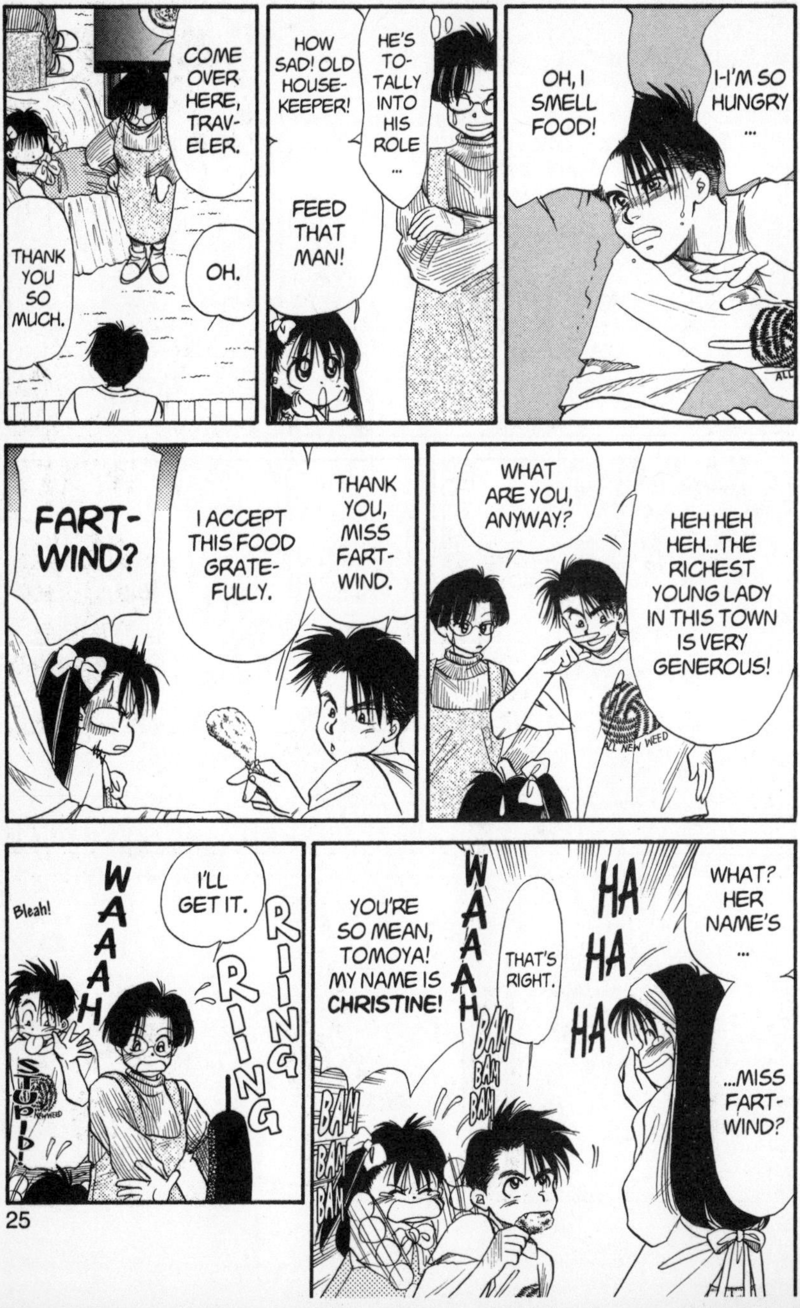
I-I'M SO HUNGRY ...
OH, I SMELL FOOD!
HE'S TOTALLY INTO HIS ROLE ...
HOW SAD! OLD HOUSEKEEPER!
FEED THAT MAN!
COME OVER HERE, TRAVELER.
OH.
THANK YOU SO MUCH.
HEH HEH HEH...THE RICHEST YOUNG LADY IN THIS TOWN IS VERY GENEROUS!
WHAT ARE YOU, ANYWAY?
ALL NEW WEED
THANK YOU, MISS FART-WIND.
I ACCEPT THIS FOOD GRATEFULLY.
FART-WIND?
WHAT? HER NAME'S ...
...MISS FART-WIND?
HA HA HA
THAT'S RIGHT.
WAAAAH
YOU'RE SO MEAN, TOMOYA! MY NAME IS CHRISTINE!
BAM BAM BAM
BAM BAM BAM
RIIING
RING
I'LL GET IT.
WAAAAH
Bleah!
STUPID!

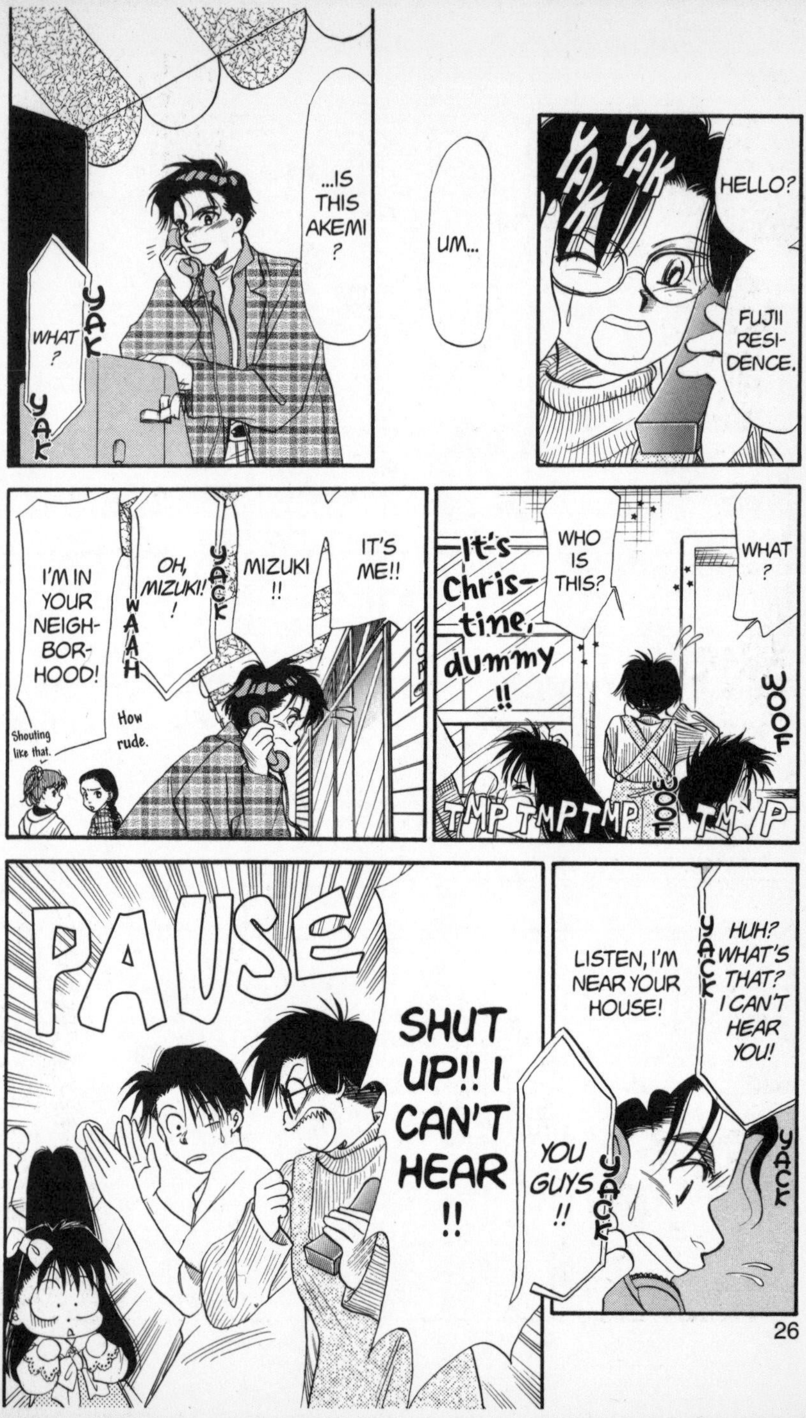
HELLO?
FUJII RESIDENCE.
YAK YAK
UM...
...IS THIS AKEMI?
WHAT?
YAK YAK
WHAT?
WHO IS THIS?
It's Christine, dummy!!
WOOF WOOF
TMP TMP TMP TMP
IT'S ME!!
MIZUKI!!
YACK
OH, MIZUKI!!
WAAH
I'M IN YOUR NEIGHBORHOOD!
How rude.
Shouting like that.
HUH? WHAT'S THAT? I CAN'T HEAR YOU!
YACK
LISTEN, I'M NEAR YOUR HOUSE!
YACK
YACK
SHUT UP!! I CAN'T HEAR YOU GUYS!!
PAUSE

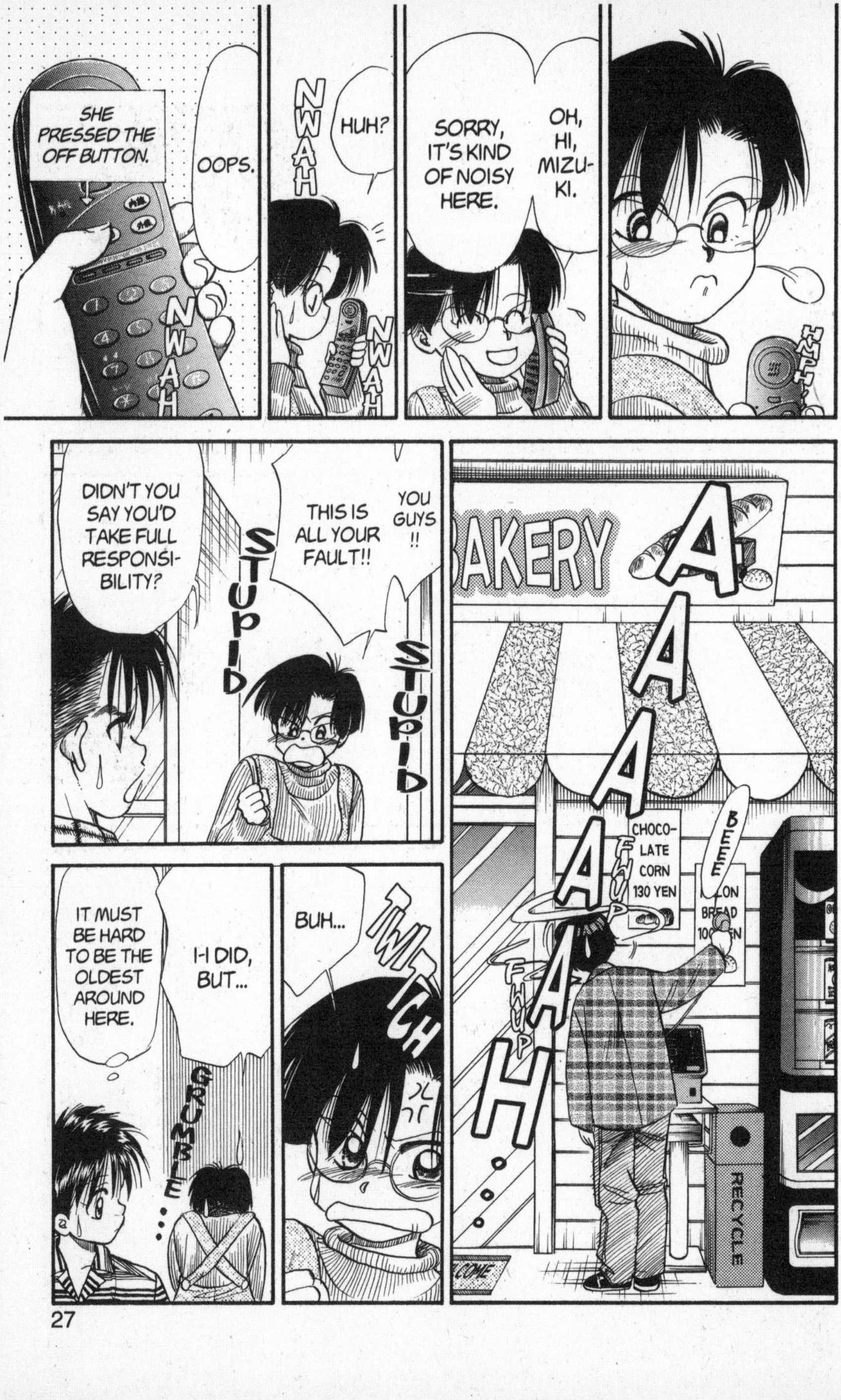
HMPH
OH, HI, MIZU-KI.
SORRY, IT'S KIND OF NOISY HERE.
NWAAH
HUH?
NWAAH
OOPS.
SHE PRESSED THE OFF BUTTON.
NWAAH
BAKERY
AAAAAAH...
BEEEP
CHOCO-LATE CORN 130 YEN
BREAD
FWUP
FWUP
RECYCLE
YOU GUYS!!
THIS IS ALL YOUR FAULT!!
STUPID
STUPID
DIDN'T YOU SAY YOU'D TAKE FULL RESPONSI-BILITY?
TWITCH
BUH...
I-I DID, BUT...
GRUMBLE...
IT MUST BE HARD TO BE THE OLDEST AROUND HERE.

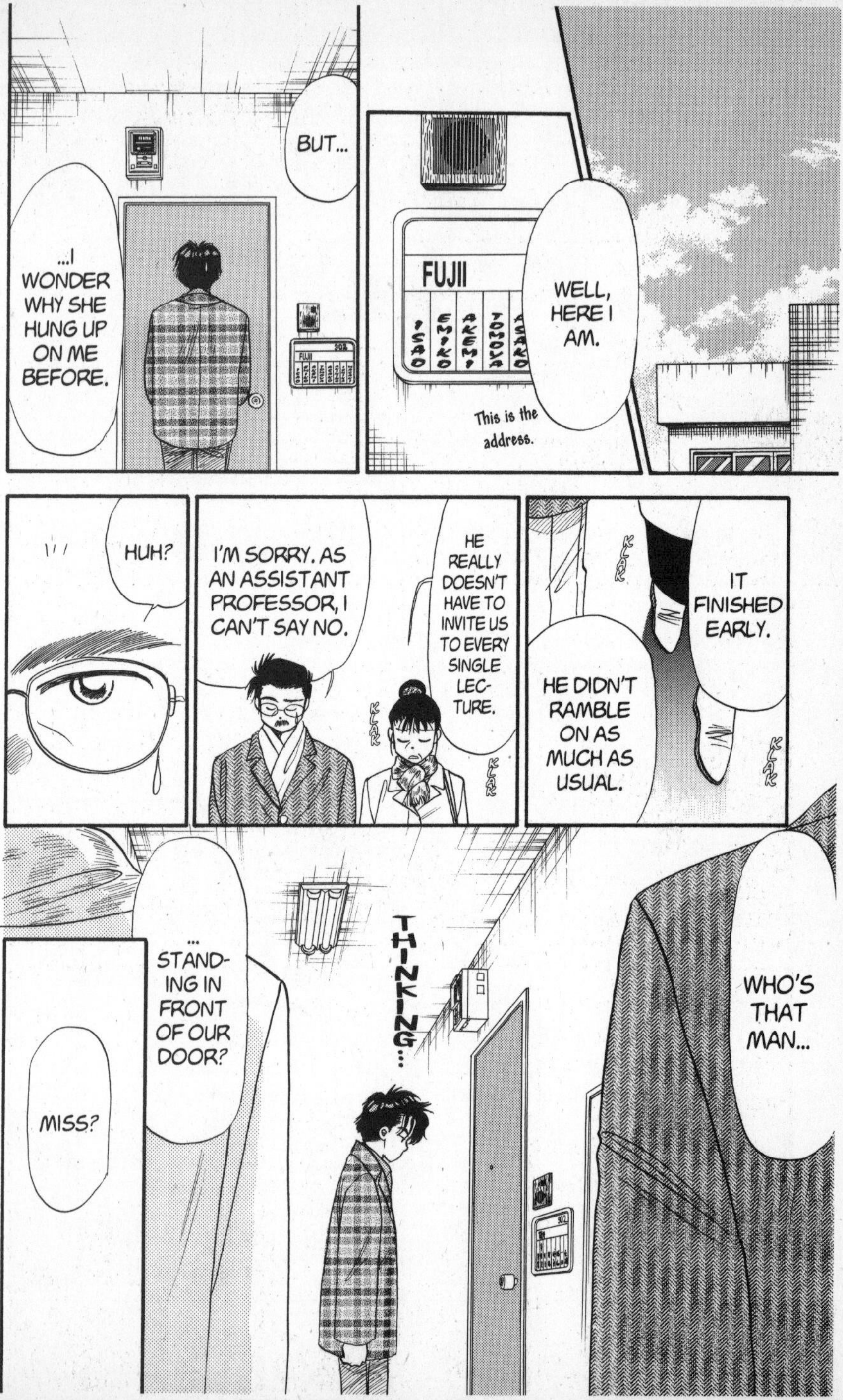
WELL, HERE I AM.
FUJII
ISAO
EMIKO
AKEMI
TOMOYA
ASAKO
This is the address.
BUT...
...I WONDER WHY SHE HUNG UP ON ME BEFORE.
KLAK
IT FINISHED EARLY.
HE DIDN'T RAMBLE ON AS MUCH AS USUAL.
KLAK
HE REALLY DOESN'T HAVE TO INVITE US TO EVERY SINGLE LEC-TURE.
KLAK
I'M SORRY. AS AN ASSISTANT PROFESSOR, I CAN'T SAY NO.
KLAK
HUH?
WHO'S THAT MAN...
THINKING...
...STAND-ING IN FRONT OF OUR DOOR?
MISS?

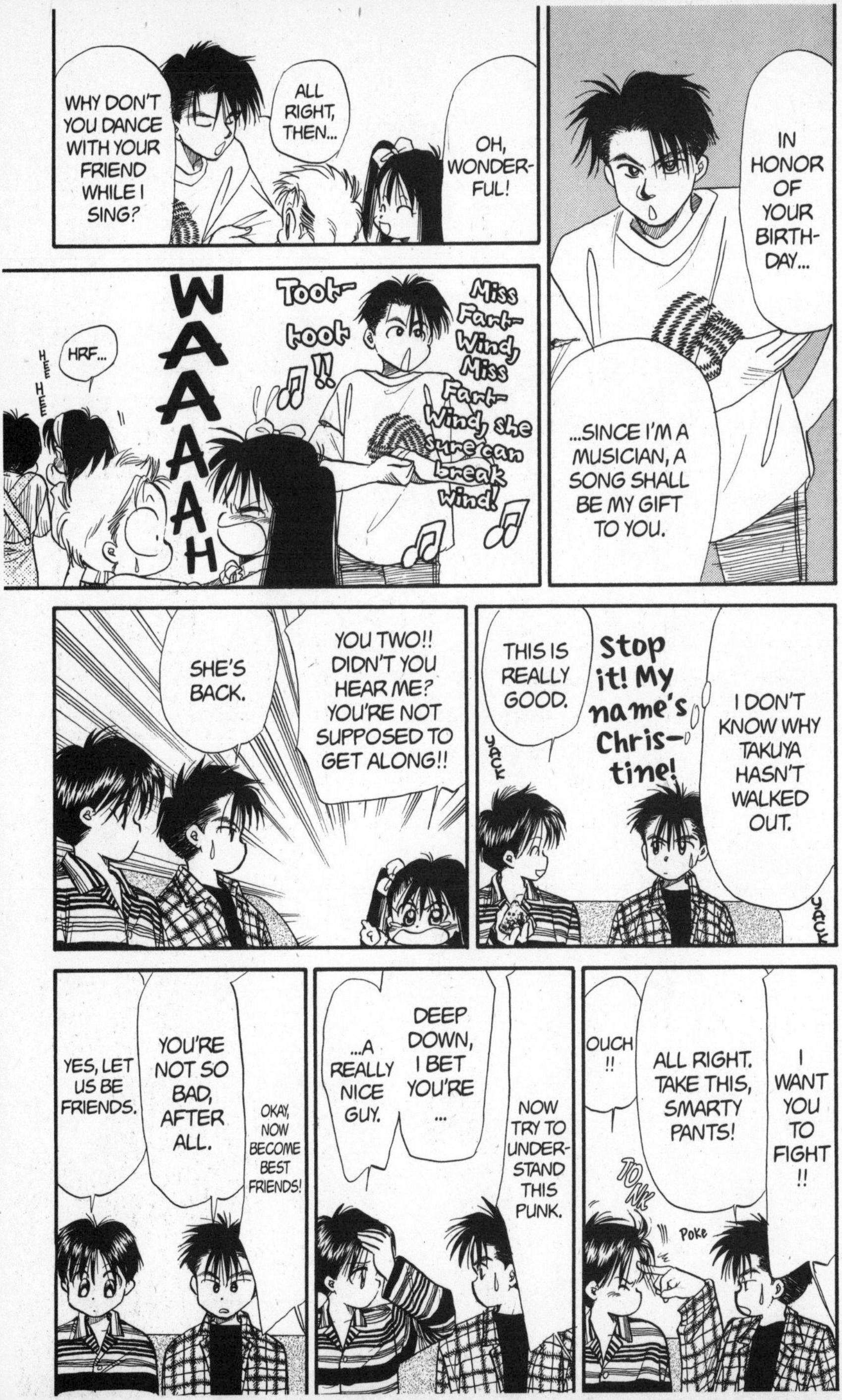
IN HONOR OF YOUR BIRTHDAY...
...SINCE I'M A MUSICIAN, A SONG SHALL BE MY GIFT TO YOU.
OH, WONDERFUL!
ALL RIGHT, THEN...
WHY DON'T YOU DANCE WITH YOUR FRIEND WHILE I SING?
Miss Fart-Wind, Miss Fart-Wind, she sure can break wind!
Took-took!!
WAAAAAH
HRF...
HEE HEE
I DON'T KNOW WHY TAKUYA HASN'T WALKED OUT.
YACK
Stop it! My name's Christine!
THIS IS REALLY GOOD.
YACK
YOU TWO!! DIDN'T YOU HEAR ME? YOU'RE NOT SUPPOSED TO GET ALONG!!
SHE'S BACK.
I WANT YOU TO FIGHT!!
ALL RIGHT. TAKE THIS, SMARTY PANTS!
OUCH!!
TONK
POKE
NOW TRY TO UNDERSTAND THIS PUNK.
DEEP DOWN, I BET YOU'RE ...
...A REALLY NICE GUY.
OKAY, NOW BECOME BEST FRIENDS!
YOU'RE NOT SO BAD, AFTER ALL.
YES, LET US BE FRIENDS.

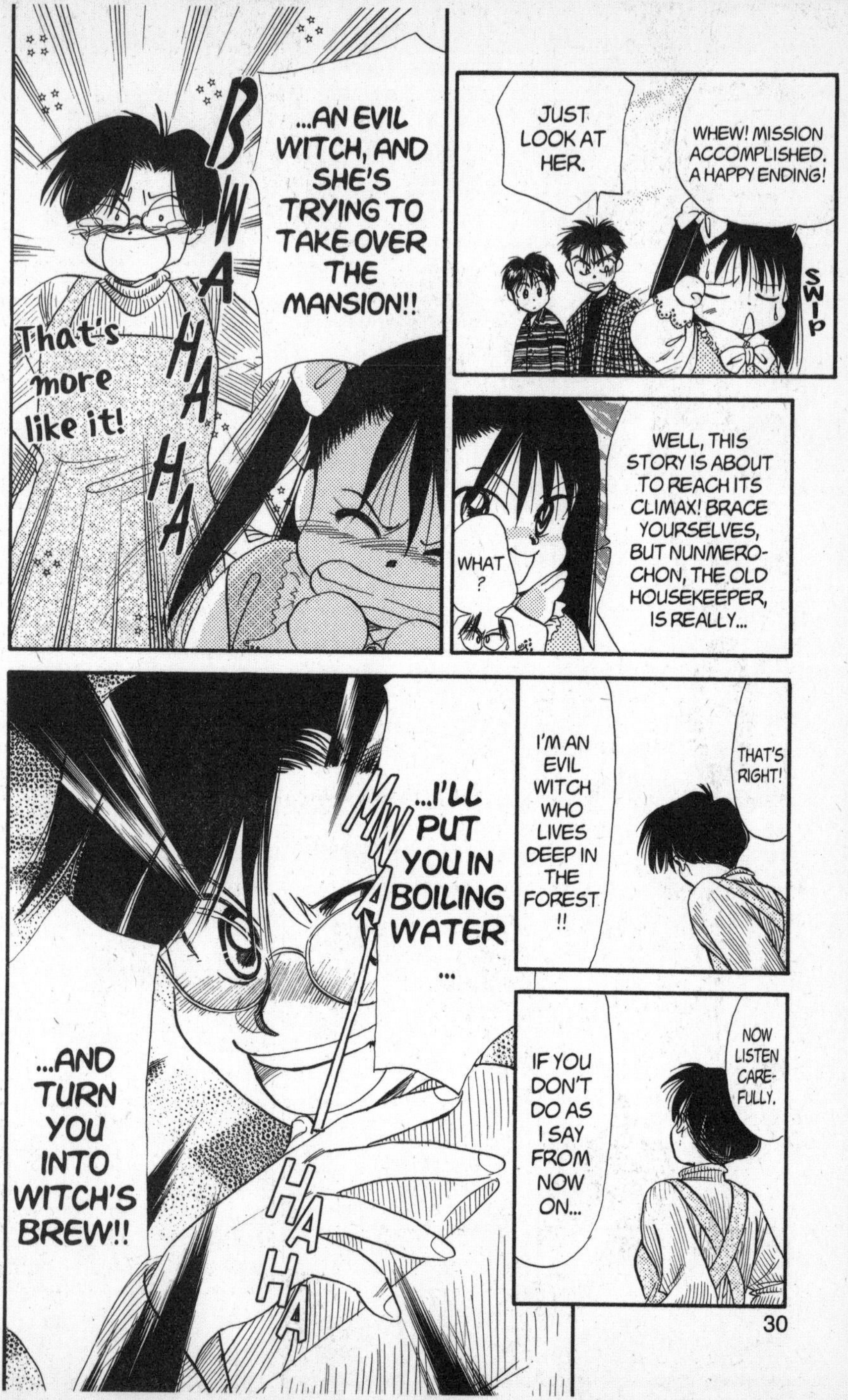
WHEW! MISSION ACCOMPLISHED. A HAPPY ENDING!
SWIP
JUST LOOK AT HER.
WELL, THIS STORY IS ABOUT TO REACH ITS CLIMAX! BRACE YOURSELVES, BUT NUNMERO-CHON, THE OLD HOUSEKEEPER, IS REALLY...
WHAT?
...AN EVIL WITCH, AND SHE'S TRYING TO TAKE OVER THE MANSION!!
BWAHAHAHA
That's more like it!
THAT'S RIGHT!
I'M AN EVIL WITCH WHO LIVES DEEP IN THE FOREST!!
NOW LISTEN CARE-FULLY.
IF YOU DON'T DO AS I SAY FROM NOW ON...
...I'LL PUT YOU IN BOILING WATER...
MWAHAHAHA
...AND TURN YOU INTO WITCH'S BREW!!

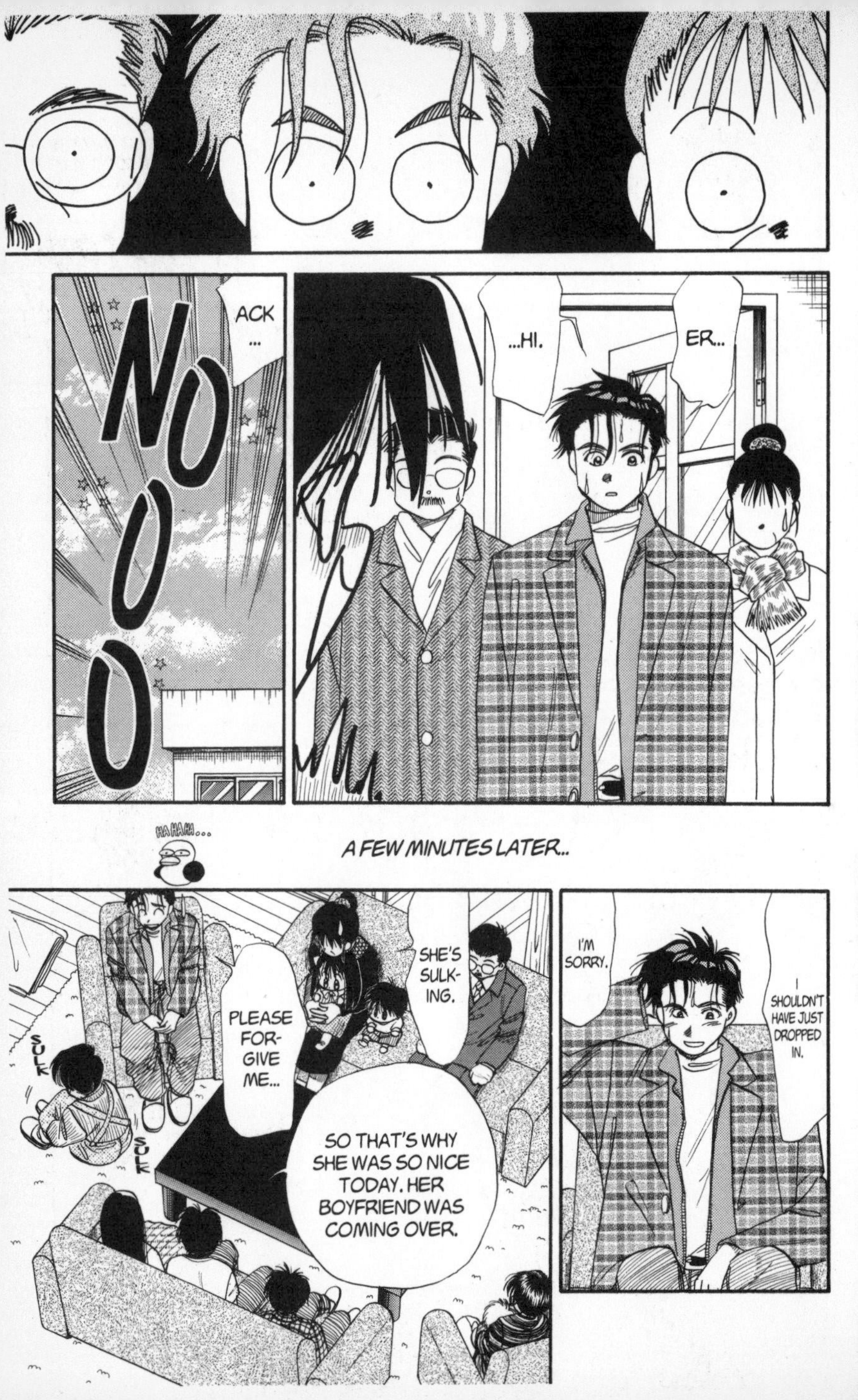
ER...
...HI.
ACK ...
NOOOO
A FEW MINUTES LATER...
HA HA HA...
I SHOULDN'T HAVE JUST DROPPED IN.
I'M SORRY.
SHE'S SULKING.
PLEASE FORGIVE ME...
SULK
SULK
SO THAT'S WHY SHE WAS SO NICE TODAY. HER BOYFRIEND WAS COMING OVER.

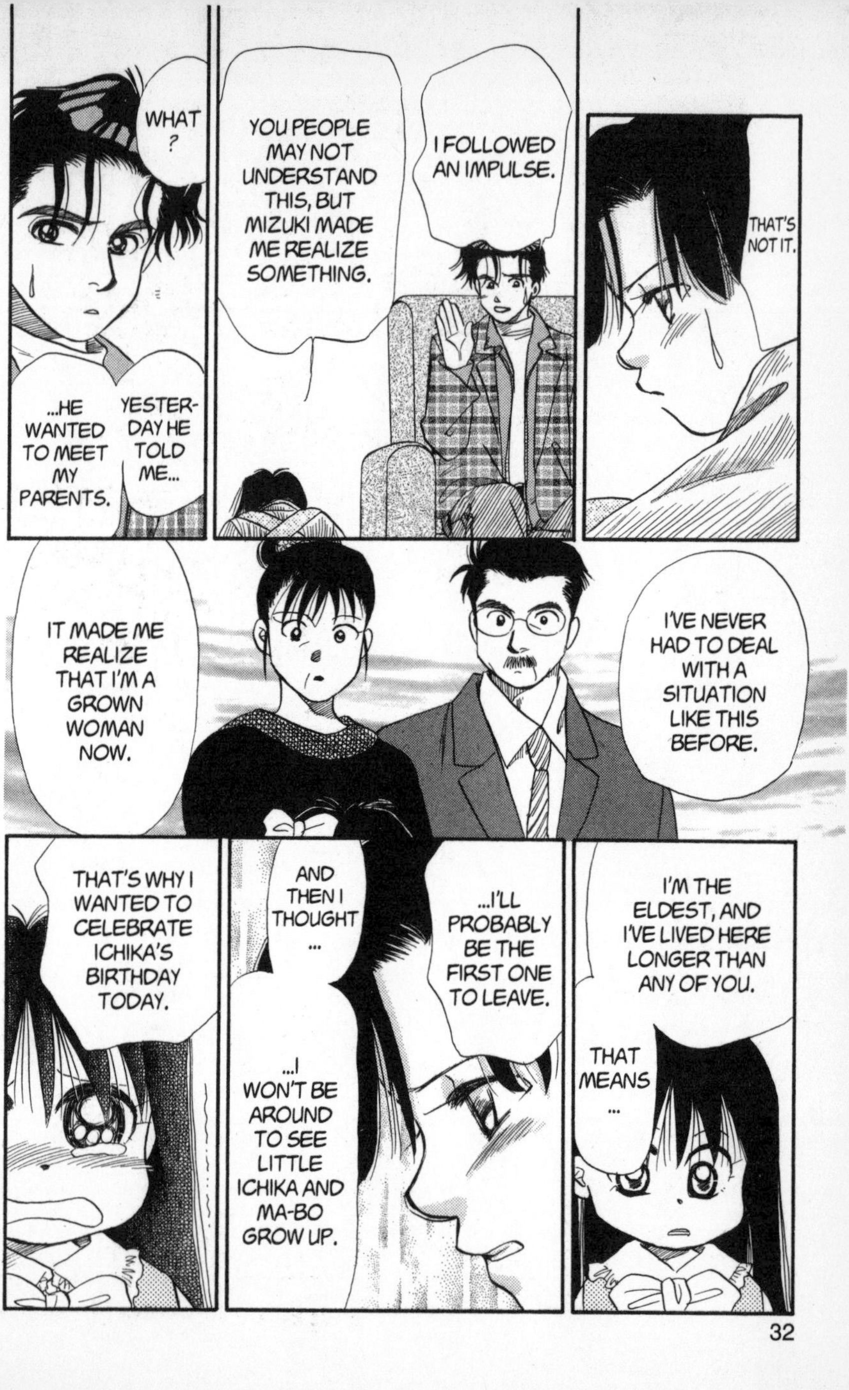
THAT'S NOT IT.
I FOLLOWED AN IMPULSE.
YOU PEOPLE MAY NOT UNDERSTAND THIS, BUT MIZUKI MADE ME REALIZE SOMETHING.
WHAT?
YESTER-DAY HE TOLD ME...
...HE WANTED TO MEET MY PARENTS.
I'VE NEVER HAD TO DEAL WITH A SITUATION LIKE THIS BEFORE.
IT MADE ME REALIZE THAT I'M A GROWN WOMAN NOW.
I'M THE ELDEST, AND I'VE LIVED HERE LONGER THAN ANY OF YOU.
THAT MEANS...
...I'LL PROBABLY BE THE FIRST ONE TO LEAVE.
AND THEN I THOUGHT...
...I WON'T BE AROUND TO SEE LITTLE ICHIKA AND MA-BO GROW UP.
THAT'S WHY I WANTED TO CELEBRATE ICHIKA'S BIRTHDAY TODAY.

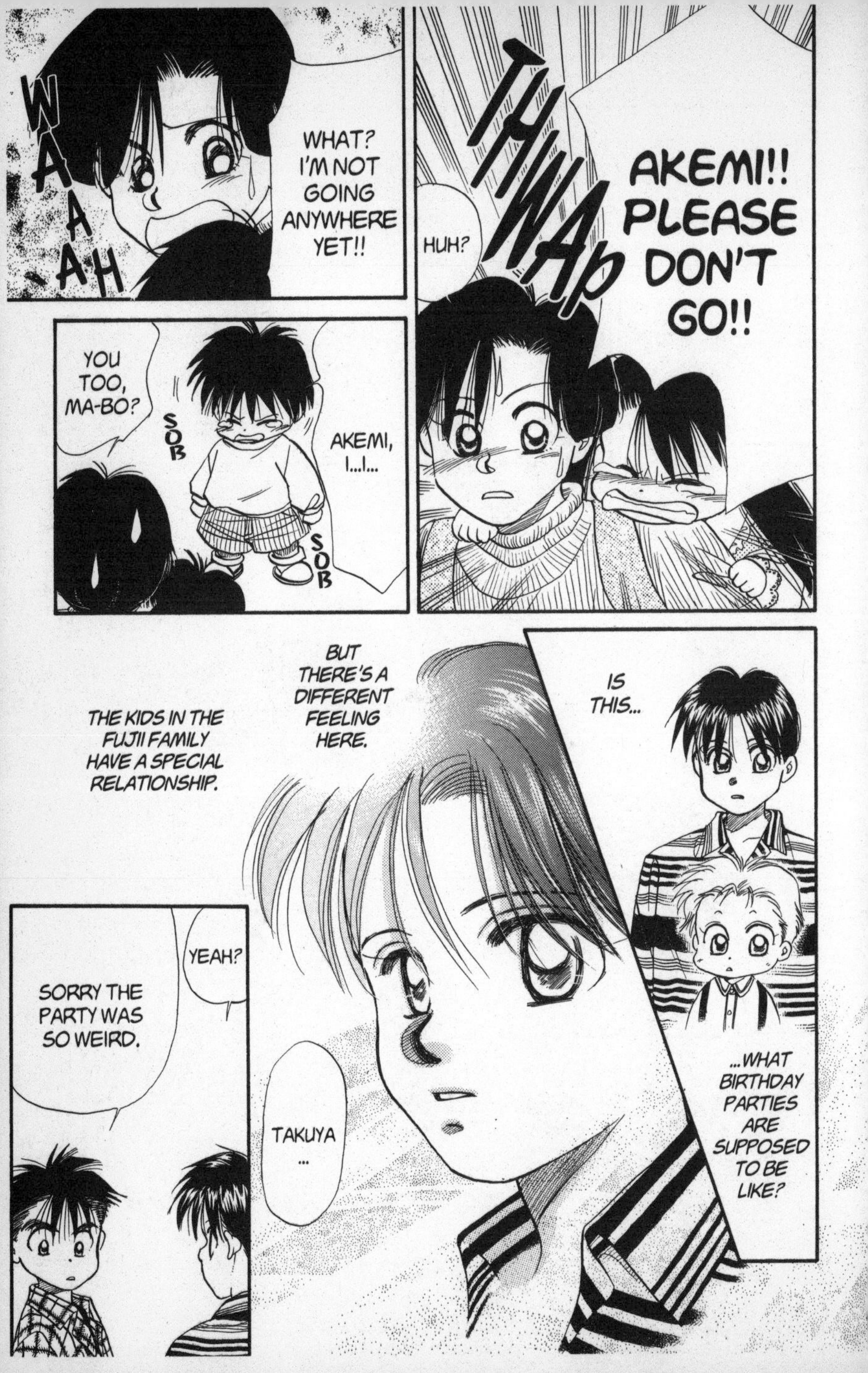
AKEMI!! PLEASE DON'T GO!!
THWAP
HUH?
WAAAH
WHAT? I'M NOT GOING ANYWHERE YET!!
AKEMI, I...I...
SOB
SOB
YOU TOO, MA-BO?
IS THIS...
...WHAT BIRTHDAY PARTIES ARE SUPPOSED TO BE LIKE?
BUT THERE'S A DIFFERENT FEELING HERE.
THE KIDS IN THE FUJII FAMILY HAVE A SPECIAL RELATIONSHIP.
TAKUYA ...
YEAH?
SORRY THE PARTY WAS SO WEIRD.

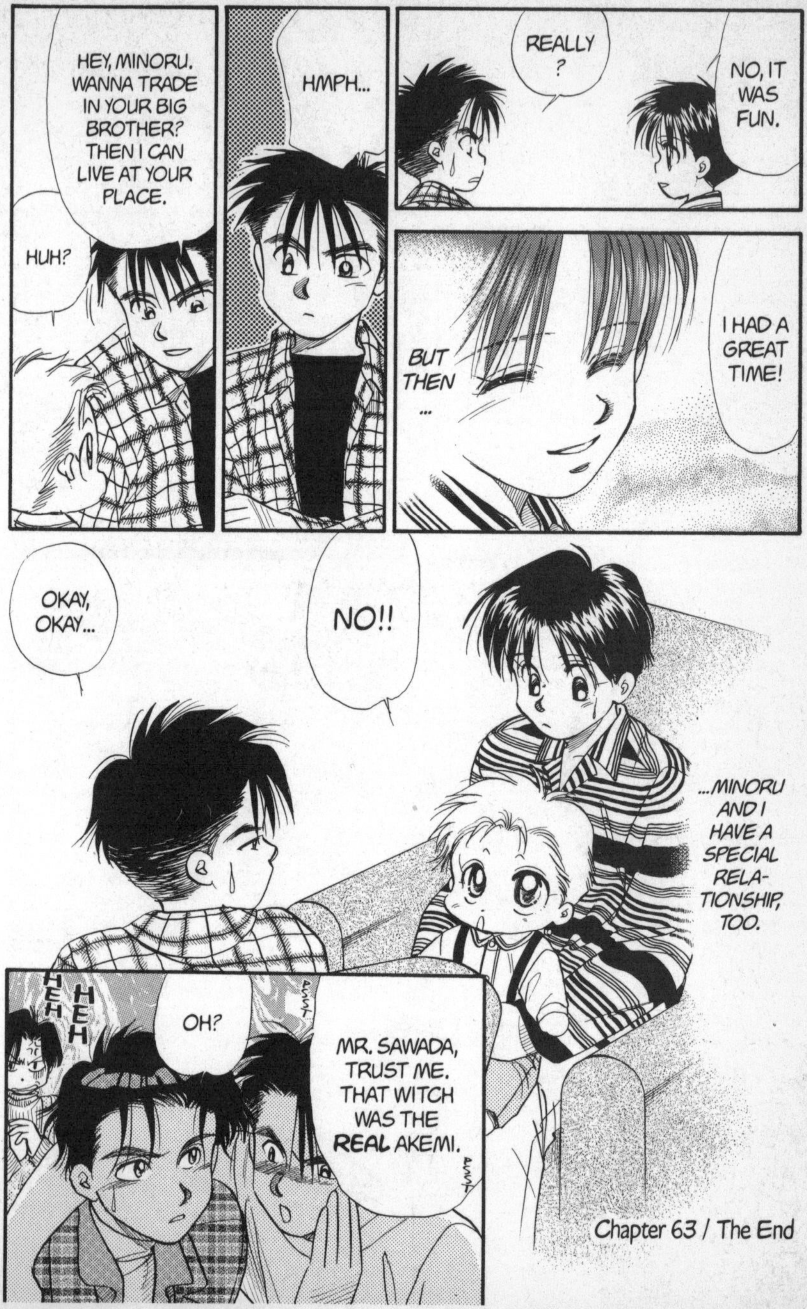
NO, IT WAS FUN.
REALLY?
I HAD A GREAT TIME!
BUT THEN...
HMPH...
HEY, MINORU. WANNA TRADE IN YOUR BIG BROTHER? THEN I CAN LIVE AT YOUR PLACE.
HUH?
...MINORU AND I HAVE A SPECIAL RELATIONSHIP, TOO.
NO!!
OKAY, OKAY...
PSST
MR. SAWADA, TRUST ME. THAT WITCH WAS THE **REAL** AKEMI.
PSST
OH?
HEH HEH
HEH

Chapter 63 / The End

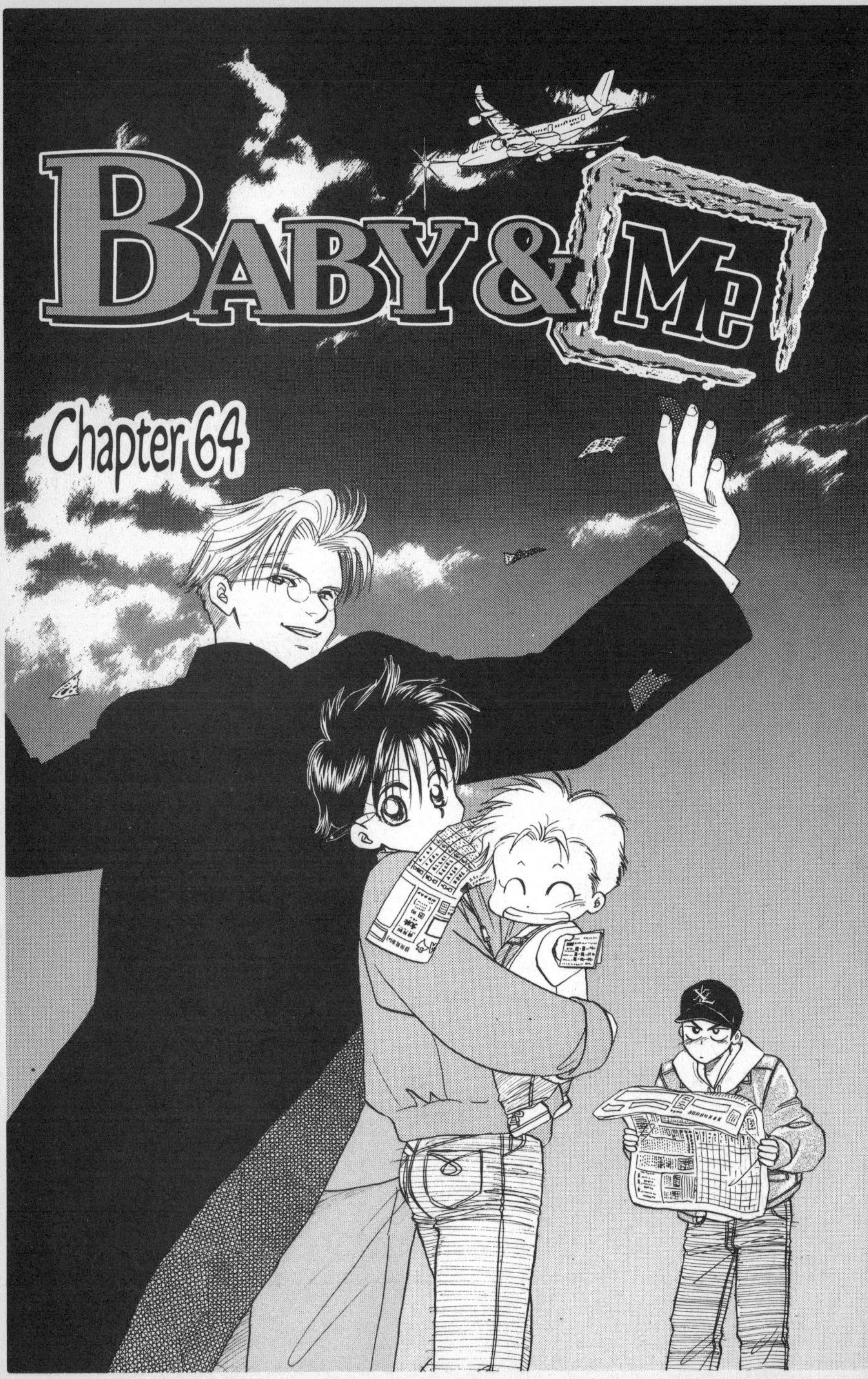

BABY & ME
Chapter 64

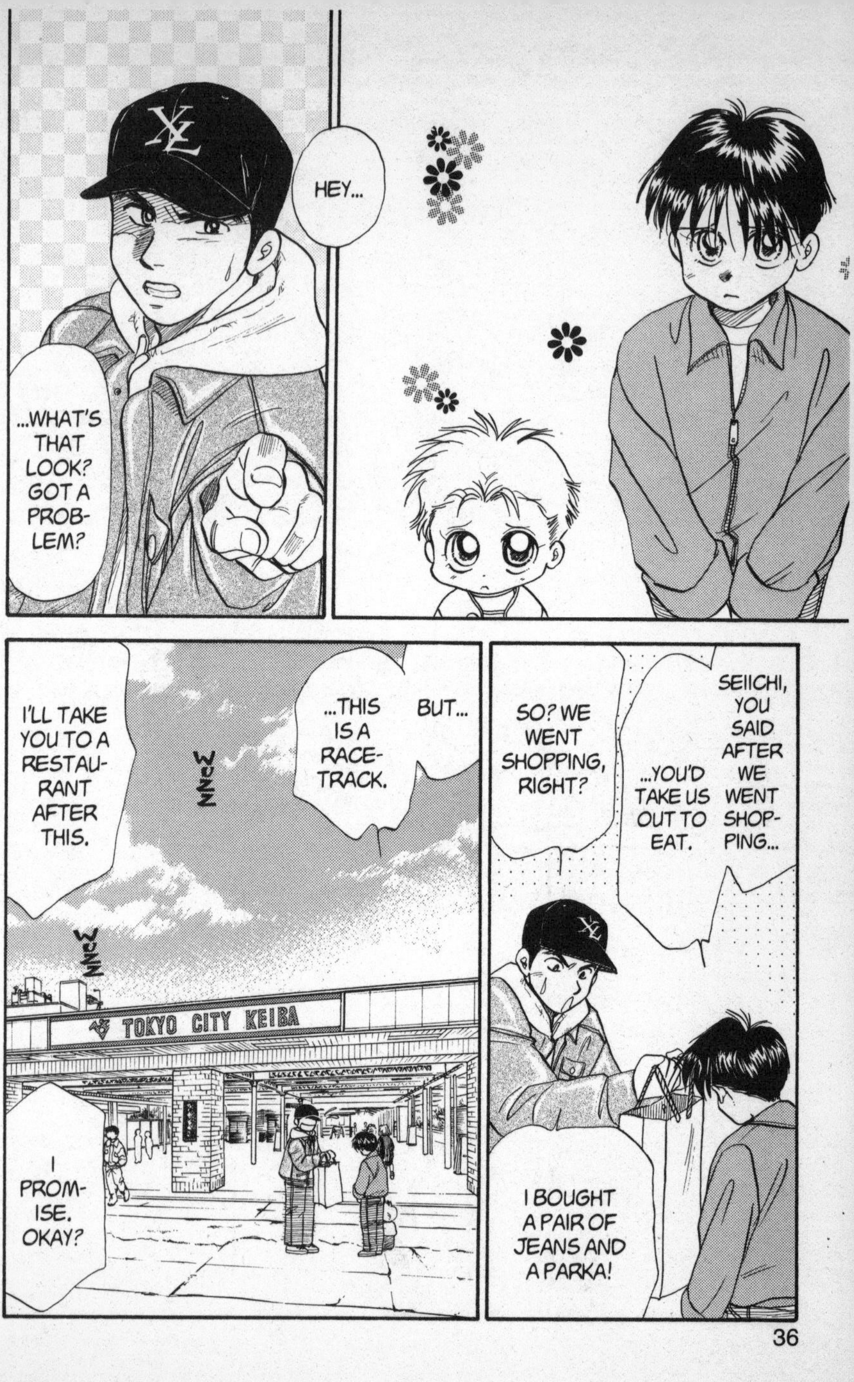
HEY...
...WHAT'S THAT LOOK? GOT A PROB-LEM?
SEIICHI, YOU SAID AFTER WE WENT SHOP-PING...
...YOU'D TAKE US OUT TO EAT.
SO? WE WENT SHOPPING, RIGHT?
I BOUGHT A PAIR OF JEANS AND A PARKA!
BUT...
...THIS IS A RACE-TRACK.
WZZN
I'LL TAKE YOU TO A RESTAU-RANT AFTER THIS.
WZZN
TOKYO CITY KEIBA
I PROM-ISE. OKAY?

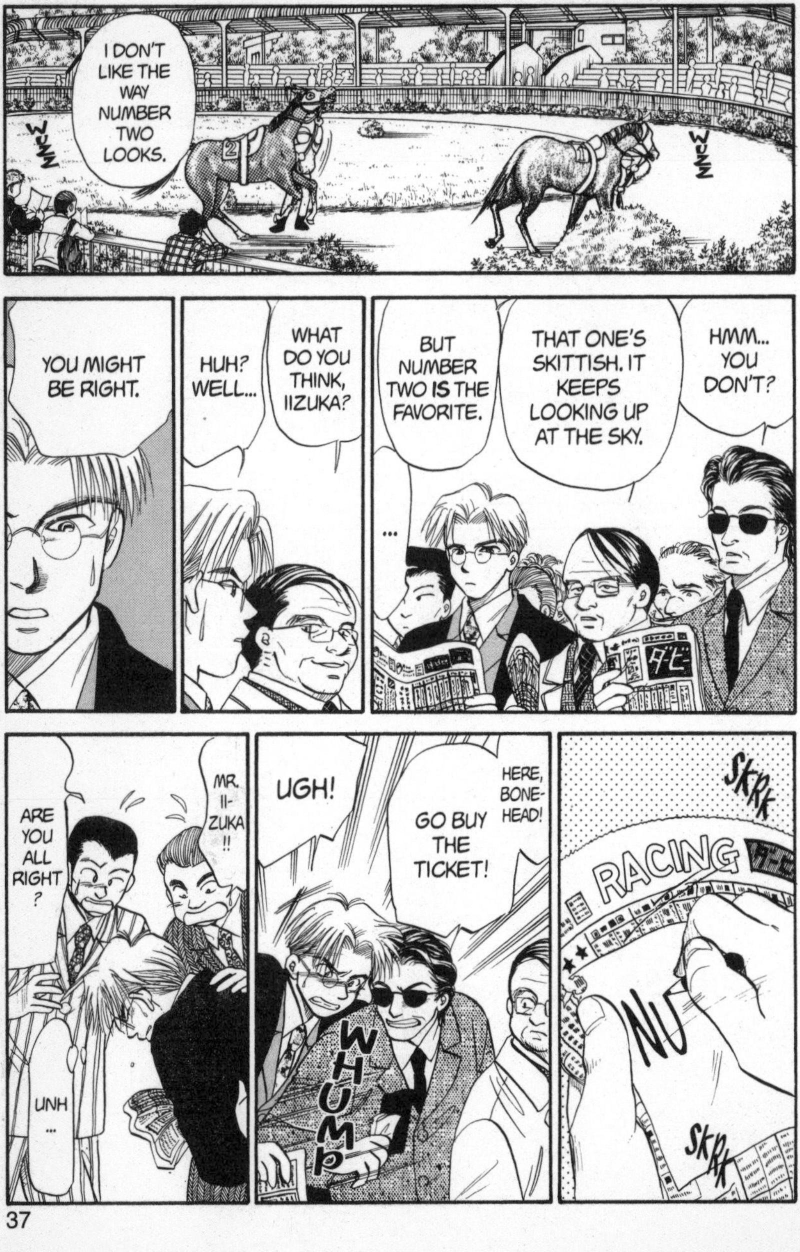
WUZZ
I DON'T LIKE THE WAY NUMBER TWO LOOKS.
WUZZ
HMM... YOU DON'T?
THAT ONE'S SKITTISH. IT KEEPS LOOKING UP AT THE SKY.
BUT NUMBER TWO IS THE FAVORITE.
...
WHAT DO YOU THINK, IIZUKA?
HUH? WELL...
YOU MIGHT BE RIGHT.
SKRK
RACING
NU
SKRK
HERE, BONE-HEAD!
GO BUY THE TICKET!
UGH!
WHUMP
MR. II-ZUKA!!
ARE YOU ALL RIGHT?
UNH...

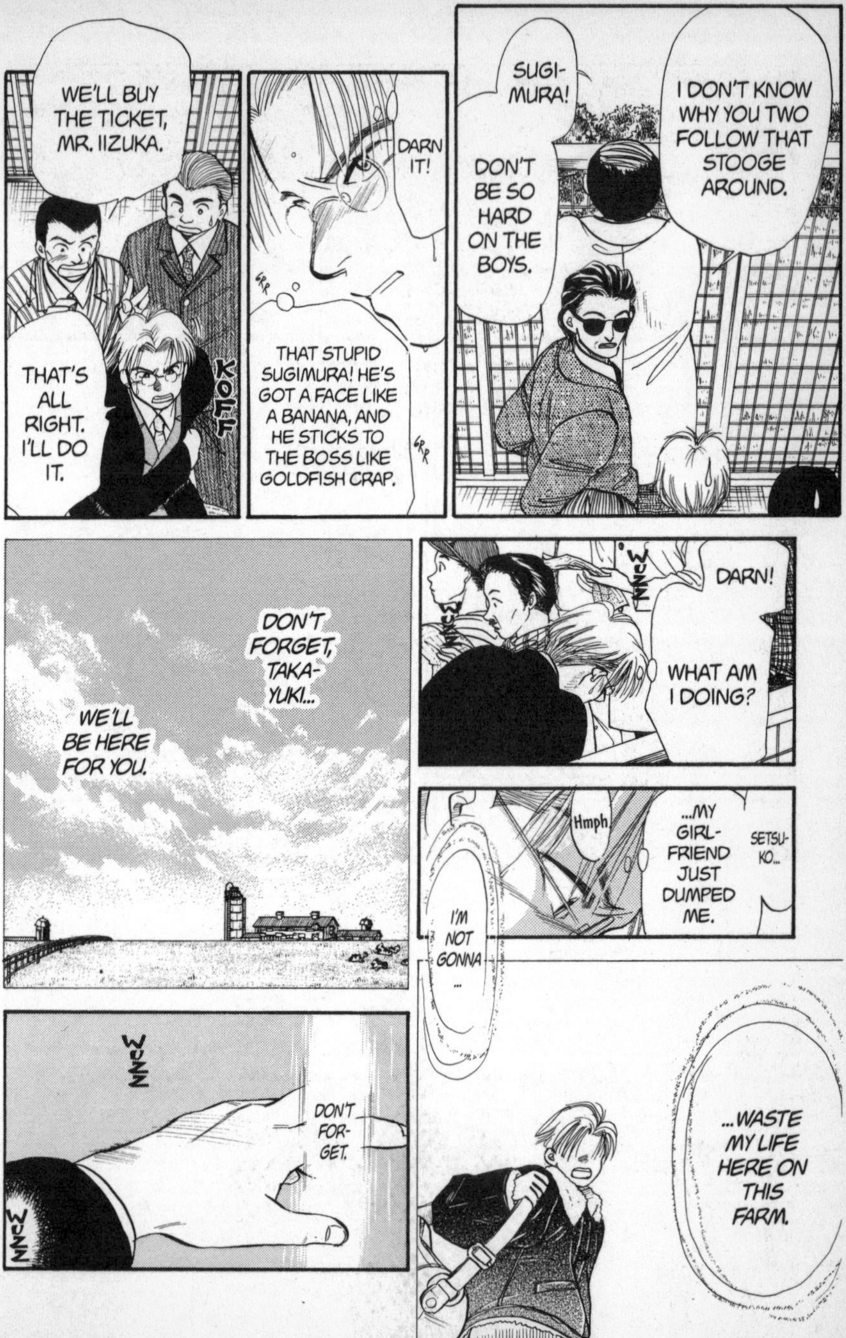
I DON'T KNOW WHY YOU TWO FOLLOW THAT STOOGE AROUND.
SUGI-MURA!
DON'T BE SO HARD ON THE BOYS.
DARN IT!
THAT STUPID SUGIMURA! HE'S GOT A FACE LIKE A BANANA, AND HE STICKS TO THE BOSS LIKE GOLDFISH CRAP.
GRR
GRR
WE'LL BUY THE TICKET, MR. IIZUKA.
KOFF
THAT'S ALL RIGHT. I'LL DO IT.
DARN!
WUZZ
WUZZ
WHAT AM I DOING?
SETSU-KO...
...MY GIRL-FRIEND JUST DUMPED ME.
Hmph
I'M NOT GONNA ...
...WASTE MY LIFE HERE ON THIS FARM.
DON'T FORGET, TAKA-YUKI...
WE'LL BE HERE FOR YOU.
WUZZ
DON'T FOR-GET.
WUZZ

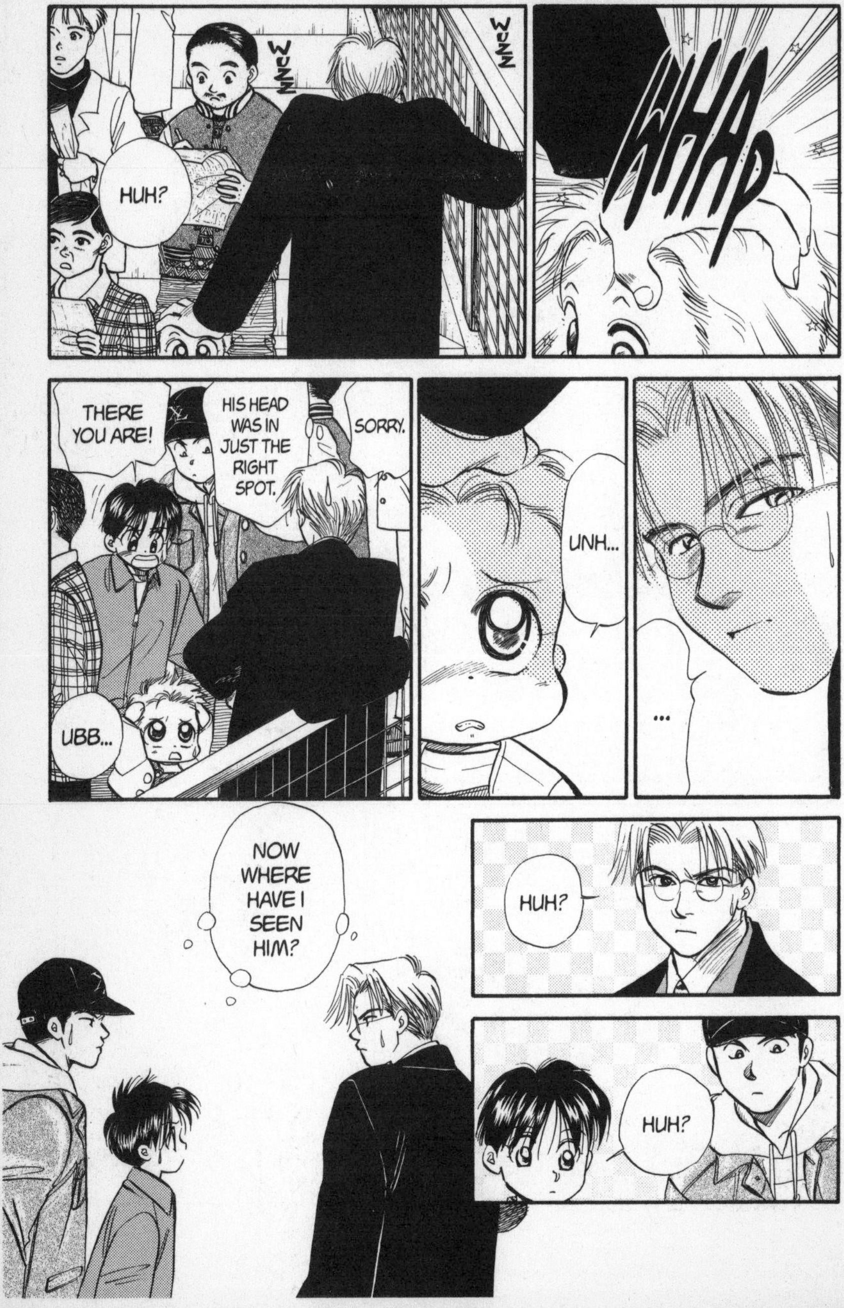
WHAP
WUZZ
WUZZ
HUH?
...
UNH...
SORRY.
HIS HEAD WAS IN JUST THE RIGHT SPOT.
THERE YOU ARE!
UBB...
HUH?
HUH?
NOW WHERE HAVE I SEEN HIM?

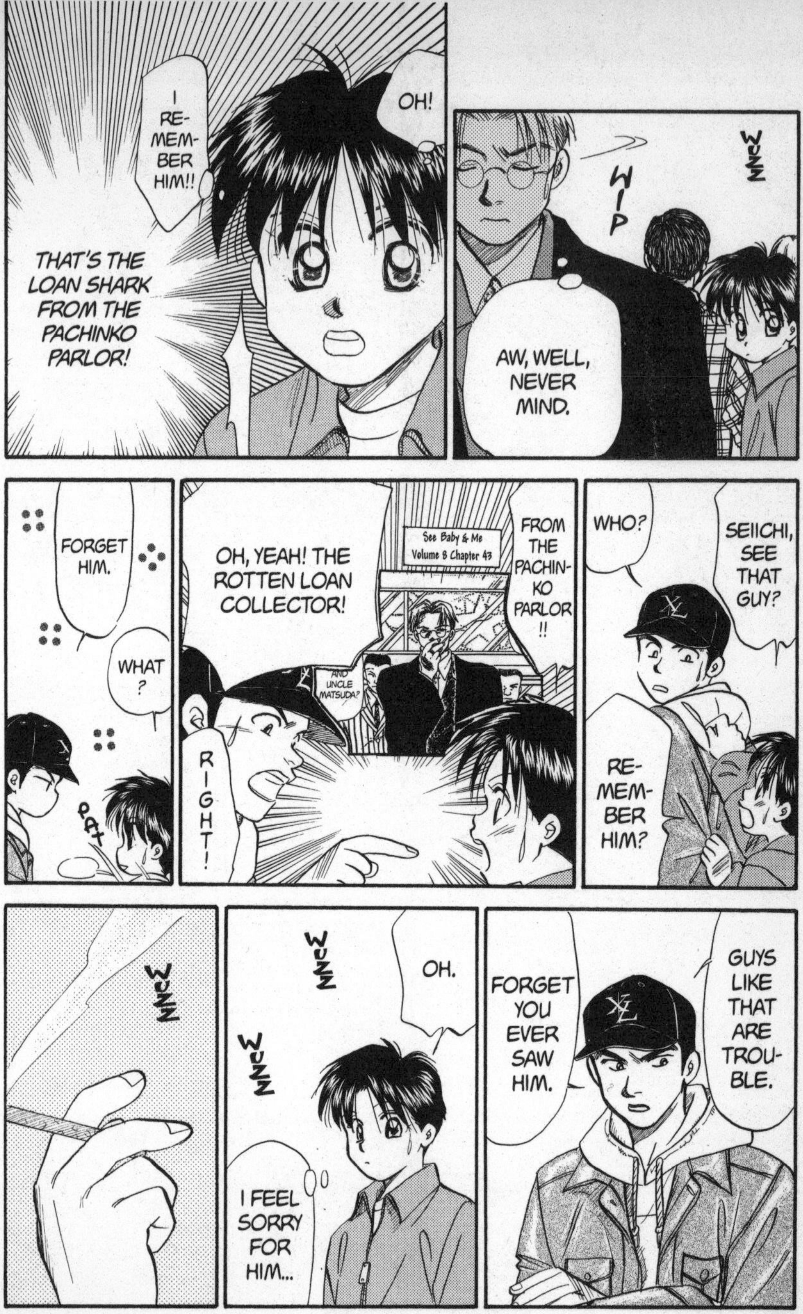
WUZZ
WIP
AW, WELL, NEVER MIND.
OH!
I REMEMBER HIM!!
THAT'S THE LOAN SHARK FROM THE PACHINKO PARLOR!
SEIICHI, SEE THAT GUY?
WHO?
REMEMBER HIM?
FROM THE PACHINKO PARLOR!!
See Baby & Me Volume 8 Chapter 43
OH, YEAH! THE ROTTEN LOAN COLLECTOR!
AND UNCLE MATSUDA?
RIGHT!
FORGET HIM.
WHAT?
PAT
GUYS LIKE THAT ARE TROUBLE.
FORGET YOU EVER SAW HIM.
OH.
WUZZ
WUZZ
I FEEL SORRY FOR HIM...
WUZZ

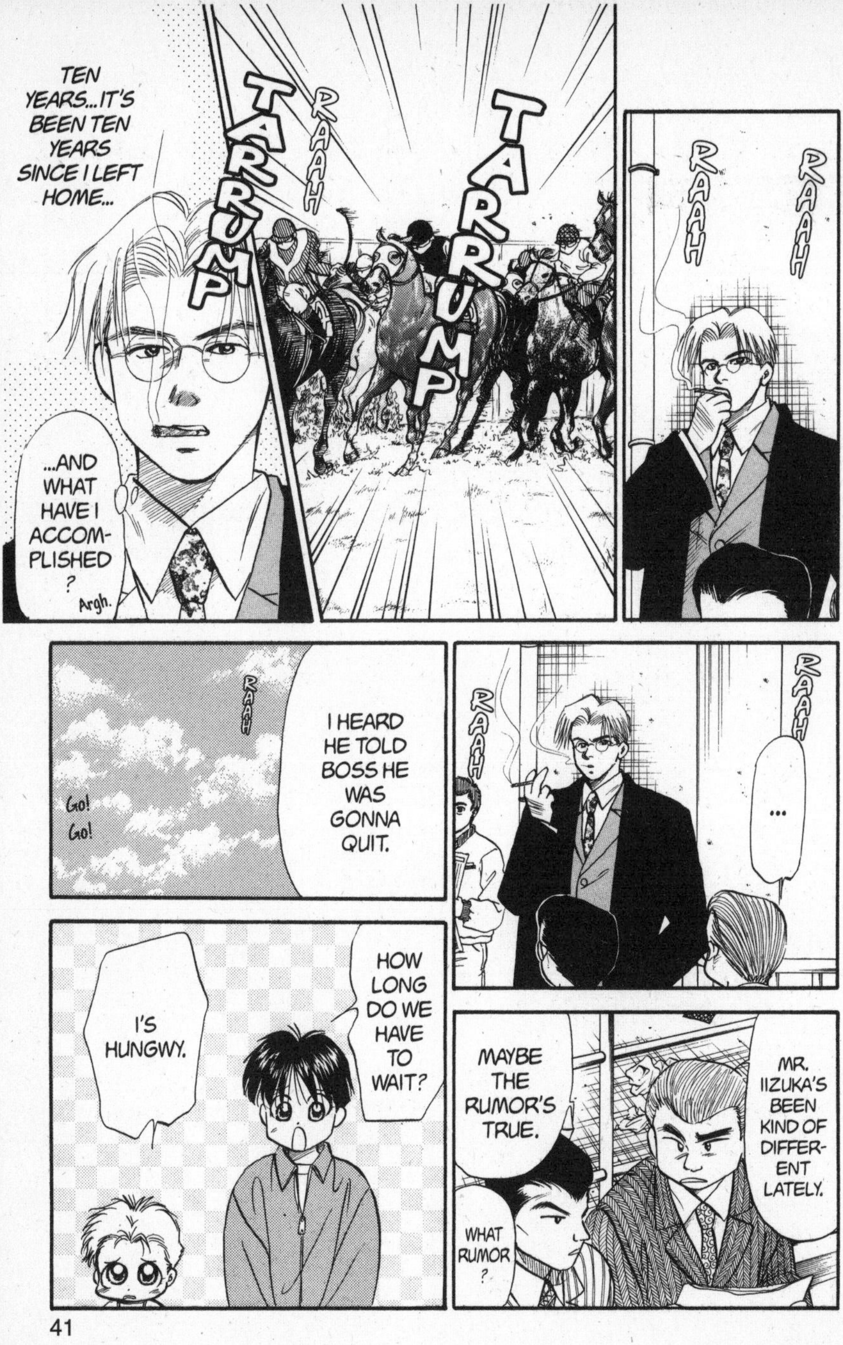
RAAAH
RAAAH
TARRUMP
RAAAH
TARRUMP
TEN YEARS...IT'S BEEN TEN YEARS SINCE I LEFT HOME...
...AND WHAT HAVE I ACCOMPLISHED?
Argh.
RAAAH
...
RAAAH
I HEARD HE TOLD BOSS HE WAS GONNA QUIT.
RAAH
Go! Go!
MR. IIZUKA'S BEEN KIND OF DIFFERENT LATELY.
MAYBE THE RUMOR'S TRUE.
WHAT RUMOR?
HOW LONG DO WE HAVE TO WAIT?
I'S HUNGWY.

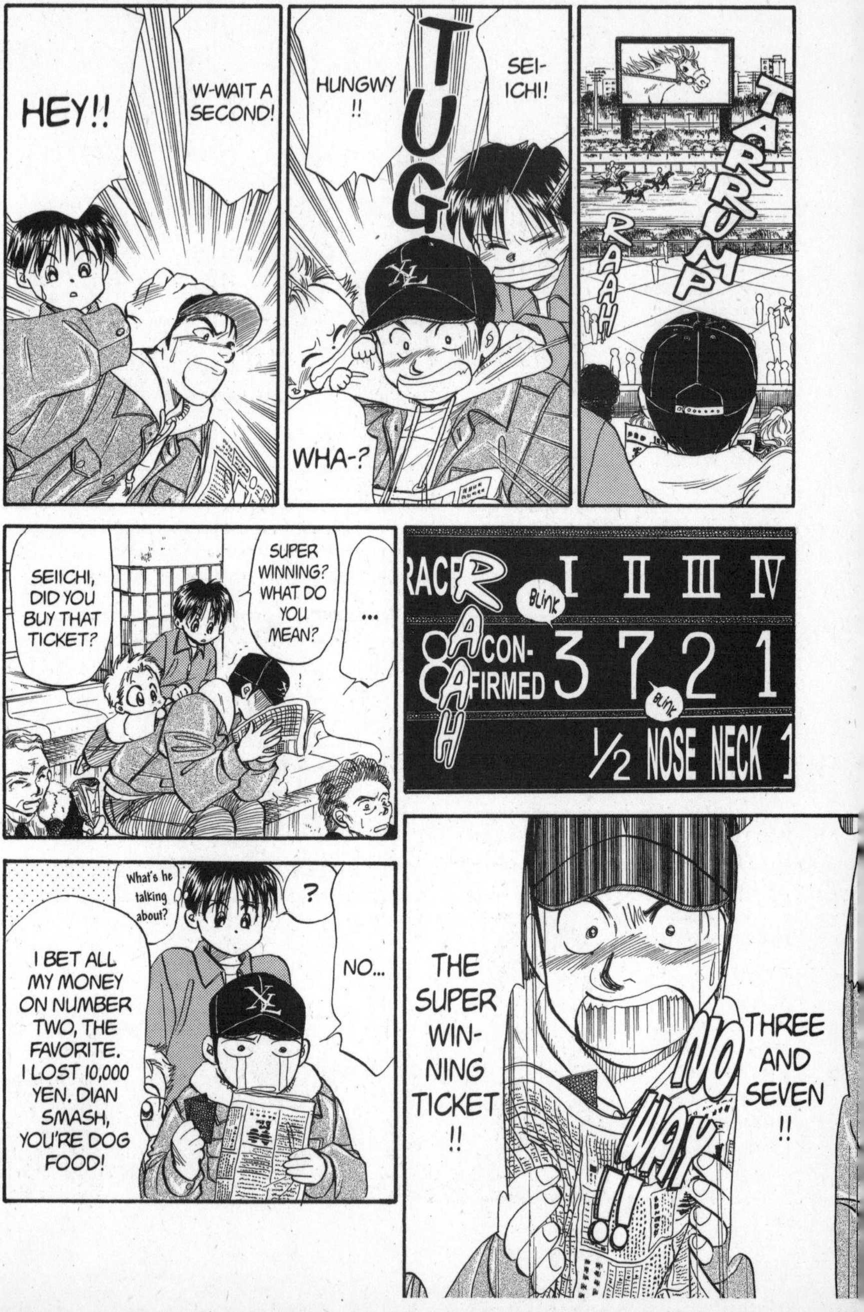
TARRUMP
RAAH
SEI-ICHI!
TUG
HUNGWY !!
WHA-?
W-WAIT A SECOND!
HEY!!
RACE RAAH I II III IV
Blink
8 CON-FIRMED 3 7 2 1
Blink
1/2 NOSE NECK 1
...
SUPER WINNING? WHAT DO YOU MEAN?
SEIICHI, DID YOU BUY THAT TICKET?
THREE AND SEVEN !!
NO WAY!!
THE SUPER WIN-NING TICKET !!
NO...
?
What's he talking about?
I BET ALL MY MONEY ON NUMBER TWO, THE FAVORITE. I LOST 10,000 YEN. DIAN SMASH, YOU'RE DOG FOOD!

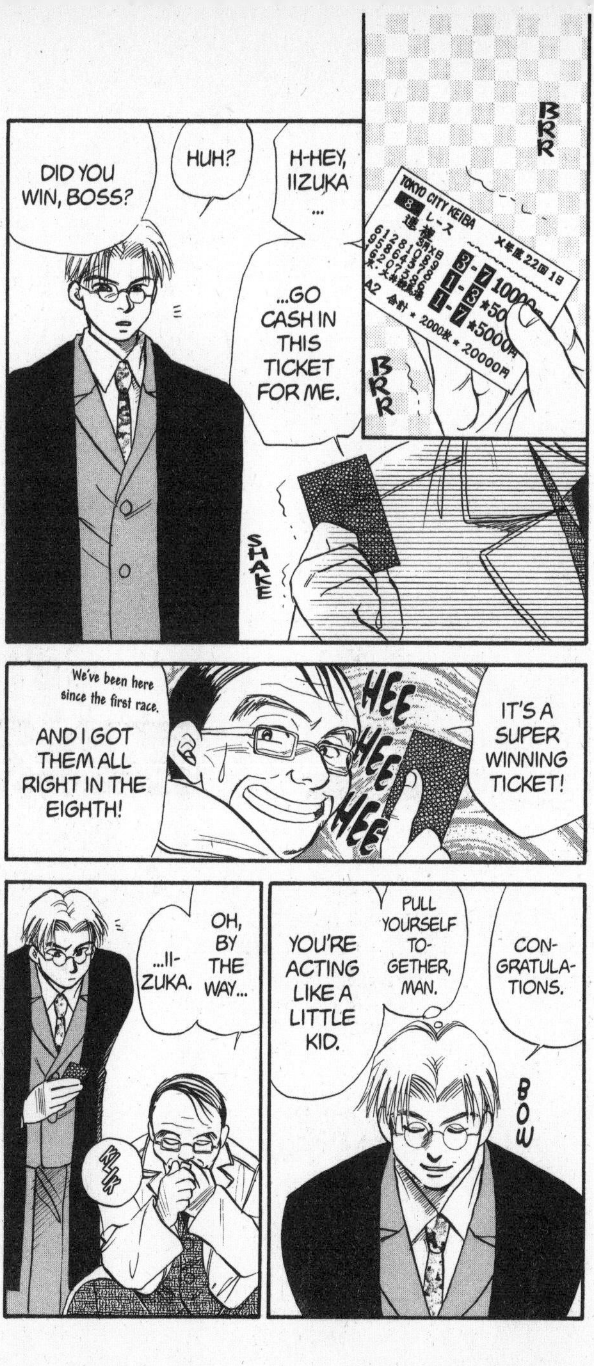
BRR
TOKYO CITY KEIBA
BRR
H-HEY, IIZUKA ...
...GO CASH IN THIS TICKET FOR ME.
SHAKE
HUH?
DID YOU WIN, BOSS?
IT'S A SUPER WINNING TICKET!
HEE HEE HEE
AND I GOT THEM ALL RIGHT IN THE EIGHTH!
We've been here since the first race.
CON-GRATULA-TIONS.
BOW
PULL YOURSELF TO-GETHER, MAN.
YOU'RE ACTING LIKE A LITTLE KID.
OH, BY THE WAY...
...II-ZUKA.

Author's Note Part 2

When I was working on this story, I was mentally exhausted. I was thinking, "Again? I've had enough!" and I didn't do a very good job. That's why my drawing is even worse than usual in this chapter.

Ever since the pachinko parlor story in which Iizuka first appeared, I've wanted to do more with him. So that made me happy.

Originally, it was unclear in the end whether Iizuka was alive or dead, but my editor, "Itchan," hates sad endings and insisted that I change it. That's why the next chapter ends like it does. But, as I'm sure you'll be able to tell, I didn't have enough pages. Hmph.

I want to sincerely thank my brother, who did research on racetracks, the monorail and Haneda Airport for me; my editor, who collected various materials from Haneda Airport and took pictures of its restrooms; and my regular and temporary assistants who frantically drew with me.

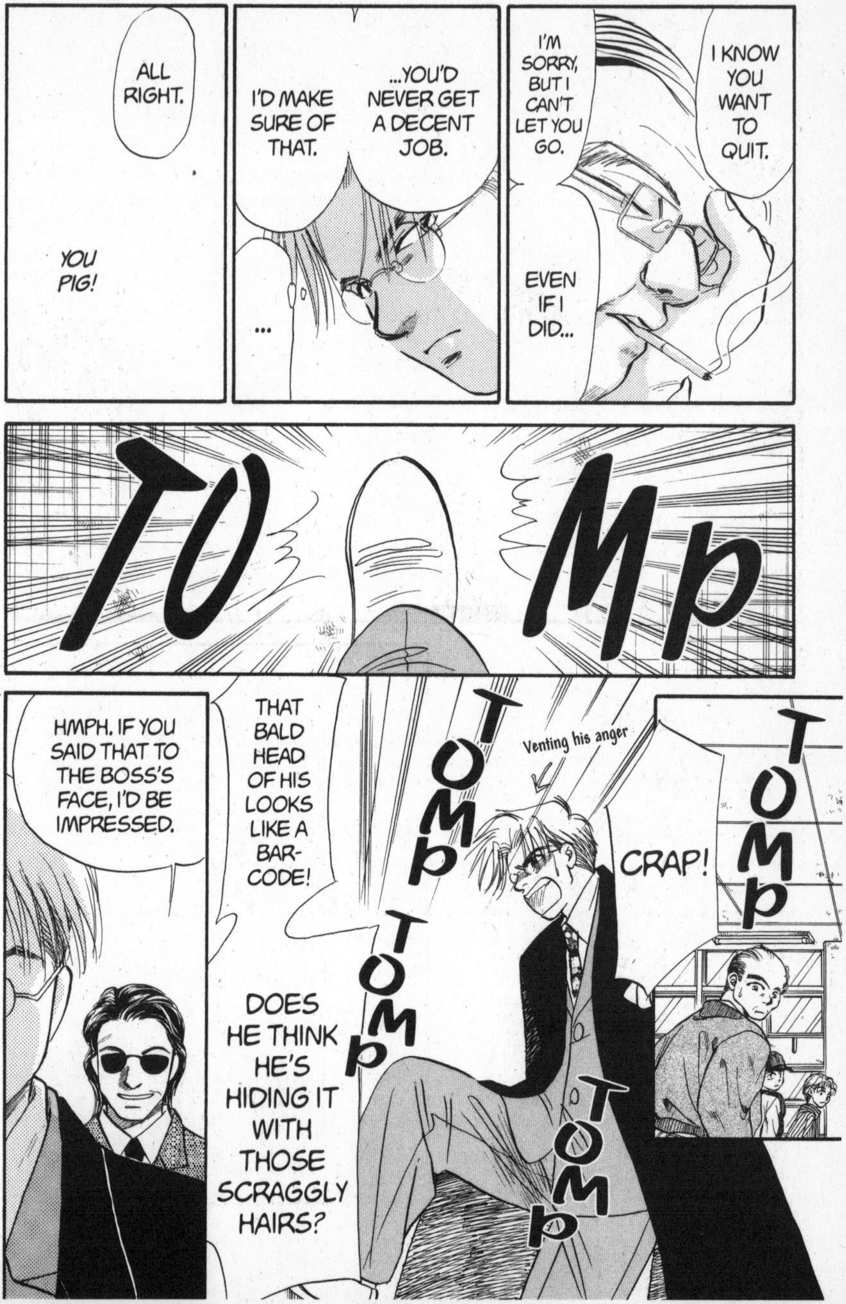
I KNOW YOU WANT TO QUIT.
I'M SORRY, BUT I CAN'T LET YOU GO.
EVEN IF I DID...
...YOU'D NEVER GET A DECENT JOB.
I'D MAKE SURE OF THAT.
...
ALL RIGHT.
YOU PIG!
TOMp
TOMp
CRAP!
Venting his anger
TOMp
THAT BALD HEAD OF HIS LOOKS LIKE A BAR-CODE!
TOMp
TOMp
DOES HE THINK HE'S HIDING IT WITH THOSE SCRAGGLY HAIRS?
HMPH. IF YOU SAID THAT TO THE BOSS'S FACE, I'D BE IMPRESSED.

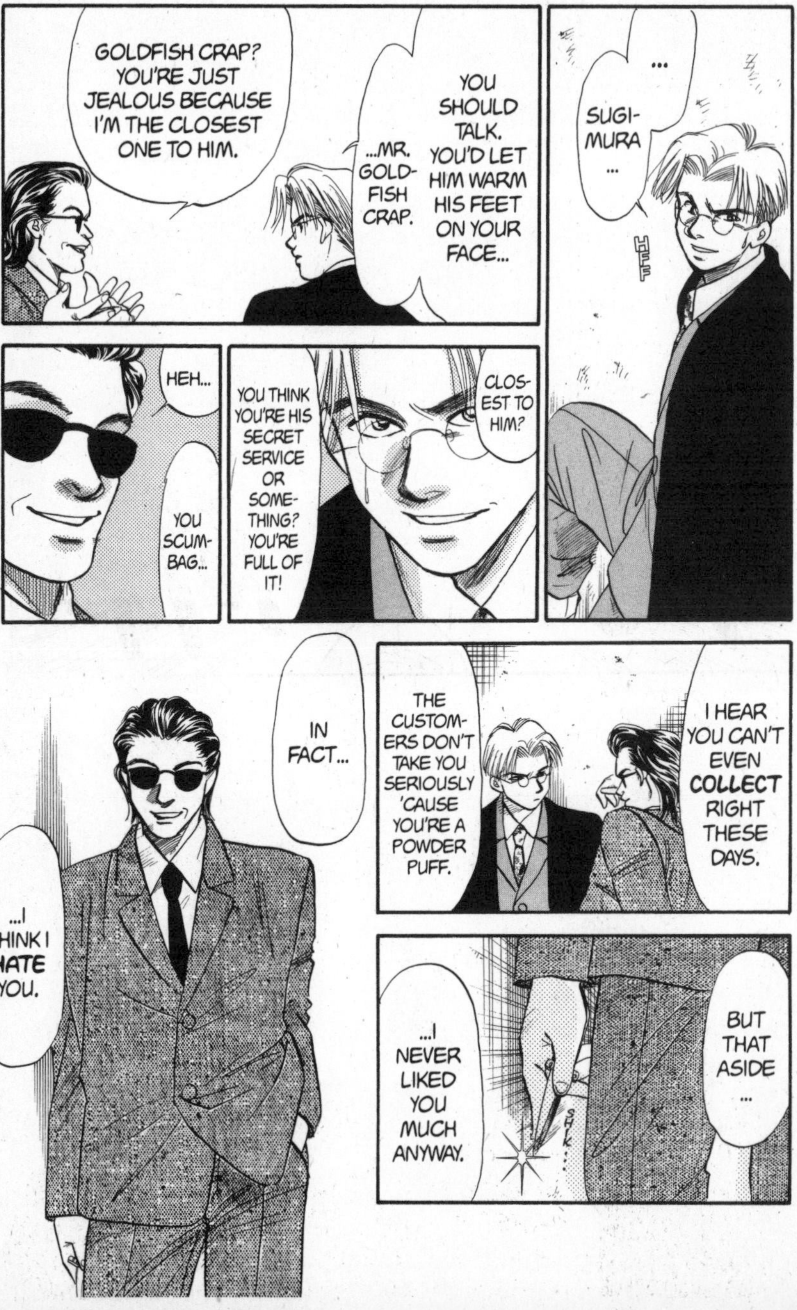
...
SUGI-MURA...
HEFF
YOU SHOULD TALK. YOU'D LET HIM WARM HIS FEET ON YOUR FACE...
...MR. GOLDFISH CRAP.
GOLDFISH CRAP? YOU'RE JUST JEALOUS BECAUSE I'M THE CLOSEST ONE TO HIM.
CLOSEST TO HIM?
YOU THINK YOU'RE HIS SECRET SERVICE OR SOMETHING? YOU'RE FULL OF IT!
HEH...
YOU SCUMBAG...
I HEAR YOU CAN'T EVEN **COLLECT** RIGHT THESE DAYS.
THE CUSTOMERS DON'T TAKE YOU SERIOUSLY 'CAUSE YOU'RE A POWDER PUFF.
BUT THAT ASIDE...
...I NEVER LIKED YOU MUCH ANYWAY.
SHIK...
IN FACT...
...I THINK I **HATE** YOU.

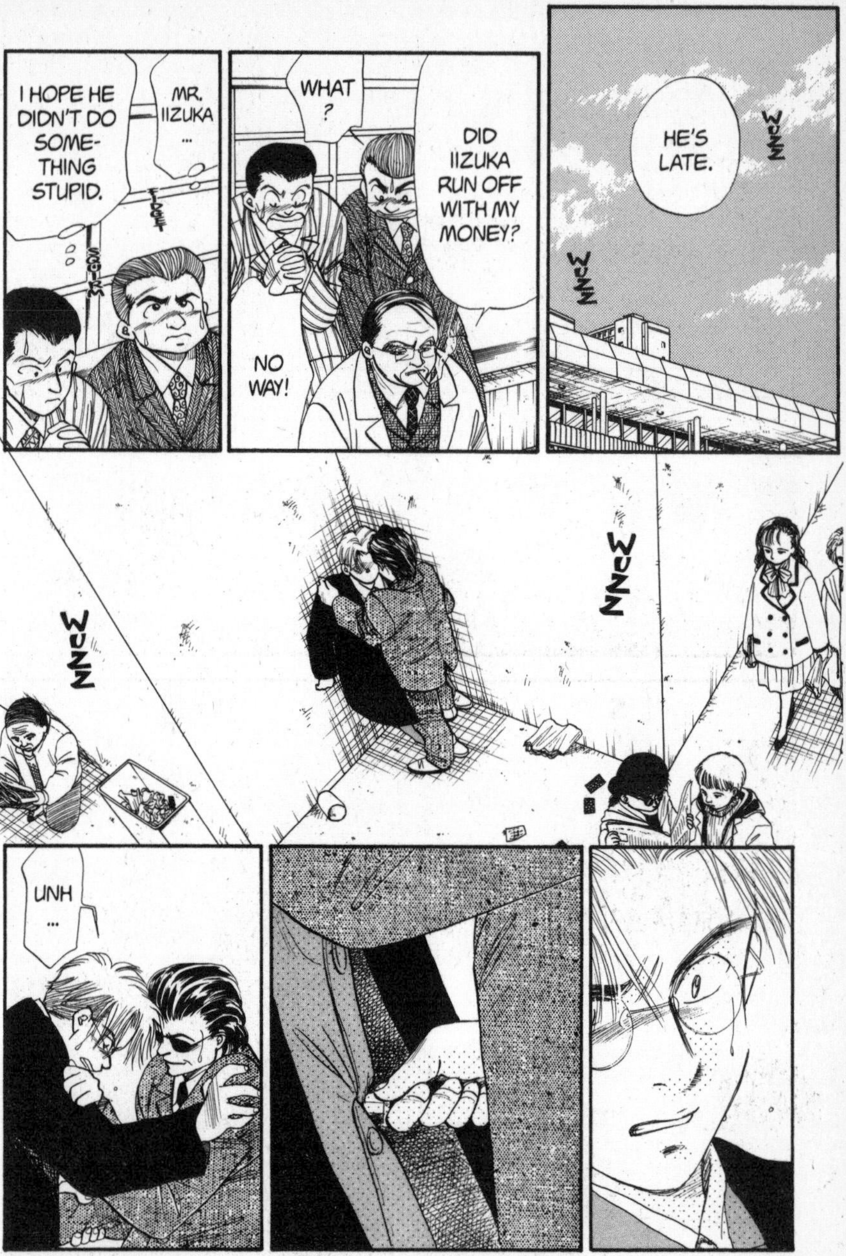
HE'S LATE.
WUZZ
WUZZ
DID IIZUKA RUN OFF WITH MY MONEY?
WHAT ?
NO WAY!
MR. IIZUKA ...
I HOPE HE DIDN'T DO SOME-THING STUPID.
FIDGET
SQUIRM
WUZZ
WUZZ
UNH ...

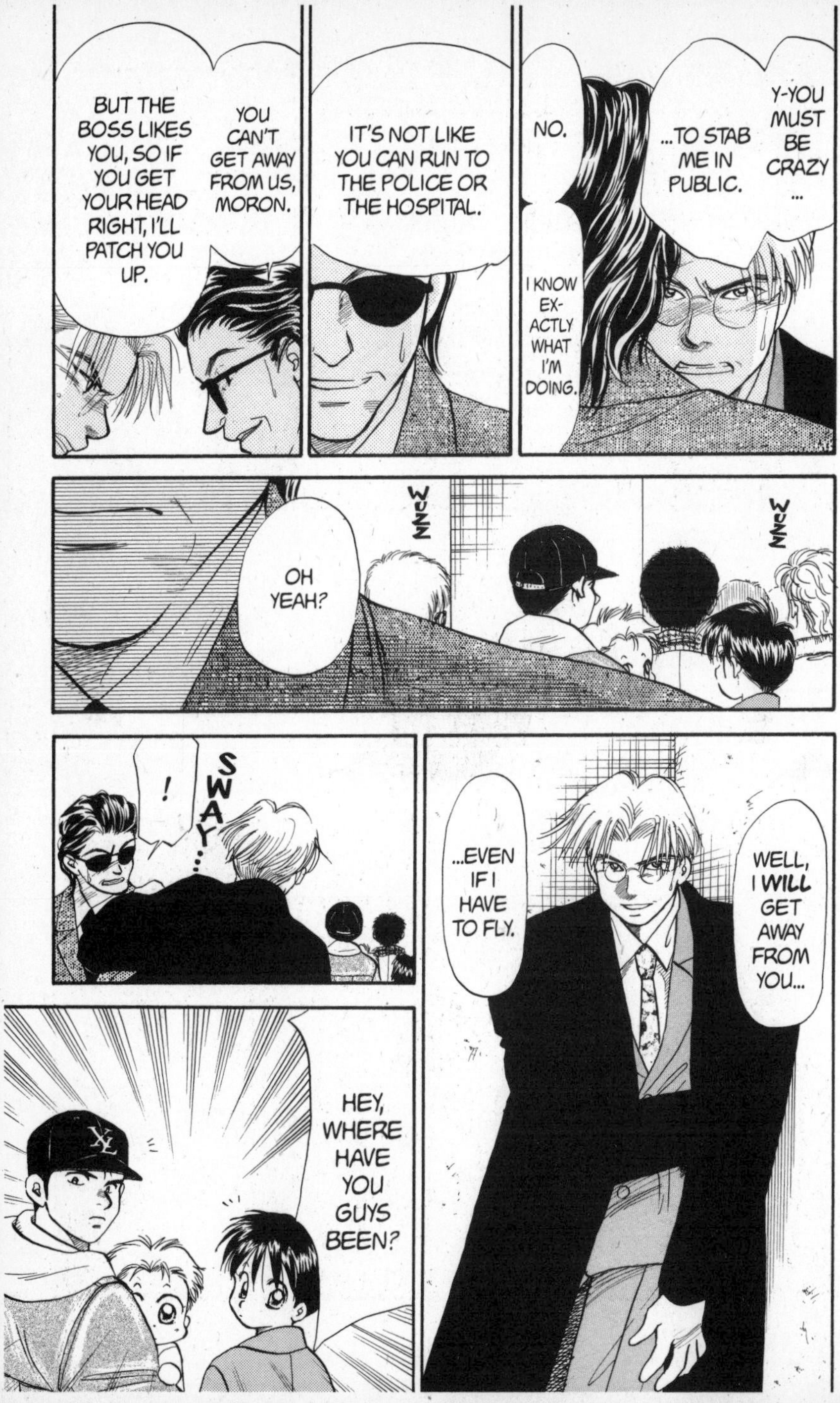
Y-YOU MUST BE CRAZY...
...TO STAB ME IN PUBLIC.
NO.
I KNOW EXACTLY WHAT I'M DOING.
IT'S NOT LIKE YOU CAN RUN TO THE POLICE OR THE HOSPITAL.
YOU CAN'T GET AWAY FROM US, MORON.
BUT THE BOSS LIKES YOU, SO IF YOU GET YOUR HEAD RIGHT, I'LL PATCH YOU UP.
WUZZ
WUZZ
OH YEAH?
WELL, I **WILL** GET AWAY FROM YOU...
...EVEN IF I HAVE TO FLY.
!
SWAY...
HEY, WHERE HAVE YOU GUYS BEEN?

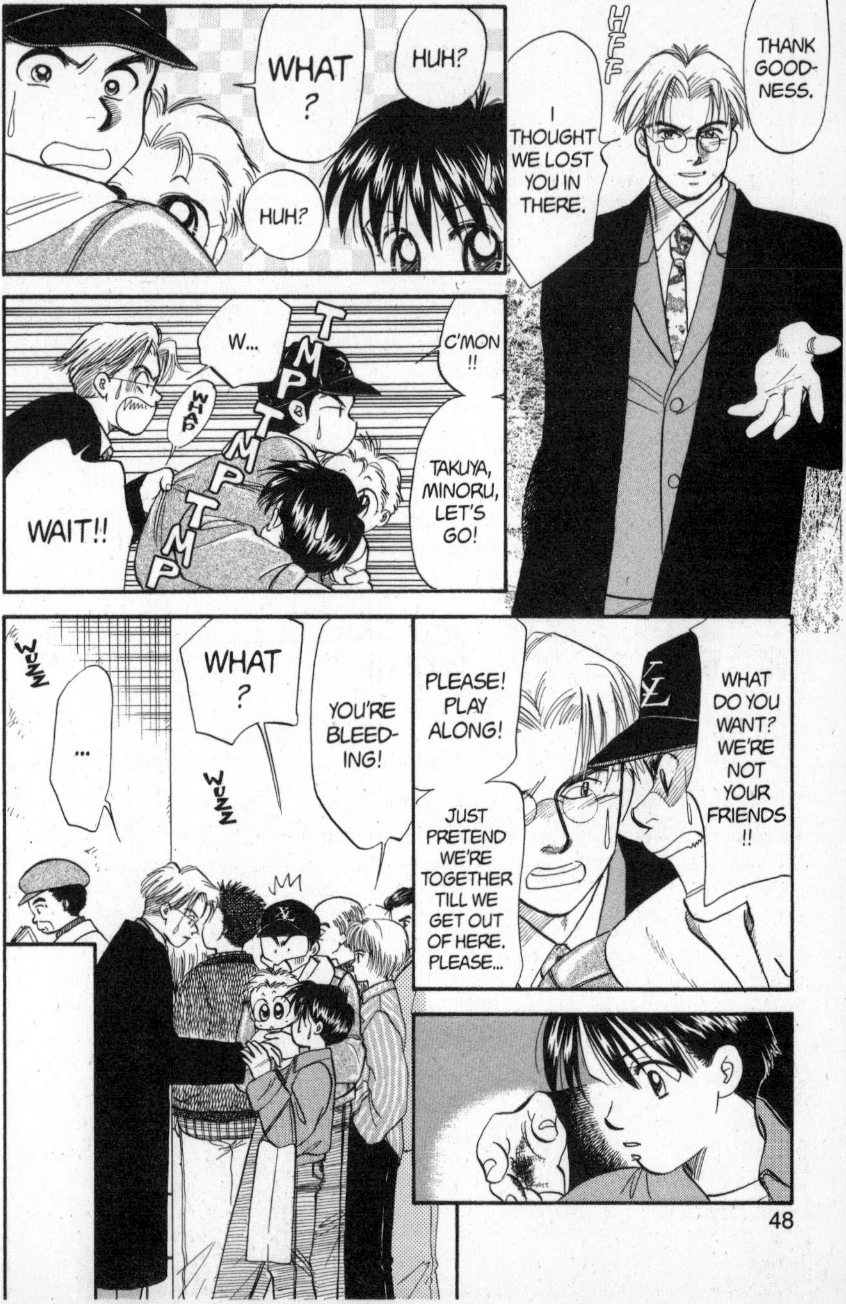
THANK GOODNESS.
HFF
I THOUGHT WE LOST YOU IN THERE.
HUH?
WHAT?
HUH?
C'MON!!
TAKUYA, MINORU, LET'S GO!
TMP TMP TMP
W...
WHAP
WAIT!!
WHAT DO YOU WANT? WE'RE NOT YOUR FRIENDS!!
PLEASE! PLAY ALONG!
JUST PRETEND WE'RE TOGETHER TILL WE GET OUT OF HERE. PLEASE...
YOU'RE BLEEDING!
WHAT?
WUZZ
...
WUZZ

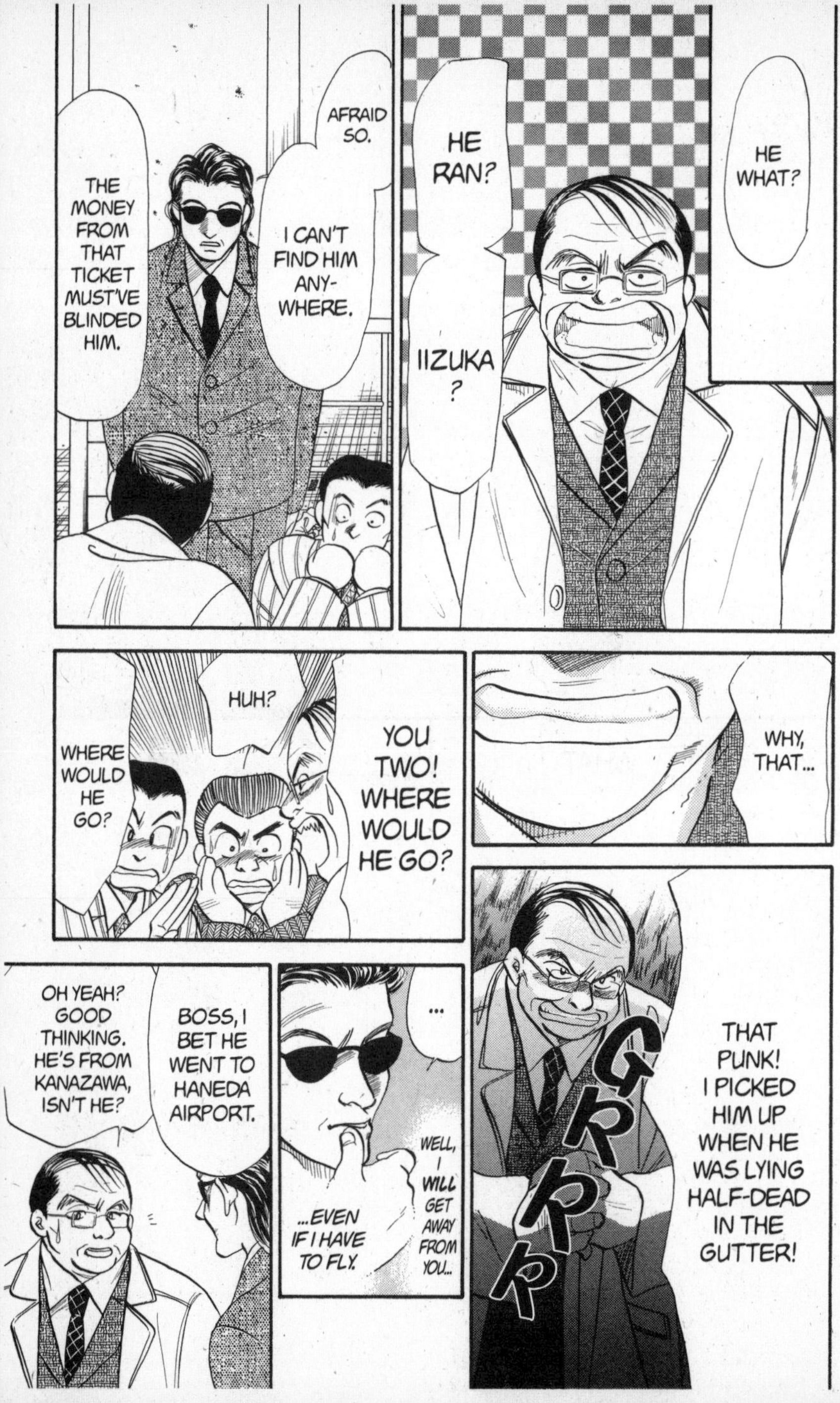
HE WHAT?
HE RAN?
IIZUKA?
AFRAID SO.
I CAN'T FIND HIM ANYWHERE.
THE MONEY FROM THAT TICKET MUST'VE BLINDED HIM.
WHY, THAT...
THAT PUNK! I PICKED HIM UP WHEN HE WAS LYING HALF-DEAD IN THE GUTTER!
GRRRR
YOU TWO! WHERE WOULD HE GO?
HUH?
WHERE WOULD HE GO?
...
WELL, I WILL GET AWAY FROM YOU...
...EVEN IF I HAVE TO FLY.
BOSS, I BET HE WENT TO HANEDA AIRPORT.
OH YEAH? GOOD THINKING. HE'S FROM KANAZAWA, ISN'T HE?

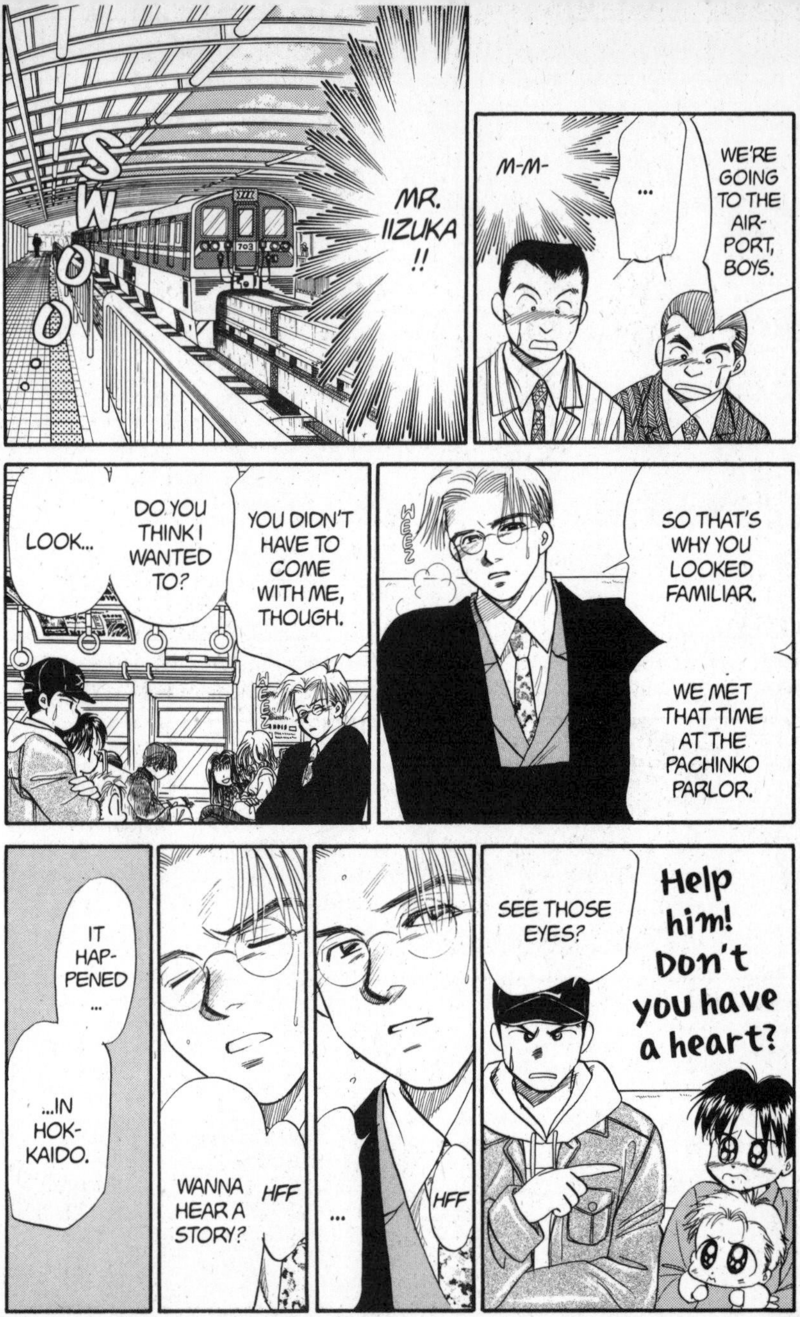
WE'RE GOING TO THE AIR-PORT, BOYS.
...
M-M-
MR. IIZUKA!!
SWOOO
SO THAT'S WHY YOU LOOKED FAMILIAR.
WE MET THAT TIME AT THE PACHINKO PARLOR.
WEEZ
YOU DIDN'T HAVE TO COME WITH ME, THOUGH.
DO YOU THINK I WANTED TO?
LOOK...
WEEZ
Help him! Don't you have a heart?
SEE THOSE EYES?
HFF
...
HFF
WANNA HEAR A STORY?
IT HAP-PENED...
...IN HOK-KAIDO.

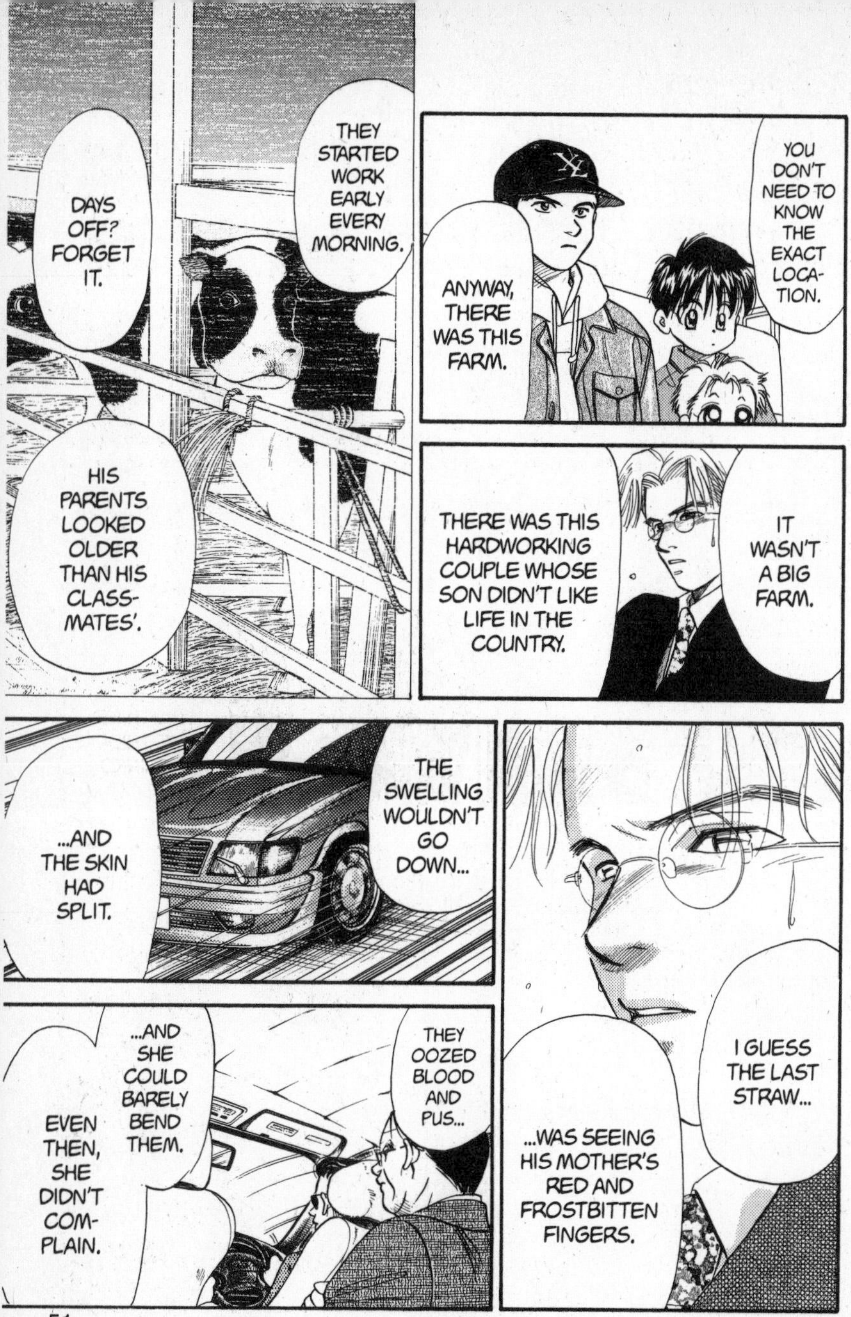
YOU DON'T NEED TO KNOW THE EXACT LOCATION.
ANYWAY, THERE WAS THIS FARM.
IT WASN'T A BIG FARM.
THERE WAS THIS HARDWORKING COUPLE WHOSE SON DIDN'T LIKE LIFE IN THE COUNTRY.
THEY STARTED WORK EARLY EVERY MORNING.
DAYS OFF? FORGET IT.
HIS PARENTS LOOKED OLDER THAN HIS CLASSMATES'.
I GUESS THE LAST STRAW...
...WAS SEEING HIS MOTHER'S RED AND FROSTBITTEN FINGERS.
THE SWELLING WOULDN'T GO DOWN...
...AND THE SKIN HAD SPLIT.
THEY OOZED BLOOD AND PUS...
...AND SHE COULD BARELY BEND THEM.
EVEN THEN, SHE DIDN'T COMPLAIN.

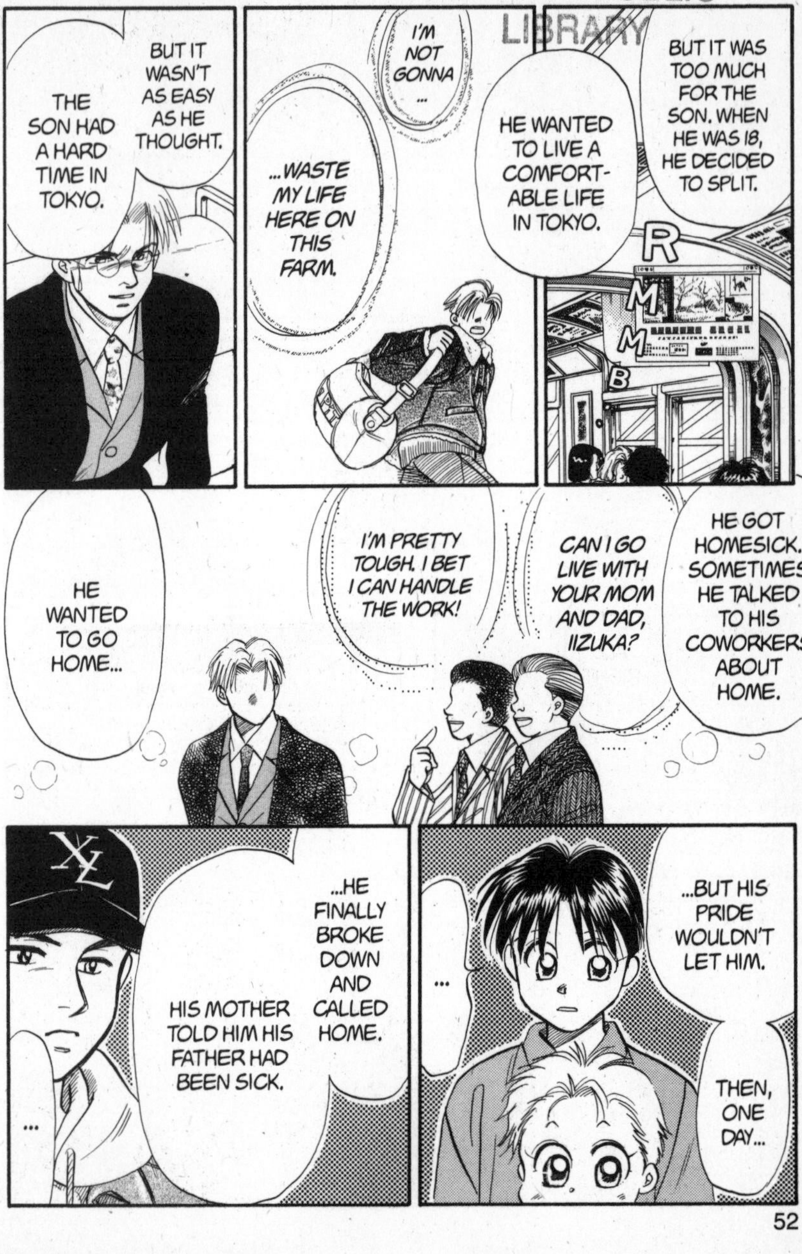
BUT IT WAS TOO MUCH FOR THE SON. WHEN HE WAS 18, HE DECIDED TO SPLIT.
HE WANTED TO LIVE A COMFORT-ABLE LIFE IN TOKYO.
RMMB
I'M NOT GONNA...
...WASTE MY LIFE HERE ON THIS FARM.
BUT IT WASN'T AS EASY AS HE THOUGHT.
THE SON HAD A HARD TIME IN TOKYO.
HE GOT HOMESICK. SOMETIMES HE TALKED TO HIS COWORKERS ABOUT HOME.
CAN I GO LIVE WITH YOUR MOM AND DAD, IIZUKA?
I'M PRETTY TOUGH. I BET I CAN HANDLE THE WORK!
HE WANTED TO GO HOME...
...BUT HIS PRIDE WOULDN'T LET HIM.
THEN, ONE DAY...
...
...HE FINALLY BROKE DOWN AND CALLED HOME.
HIS MOTHER TOLD HIM HIS FATHER HAD BEEN SICK.
...

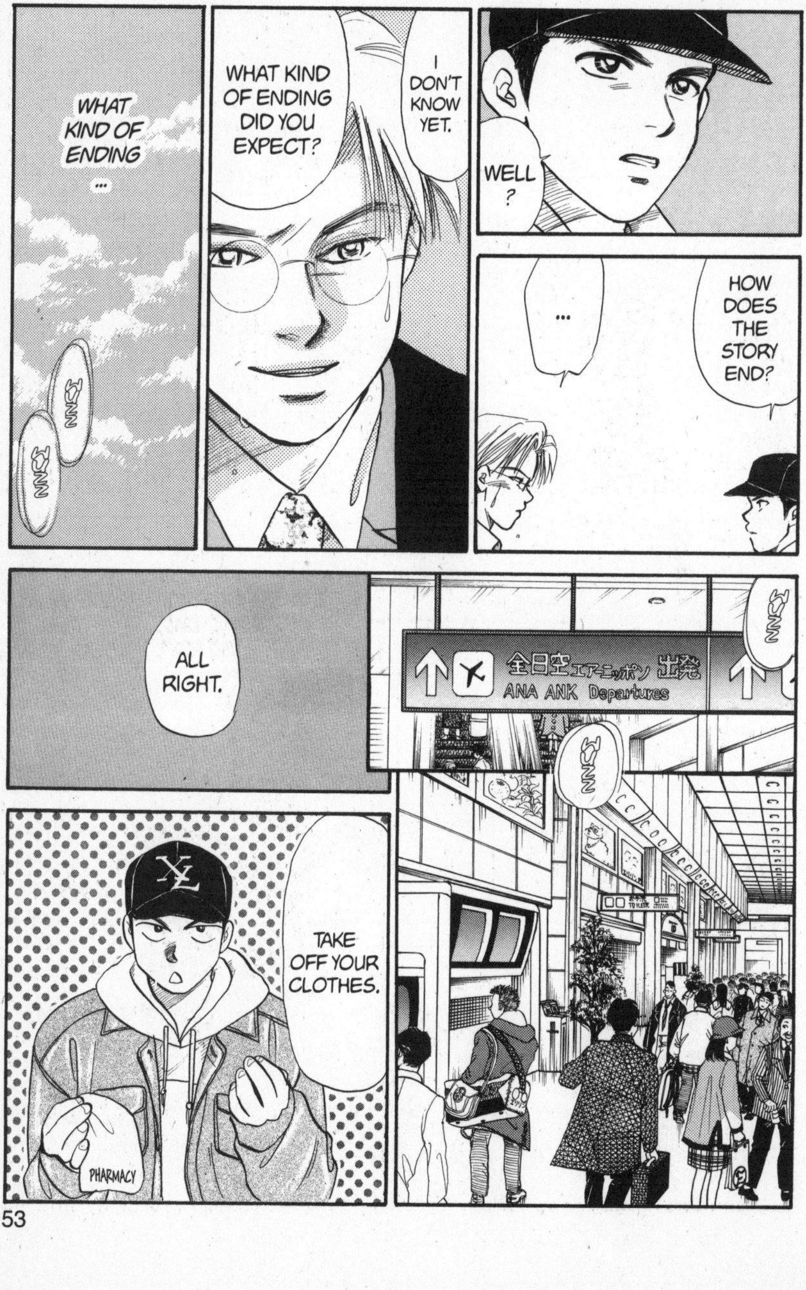
WELL?
HOW DOES THE STORY END?
...
I DON'T KNOW YET.
WHAT KIND OF ENDING DID YOU EXPECT?
WHAT KIND OF ENDING ...
全日空エアーニッポン 出発
ANA ANK Departures
ALL RIGHT.
TAKE OFF YOUR CLOTHES.
PHARMACY

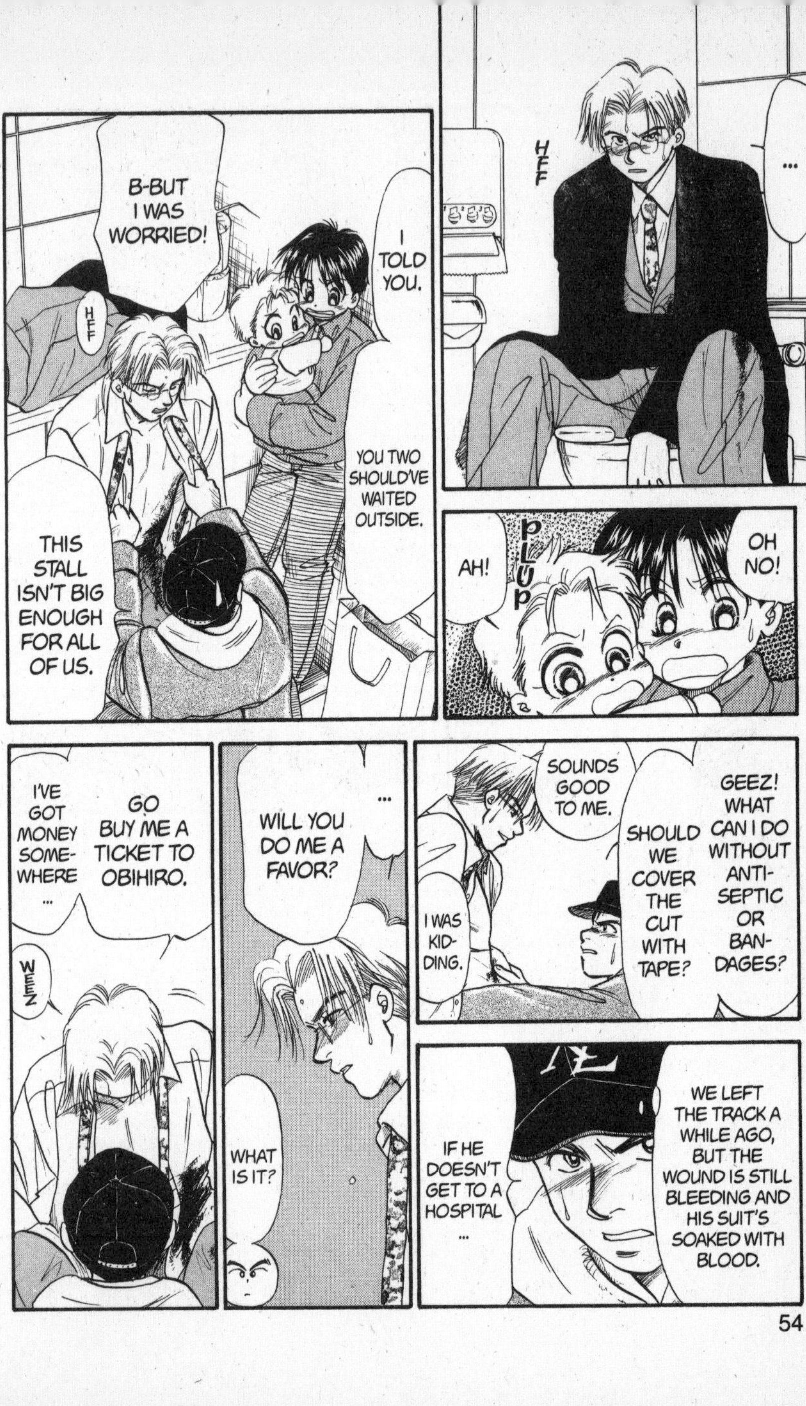
...
HFF
OH NO!
PLUP
AH!
I TOLD YOU.
B-BUT I WAS WORRIED!
HFF
YOU TWO SHOULD'VE WAITED OUTSIDE.
THIS STALL ISN'T BIG ENOUGH FOR ALL OF US.
GEEZ! WHAT CAN I DO WITHOUT ANTISEPTIC OR BANDAGES?
SHOULD WE COVER THE CUT WITH TAPE?
SOUNDS GOOD TO ME.
I WAS KIDDING.
WE LEFT THE TRACK A WHILE AGO, BUT THE WOUND IS STILL BLEEDING AND HIS SUIT'S SOAKED WITH BLOOD.
IF HE DOESN'T GET TO A HOSPITAL ...
...
WILL YOU DO ME A FAVOR?
WHAT IS IT?
GO BUY ME A TICKET TO OBIHIRO.
I'VE GOT MONEY SOMEWHERE ...
WEEZ

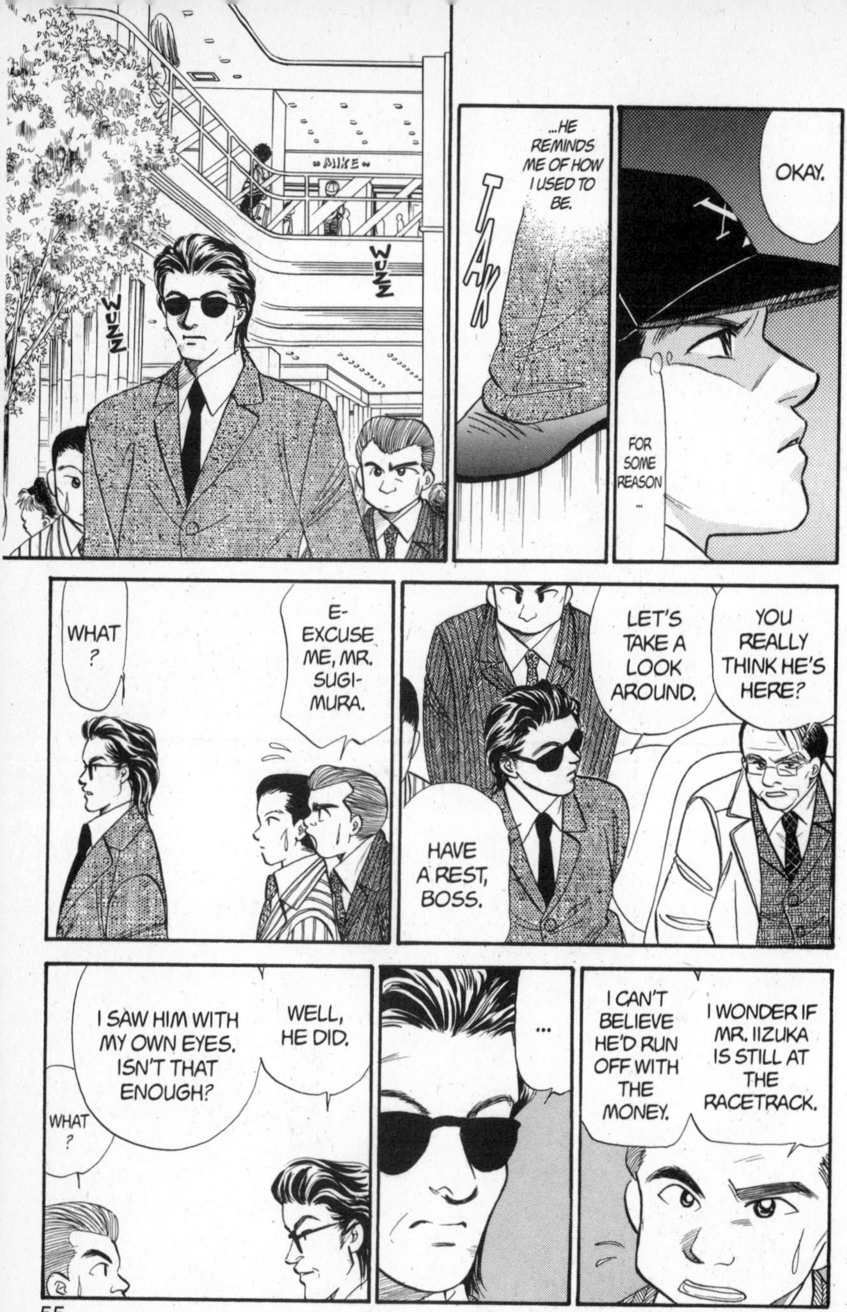
OKAY.
FOR SOME REASON...
...HE REMINDS ME OF HOW I USED TO BE.
TAK
WUZZ
WUZZ
YOU REALLY THINK HE'S HERE?
LET'S TAKE A LOOK AROUND.
HAVE A REST, BOSS.
E-EXCUSE ME, MR. SUGI-MURA.
WHAT?
I WONDER IF MR. IIZUKA IS STILL AT THE RACETRACK.
I CAN'T BELIEVE HE'D RUN OFF WITH THE MONEY.
...
WELL, HE DID.
I SAW HIM WITH MY OWN EYES. ISN'T THAT ENOUGH?
WHAT?

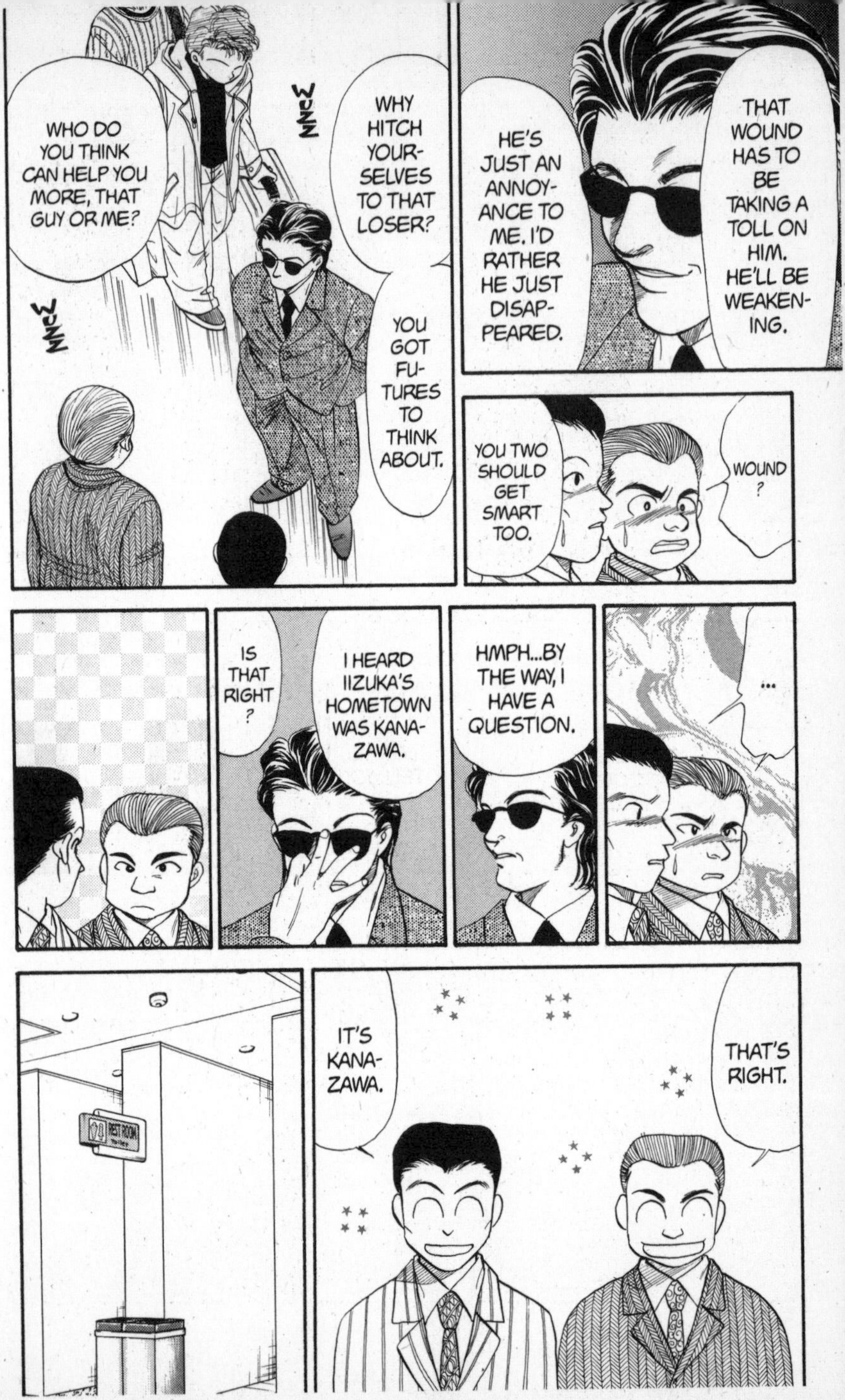
THAT WOUND HAS TO BE TAKING A TOLL ON HIM. HE'LL BE WEAKENING.
HE'S JUST AN ANNOYANCE TO ME. I'D RATHER HE JUST DISAPPEARED.
WOUND?
YOU TWO SHOULD GET SMART TOO.
WHY HITCH YOURSELVES TO THAT LOSER?
YOU GOT FUTURES TO THINK ABOUT.
WUZZ
WHO DO YOU THINK CAN HELP YOU MORE, THAT GUY OR ME?
WUZZ
...
HMPH...BY THE WAY, I HAVE A QUESTION.
I HEARD IIZUKA'S HOMETOWN WAS KANAZAWA.
IS THAT RIGHT?
THAT'S RIGHT.
IT'S KANAZAWA.
REST ROOM

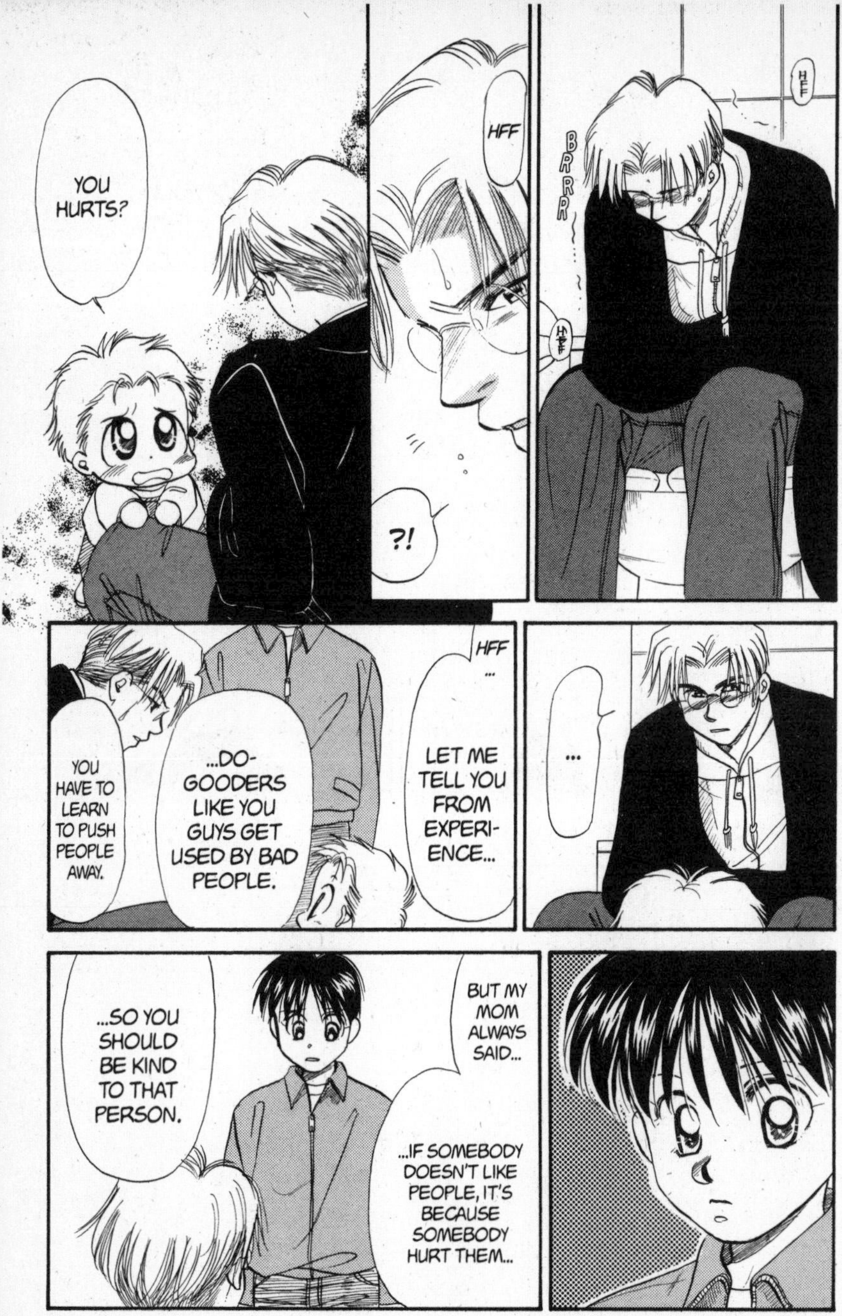
HFF
BRRR
HFF
HFF
?!
YOU HURTS?
...
HFF...
LET ME TELL YOU FROM EXPERIENCE...
...DO-GOODERS LIKE YOU GUYS GET USED BY BAD PEOPLE.
YOU HAVE TO LEARN TO PUSH PEOPLE AWAY.
BUT MY MOM ALWAYS SAID...
...IF SOMEBODY DOESN'T LIKE PEOPLE, IT'S BECAUSE SOMEBODY HURT THEM...
...SO YOU SHOULD BE KIND TO THAT PERSON.

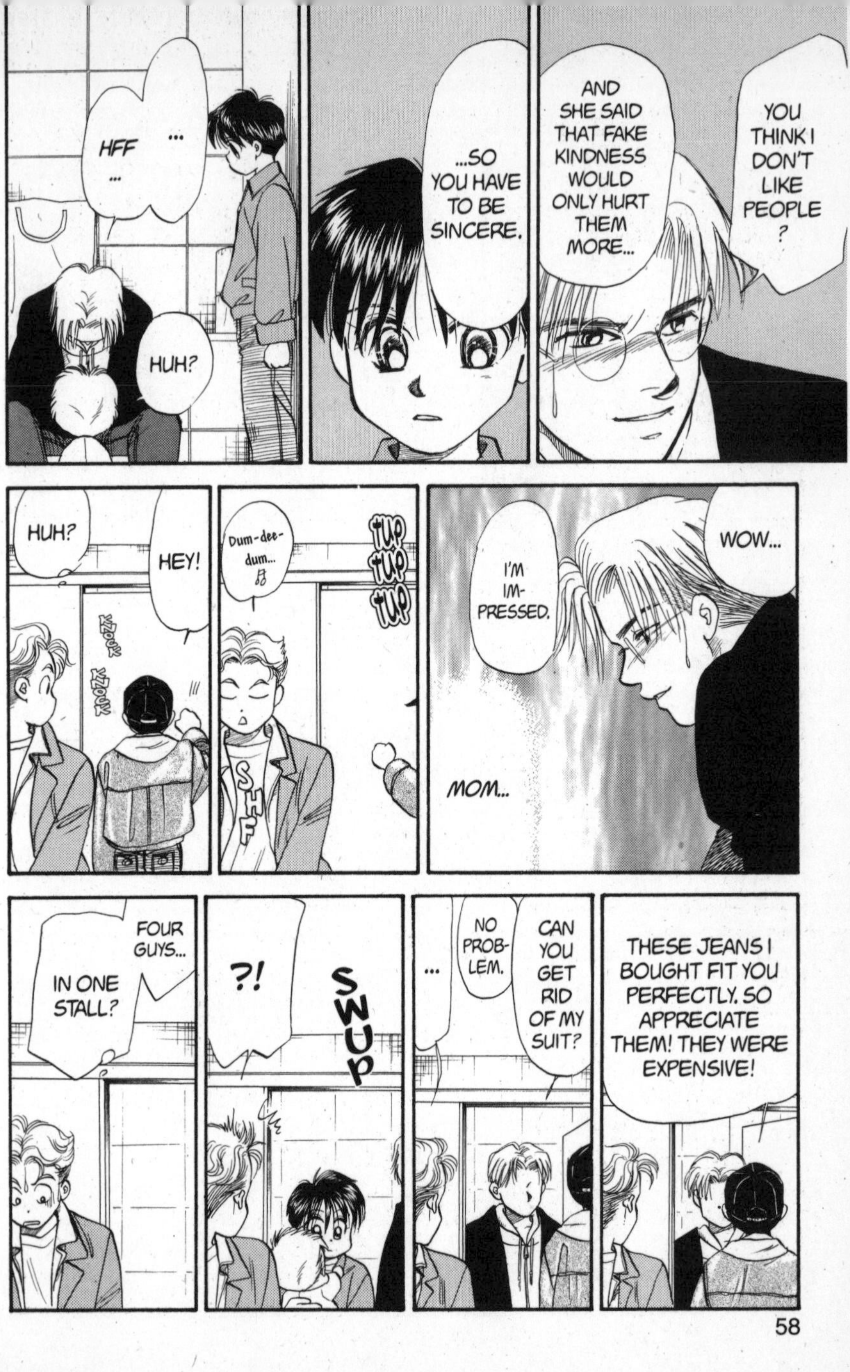
YOU THINK I DON'T LIKE PEOPLE?
AND SHE SAID THAT FAKE KINDNESS WOULD ONLY HURT THEM MORE...
...SO YOU HAVE TO BE SINCERE.
...
HFF ...
HUH?
WOW...
I'M IM-PRESSED.
MOM...
TUP TUP TUP
Dum-dee-dum...
HEY!
HUH?
KNOCK KNOCK
THESE JEANS I BOUGHT FIT YOU PERFECTLY. SO APPRECIATE THEM! THEY WERE EXPENSIVE!
CAN YOU GET RID OF MY SUIT?
NO PROB-LEM.
...
SWUP
?!
FOUR GUYS...
IN ONE STALL?

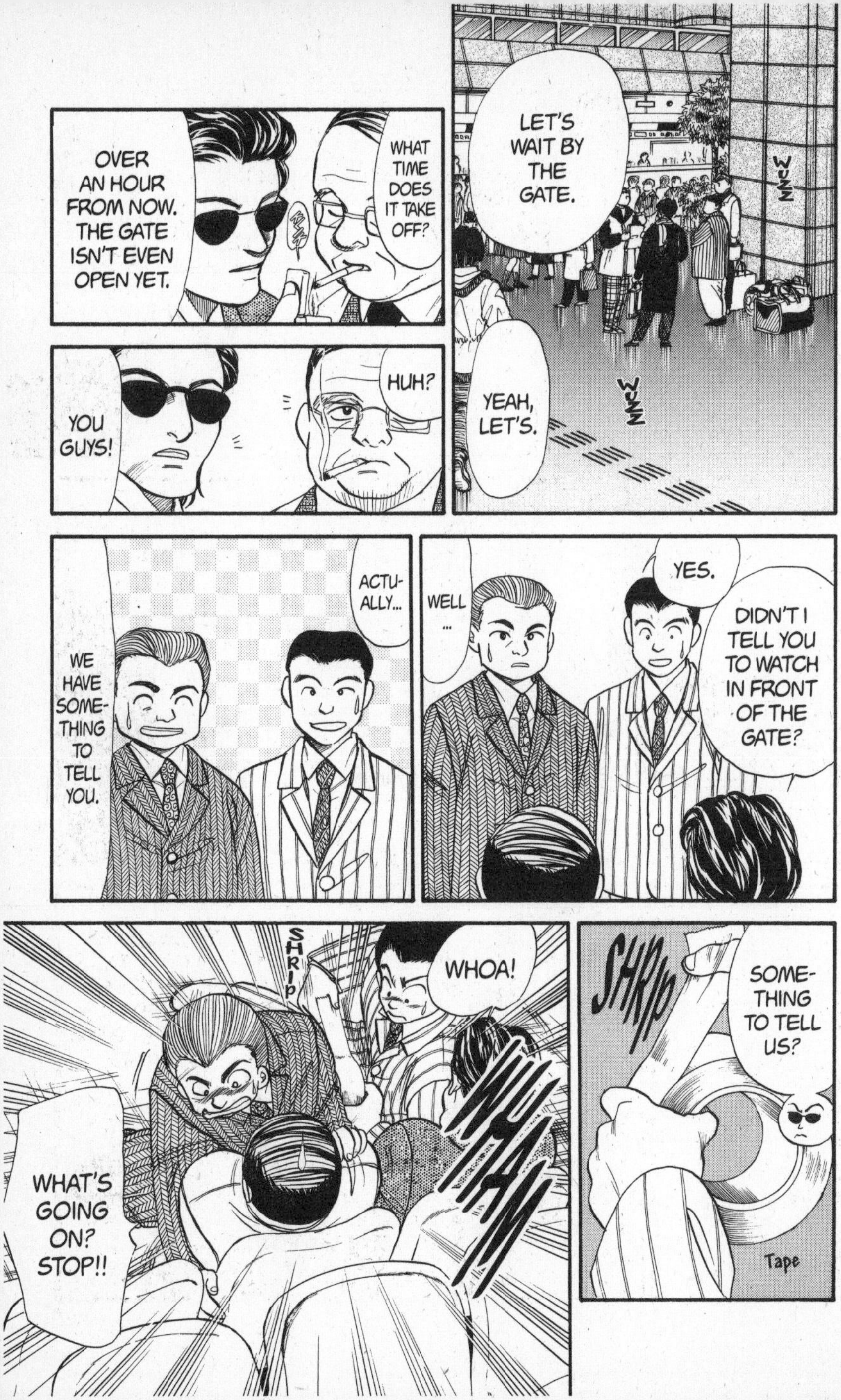
LET'S WAIT BY THE GATE.
WUZZ
YEAH, LET'S.
WUZZ
WHAT TIME DOES IT TAKE OFF?
OVER AN HOUR FROM NOW. THE GATE ISN'T EVEN OPEN YET.
HUH?
YOU GUYS!
YES.
DIDN'T I TELL YOU TO WATCH IN FRONT OF THE GATE?
WELL...
ACTU-ALLY...
WE HAVE SOME-THING TO TELL YOU.
SHRIP
SOME-THING TO TELL US?
Tape
SHRIP
WHOA!
WHAT'S GOING ON? STOP!!

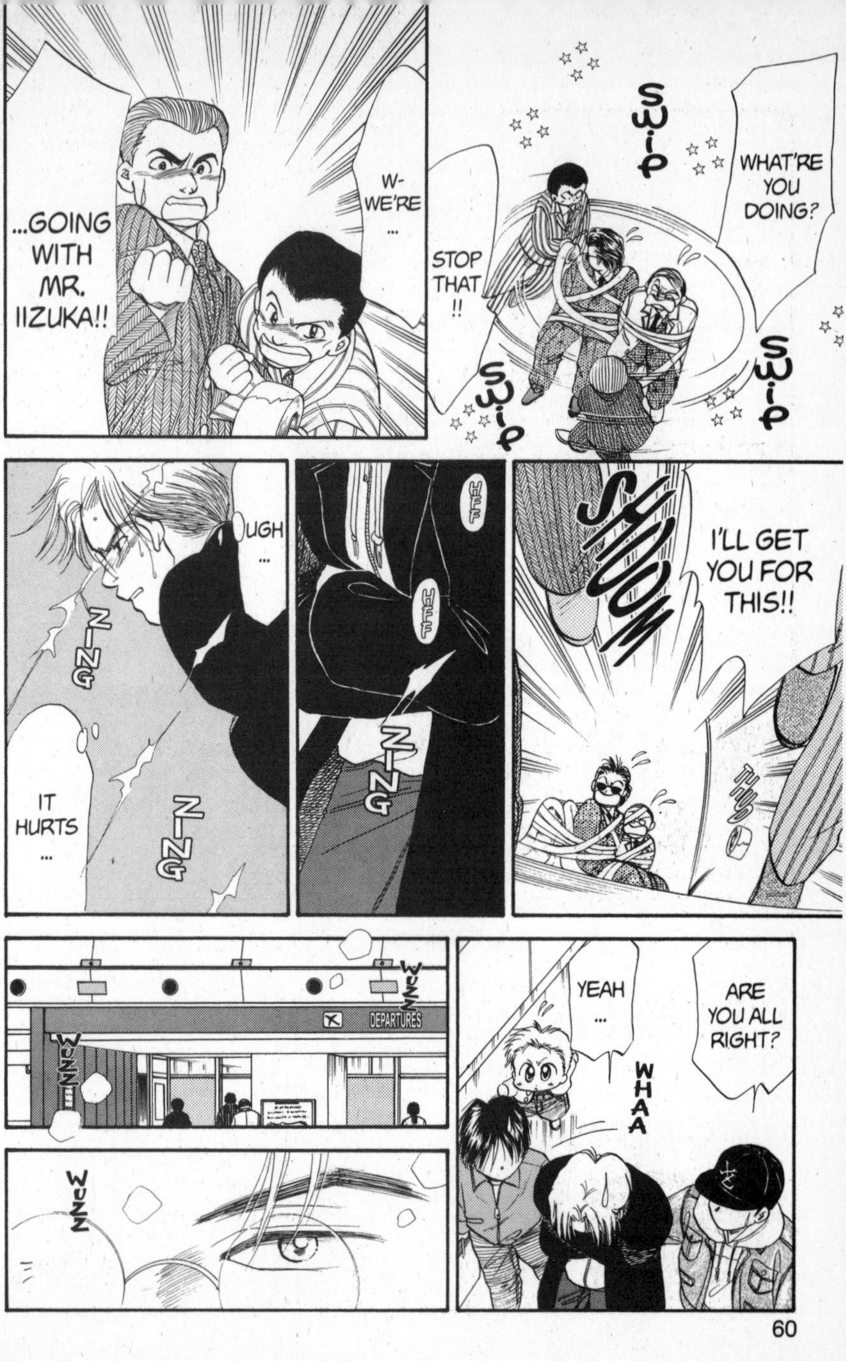
SWIP
WHAT'RE YOU DOING?
SWIP
STOP THAT!!
SWIP
W-WE'RE...
...GOING WITH MR. IIZUKA!!
SHOOM
I'LL GET YOU FOR THIS!!
THUD
HFF
HFF
ZING
UGH...
ZING
IT HURTS...
ZING
ARE YOU ALL RIGHT?
YEAH...
WHAA
WUZZ
DEPARTURES
WUZZ
WUZZ

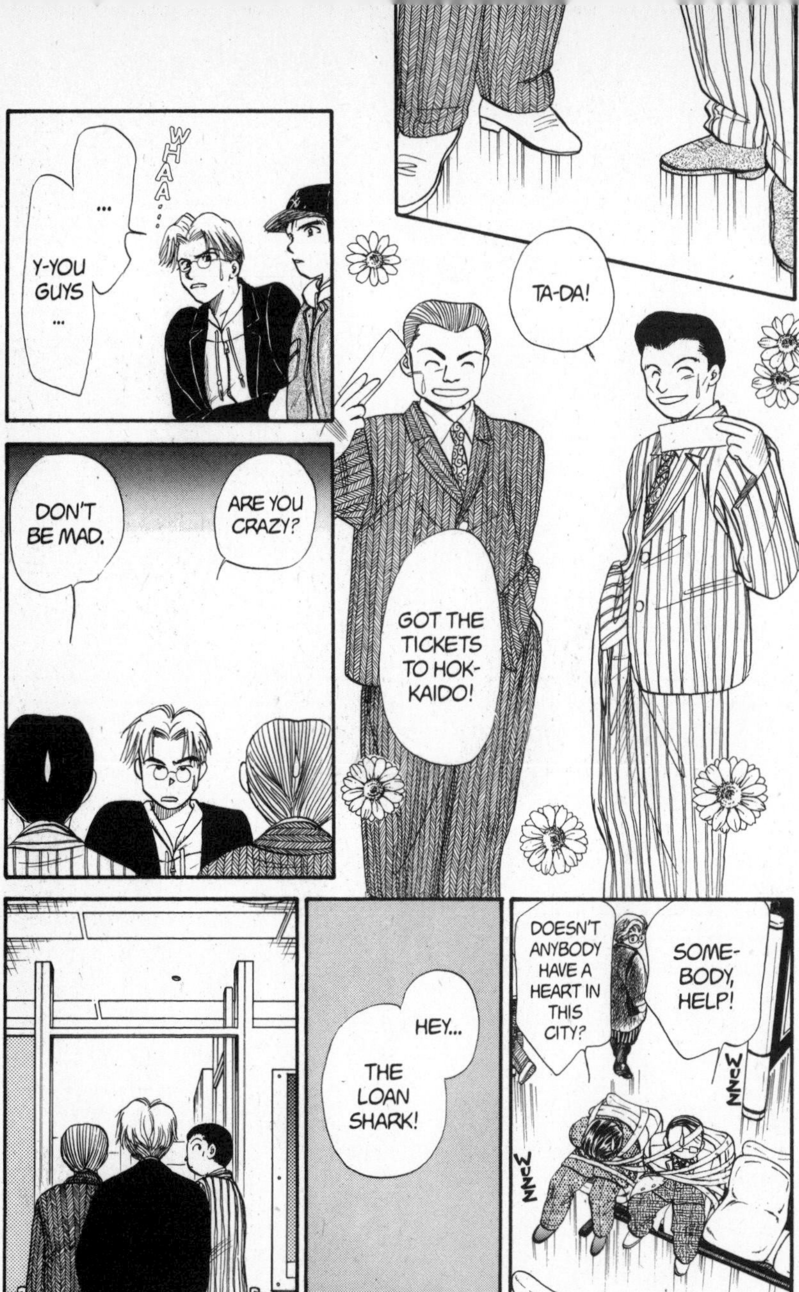
TA-DA!
GOT THE TICKETS TO HOK-KAIDO!
WHAA...
...
Y-YOU GUYS ...
ARE YOU CRAZY?
DON'T BE MAD.
SOME-BODY, HELP!
DOESN'T ANYBODY HAVE A HEART IN THIS CITY?
WUZZ
WUZZ
HEY...
THE LOAN SHARK!

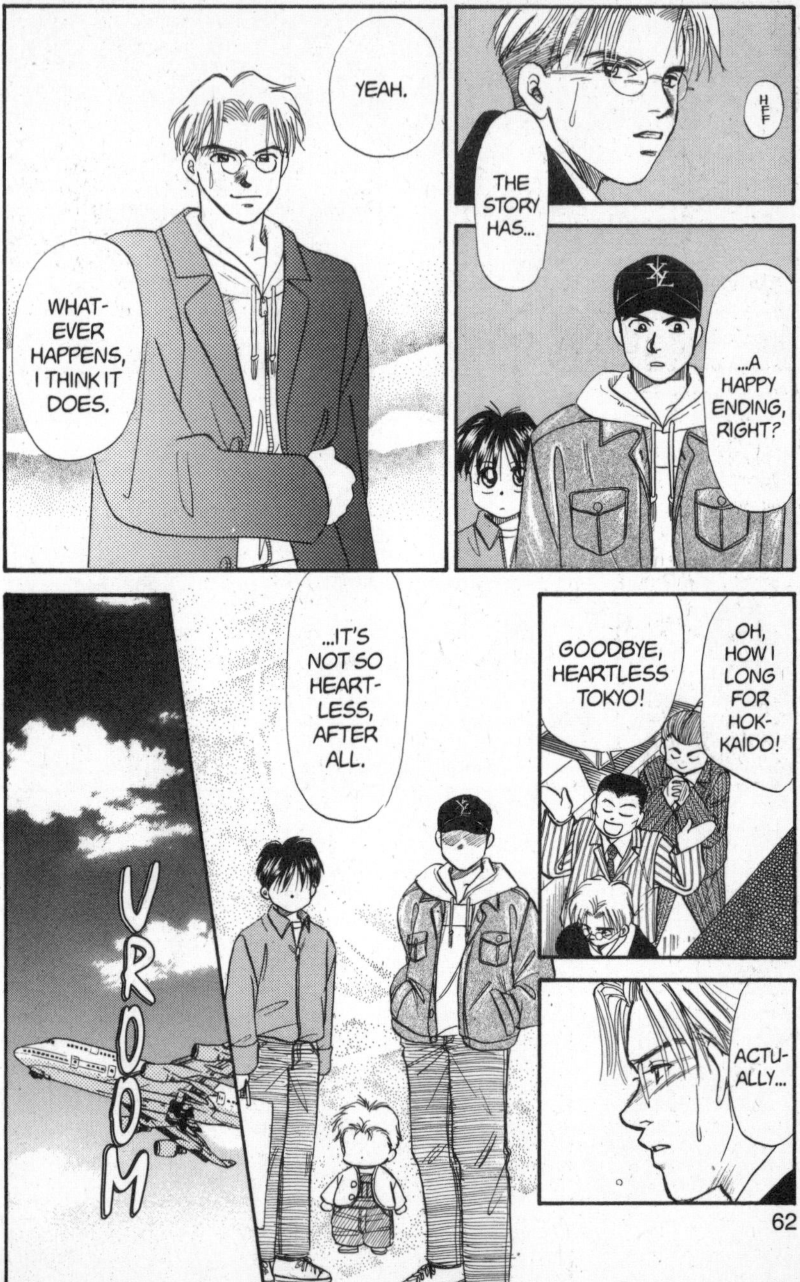
HFF
THE STORY HAS...
...A HAPPY ENDING, RIGHT?
YEAH.
WHAT-EVER HAPPENS, I THINK IT DOES.
OH, HOW I LONG FOR HOK-KAIDO!
GOODBYE, HEARTLESS TOKYO!
ACTU-ALLY...
...IT'S NOT SO HEART-LESS, AFTER ALL.
VROOM

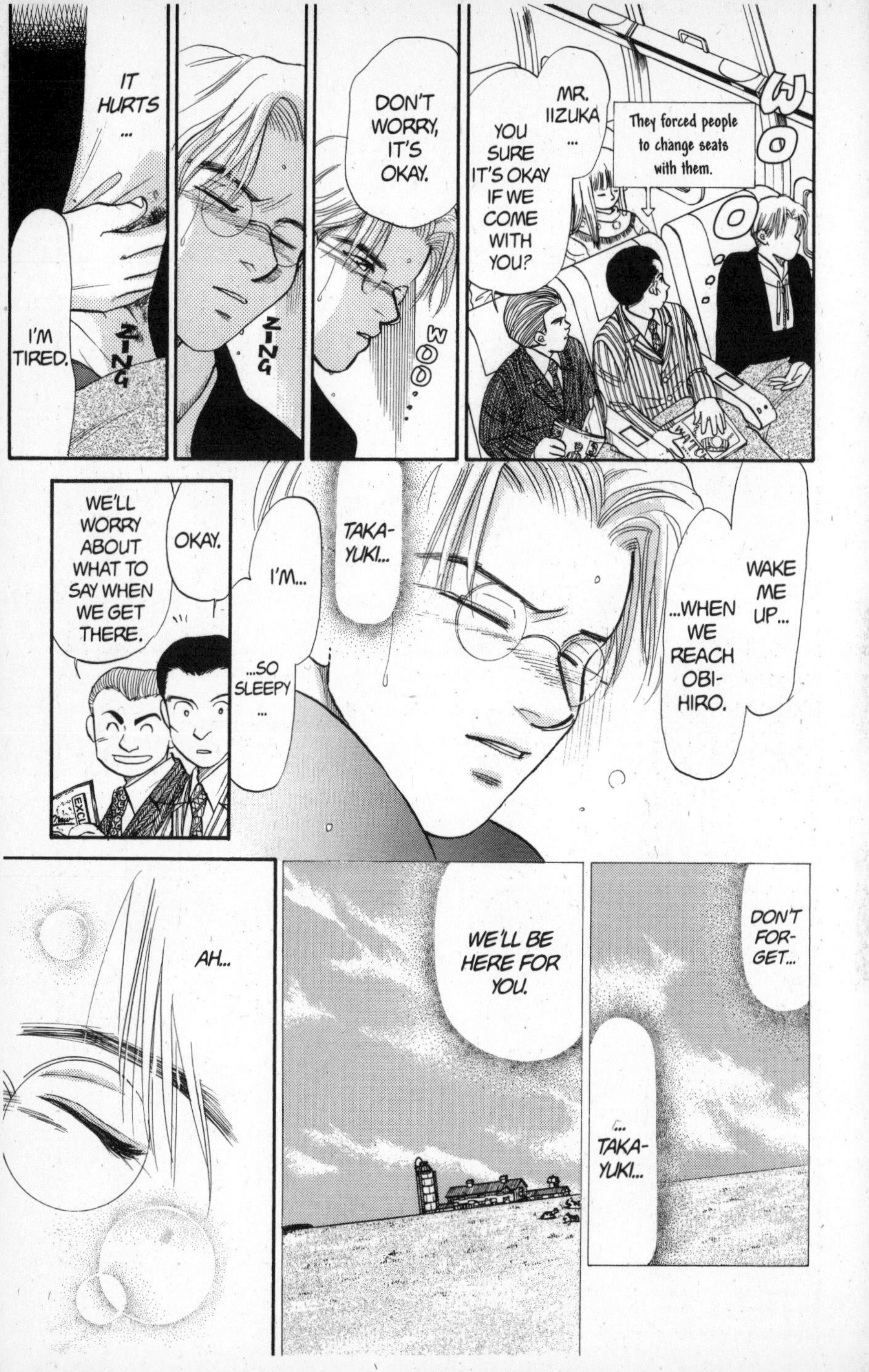

MR. IIZUKA ...
YOU SURE IT'S OKAY IF WE COME WITH YOU?
They forced people to change seats with them.
WOO
DON'T WORRY, IT'S OKAY.
WOO
ZING
IT HURTS ...
I'M TIRED.
ZING
WAKE ME UP...
...WHEN WE REACH OBI-HIRO.
TAKA-YUKI...
I'M...
...SO SLEEPY ...
OKAY.
WE'LL WORRY ABOUT WHAT TO SAY WHEN WE GET THERE.
DON'T FOR-GET...
... TAKA-YUKI...
WE'LL BE HERE FOR YOU.
AH...

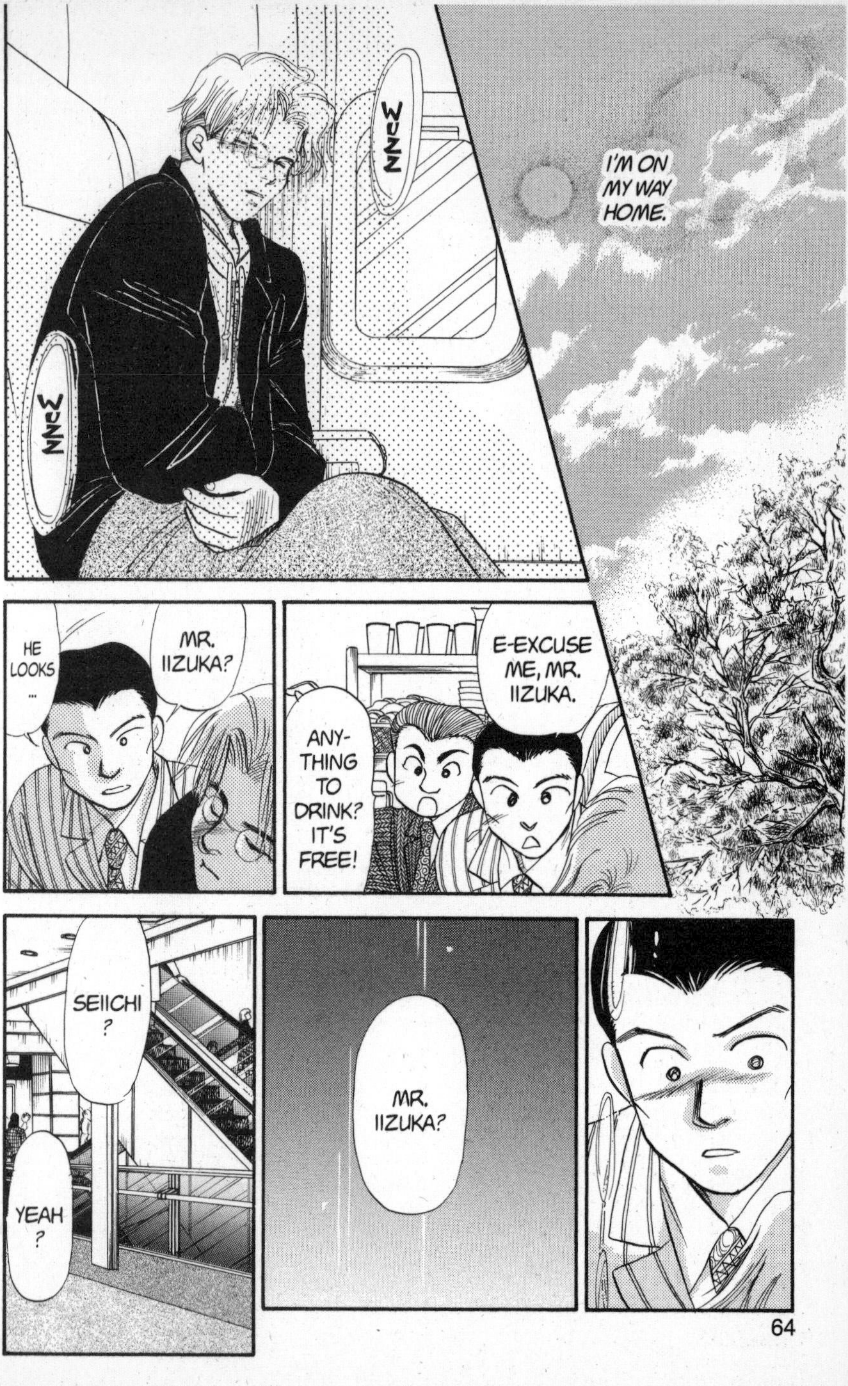
I'M ON MY WAY HOME.
WUZZ
WUZZ
E-EXCUSE ME, MR. IIZUKA.
ANYTHING TO DRINK? IT'S FREE!
MR. IIZUKA?
HE LOOKS ...
MR. IIZUKA?
SEIICHI?
YEAH?

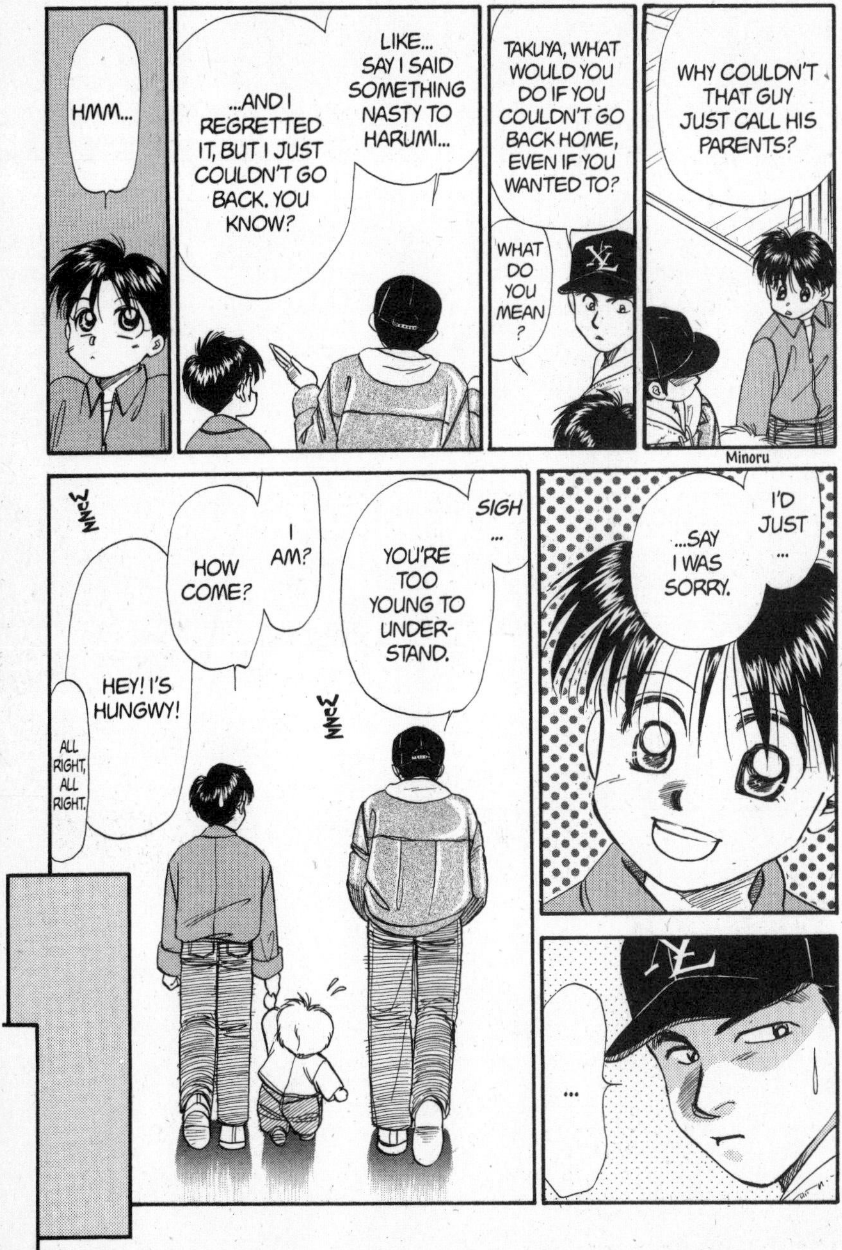
WHY COULDN'T THAT GUY JUST CALL HIS PARENTS?
Minoru
TAKUYA, WHAT WOULD YOU DO IF YOU COULDN'T GO BACK HOME, EVEN IF YOU WANTED TO?
WHAT DO YOU MEAN?
LIKE... SAY I SAID SOMETHING NASTY TO HARUMI...
...AND I REGRETTED IT, BUT I JUST COULDN'T GO BACK. YOU KNOW?
HMM...
I'D JUST...
...SAY I WAS SORRY.
...
SIGH...
YOU'RE TOO YOUNG TO UNDER-STAND.
I AM?
HOW COME?
HEY! I'S HUNGWY!
ALL RIGHT, ALL RIGHT.

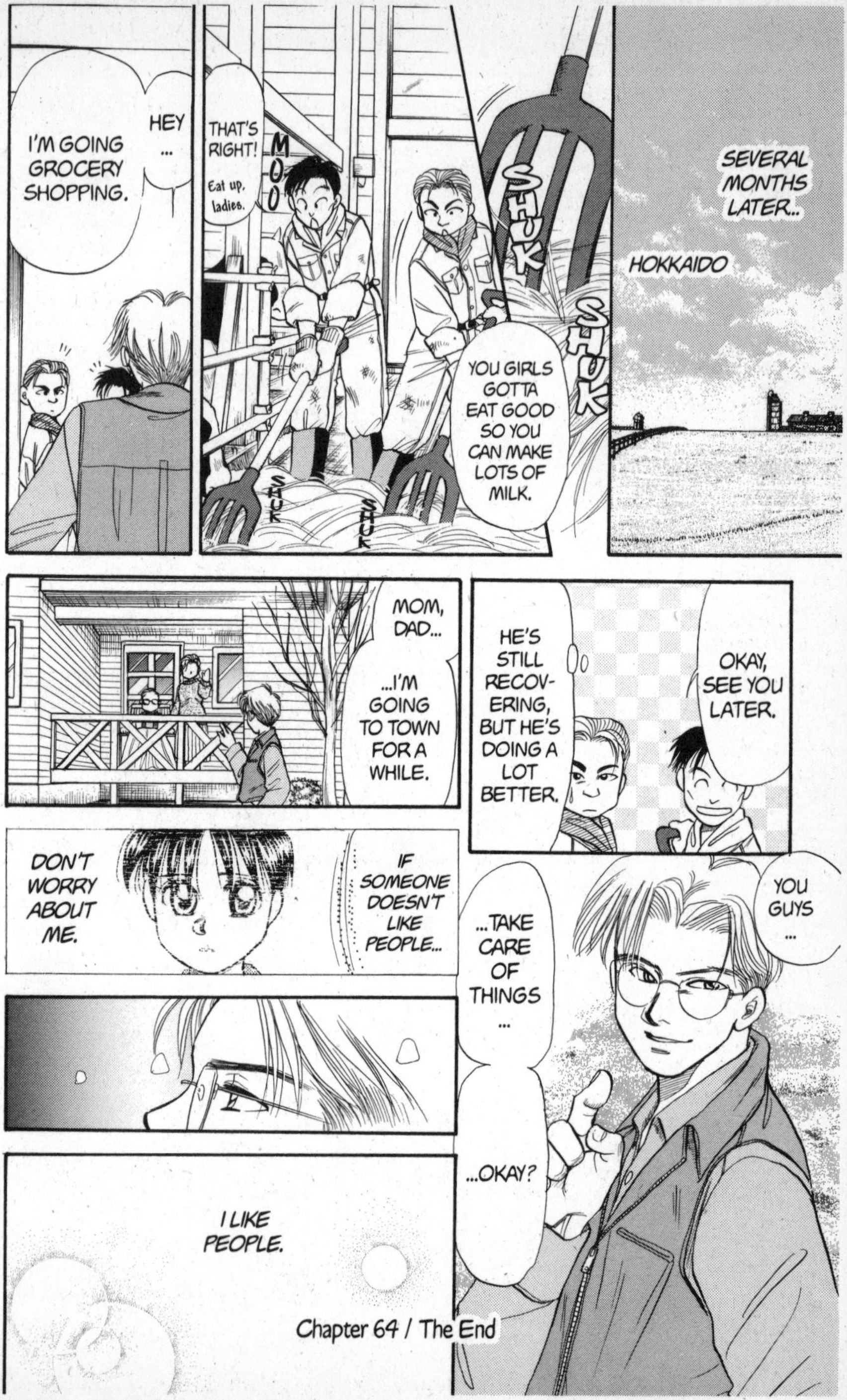
SEVERAL MONTHS LATER..
HOKKAIDO
SHUK
SHUK
YOU GIRLS GOTTA EAT GOOD SO YOU CAN MAKE LOTS OF MILK.
SHUK
SHUK
MOO
THAT'S RIGHT!
Eat up, ladies.
HEY ...
I'M GOING GROCERY SHOPPING.
OKAY, SEE YOU LATER.
HE'S STILL RECOVER-ERING, BUT HE'S DOING A LOT BETTER.
MOM, DAD...
...I'M GOING TO TOWN FOR A WHILE.
YOU GUYS ...
...TAKE CARE OF THINGS ...
...OKAY?
IF SOMEONE DOESN'T LIKE PEOPLE...
DON'T WORRY ABOUT ME.
I LIKE PEOPLE.
Chapter 64 / The End

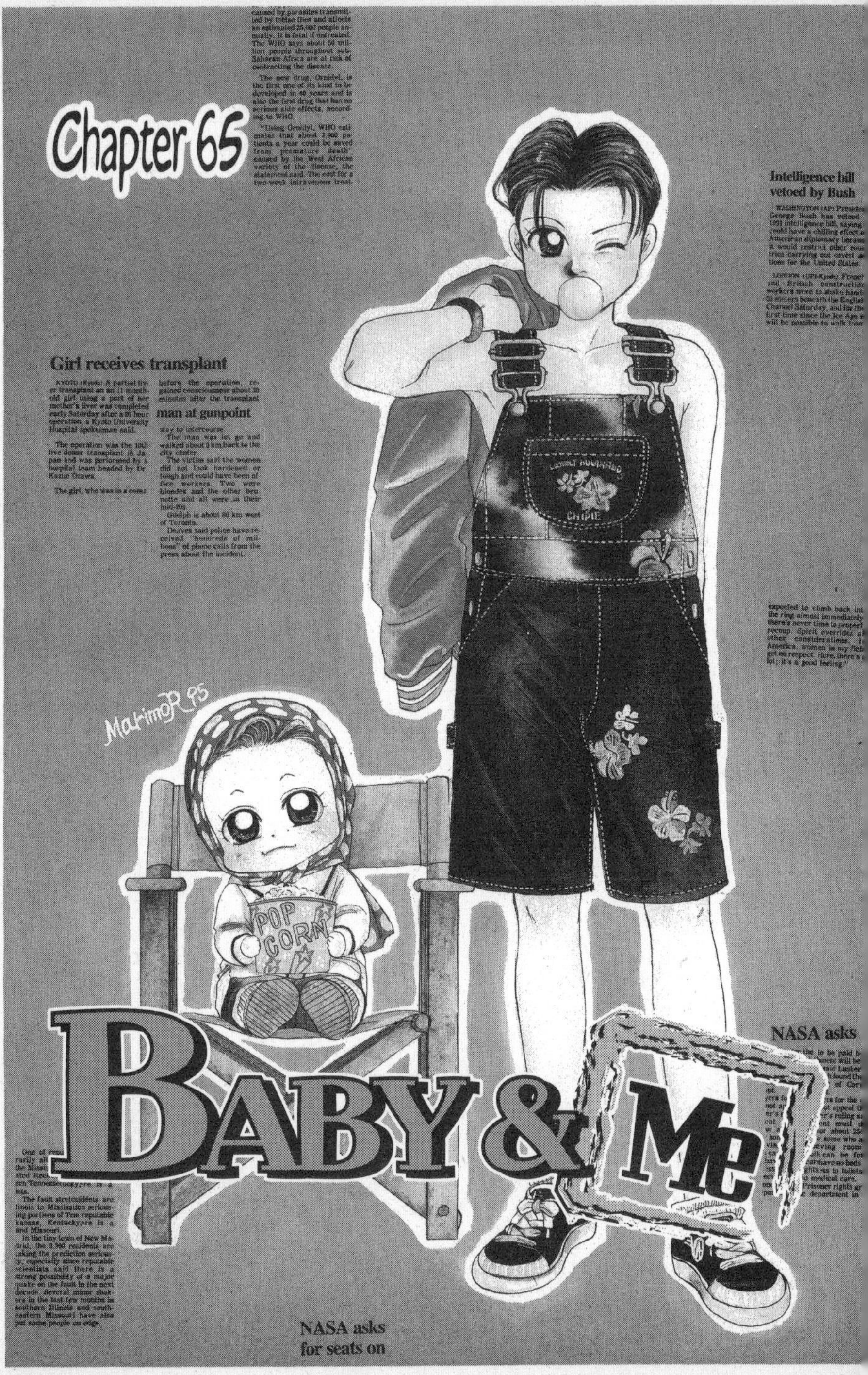

Chapter 65
BABY & Me
MarimoR '95
POP CORN
CHIPIE
Girl receives transplant
man at gunpoint
Intelligence bill vetoed by Bush
NASA asks
NASA asks for seats on

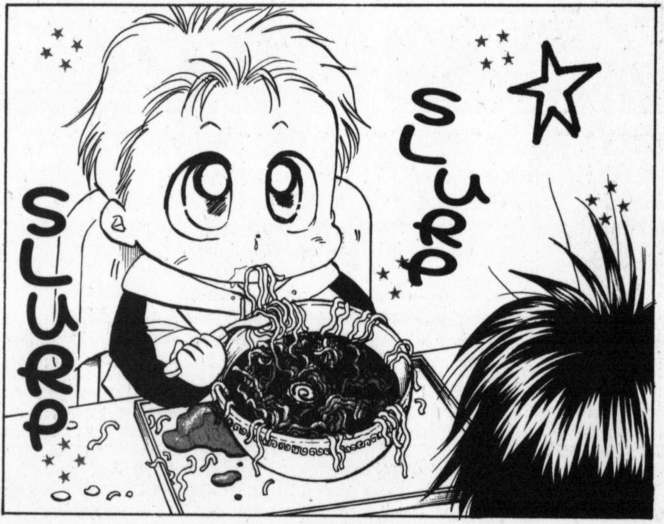
SLURP
SLURP

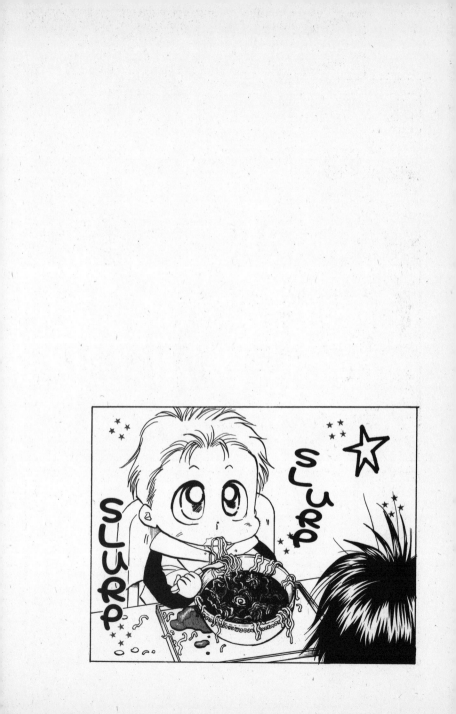

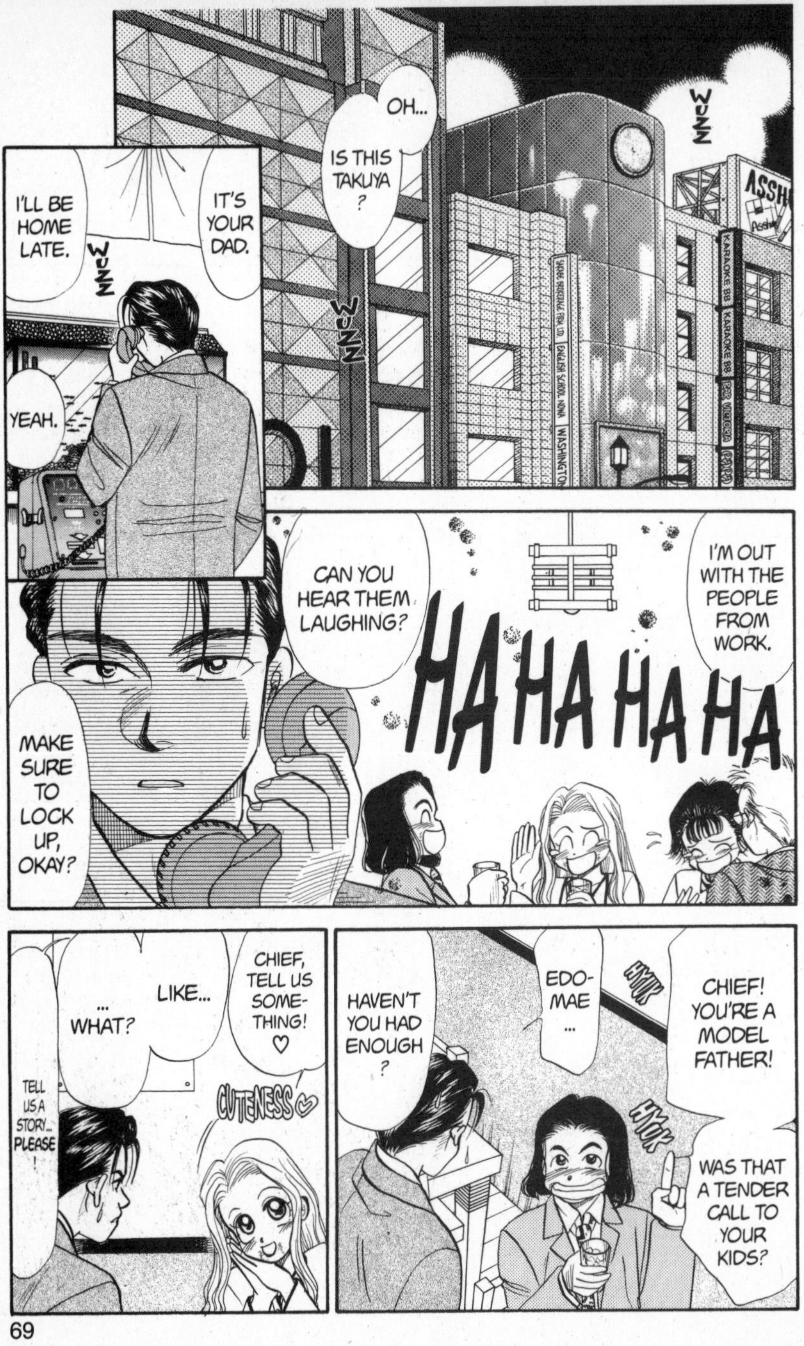

WUZZ
OH...
IS THIS TAKUYA?
WUZZ
IT'S YOUR DAD.
I'LL BE HOME LATE.
WUZZ
YEAH.
I'M OUT WITH THE PEOPLE FROM WORK.
HA HA HA HA HA
CAN YOU HEAR THEM LAUGHING?
MAKE SURE TO LOCK UP, OKAY?
CHIEF! YOU'RE A MODEL FATHER!
HYUK
EDO-MAE...
HAVEN'T YOU HAD ENOUGH?
HYUK
WAS THAT A TENDER CALL TO YOUR KIDS?
CHIEF, TELL US SOME-THING! ♡
LIKE...
...WHAT?
CUTENESS♡
TELL US A STORY... PLEASE!

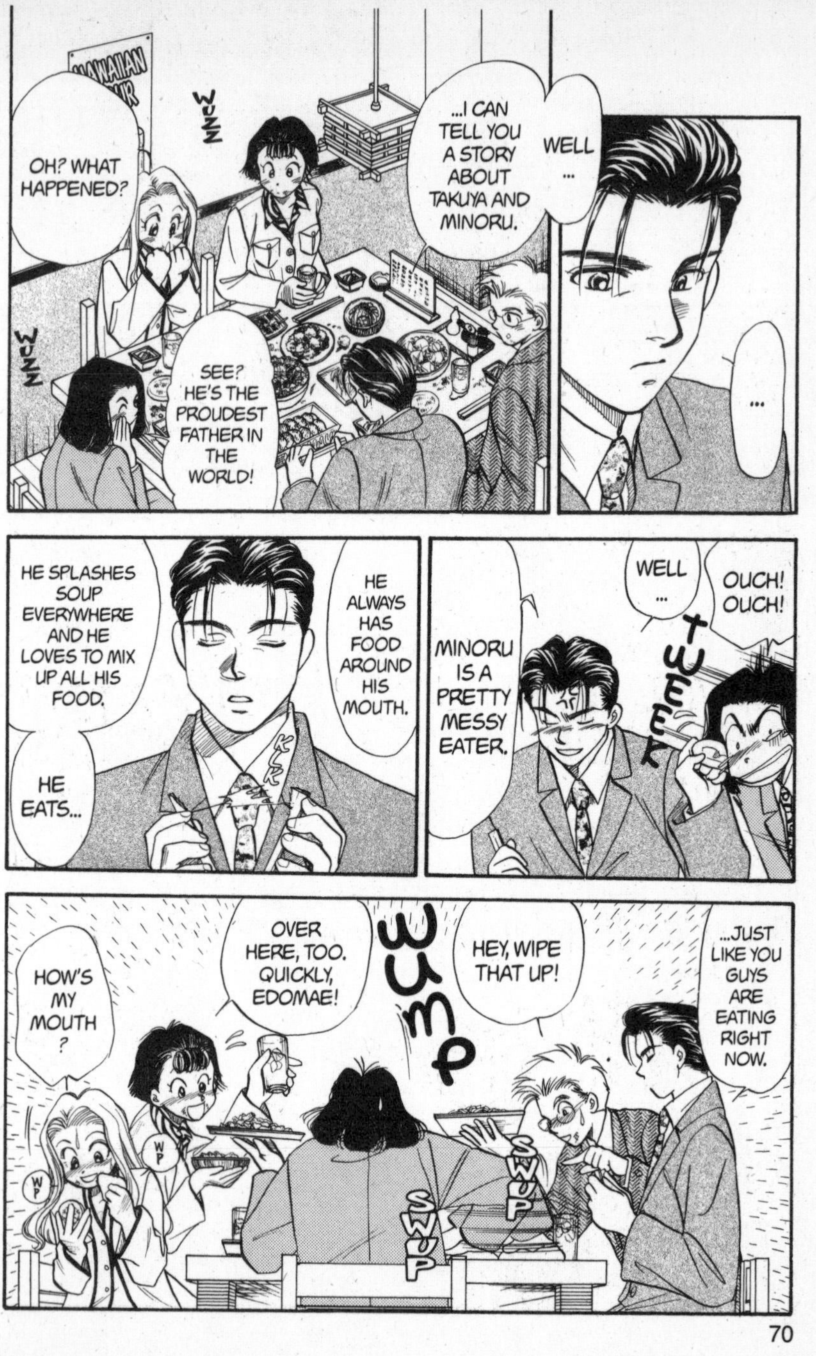
...
WELL ...
...I CAN TELL YOU A STORY ABOUT TAKUYA AND MINORU.
WUZZ
OH? WHAT HAPPENED?
SEE? HE'S THE PROUDEST FATHER IN THE WORLD!
WUZZ
OUCH! OUCH!
WELL ...
TWEEK
MINORU IS A PRETTY MESSY EATER.
HE ALWAYS HAS FOOD AROUND HIS MOUTH.
HE SPLASHES SOUP EVERYWHERE AND HE LOVES TO MIX UP ALL HIS FOOD.
KLK
HE EATS...
...JUST LIKE YOU GUYS ARE EATING RIGHT NOW.
HEY, WIPE THAT UP!
WUMP
SWUP
SWUP
OVER HERE, TOO. QUICKLY, EDOMAE!
HOW'S MY MOUTH?
WP
WP

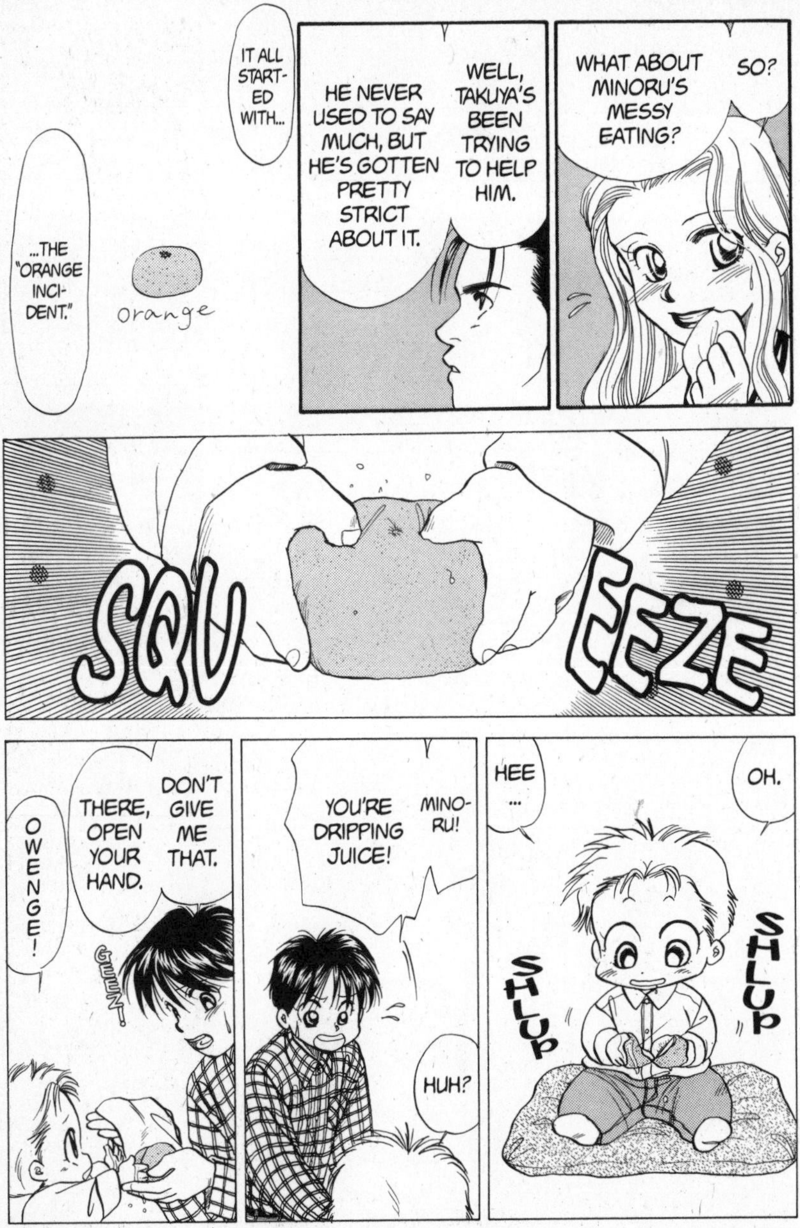
SO?
WHAT ABOUT MINORU'S MESSY EATING?
WELL, TAKUYA'S BEEN TRYING TO HELP HIM.
HE NEVER USED TO SAY MUCH, BUT HE'S GOTTEN PRETTY STRICT ABOUT IT.
IT ALL START-ED WITH...
...THE "ORANGE INCI-DENT."
orange
SQUEEZE
OH.
HEE ...
SHLUP
SHLUP
MINO-RU!
YOU'RE DRIPPING JUICE!
HUH?
DON'T GIVE ME THAT.
THERE, OPEN YOUR HAND.
OWENGE!
GEEZ!

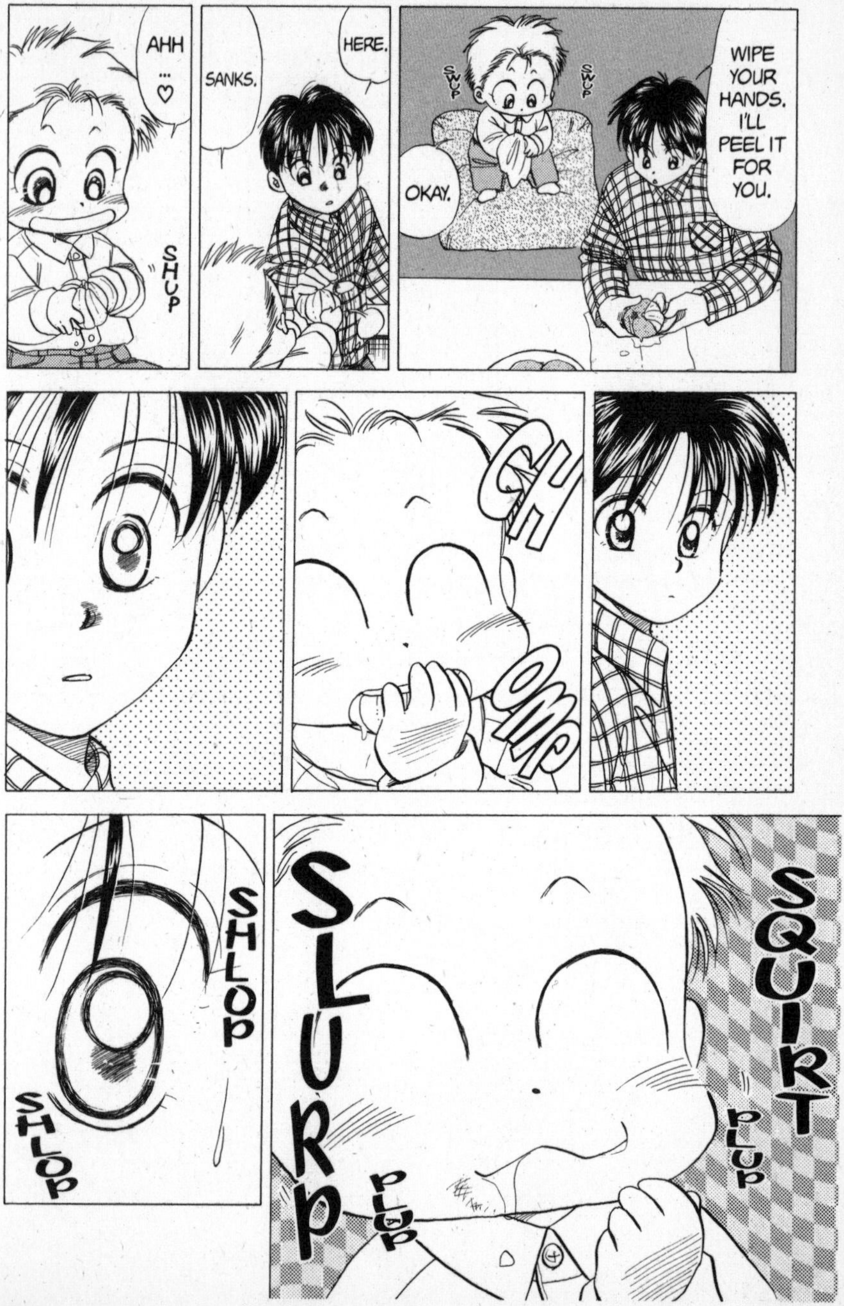
WIPE YOUR HANDS. I'LL PEEL IT FOR YOU.
SWUP
SWUP
OKAY.
HERE.
SANKS.
AHH ... ♡
SHUP
CHOMP
SQUIRT
PLUP
SLURP
PLUP
SHLOP
SHLOP

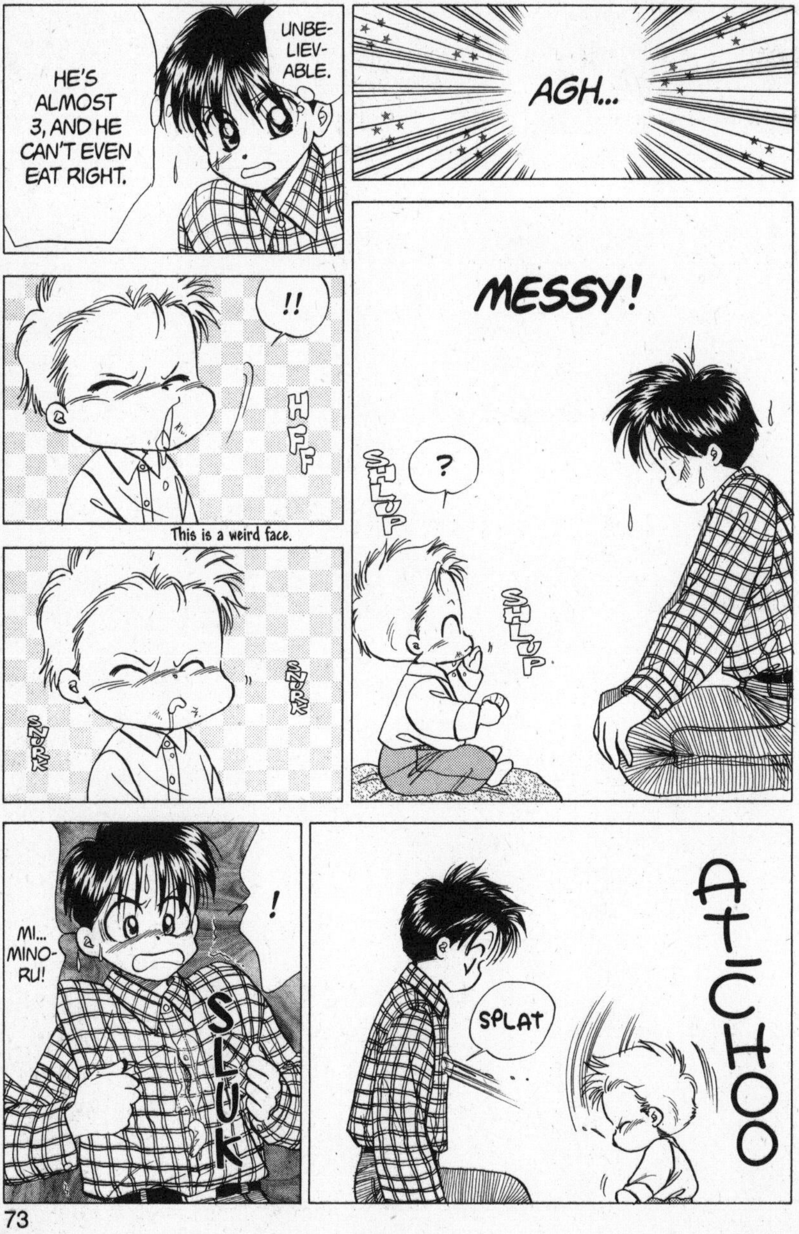
AGH...
UNBE-LIEV-ABLE.
HE'S ALMOST 3, AND HE CAN'T EVEN EAT RIGHT.
MESSY!
SHLUP
?
SHLUP
!!
HFF
This is a weird face.
SNURK
SNURK
ATCHOO
SPLAT
..
!
MI... MINO-RU!
SLUK

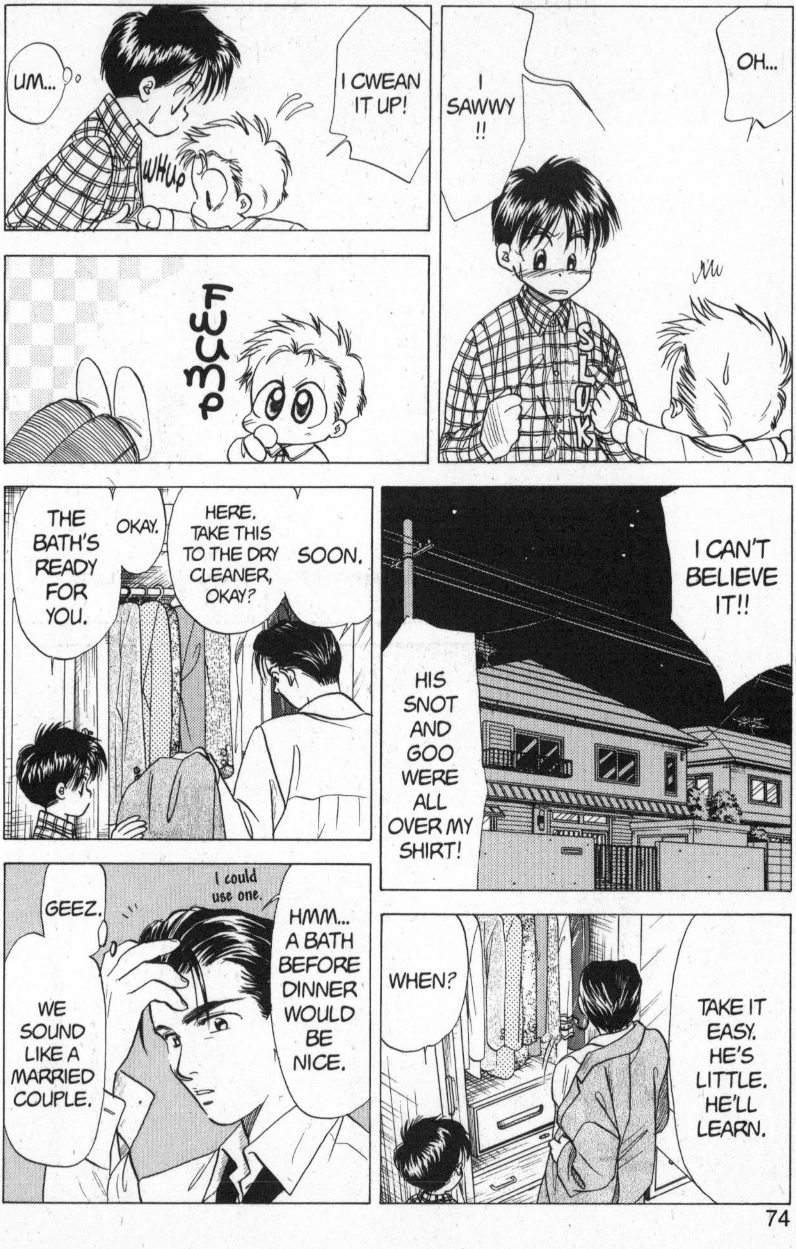
OH...
I SAWWY !!
SLUK
I CWEAN IT UP!
UM...
WHUP
FWUMP
I CAN'T BELIEVE IT!!
HIS SNOT AND GOO WERE ALL OVER MY SHIRT!
SOON.
HERE. TAKE THIS TO THE DRY CLEANER, OKAY?
OKAY.
THE BATH'S READY FOR YOU.
TAKE IT EASY. HE'S LITTLE. HE'LL LEARN.
WHEN?
HMM... A BATH BEFORE DINNER WOULD BE NICE.
I could use one.
GEEZ.
WE SOUND LIKE A MARRIED COUPLE.

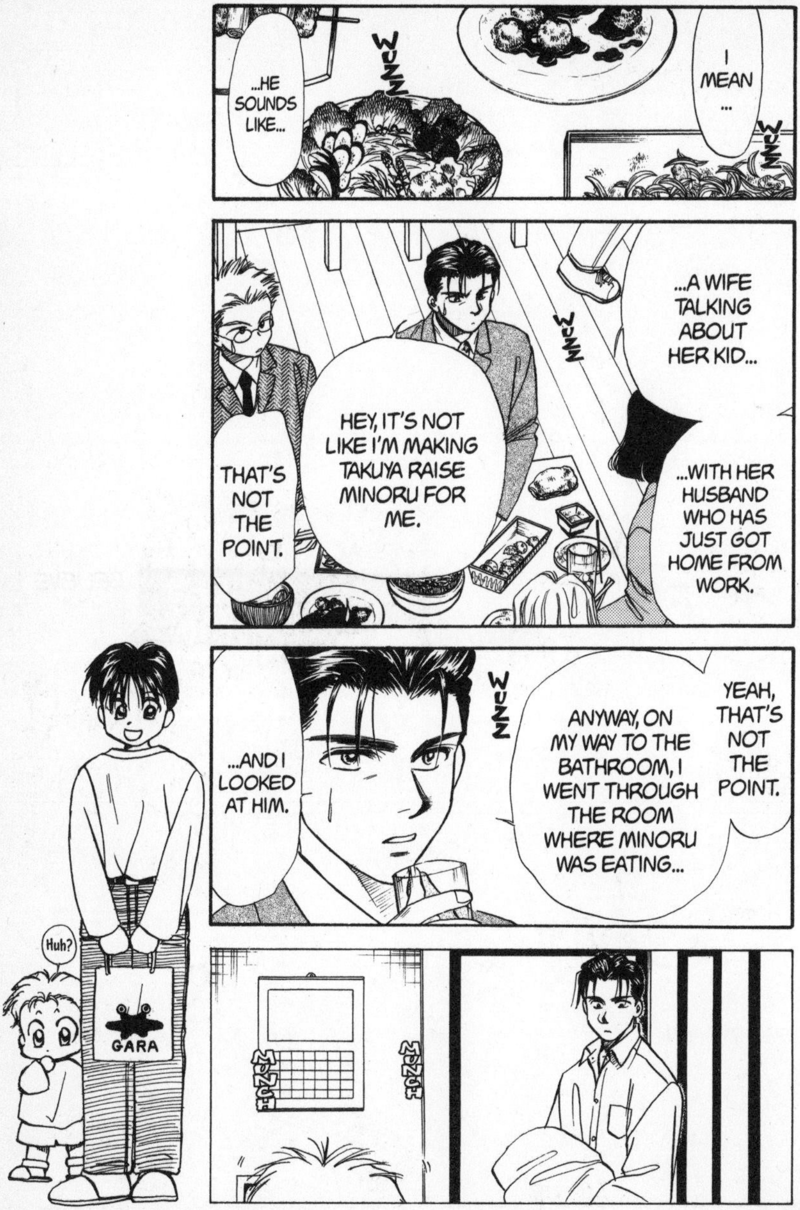
I MEAN ...
WUZZ
WUZZ
...HE SOUNDS LIKE...
...A WIFE TALKING ABOUT HER KID...
...WITH HER HUSBAND WHO HAS JUST GOT HOME FROM WORK.
WUZZ
HEY, IT'S NOT LIKE I'M MAKING TAKUYA RAISE MINORU FOR ME.
THAT'S NOT THE POINT.
YEAH, THAT'S NOT THE POINT.
ANYWAY, ON MY WAY TO THE BATHROOM, I WENT THROUGH THE ROOM WHERE MINORU WAS EATING...
WUZZ
...AND I LOOKED AT HIM.
MUNCH
MUNCH
Huh?
GARA

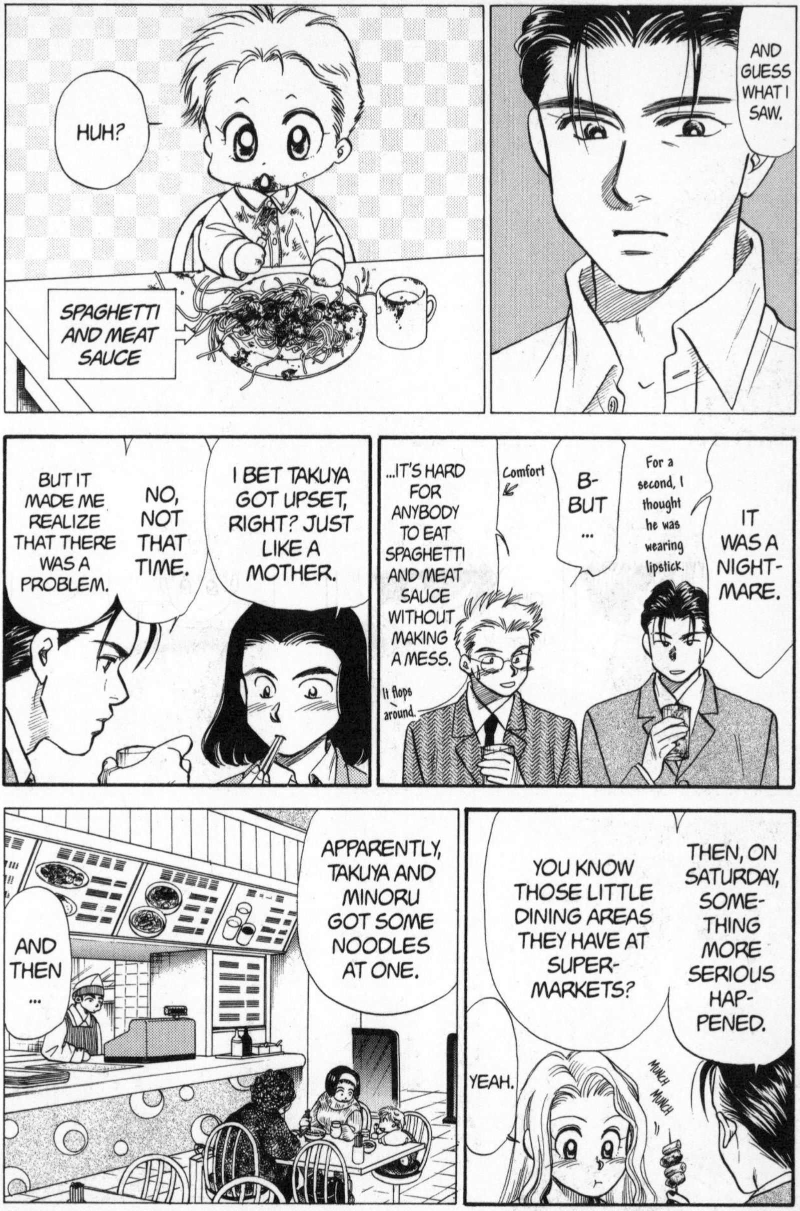
AND GUESS WHAT I SAW.
HUH?
SPAGHETTI AND MEAT SAUCE
IT WAS A NIGHTMARE.
For a second, I thought he was wearing lipstick.
B-BUT ...
Comfort
...IT'S HARD FOR ANYBODY TO EAT SPAGHETTI AND MEAT SAUCE WITHOUT MAKING A MESS.
It flops around.
I BET TAKUYA GOT UPSET, RIGHT? JUST LIKE A MOTHER.
NO, NOT THAT TIME.
BUT IT MADE ME REALIZE THAT THERE WAS A PROBLEM.
THEN, ON SATURDAY, SOMETHING MORE SERIOUS HAPPENED.
YOU KNOW THOSE LITTLE DINING AREAS THEY HAVE AT SUPERMARKETS?
MUNCH MUNCH
YEAH.
APPARENTLY, TAKUYA AND MINORU GOT SOME NOODLES AT ONE.
AND THEN ...

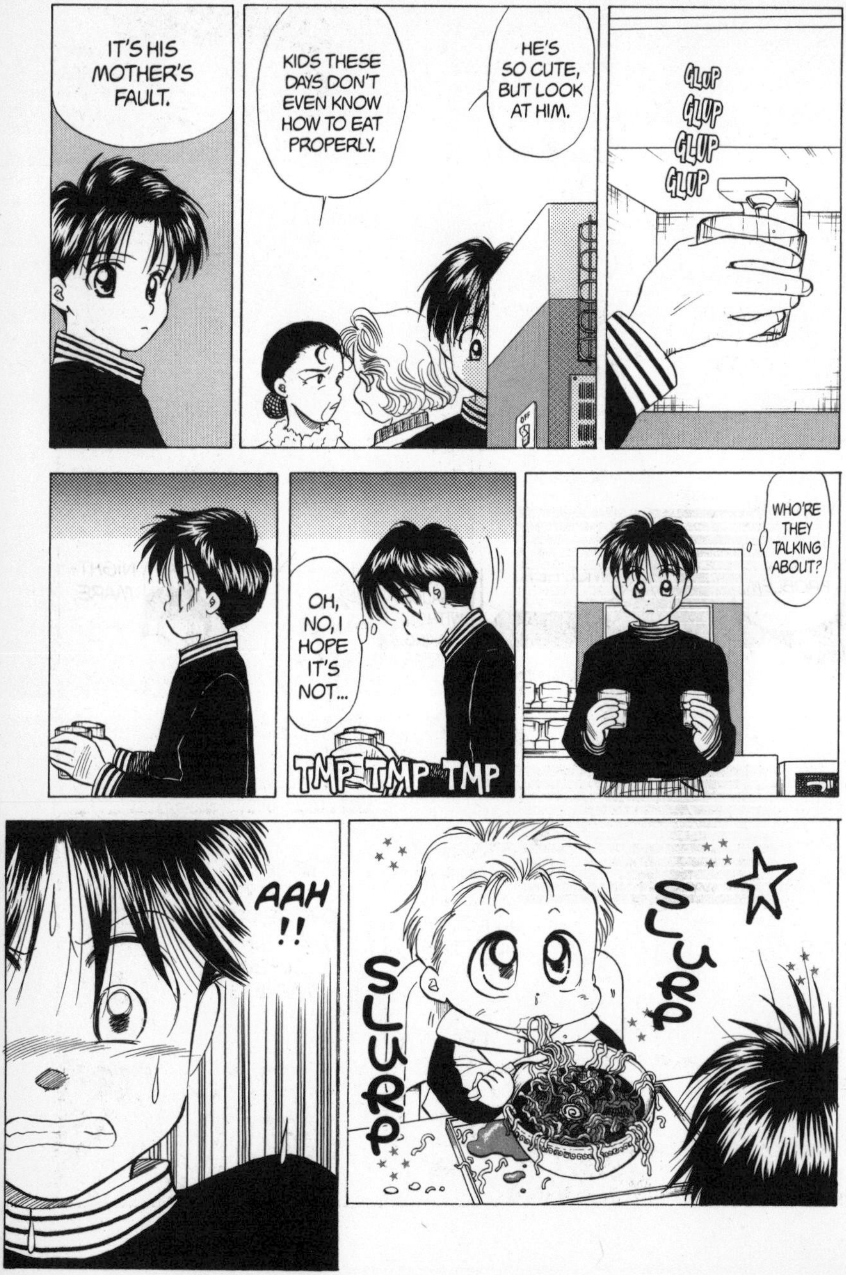
GLUP GLUP GLUP GLUP
HE'S SO CUTE, BUT LOOK AT HIM.
KIDS THESE DAYS DON'T EVEN KNOW HOW TO EAT PROPERLY.
IT'S HIS MOTHER'S FAULT.
WHO'RE THEY TALKING ABOUT?
OH, NO, I HOPE IT'S NOT...
TMP TMP TMP
SLURP
SLURP
AAH !!

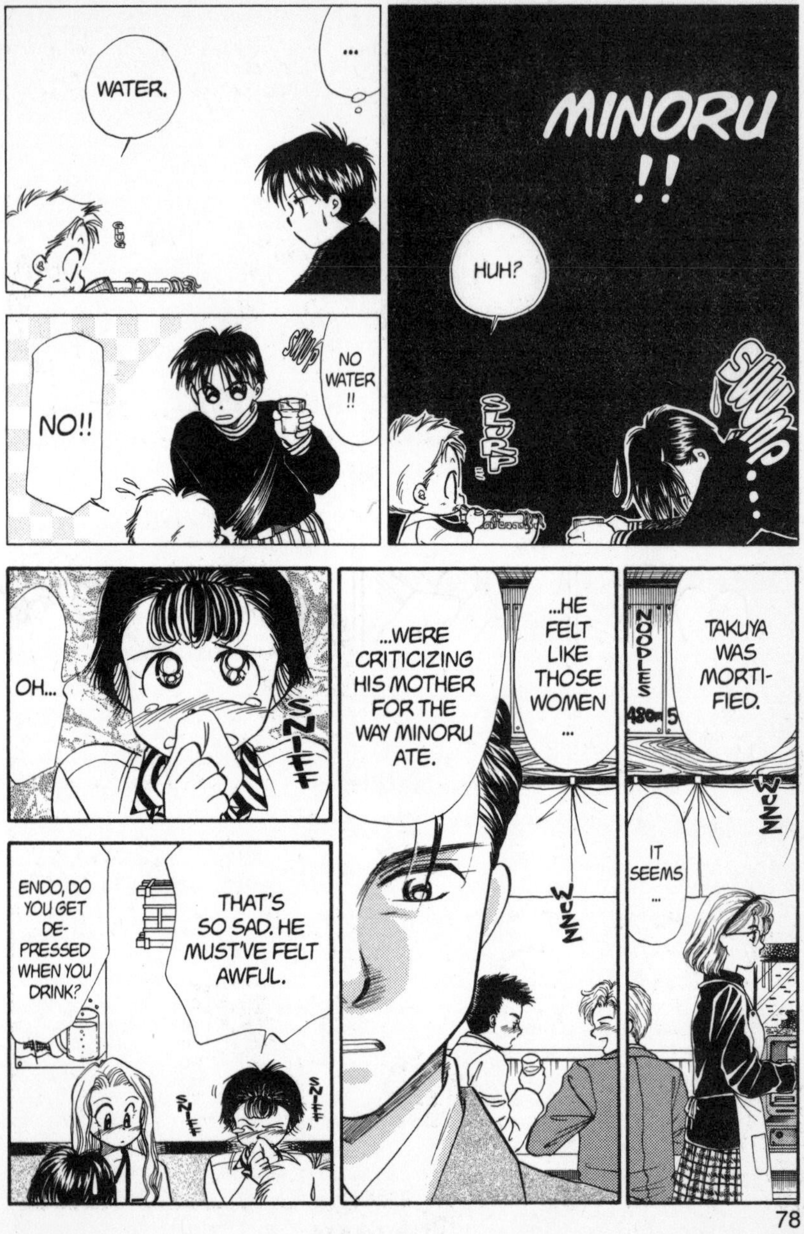
MINORU !!
HUH?
SLURP
SWUMP...
...
WATER.
NO WATER !!
NO!!
TAKUYA WAS MORTIFIED.
NOODLES
480
WUZZ
IT SEEMS ...
...HE FELT LIKE THOSE WOMEN ...
...WERE CRITICIZING HIS MOTHER FOR THE WAY MINORU ATE.
WUZZ
OH...
SNIFF
THAT'S SO SAD. HE MUST'VE FELT AWFUL.
ENDO, DO YOU GET DE-PRESSED WHEN YOU DRINK?
SNIFF
SNIFF

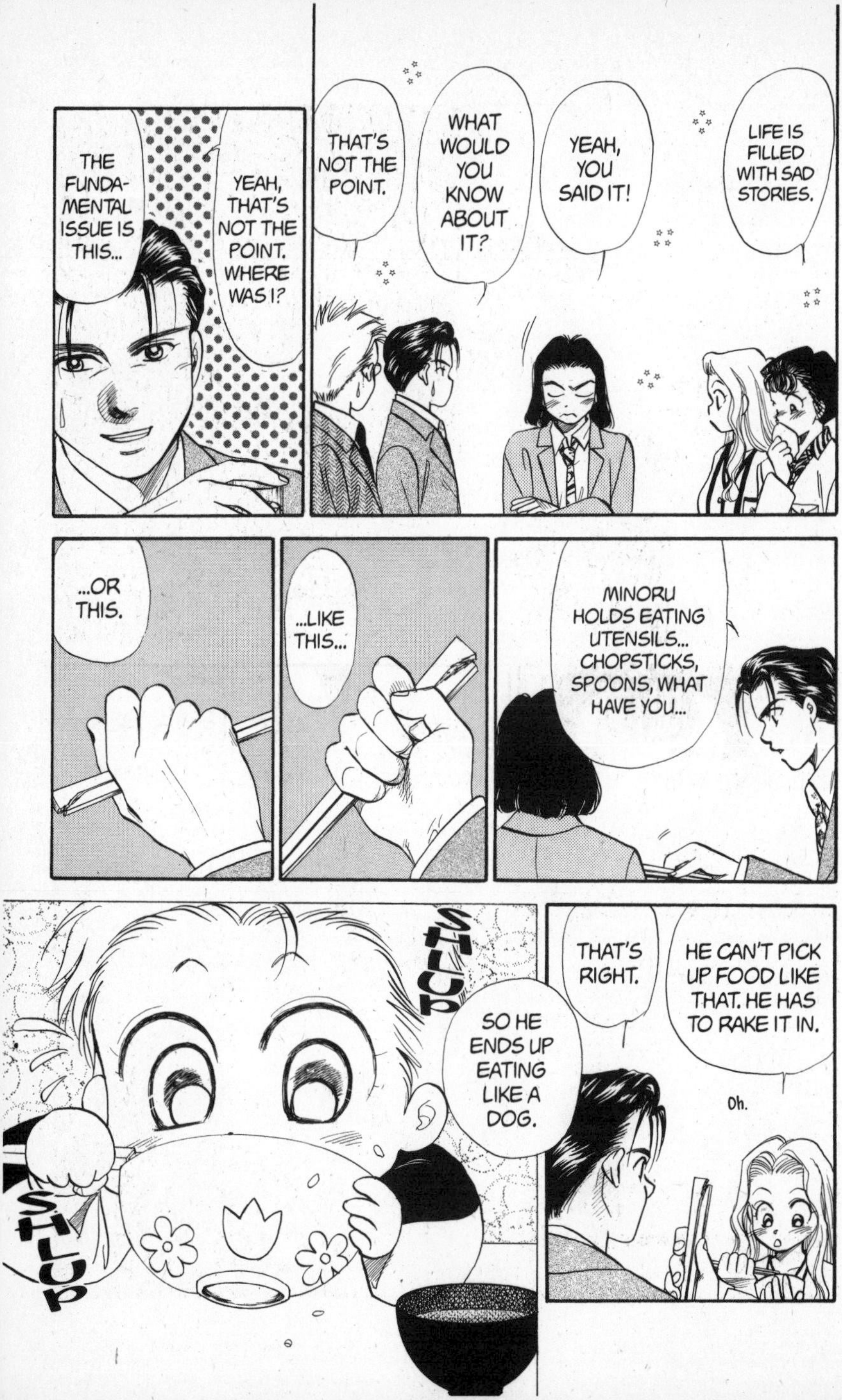
LIFE IS FILLED WITH SAD STORIES.
YEAH, YOU SAID IT!
WHAT WOULD YOU KNOW ABOUT IT?
THAT'S NOT THE POINT.
YEAH, THAT'S NOT THE POINT. WHERE WAS I?
THE FUNDAMENTAL ISSUE IS THIS...
MINORU HOLDS EATING UTENSILS... CHOPSTICKS, SPOONS, WHAT HAVE YOU...
...LIKE THIS...
...OR THIS.
HE CAN'T PICK UP FOOD LIKE THAT. HE HAS TO RAKE IT IN.
THAT'S RIGHT.
Oh.
SO HE ENDS UP EATING LIKE A DOG.
SHLUP
SHLUP

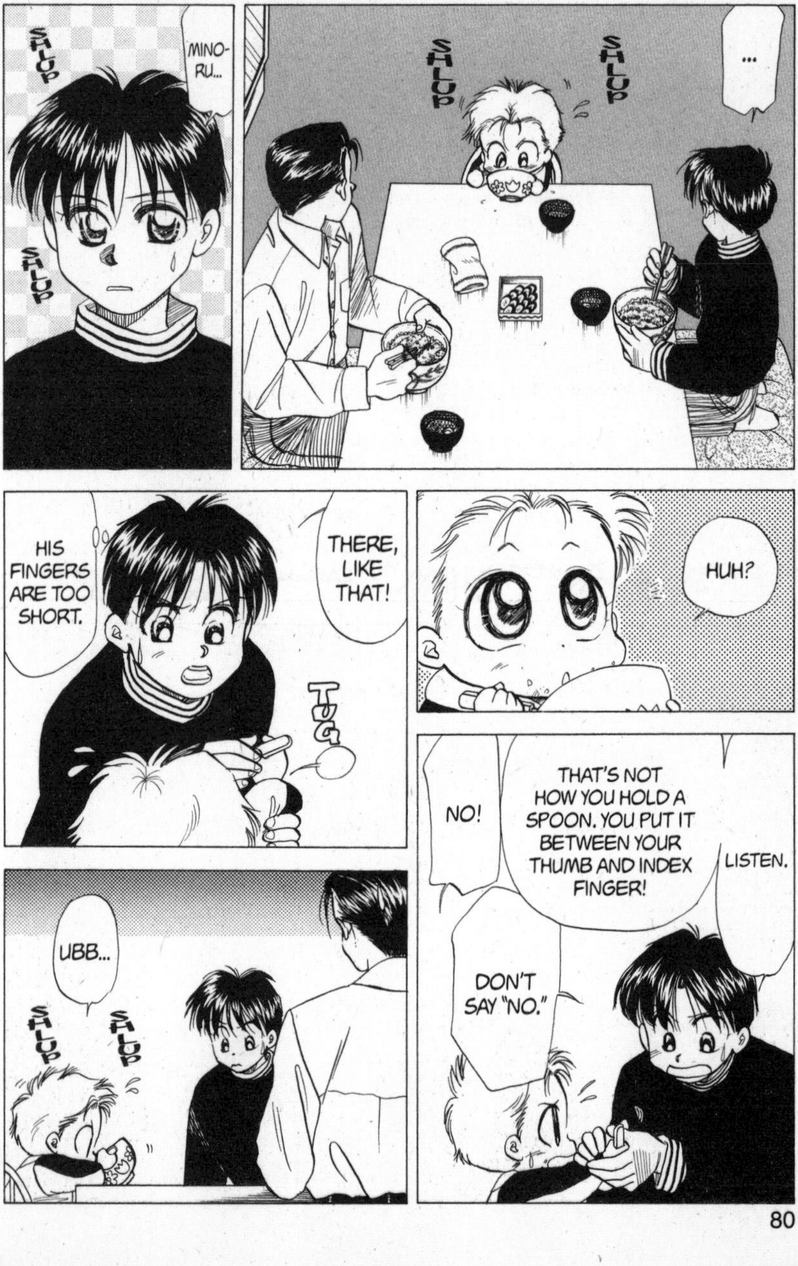
...
SHLUP
SHLUP
MINO-RU...
SHLUP
SHLUP
HUH?
THERE, LIKE THAT!
HIS FINGERS ARE TOO SHORT.
TUG
LISTEN.
THAT'S NOT HOW YOU HOLD A SPOON. YOU PUT IT BETWEEN YOUR THUMB AND INDEX FINGER!
NO!
DON'T SAY "NO."
UBB...
SHLUP
SHLUP

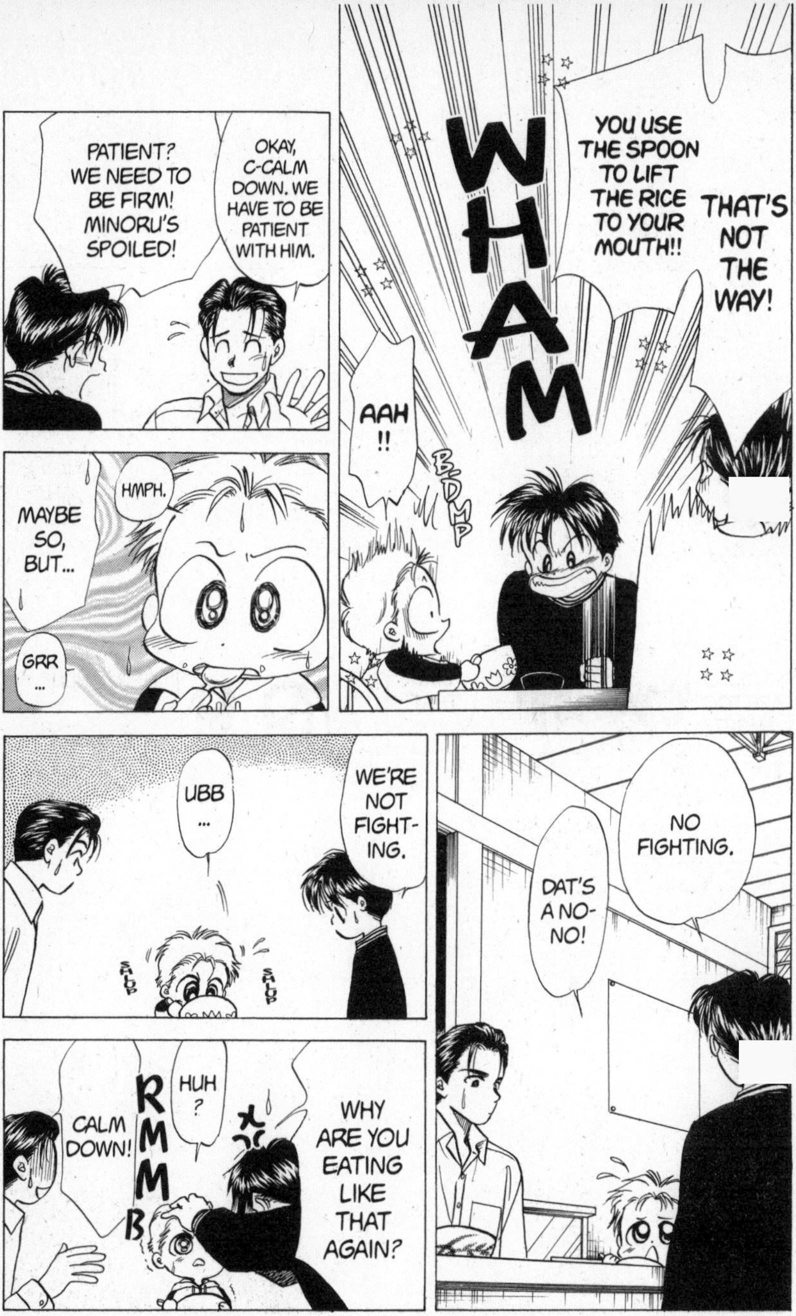
THAT'S NOT THE WAY!
YOU USE THE SPOON TO LIFT THE RICE TO YOUR MOUTH!!
WHAM
AAH !!
B-DMP
OKAY, C-CALM DOWN. WE HAVE TO BE PATIENT WITH HIM.
PATIENT? WE NEED TO BE FIRM! MINORU'S SPOILED!
HMPH.
MAYBE SO, BUT...
GRR ...
NO FIGHTING.
DAT'S A NO-NO!
WE'RE NOT FIGHT-ING.
UBB ...
SHLUP
SHLUP
WHY ARE YOU EATING LIKE THAT AGAIN?
RMMB
HUH ?
CALM DOWN!

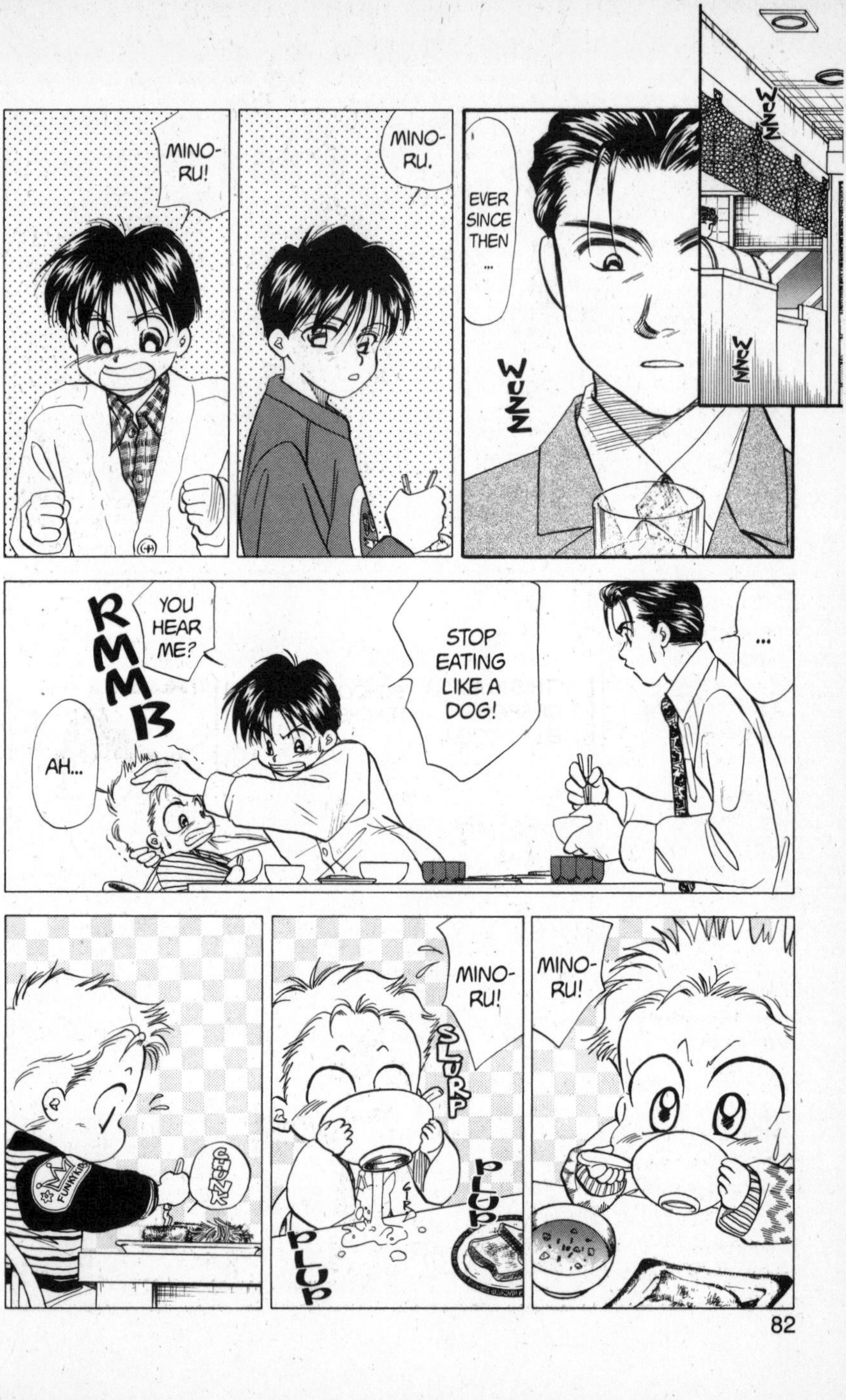
WUZZ
WUZZ
EVER SINCE THEN ...
WUZZ
MINO-RU.
MINO-RU!
...
STOP EATING LIKE A DOG!
YOU HEAR ME?
RMMB
AH...
MINO-RU!
MINO-RU!
SLURP
PLUP
GIR
PLUP
CHUNK
FUNKY KIDS

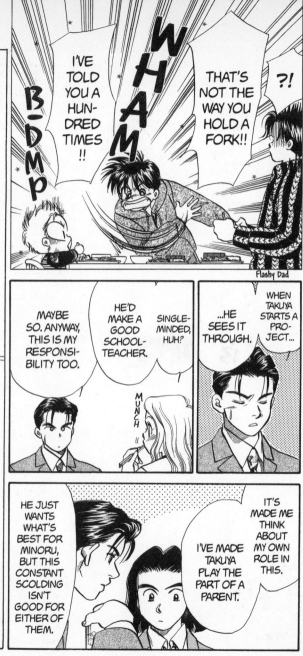

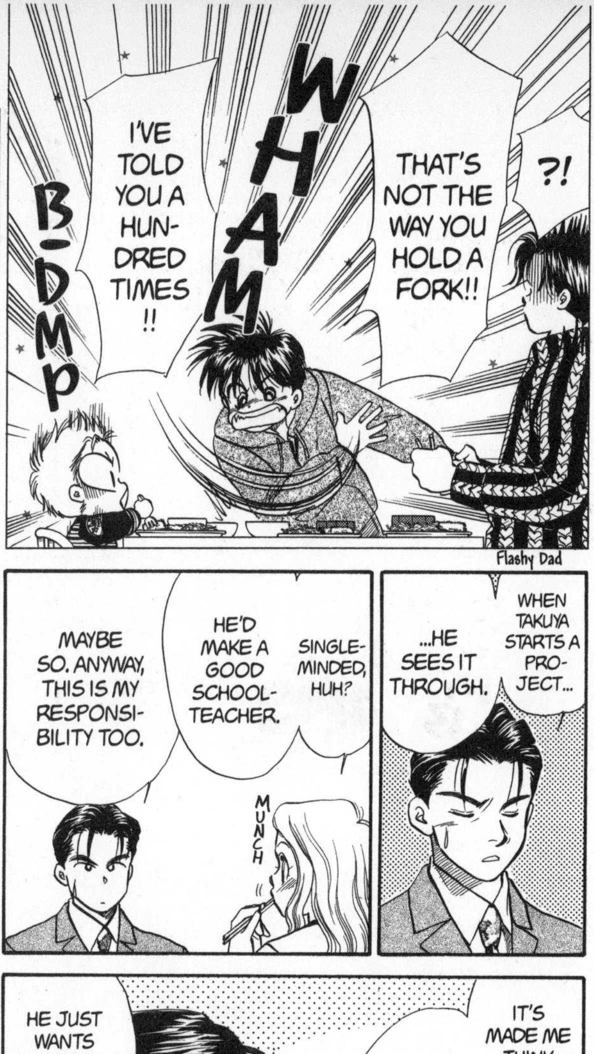
?!
THAT'S NOT THE WAY YOU HOLD A FORK!!
WHAM
I'VE TOLD YOU A HUNDRED TIMES!!
B-DMP
Flashy Dad
WHEN TAKUYA STARTS A PROJECT...
...HE SEES IT THROUGH.
SINGLE-MINDED, HUH?
HE'D MAKE A GOOD SCHOOLTEACHER.
MAYBE SO. ANYWAY, THIS IS MY RESPONSIBILITY TOO.
MUNCH
IT'S MADE ME THINK ABOUT MY OWN ROLE IN THIS.
I'VE MADE TAKUYA PLAY THE PART OF A PARENT.
HE JUST WANTS WHAT'S BEST FOR MINORU, BUT THIS CONSTANT SCOLDING ISN'T GOOD FOR EITHER OF THEM.

Author's Note Part 3

When I showed you my younger brother's drawing last time, it was very popular, so I made him draw another one. He got fed up, tore up all of his drawings and threw them away! But you weren't careful enough, Brother! I searched your trash can and found something! That's right. Call me a meanie if you want. Anyway, here's a picture he drew.

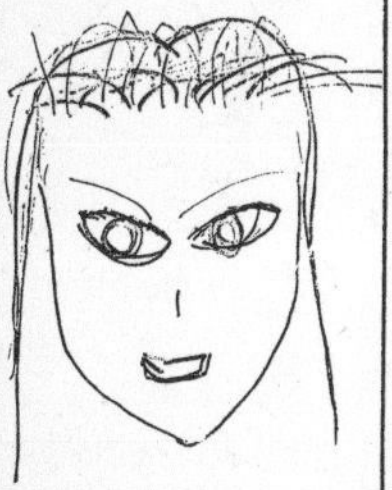

He'll probably become even more guarded now and maybe even stop drawing altogether.

It's 6:30 in the morning, and he's arranging emergency disaster supplies in the entry hall. He has no idea what I'm doing...Hee hee hee...

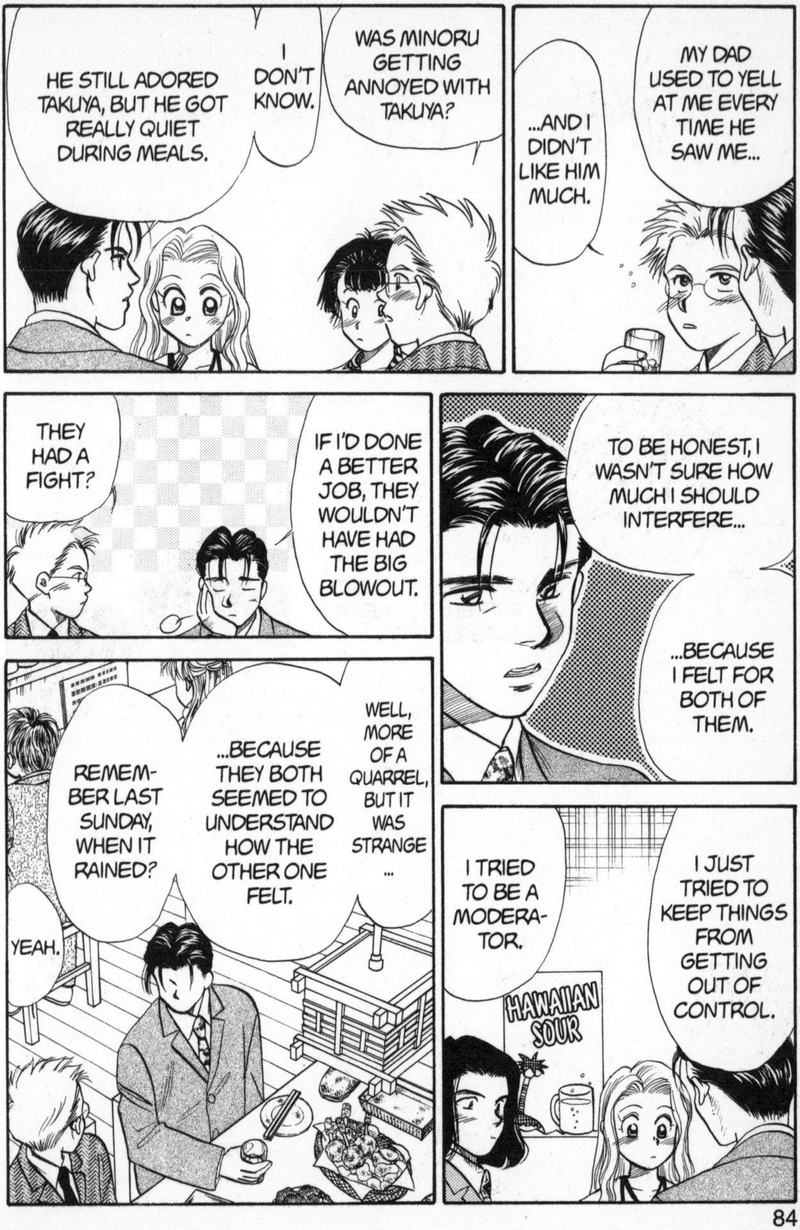
MY DAD USED TO YELL AT ME EVERY TIME HE SAW ME...
...AND I DIDN'T LIKE HIM MUCH.
WAS MINORU GETTING ANNOYED WITH TAKUYA?
I DON'T KNOW.
HE STILL ADORED TAKUYA, BUT HE GOT REALLY QUIET DURING MEALS.
TO BE HONEST, I WASN'T SURE HOW MUCH I SHOULD INTERFERE...
...BECAUSE I FELT FOR BOTH OF THEM.
I JUST TRIED TO KEEP THINGS FROM GETTING OUT OF CONTROL.
I TRIED TO BE A MODERATOR.
HAWAIIAN SOUR
IF I'D DONE A BETTER JOB, THEY WOULDN'T HAVE HAD THE BIG BLOWOUT.
THEY HAD A FIGHT?
WELL, MORE OF A QUARREL, BUT IT WAS STRANGE...
...BECAUSE THEY BOTH SEEMED TO UNDERSTAND HOW THE OTHER ONE FELT.
REMEMBER LAST SUNDAY, WHEN IT RAINED?
YEAH.

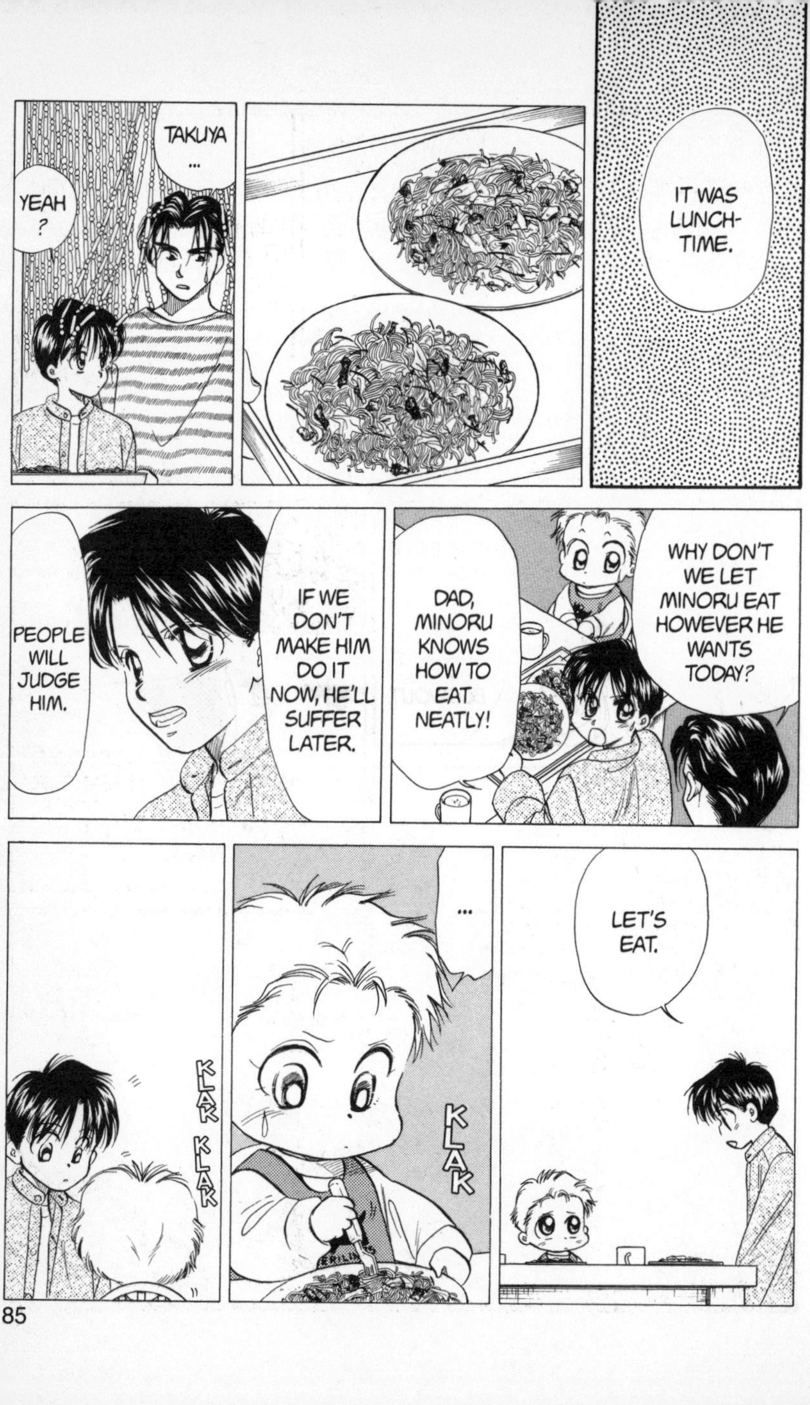
IT WAS LUNCH-TIME.
TAKUYA ...
YEAH ?
WHY DON'T WE LET MINORU EAT HOWEVER HE WANTS TODAY?
DAD, MINORU KNOWS HOW TO EAT NEATLY!
IF WE DON'T MAKE HIM DO IT NOW, HE'LL SUFFER LATER.
PEOPLE WILL JUDGE HIM.
LET'S EAT.
...
KLAK
KLAK KLAK KLAK

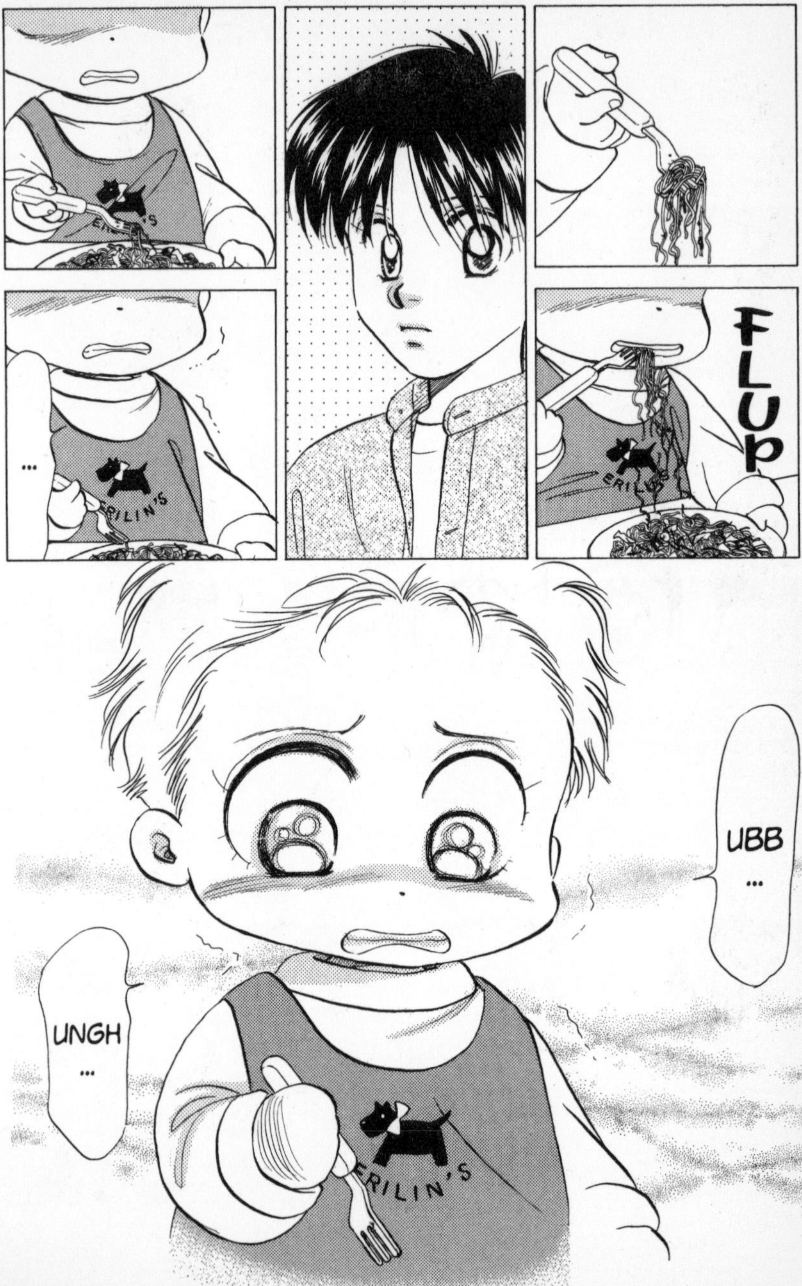
FLUP
...
UBB ...
UNGH ...

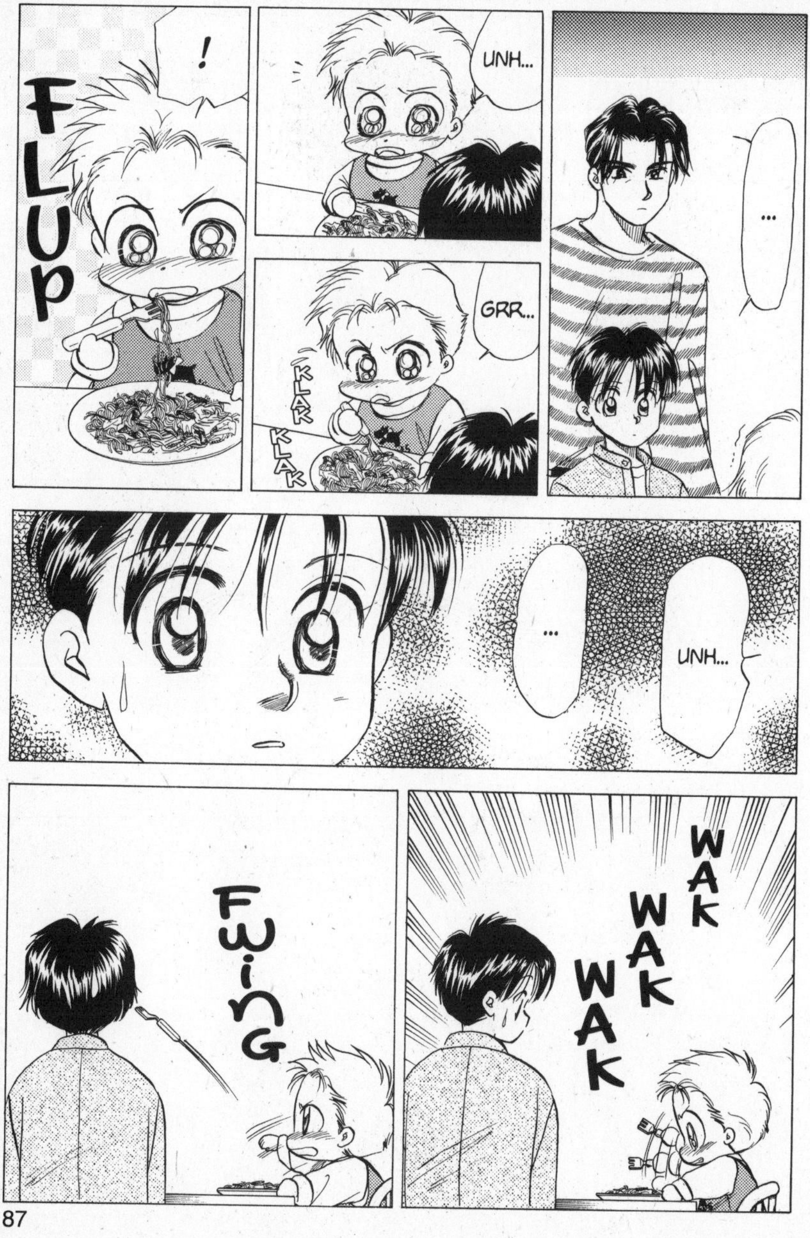
...
UNH...
GRR...
KLAK KLAK
!
FLUP
UNH...
...
WAK WAK WAK
FWING

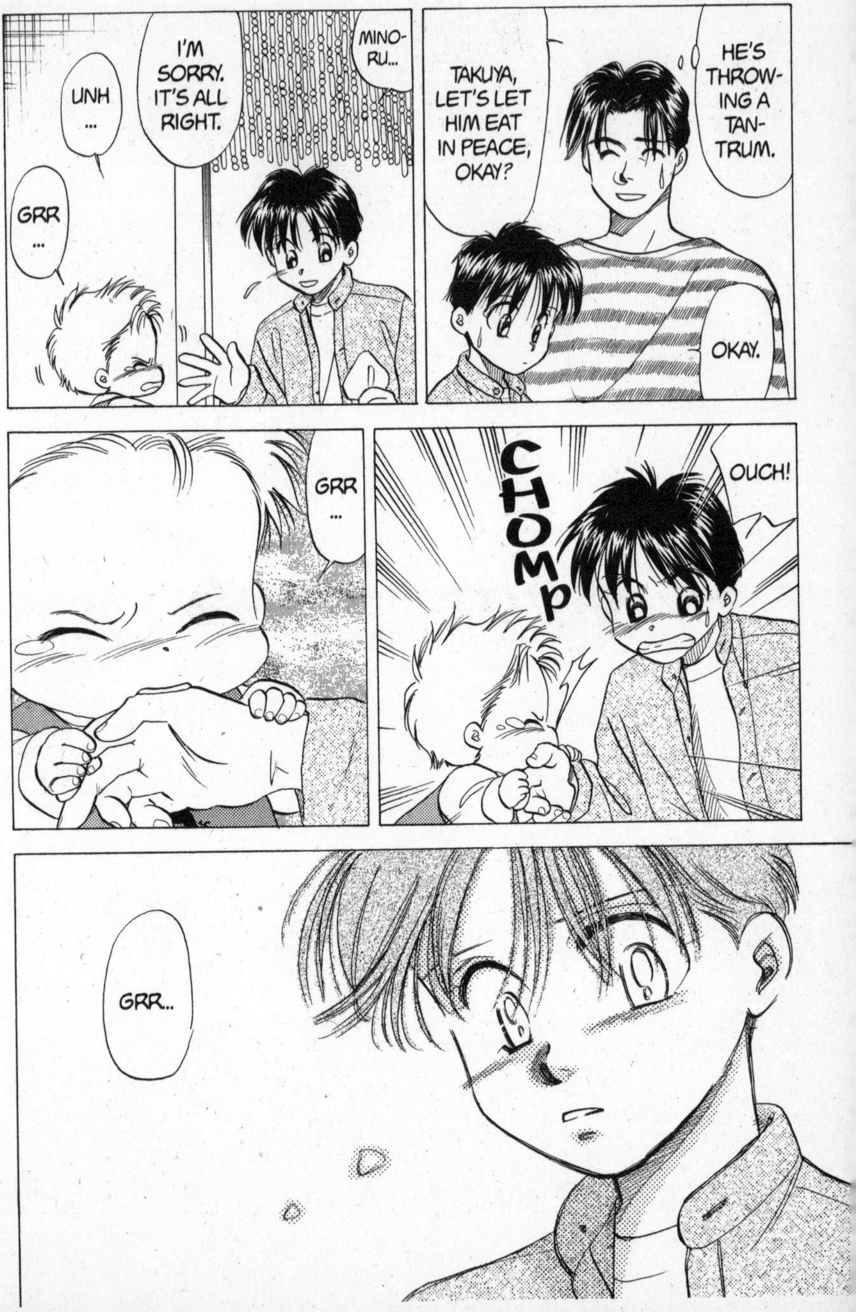
HE'S THROWING A TAN-TRUM.
TAKUYA, LET'S LET HIM EAT IN PEACE, OKAY?
OKAY.
MINO-RU...
I'M SORRY. IT'S ALL RIGHT.
UNH ...
GRR ...
OUCH!
CHOMP
GRR ...
GRR...

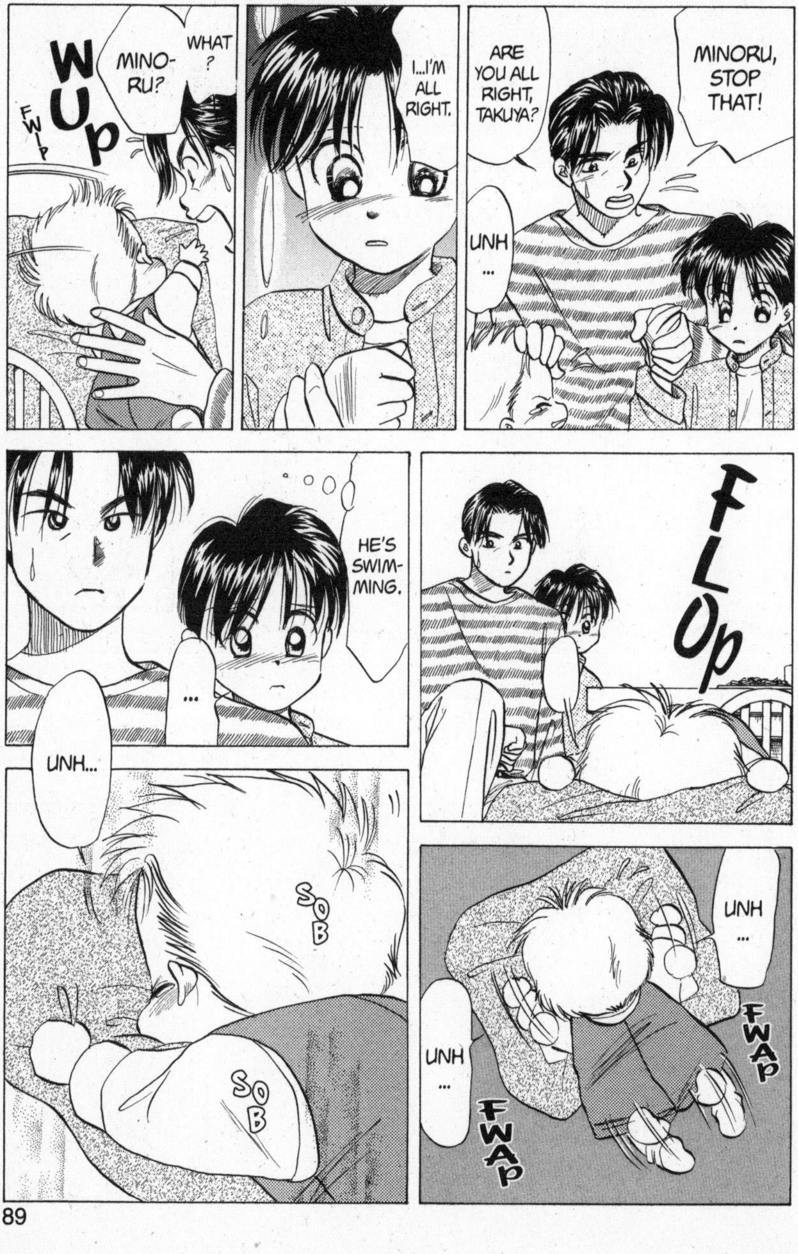
MINORU, STOP THAT!
ARE YOU ALL RIGHT, TAKUYA?
UNH ...
I...I'M ALL RIGHT.
WHAT ?
MINO-RU?
WUp
FWIP
FLOp
HE'S SWIM-MING.
...
UNH...
UNH ...
FWAP
UNH ...
FWAP
SOB
SOB

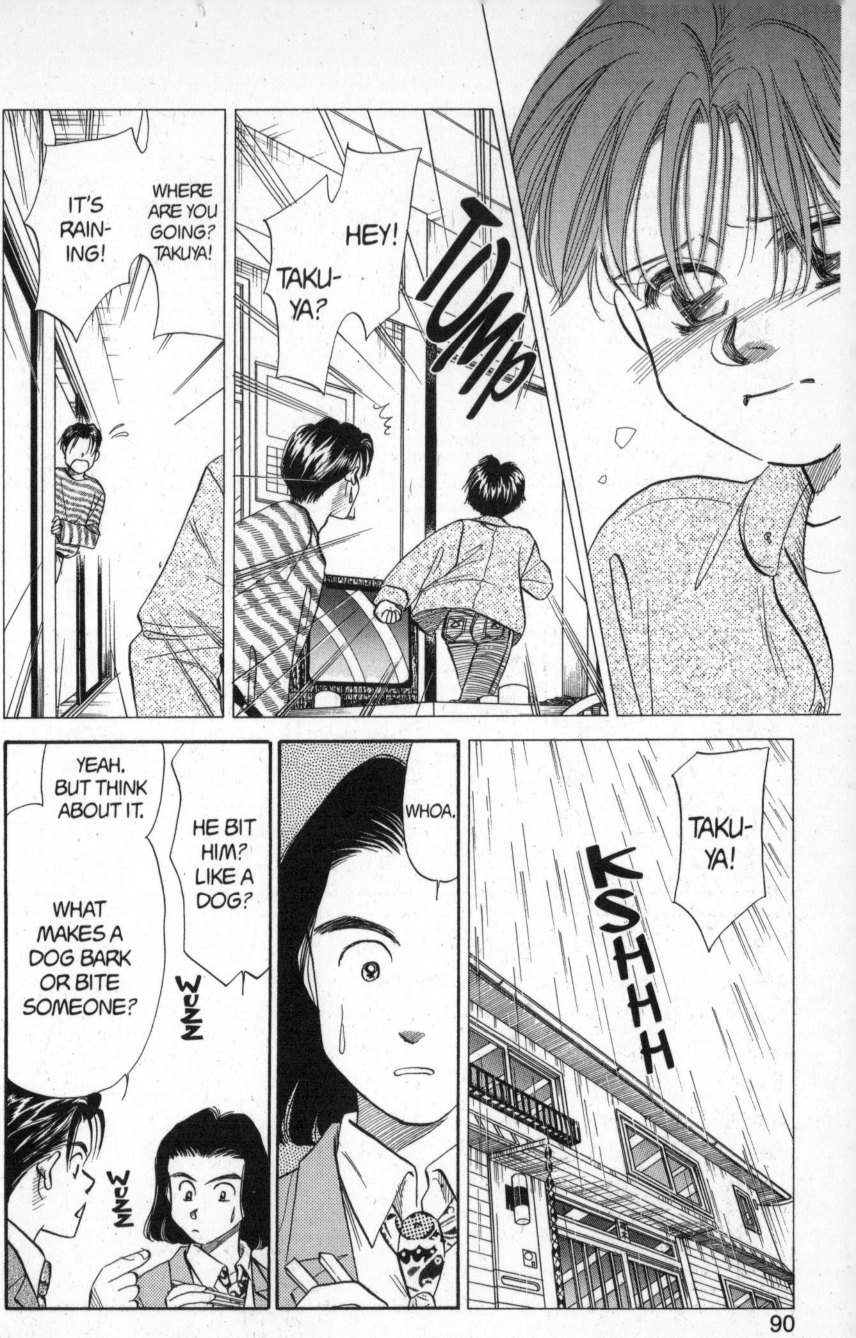
TUMP
HEY!
TAKU-YA?
WHERE ARE YOU GOING? TAKUYA!
IT'S RAIN-ING!
TAKU-YA!
KSHHH
WHOA.
HE BIT HIM? LIKE A DOG?
YEAH. BUT THINK ABOUT IT.
WHAT MAKES A DOG BARK OR BITE SOMEONE?
WUZZ
WUZZ

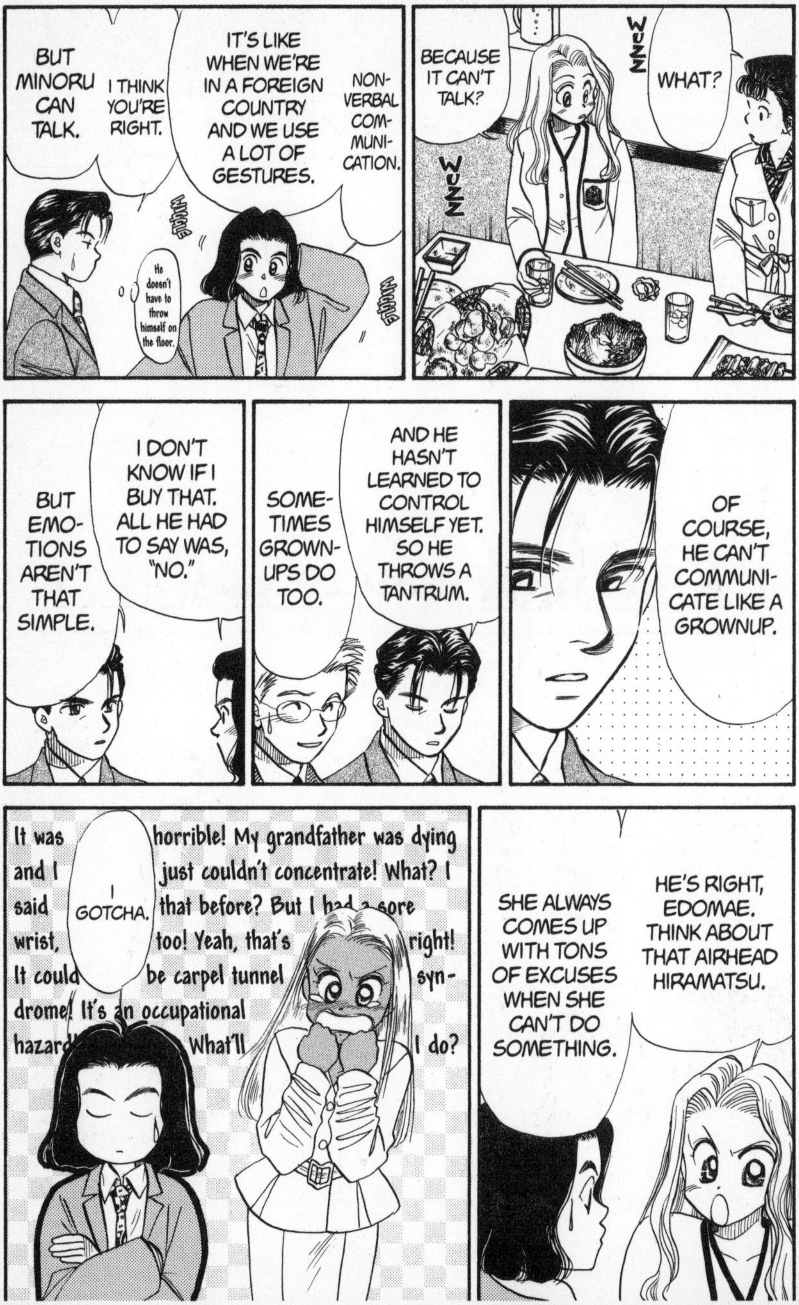
WHAT?
WUZZ
BECAUSE IT CAN'T TALK?
WUZZ
NON-VERBAL COM-MUNI-CATION.
IT'S LIKE WHEN WE'RE IN A FOREIGN COUNTRY AND WE USE A LOT OF GESTURES.
I THINK YOU'RE RIGHT.
BUT MINORU CAN TALK.
WIGGLE
He doesn't have to throw himself on the floor.
WIGGLE
OF COURSE, HE CAN'T COMMUNI-CATE LIKE A GROWNUP.
AND HE HASN'T LEARNED TO CONTROL HIMSELF YET. SO HE THROWS A TANTRUM.
SOME-TIMES GROWN-UPS DO TOO.
I DON'T KNOW IF I BUY THAT. ALL HE HAD TO SAY WAS, "NO."
BUT EMO-TIONS AREN'T THAT SIMPLE.
HE'S RIGHT, EDOMAE. THINK ABOUT THAT AIRHEAD HIRAMATSU.
SHE ALWAYS COMES UP WITH TONS OF EXCUSES WHEN SHE CAN'T DO SOMETHING.
I GOTCHA.
It was horrible! My grandfather was dying and I just couldn't concentrate! What? I said that before? But I had a sore wrist, too! Yeah, that's right! It could be carpel tunnel syn-drome! It's an occupational hazard What'll I do?

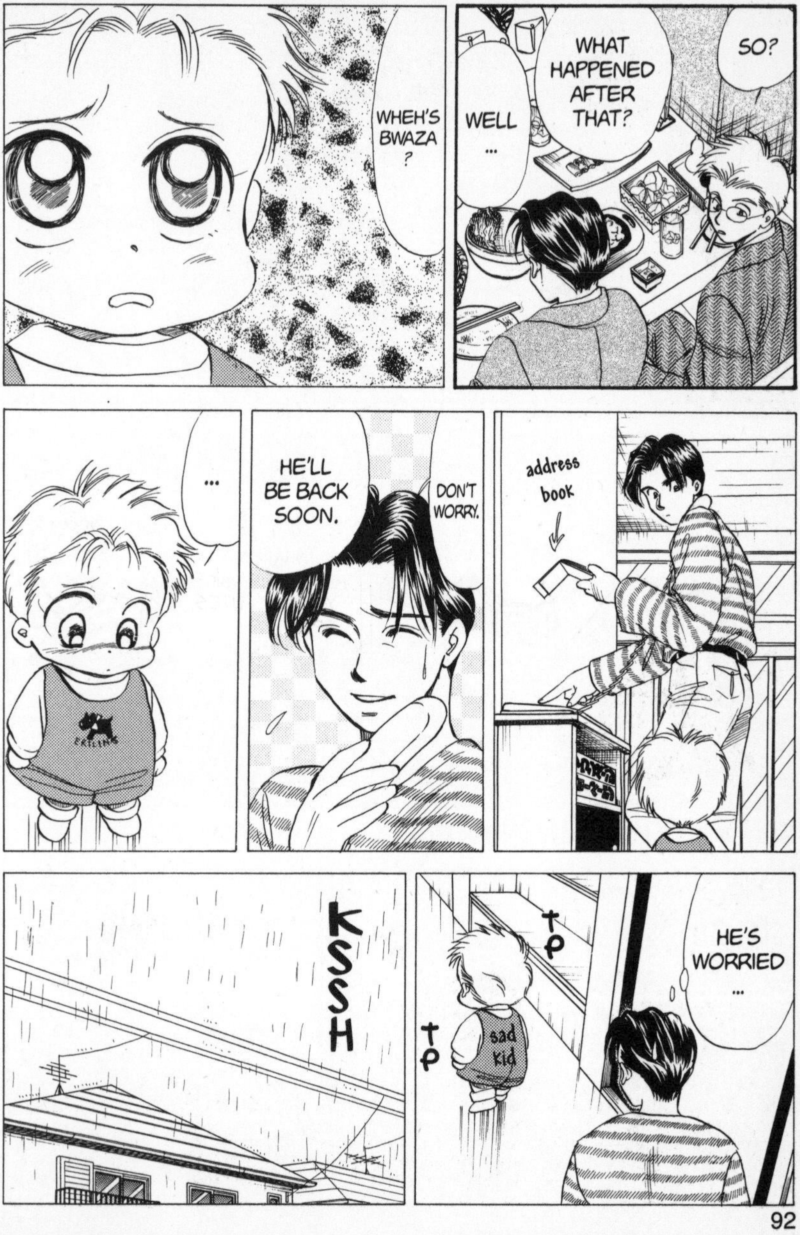
SO?
WHAT HAPPENED AFTER THAT?
WELL ...
WHEH'S BWAZA ?
address book
DON'T WORRY.
HE'LL BE BACK SOON.
...
HE'S WORRIED ...
TP
sad kid
TP
KSSH

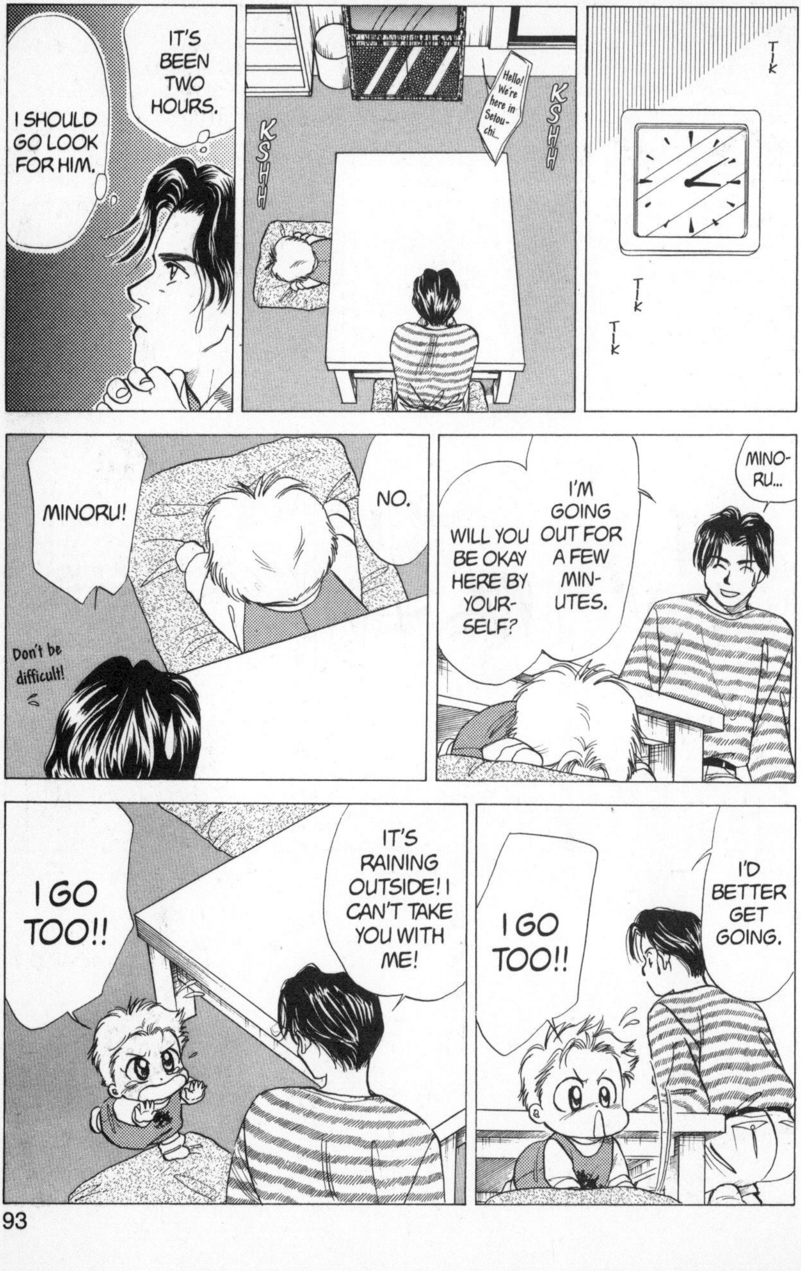
TIK
TIK
TIK
KSHHH
Hello! We're here in Setouchi..
KSHHH
IT'S BEEN TWO HOURS.
I SHOULD GO LOOK FOR HIM.
MINO-RU...
I'M GOING OUT FOR A FEW MIN-UTES.
WILL YOU BE OKAY HERE BY YOUR-SELF?
NO.
MINORU!
Don't be difficult!
I'D BETTER GET GOING.
I GO TOO!!
IT'S RAINING OUTSIDE! I CAN'T TAKE YOU WITH ME!
I GO TOO!!

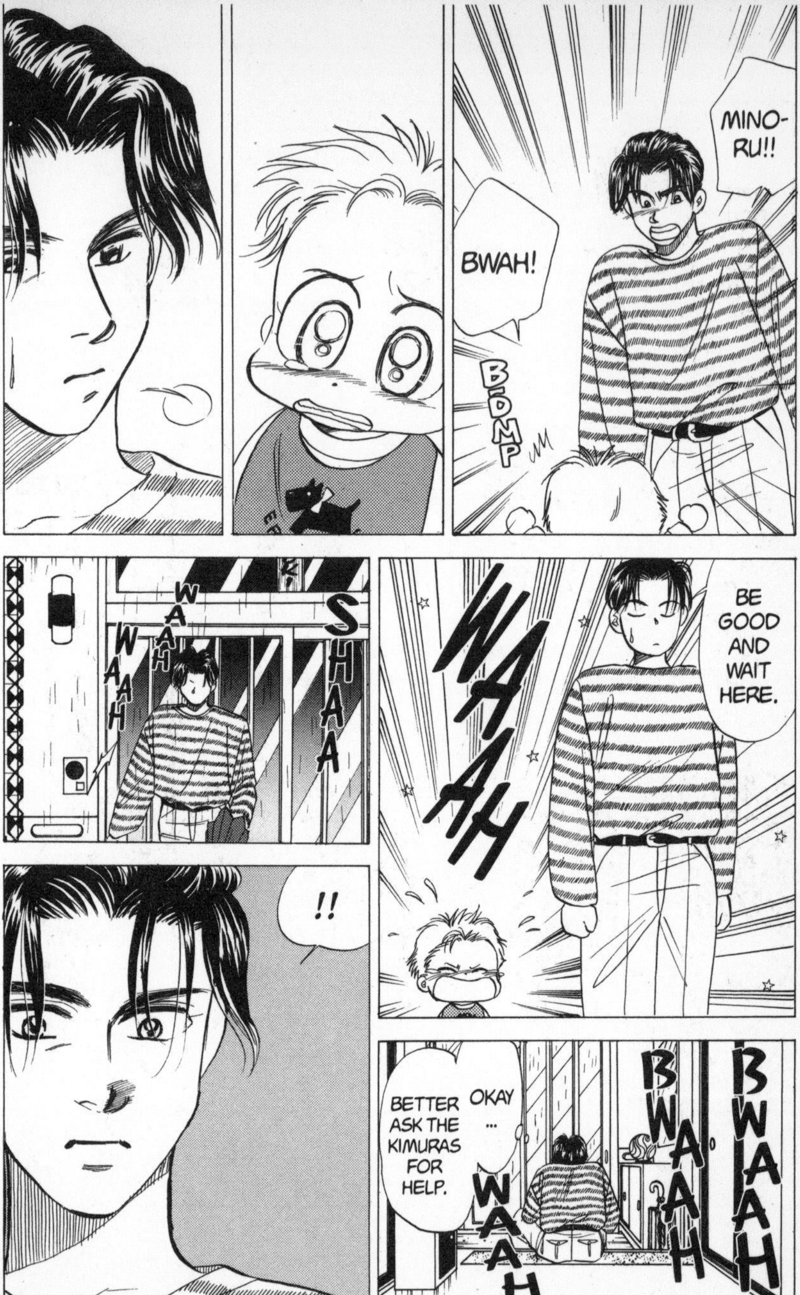
MINO-RU!!
BWAH!
B-DMP
BE GOOD AND WAIT HERE.
WAAAH
WAAH
WAAH
SHAAA
!!
OKAY ...
BETTER ASK THE KIMURAS FOR HELP.
BWAAAH
BWAAAH
WAAH

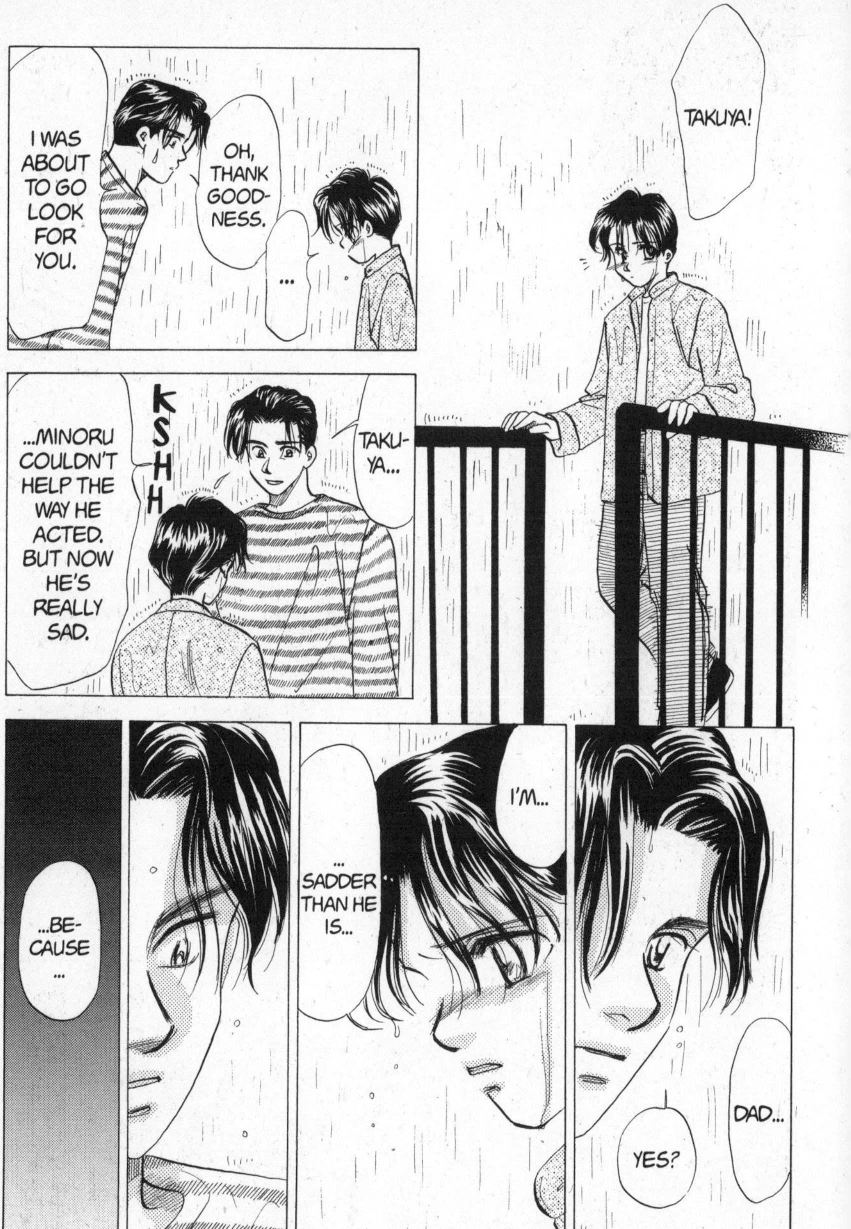
TAKUYA!
OH, THANK GOODNESS.
...
I WAS ABOUT TO GO LOOK FOR YOU.
TAKU-YA...
KSHH
...MINORU COULDN'T HELP THE WAY HE ACTED. BUT NOW HE'S REALLY SAD.
DAD...
YES?
I'M...
...SADDER THAN HE IS...
...BE-CAUSE ...

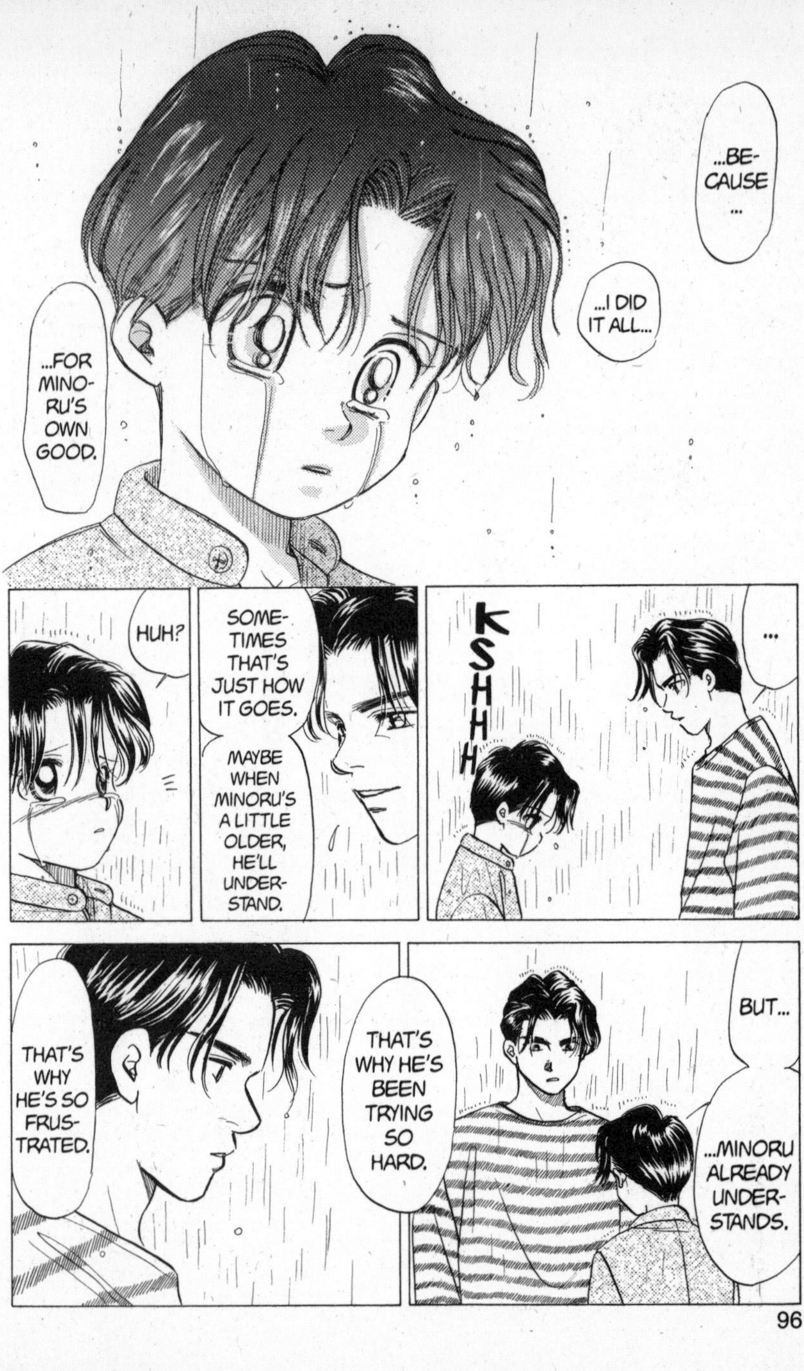
...BE-CAUSE ...
...I DID IT ALL...
...FOR MINO-RU'S OWN GOOD.
KSHHH
...
SOME-TIMES THAT'S JUST HOW IT GOES.
MAYBE WHEN MINORU'S A LITTLE OLDER, HE'LL UNDER-STAND.
HUH?
BUT...
...MINORU ALREADY UNDER-STANDS.
THAT'S WHY HE'S BEEN TRYING SO HARD.
THAT'S WHY HE'S SO FRUS-TRATED.

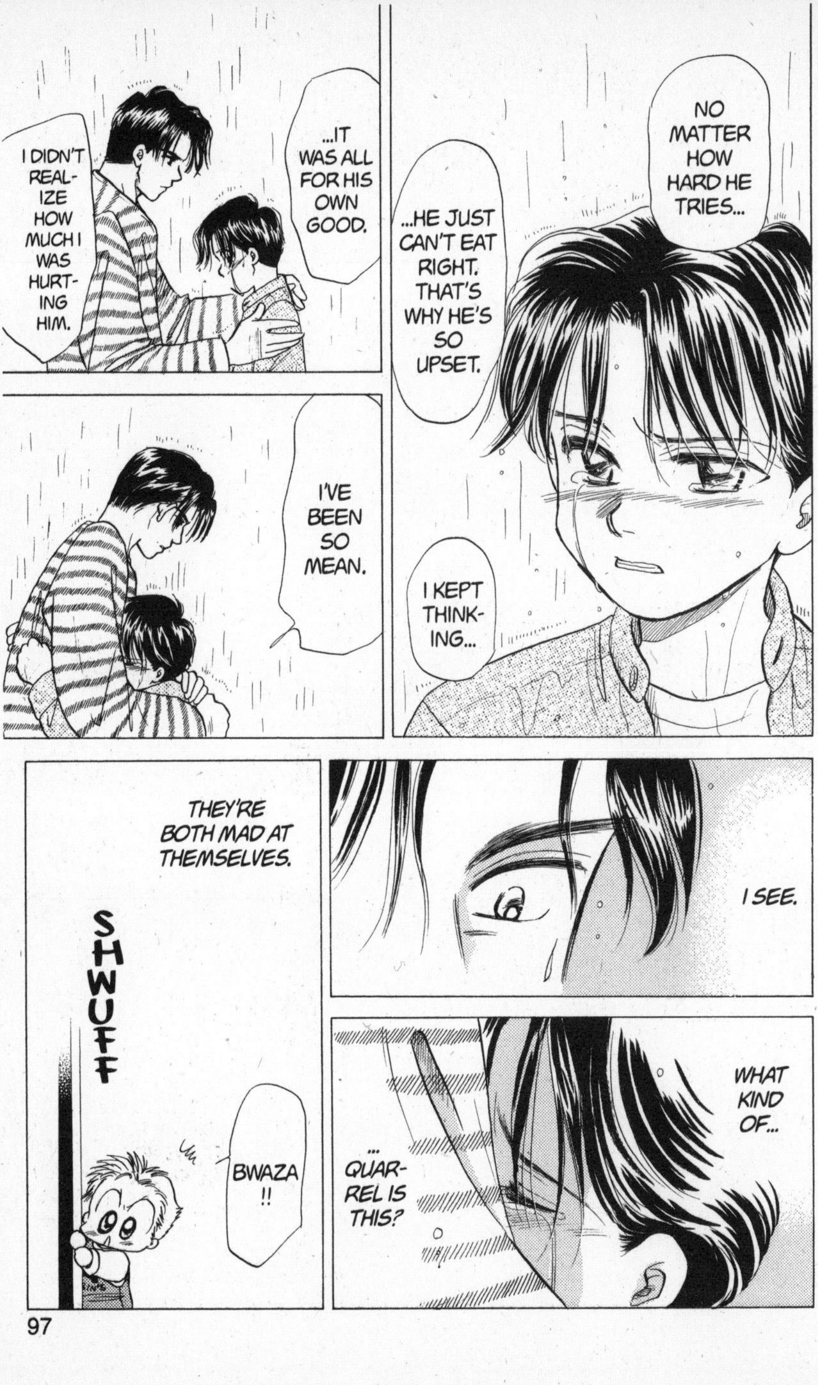
NO MATTER HOW HARD HE TRIES...
...HE JUST CAN'T EAT RIGHT. THAT'S WHY HE'S SO UPSET.
I KEPT THINKING...
...IT WAS ALL FOR HIS OWN GOOD.
I DIDN'T REALIZE HOW MUCH I WAS HURTING HIM.
I'VE BEEN SO MEAN.
I SEE.
WHAT KIND OF...
...QUARREL IS THIS?
THEY'RE BOTH MAD AT THEMSELVES.
SHWUFF
BWAZA!!

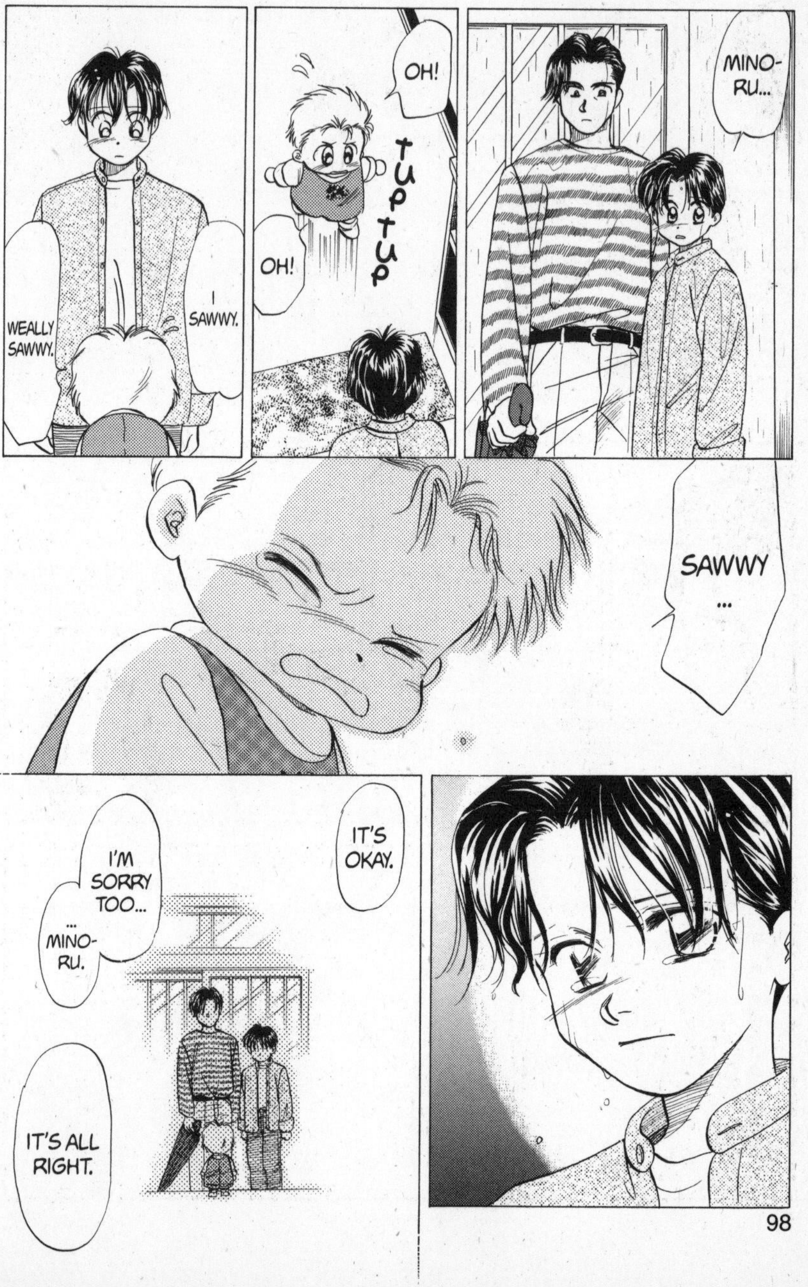
MINO-RU...
OH!
TUP TUP
OH!
I SAWWY.
WEALLY SAWWY.
SAWWY ...
IT'S OKAY.
I'M SORRY TOO... ... MINO-RU.
IT'S ALL RIGHT.

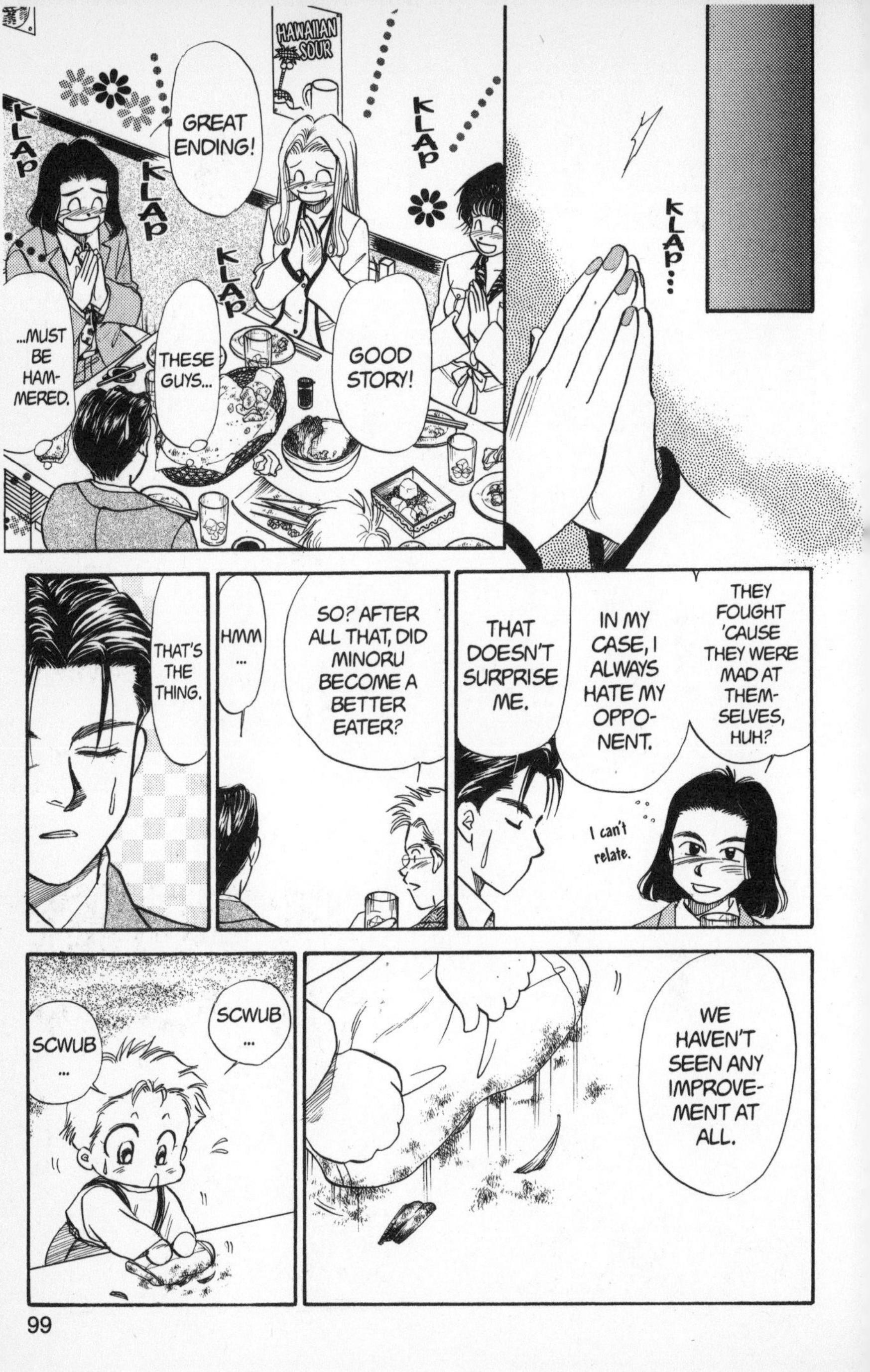
KLAP...
HAWAIIAN SOUR
KLAP
GREAT ENDING!
KLAP
KLAP
GOOD STORY!
THESE GUYS...
...MUST BE HAMMERED.
KLAP
THEY FOUGHT 'CAUSE THEY WERE MAD AT THEMSELVES, HUH?
IN MY CASE, I ALWAYS HATE MY OPPONENT.
I can't relate.
THAT DOESN'T SURPRISE ME.
SO? AFTER ALL THAT, DID MINORU BECOME A BETTER EATER?
HMM...
THAT'S THE THING.
WE HAVEN'T SEEN ANY IMPROVEMENT AT ALL.
SCWUB...
SCWUB...

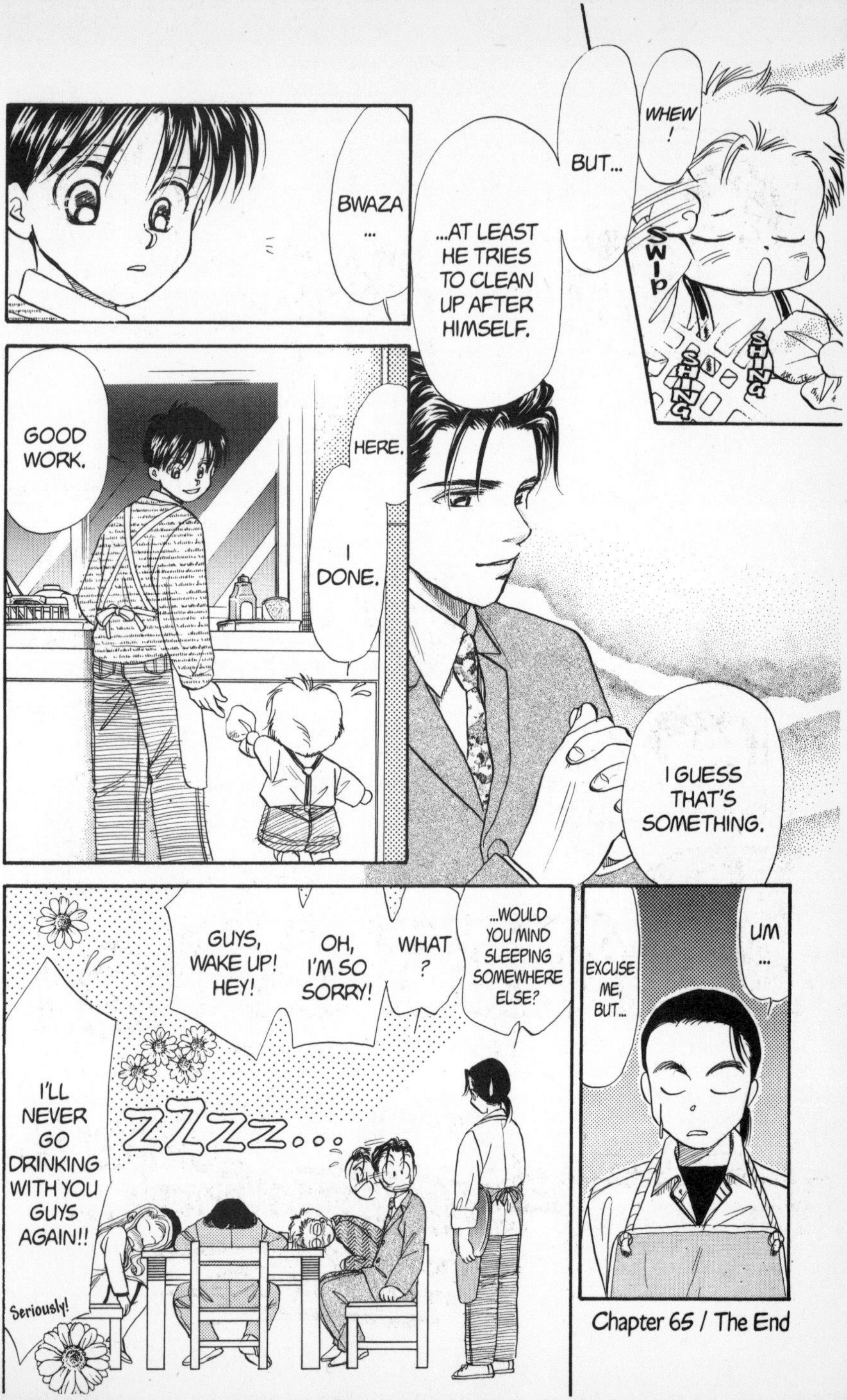
WHEW!
SWIP
SHING
SHING
BUT...
...AT LEAST HE TRIES TO CLEAN UP AFTER HIMSELF.
BWAZA ...
HERE.
I DONE.
GOOD WORK.
I GUESS THAT'S SOMETHING.
UM ...
EXCUSE ME, BUT...
...WOULD YOU MIND SLEEPING SOMEWHERE ELSE?
WHAT?
OH, I'M SO SORRY!
GUYS, WAKE UP! HEY!
ZZZZ...
I'LL NEVER GO DRINKING WITH YOU GUYS AGAIN!!
Seriously!

Chapter 65 / The End

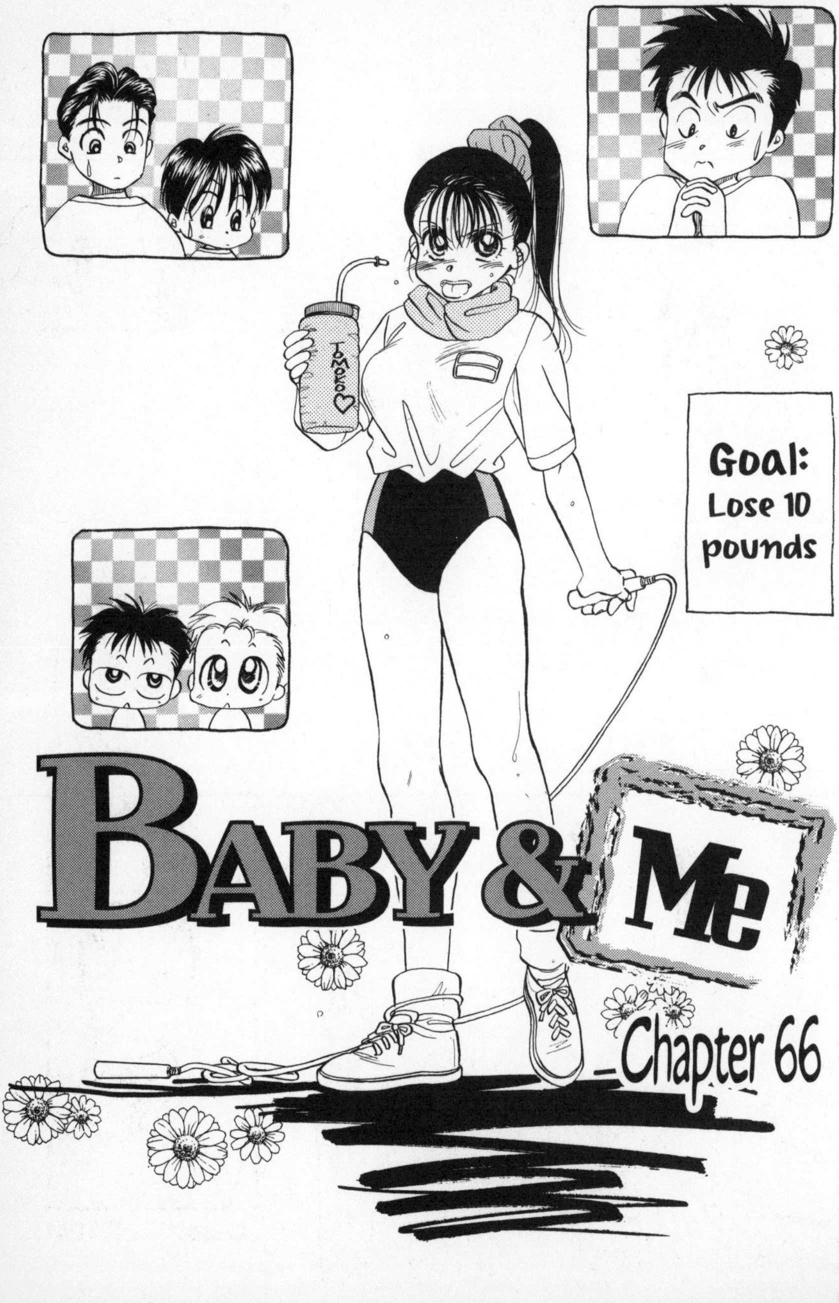
TOMOKO
Goal: Lose 10 pounds
BABY & ME
Chapter 66

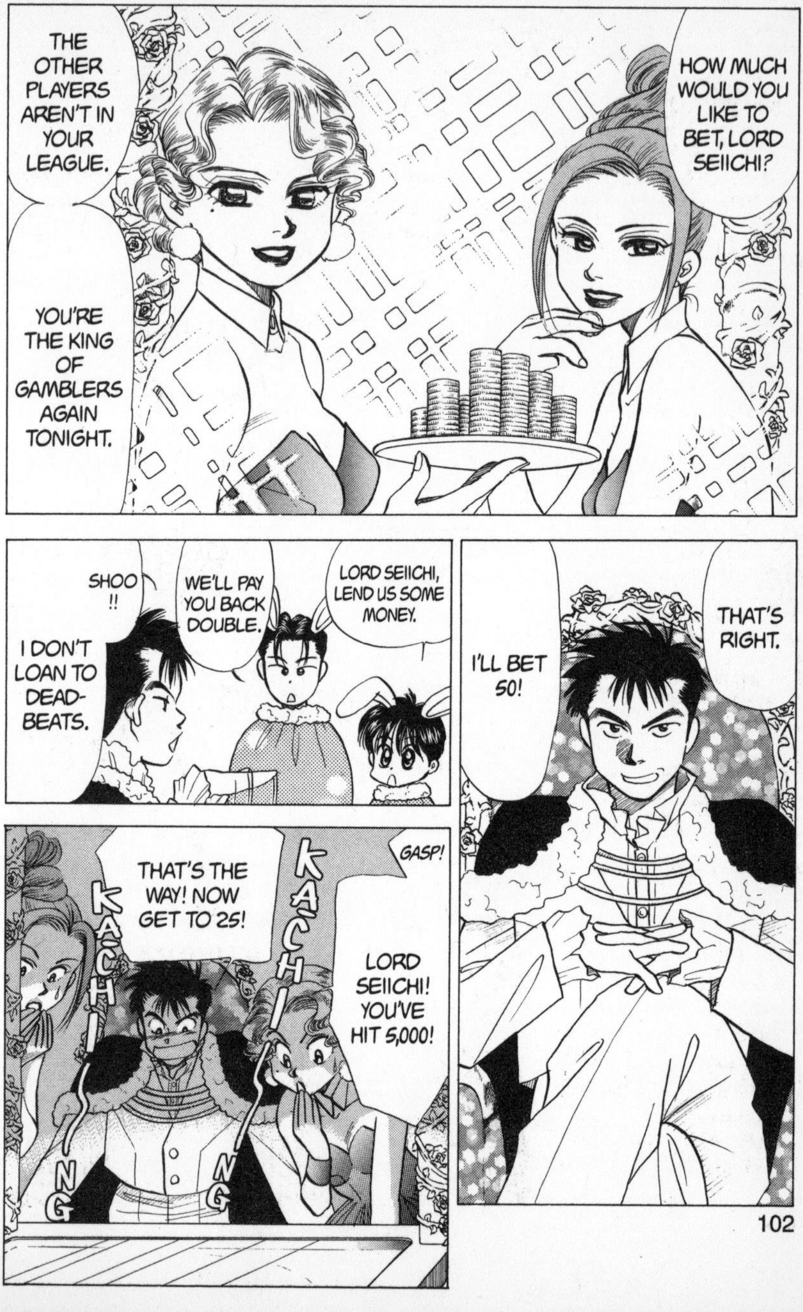

HOW MUCH WOULD YOU LIKE TO BET, LORD SEIICHI?
THE OTHER PLAYERS AREN'T IN YOUR LEAGUE.
YOU'RE THE KING OF GAMBLERS AGAIN TONIGHT.
THAT'S RIGHT.
I'LL BET 50!
LORD SEIICHI, LEND US SOME MONEY.
WE'LL PAY YOU BACK DOUBLE.
SHOO !!
I DON'T LOAN TO DEAD-BEATS.
GASP!
LORD SEIICHI! YOU'VE HIT 5,000!
KACHI-NG
THAT'S THE WAY! NOW GET TO 25!
KACHI-NG

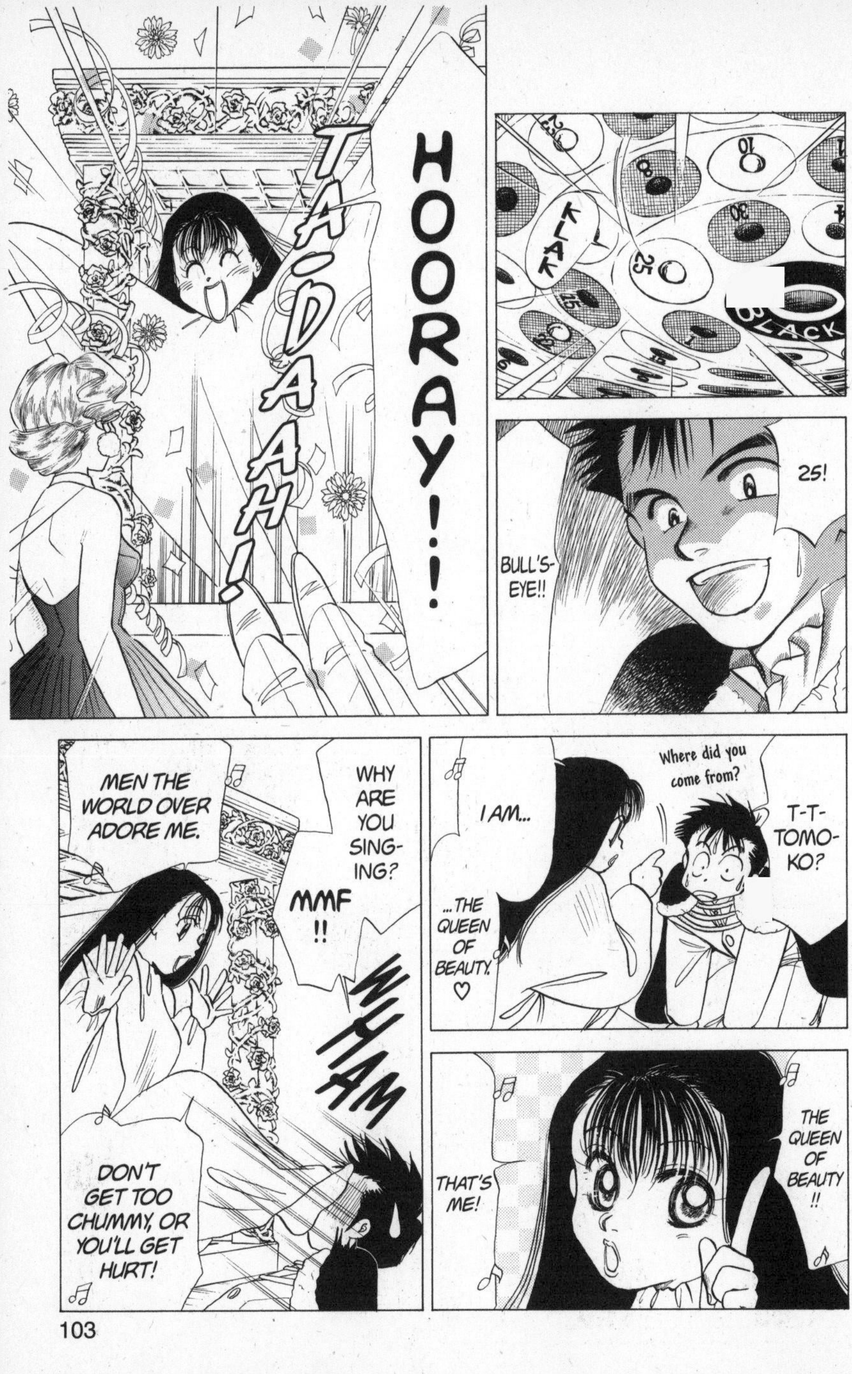
KLAK
BLACK
25!
BULL'S-EYE!!
HOORAY!!
TA-DA-AH!
Where did you come from?
T-T-TOMO-KO?
I AM...
...THE QUEEN OF BEAUTY. ♡
THE QUEEN OF BEAUTY!!
THAT'S ME!
WHY ARE YOU SING-ING?
MEN THE WORLD OVER ADORE ME.
MMF!!
WHAM
DON'T GET TOO CHUMMY, OR YOU'LL GET HURT!

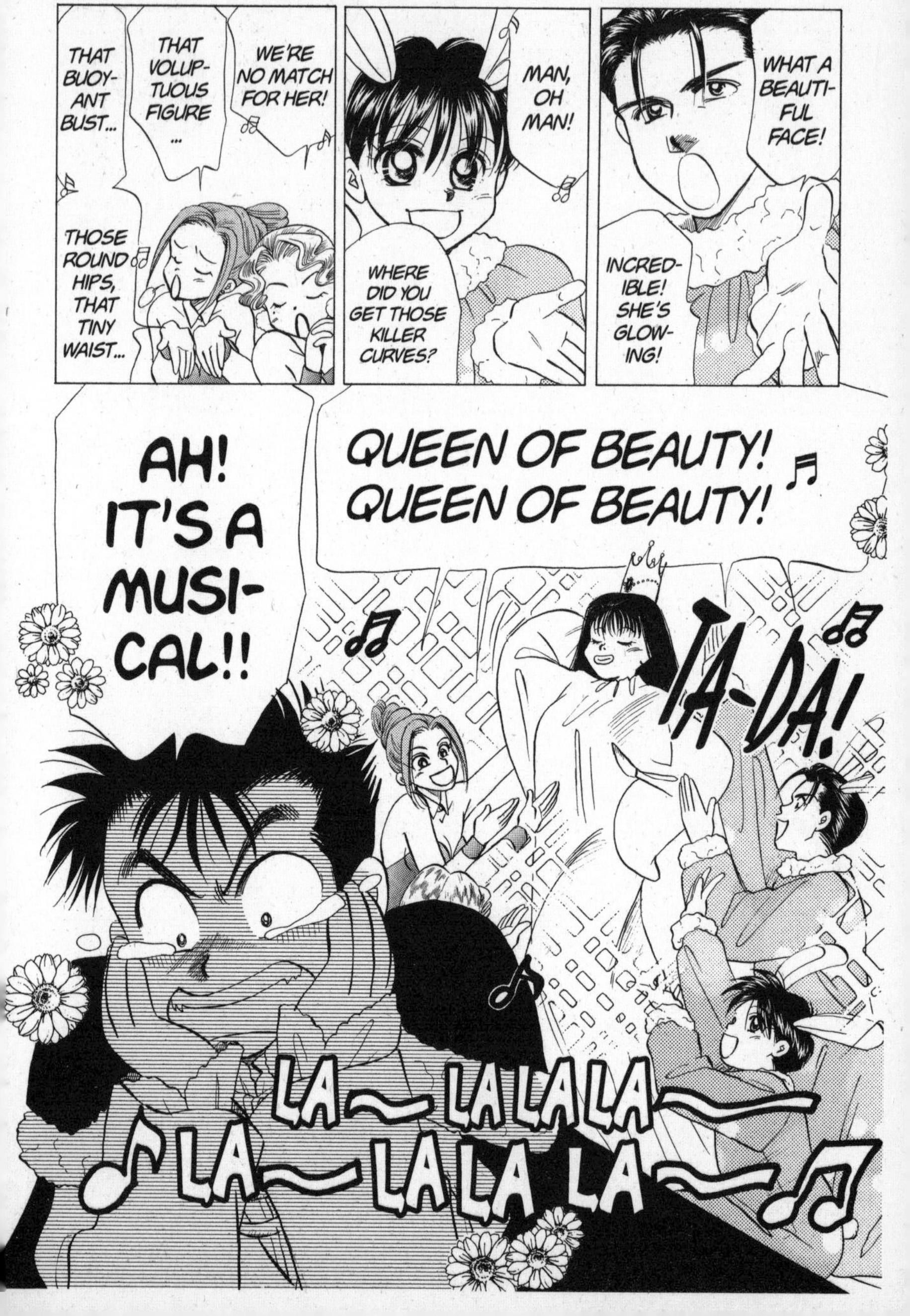
WHAT A BEAUTIFUL FACE!
INCREDIBLE! SHE'S GLOWING!
MAN, OH MAN!
WHERE DID YOU GET THOSE KILLER CURVES?
WE'RE NO MATCH FOR HER!
THAT VOLUPTUOUS FIGURE...
THAT BUOYANT BUST...
THOSE ROUND HIPS, THAT TINY WAIST...
QUEEN OF BEAUTY! QUEEN OF BEAUTY!
TA-DA!
AH! IT'S A MUSICAL!!
LA~ LALALA~
LA~ LA LA LA~

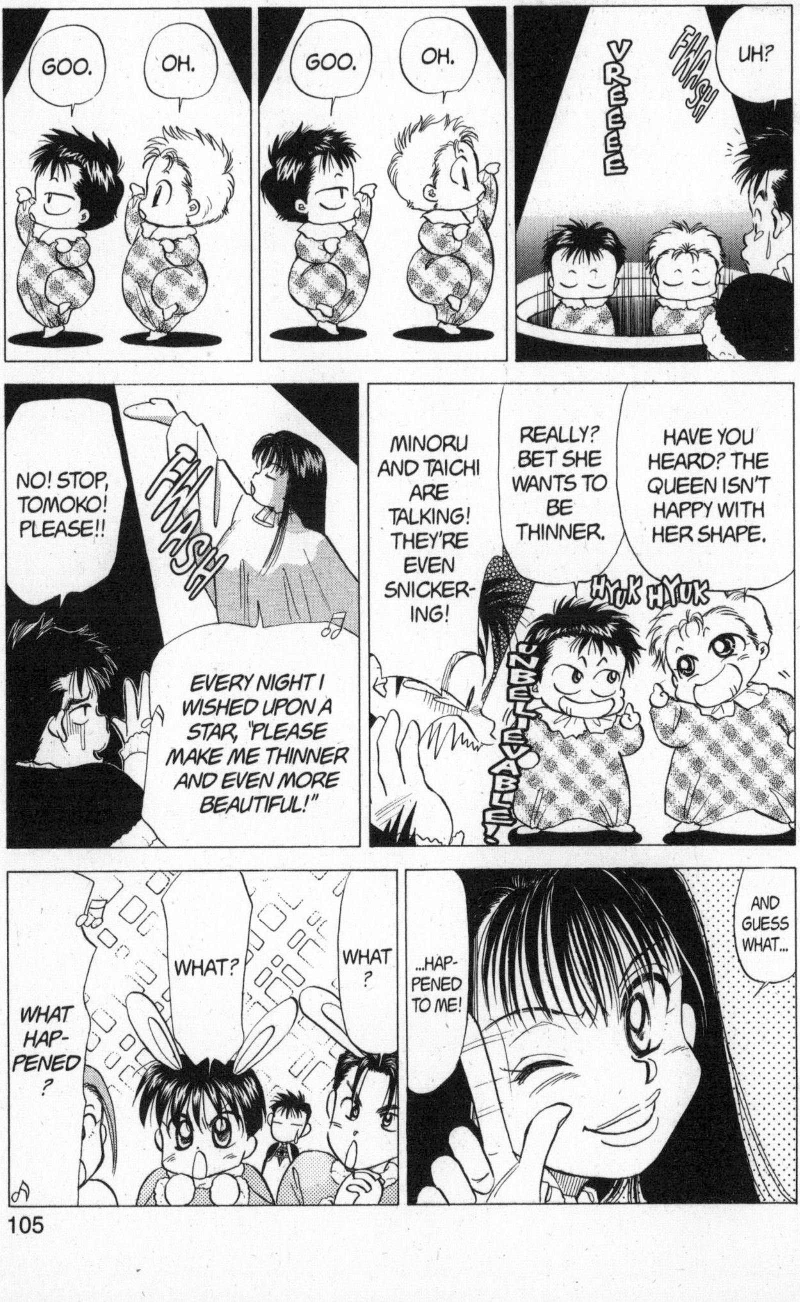
FWASH
VREEEE
UH?
OH.
GOO.
OH.
GOO.
HAVE YOU HEARD? THE QUEEN ISN'T HAPPY WITH HER SHAPE.
REALLY? BET SHE WANTS TO BE THINNER.
MINORU AND TAICHI ARE TALKING! THEY'RE EVEN SNICKERING!
HYUK HYUK
UNBELIEVABLE!
FWASH
NO! STOP, TOMOKO! PLEASE!!
EVERY NIGHT I WISHED UPON A STAR, "PLEASE MAKE ME THINNER AND EVEN MORE BEAUTIFUL!"
AND GUESS WHAT...
...HAPPENED TO ME!
WHAT?
WHAT?
WHAT HAPPENED?

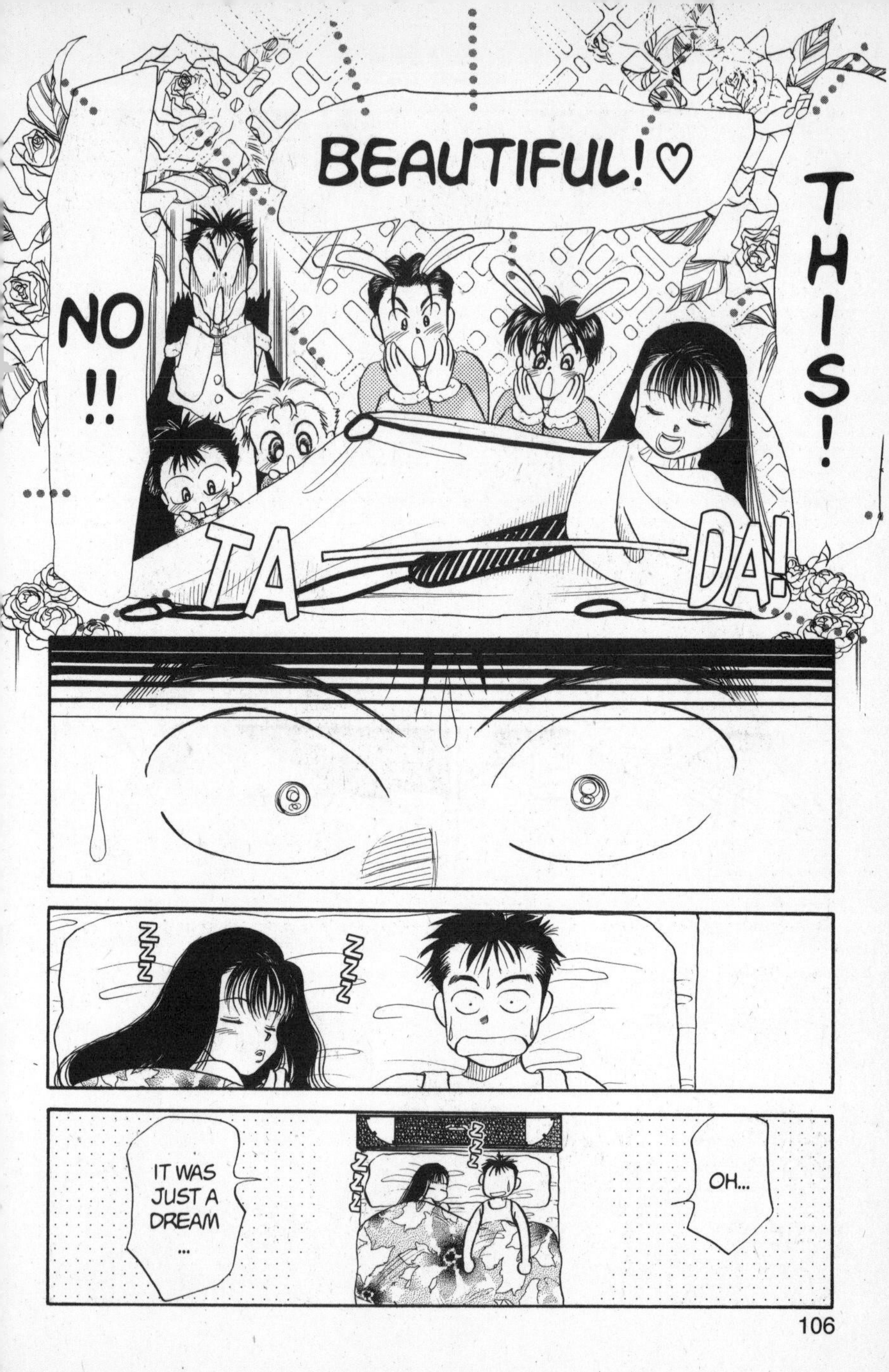
THIS!
BEAUTIFUL! ♡
NO !! ....
TA—DA!
ZZZ
ZZZ
OH...
ZZZ
ZZZ
IT WAS JUST A DREAM ...

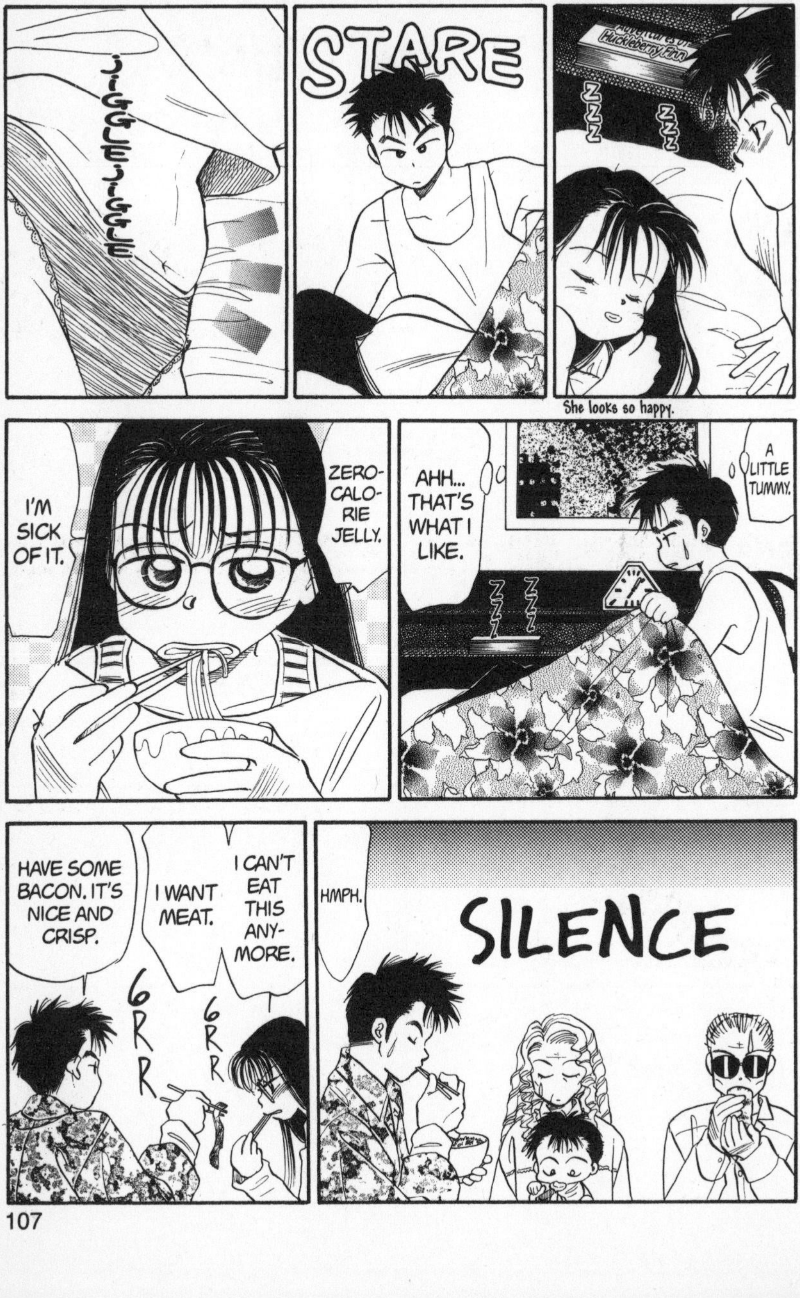
Huckleberry Finn
ZZZ
ZZZ
She looks so happy.
STARE
JIGGLE JIGGLE
A LITTLE TUMMY.
AHH... THAT'S WHAT I LIKE.
ZZZ
ZZZ
ZERO-CALORIE JELLY.
I'M SICK OF IT.
HMPH.
SILENCE
I CAN'T EAT THIS ANYMORE.
I WANT MEAT.
HAVE SOME BACON. IT'S NICE AND CRISP.
GRR
GRR

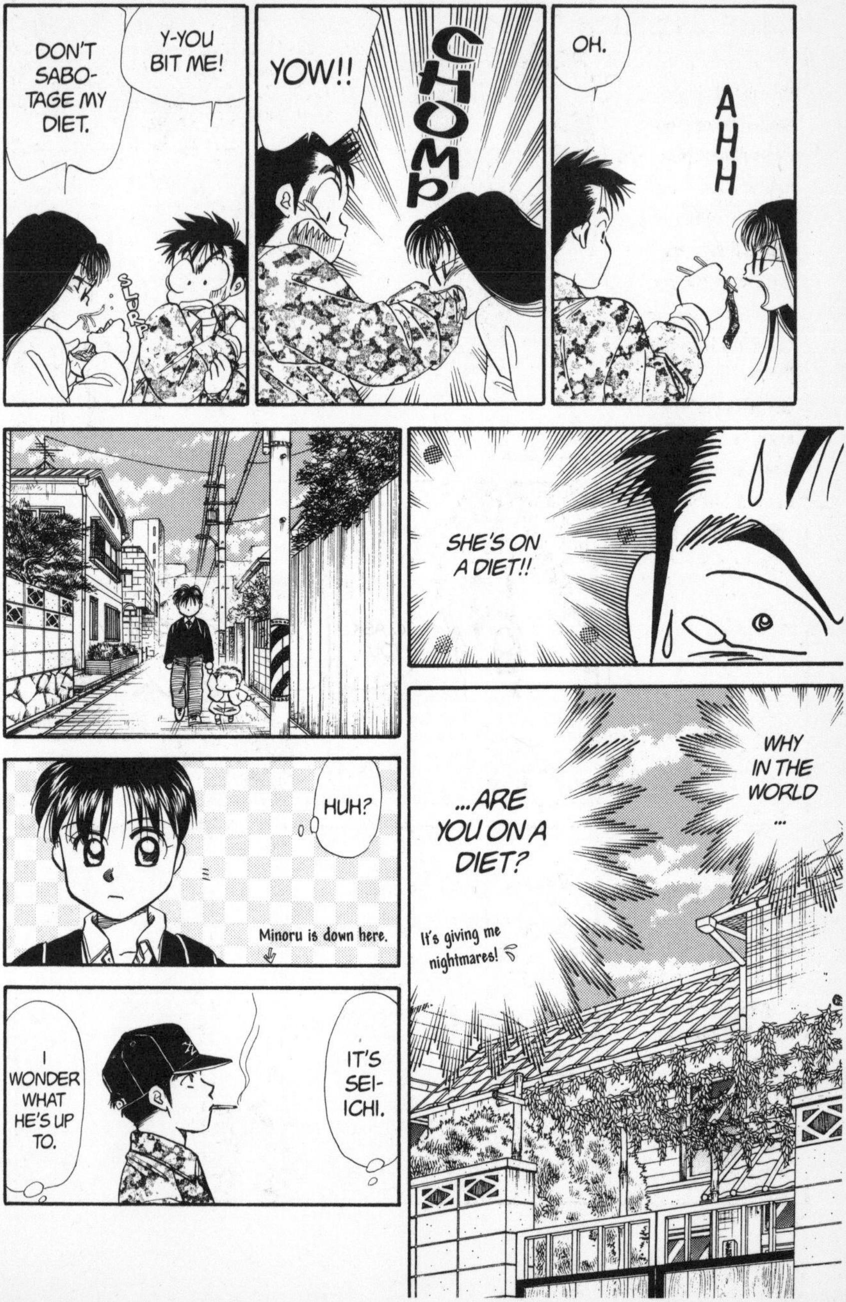
OH.
AHHH
YOW!!
CHOMP
Y-YOU BIT ME!
DON'T SABOTAGE MY DIET.
SLURP
SHE'S ON A DIET!!
WHY IN THE WORLD ...
...ARE YOU ON A DIET?
It's giving me nightmares!
HUH?
Minoru is down here.
IT'S SEI-ICHI.
I WONDER WHAT HE'S UP TO.

Author's Note Part 4

Whenever I see someone drawing skillfully without any extra lines, I feel envious. When I draw, there are lines everywhere. My drafts are all black by the time they're finished. Sometimes I don't even know which lines to ink. When I draw a body, I usually draw the frame first.

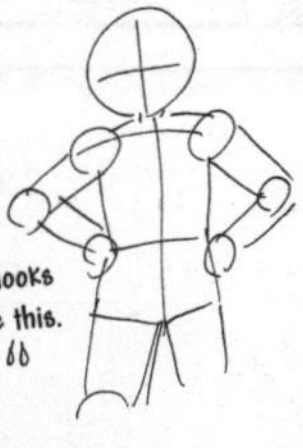

It looks like this.

What about you?

Here's what I wish for: a brain that can think of good stories, a hand that can draw super fast, and a good sense of composition and character design. Please, God! ♡ Smack!

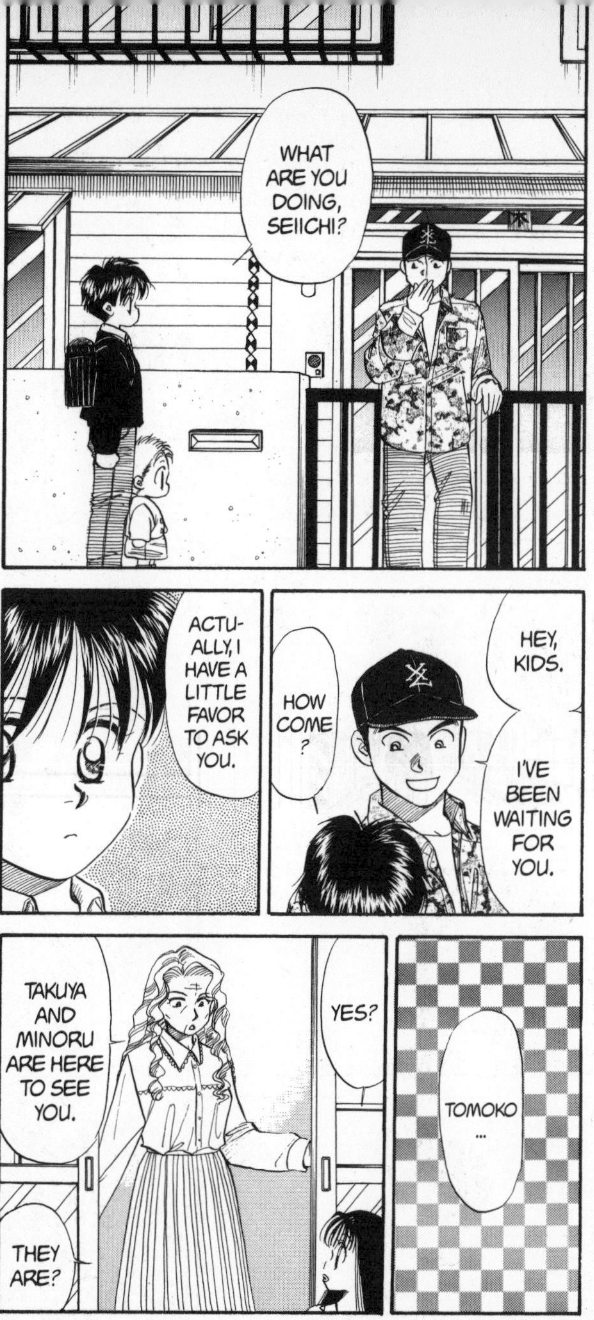
WHAT ARE YOU DOING, SEIICHI?
HEY, KIDS.
I'VE BEEN WAITING FOR YOU.
HOW COME?
ACTUALLY, I HAVE A LITTLE FAVOR TO ASK YOU.
TOMOKO...
YES?
TAKUYA AND MINORU ARE HERE TO SEE YOU.
THEY ARE?

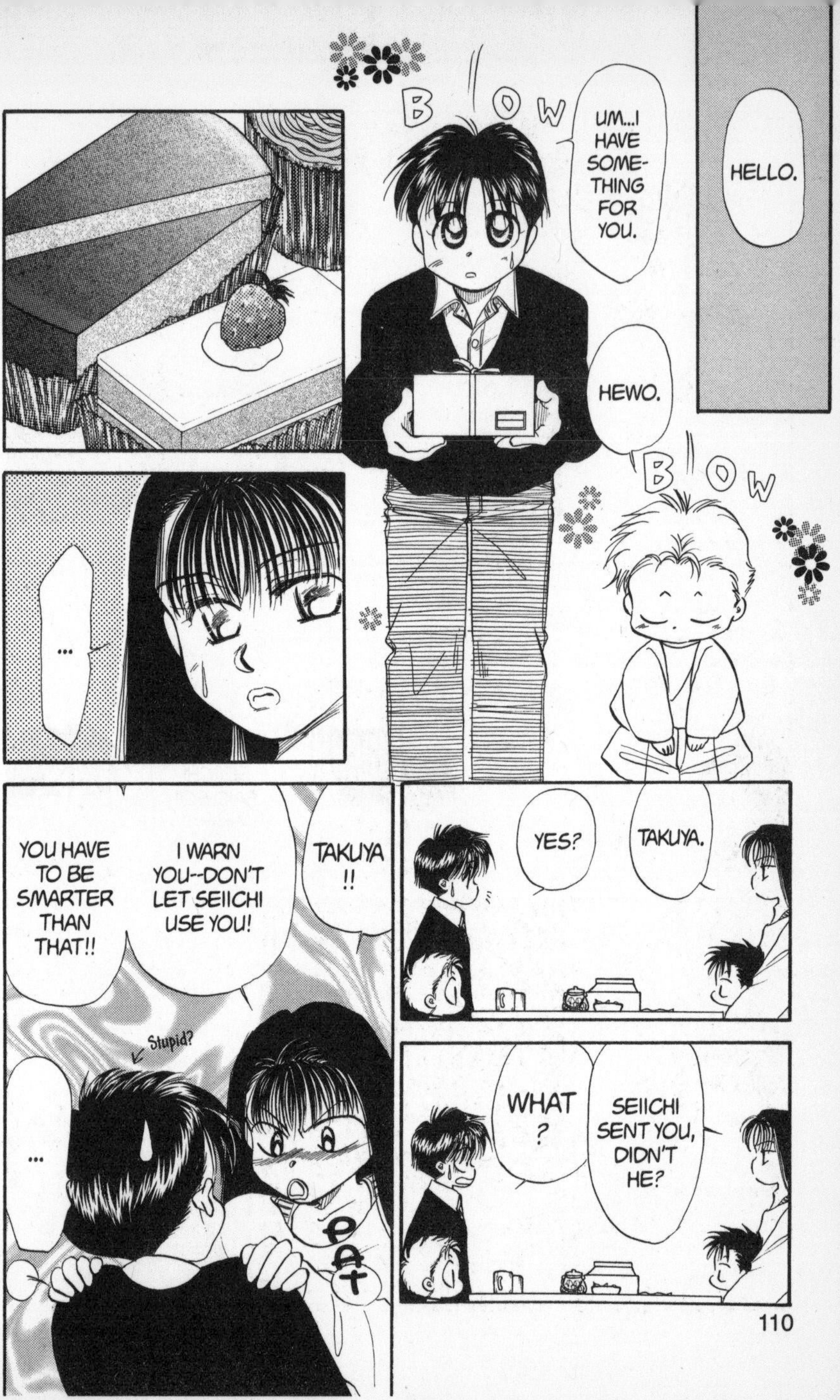
HELLO.
BOW
UM...I HAVE SOMETHING FOR YOU.
HEWO.
BOW
...
TAKUYA.
YES?
SEIICHI SENT YOU, DIDN'T HE?
WHAT?
TAKUYA!!
I WARN YOU--DON'T LET SEIICHI USE YOU!
YOU HAVE TO BE SMARTER THAN THAT!!
Stupid?
...
PAT

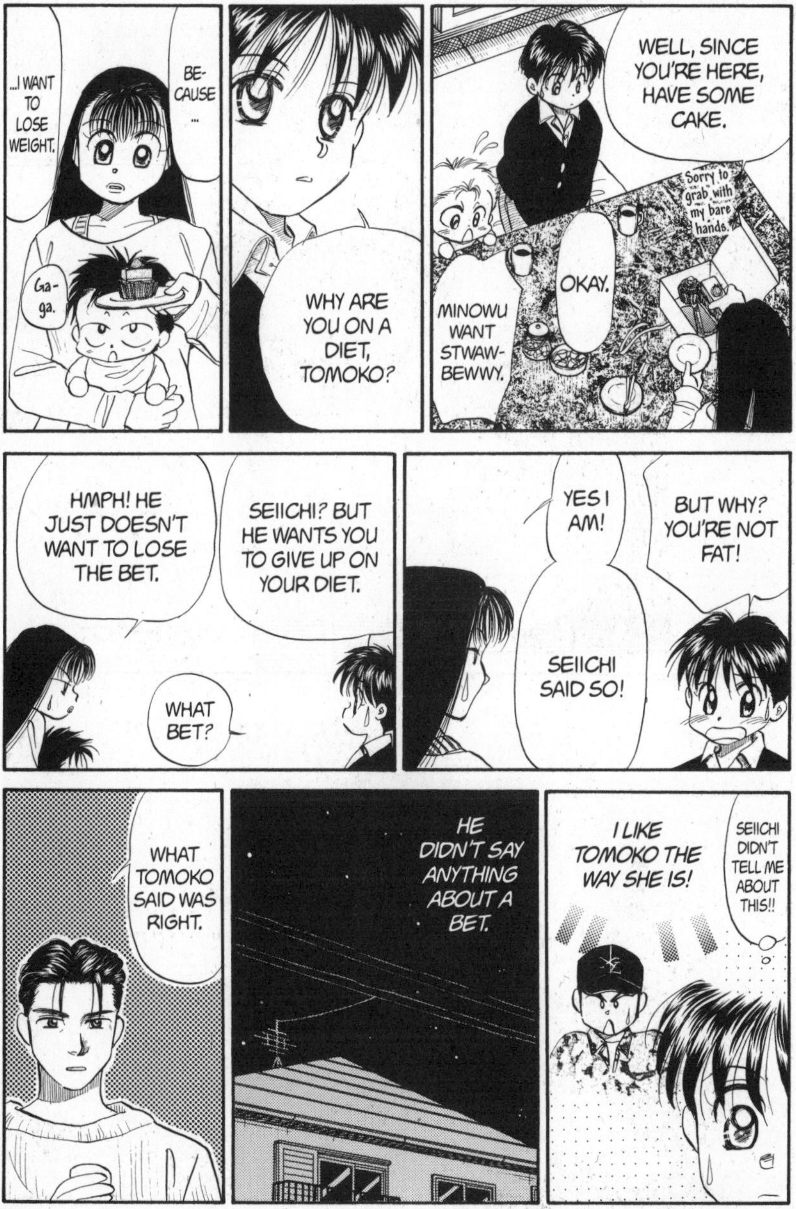
WELL, SINCE YOU'RE HERE, HAVE SOME CAKE.
Sorry to grab with my bare hands.
OKAY.
MINOWU WANT STWAW-BEWWY.
WHY ARE YOU ON A DIET, TOMOKO?
BE-CAUSE ...
...I WANT TO LOSE WEIGHT.
Ga-ga.
BUT WHY? YOU'RE NOT FAT!
YES I AM!
SEIICHI SAID SO!
SEIICHI? BUT HE WANTS YOU TO GIVE UP ON YOUR DIET.
HMPH! HE JUST DOESN'T WANT TO LOSE THE BET.
WHAT BET?
SEIICHI DIDN'T TELL ME ABOUT THIS!!
I LIKE TOMOKO THE WAY SHE IS!
HE DIDN'T SAY ANYTHING ABOUT A BET.
WHAT TOMOKO SAID WAS RIGHT.

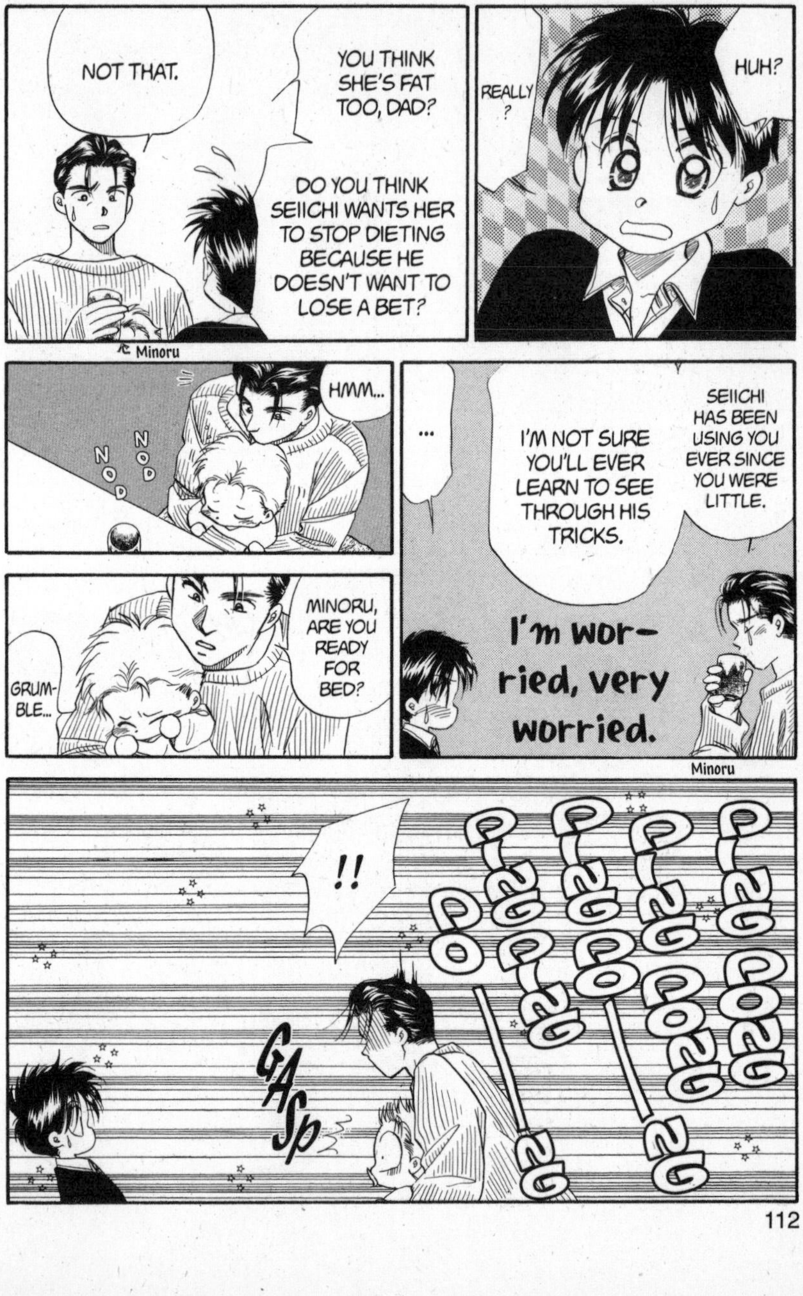
HUH?
REALLY?
YOU THINK SHE'S FAT TOO, DAD?
DO YOU THINK SEIICHI WANTS HER TO STOP DIETING BECAUSE HE DOESN'T WANT TO LOSE A BET?
NOT THAT.
Minoru
SEIICHI HAS BEEN USING YOU EVER SINCE YOU WERE LITTLE.
I'M NOT SURE YOU'LL EVER LEARN TO SEE THROUGH HIS TRICKS.
...
I'm wor-ried, very worried.
Minoru
HMM...
NOD NOD
MINORU, ARE YOU READY FOR BED?
GRUM-BLE...
PING PONG PING PONG PING PONG
PING PONG PING PONG PING PONG
!!
GASP

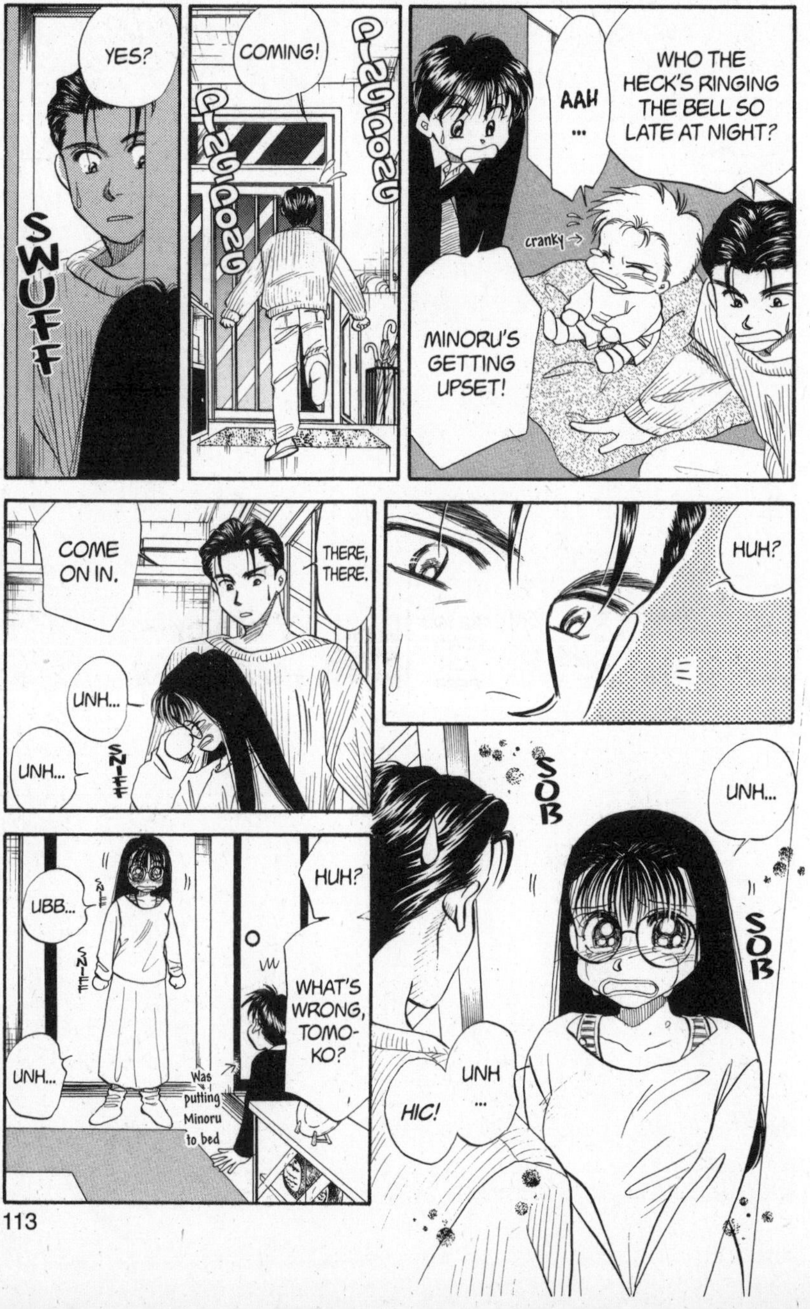
WHO THE HECK'S RINGING THE BELL SO LATE AT NIGHT?
AAH ...
cranky
MINORU'S GETTING UPSET!
PINGDONG
PINGDONG
COMING!
YES?
SWUFF
HUH?
THERE, THERE.
COME ON IN.
UNH...
UNH...
SNIFF
SOB
UNH...
SOB
UNH ...
HIC!
HUH?
WHAT'S WRONG, TOMO-KO?
Was putting Minoru to bed
UBB...
SNIFF
SNIFF
UNH...

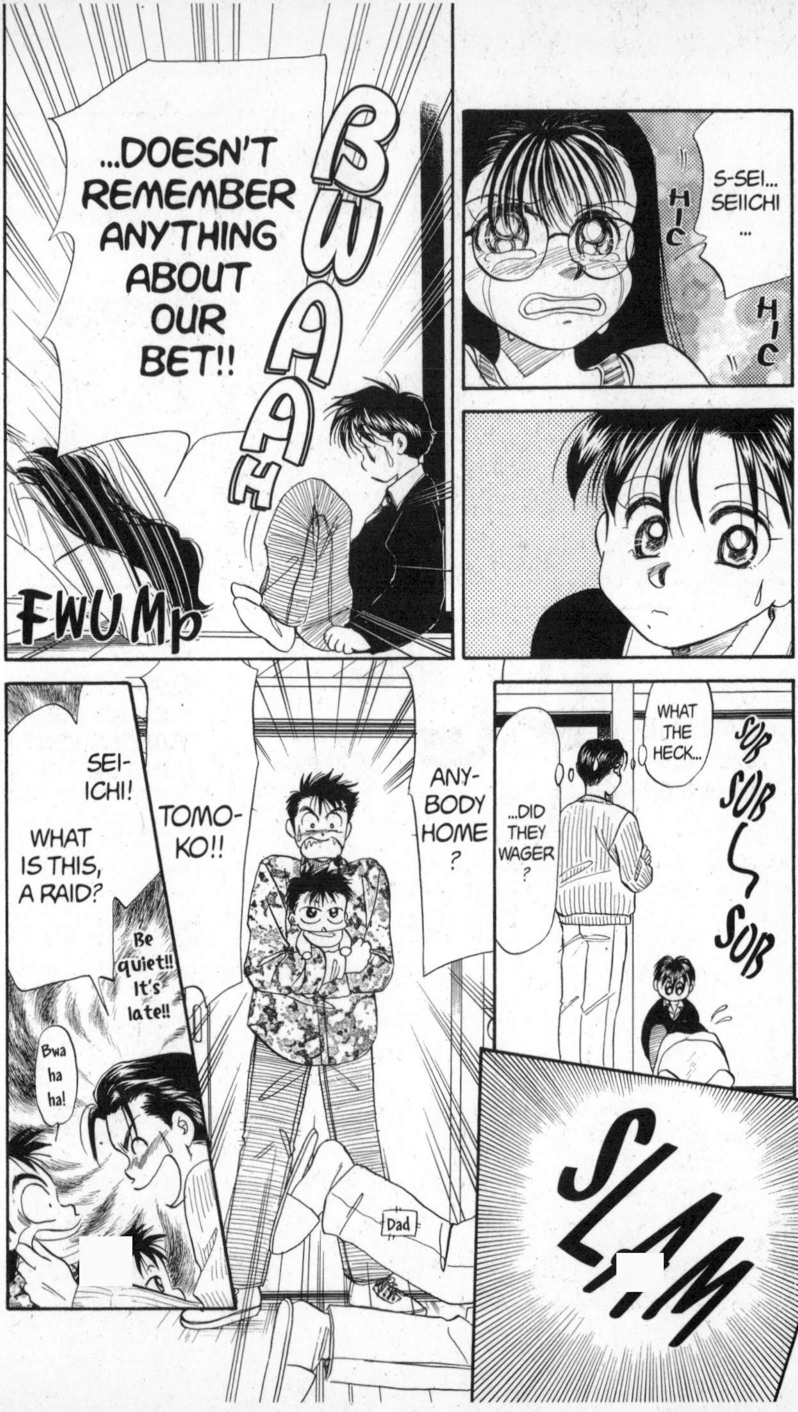
S-SEI... SEIICHI ...
HIC
HIC
...DOESN'T REMEMBER ANYTHING ABOUT OUR BET!!
BWAAAH
FWUMp
WHAT THE HECK...
...DID THEY WAGER?
SOB SOB SOB
SLAM!!
ANY-BODY HOME?
TOMO-KO!!
Dad
SEI-ICHI!
WHAT IS THIS, A RAID?
Be quiet!! It's late!!
Bwa ha ha!

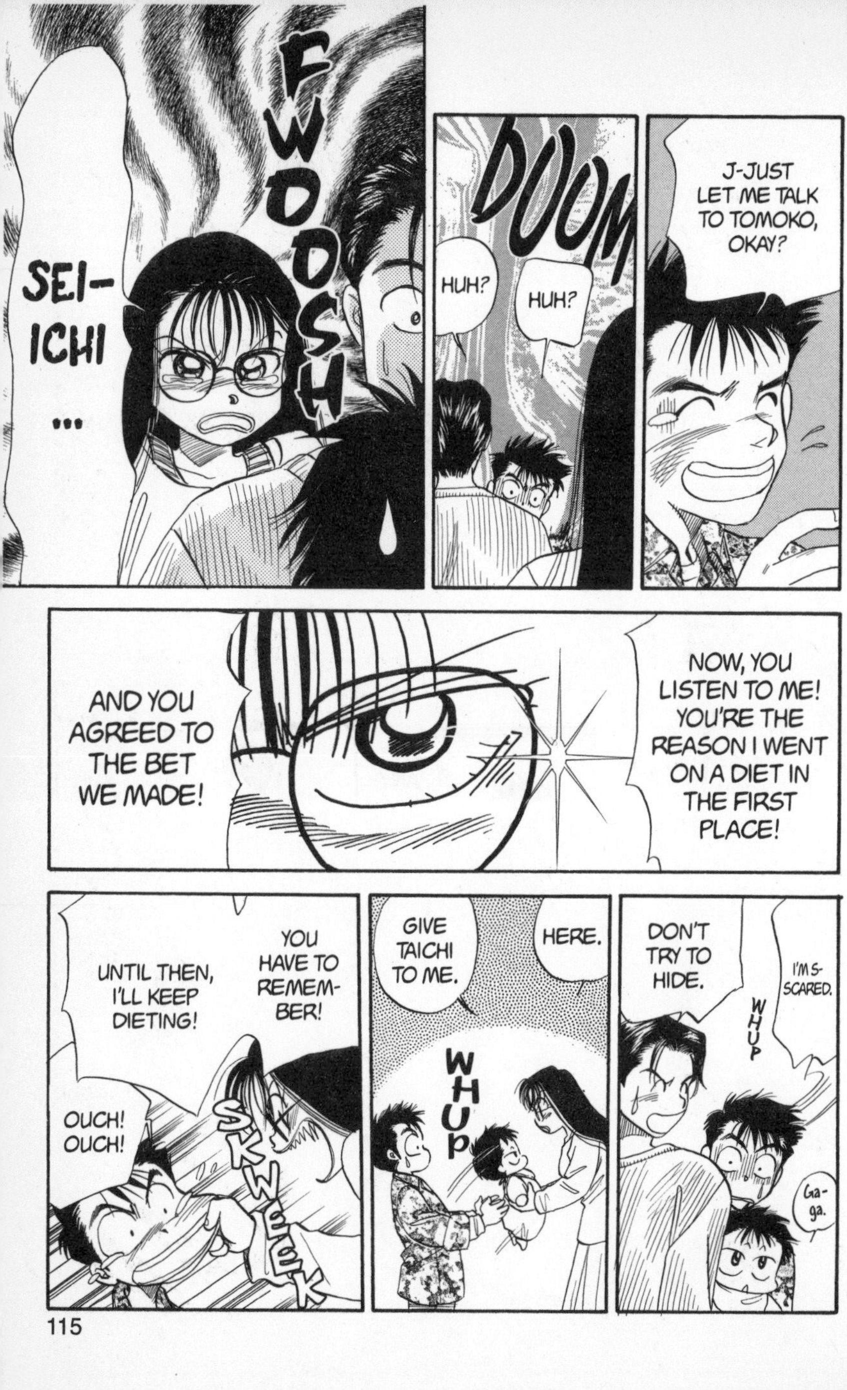
J-JUST LET ME TALK TO TOMOKO, OKAY?
DOOM
HUH?
HUH?
FWOOSH
SEI-ICHI ...
NOW, YOU LISTEN TO ME! YOU'RE THE REASON I WENT ON A DIET IN THE FIRST PLACE!
AND YOU AGREED TO THE BET WE MADE!
DON'T TRY TO HIDE.
I'M S-SCARED.
WHUP
Ga-ga.
HERE.
GIVE TAICHI TO ME.
WHUP
YOU HAVE TO REMEMBER!
UNTIL THEN, I'LL KEEP DIETING!
SKWEEEK
OUCH! OUCH!

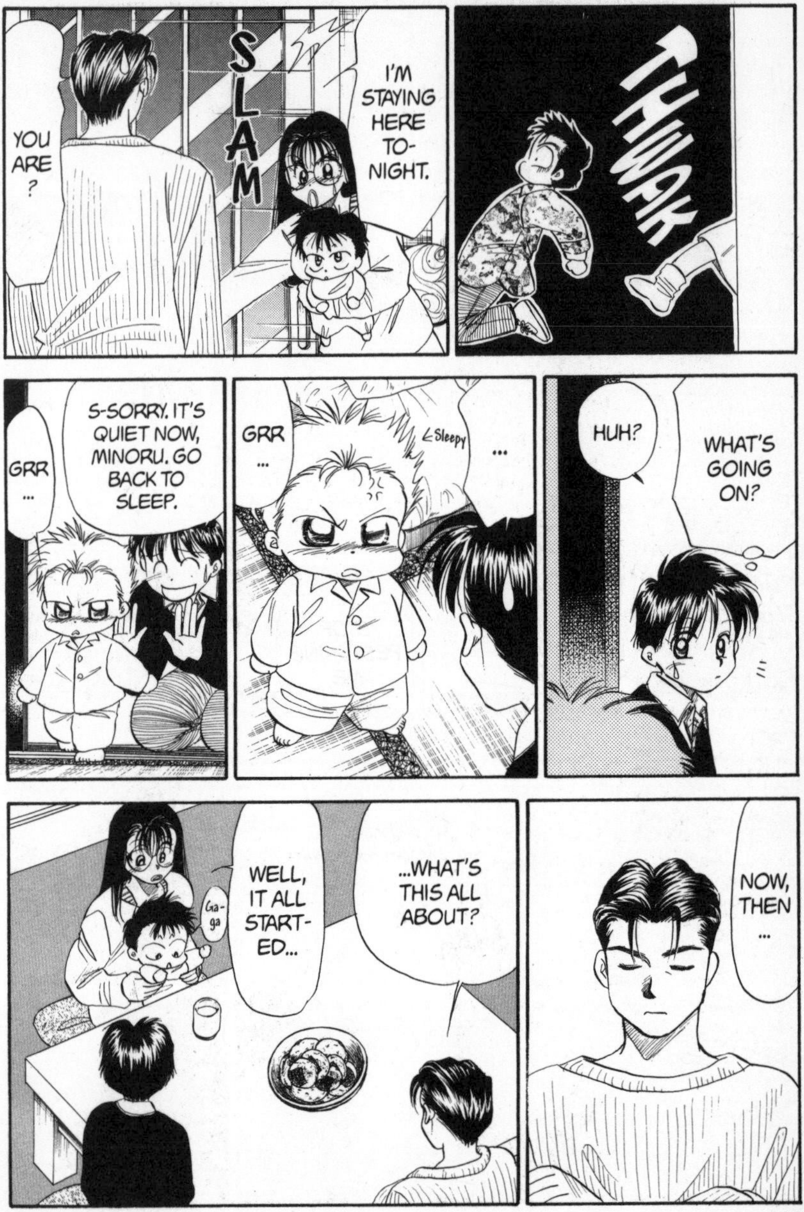
THWAK
I'M STAYING HERE TO-NIGHT.
SLAM
YOU ARE ?
WHAT'S GOING ON?
HUH?
...
Sleepy
GRR ...
S-SORRY. IT'S QUIET NOW, MINORU. GO BACK TO SLEEP.
GRR ...
NOW, THEN ...
...WHAT'S THIS ALL ABOUT?
WELL, IT ALL START-ED...
Ga-ga

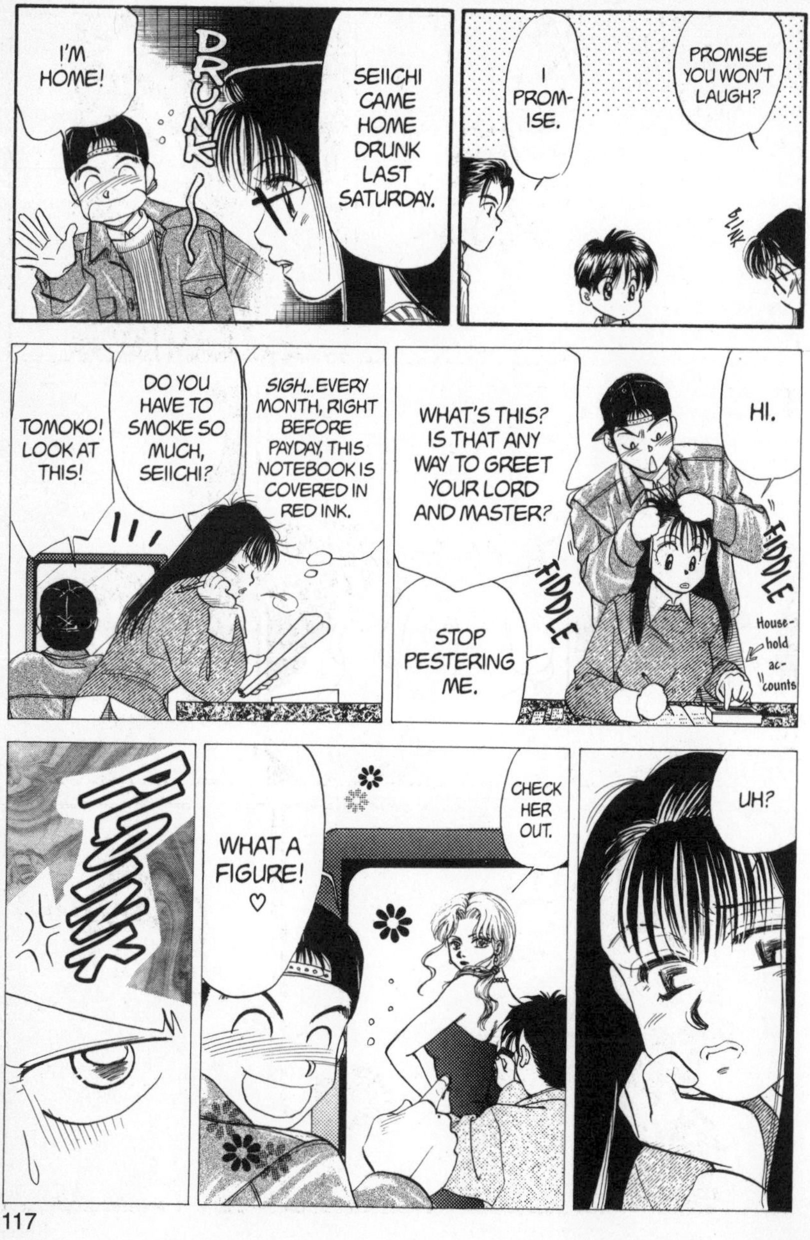
PROMISE YOU WON'T LAUGH?
I PROMISE.
BLINK
SEIICHI CAME HOME DRUNK LAST SATURDAY.
DRUNK
I'M HOME!
HI.
FIDDLE
WHAT'S THIS? IS THAT ANY WAY TO GREET YOUR LORD AND MASTER?
FIDDLE
STOP PESTERING ME.
Household accounts
SIGH... EVERY MONTH, RIGHT BEFORE PAYDAY, THIS NOTEBOOK IS COVERED IN RED INK.
DO YOU HAVE TO SMOKE SO MUCH, SEIICHI?
TOMOKO! LOOK AT THIS!
UH?
CHECK HER OUT.
WHAT A FIGURE! ♡
PLONK

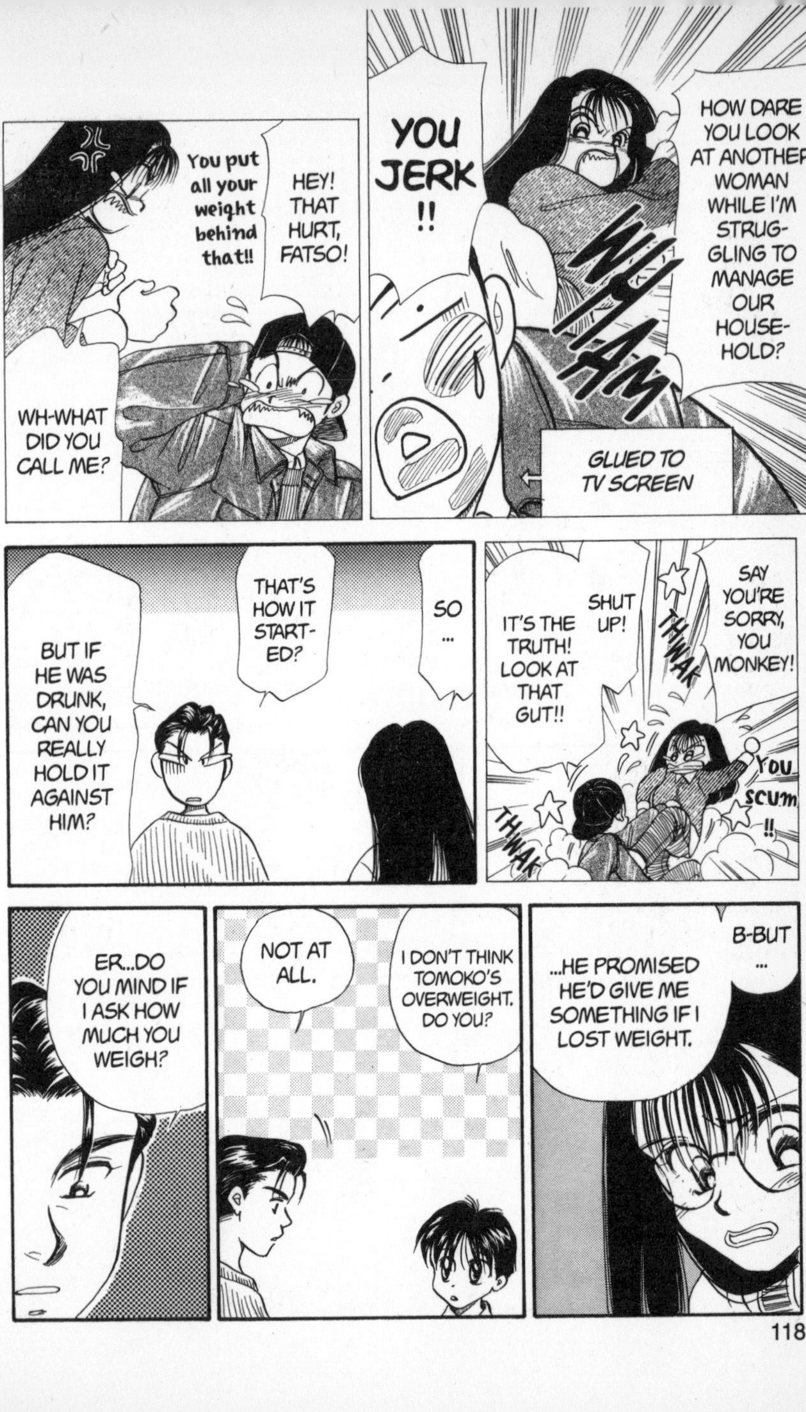
HOW DARE YOU LOOK AT ANOTHER WOMAN WHILE I'M STRUG-GLING TO MANAGE OUR HOUSE-HOLD?
YOU JERK !!
WHAM
GLUED TO TV SCREEN
HEY! THAT HURT, FATSO!
You put all your weight behind that!!
WH-WHAT DID YOU CALL ME?
SAY YOU'RE SORRY, YOU MONKEY!
THWAK
SHUT UP!
IT'S THE TRUTH! LOOK AT THAT GUT!!
YOU SCUM !!
THWAK
SO ...
THAT'S HOW IT START-ED?
BUT IF HE WAS DRUNK, CAN YOU REALLY HOLD IT AGAINST HIM?
B-BUT ...
...HE PROMISED HE'D GIVE ME SOMETHING IF I LOST WEIGHT.
I DON'T THINK TOMOKO'S OVERWEIGHT. DO YOU?
NOT AT ALL.
ER...DO YOU MIND IF I ASK HOW MUCH YOU WEIGH?

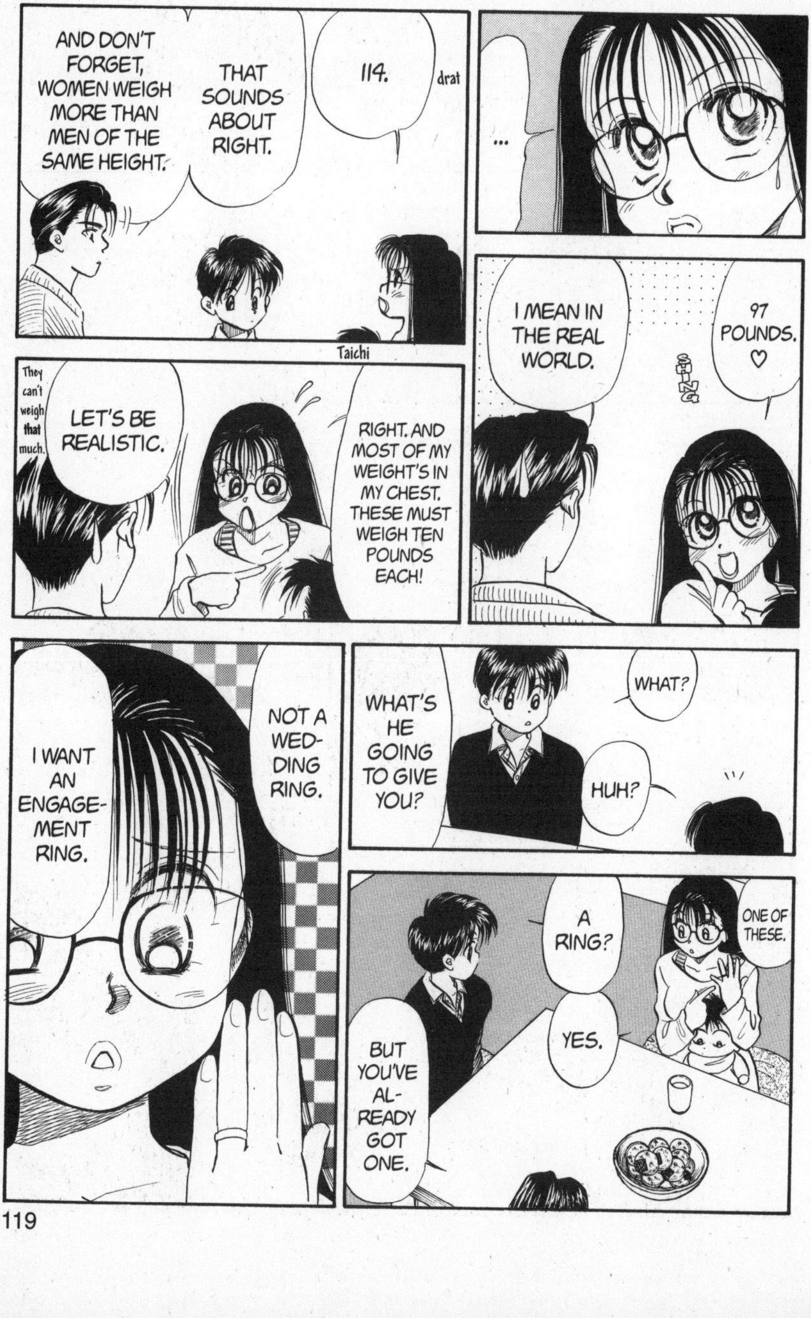
...
drat
114.
THAT SOUNDS ABOUT RIGHT.
AND DON'T FORGET, WOMEN WEIGH MORE THAN MEN OF THE SAME HEIGHT.
Taichi
97 POUNDS. ♡
SHING
I MEAN IN THE REAL WORLD.
RIGHT. AND MOST OF MY WEIGHT'S IN MY CHEST. THESE MUST WEIGH TEN POUNDS EACH!
LET'S BE REALISTIC.
They can't weigh **that** much.
WHAT?
HUH?
WHAT'S HE GOING TO GIVE YOU?
ONE OF THESE.
A RING?
YES.
BUT YOU'VE AL-READY GOT ONE.
NOT A WED-DING RING.
I WANT AN ENGAGE-MENT RING.

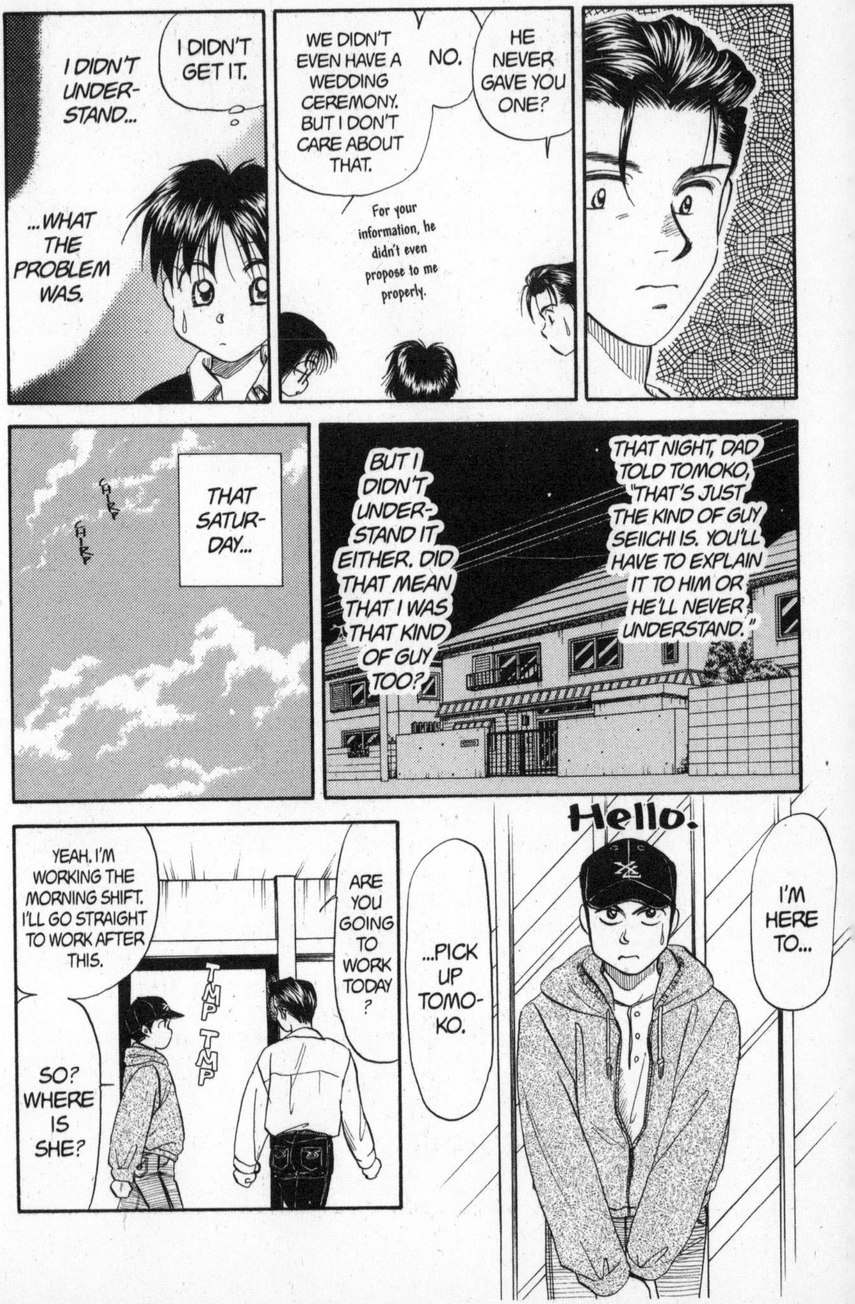
HE NEVER GAVE YOU ONE?
NO.
WE DIDN'T EVEN HAVE A WEDDING CEREMONY. BUT I DON'T CARE ABOUT THAT.
For your information, he didn't even propose to me properly.
I DIDN'T GET IT.
I DIDN'T UNDER-STAND...
...WHAT THE PROBLEM WAS.
THAT NIGHT, DAD TOLD TOMOKO, "THAT'S JUST THE KIND OF GUY SEIICHI IS. YOU'LL HAVE TO EXPLAIN IT TO HIM OR HE'LL NEVER UNDERSTAND."
BUT I DIDN'T UNDER-STAND IT EITHER. DID THAT MEAN THAT I WAS THAT KIND OF GUY TOO?
THAT SATUR-DAY...
CHK
CHK
Hello.
I'M HERE TO...
...PICK UP TOMO-KO.
ARE YOU GOING TO WORK TODAY?
YEAH. I'M WORKING THE MORNING SHIFT. I'LL GO STRAIGHT TO WORK AFTER THIS.
TMP TMP
SO? WHERE IS SHE?

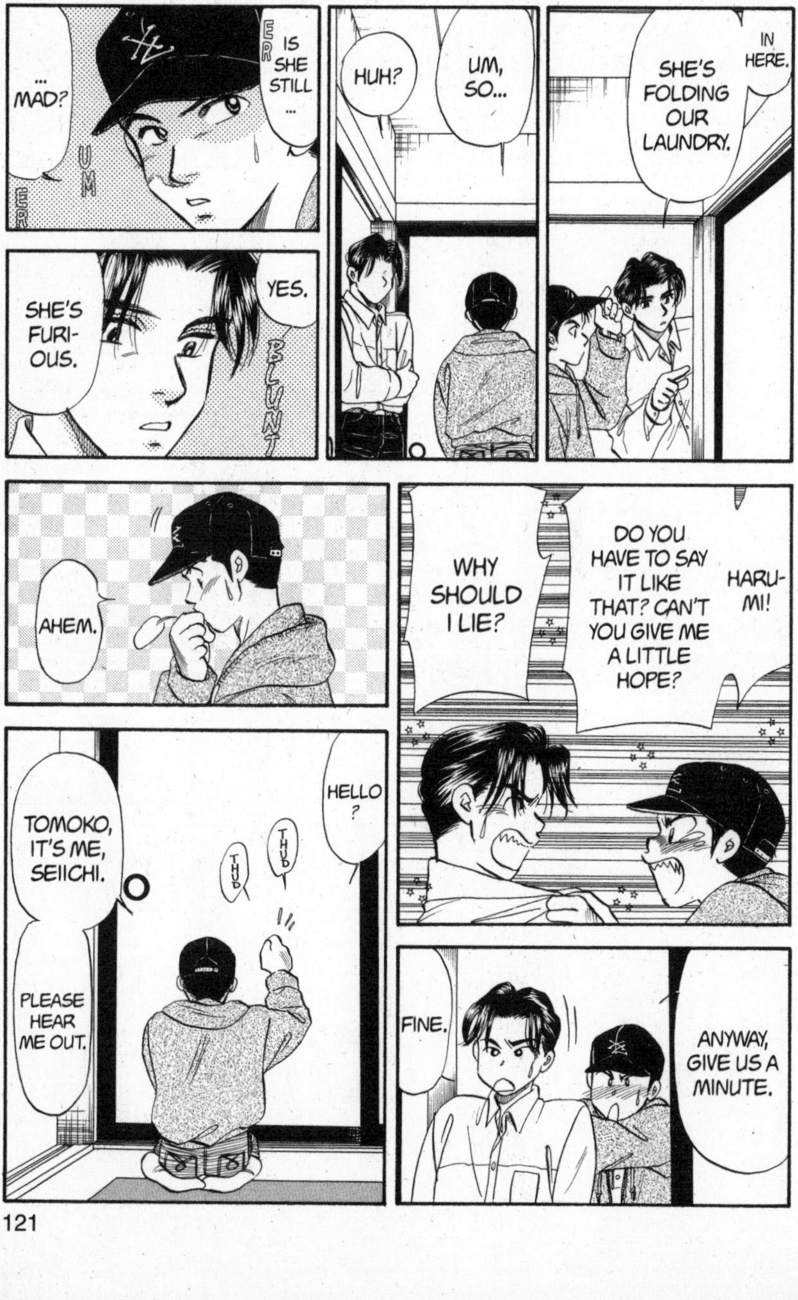
IN HERE.
SHE'S FOLDING OUR LAUNDRY.
UM, SO...
HUH?
IS SHE STILL ...
ER
... MAD?
UM
ER
YES.
SHE'S FURI-OUS.
BLUNT
HARU-MI!
DO YOU HAVE TO SAY IT LIKE THAT? CAN'T YOU GIVE ME A LITTLE HOPE?
WHY SHOULD I LIE?
AHEM.
ANYWAY, GIVE US A MINUTE.
FINE.
HELLO ?
THUD
THUD
TOMOKO, IT'S ME, SEIICHI.
PLEASE HEAR ME OUT.

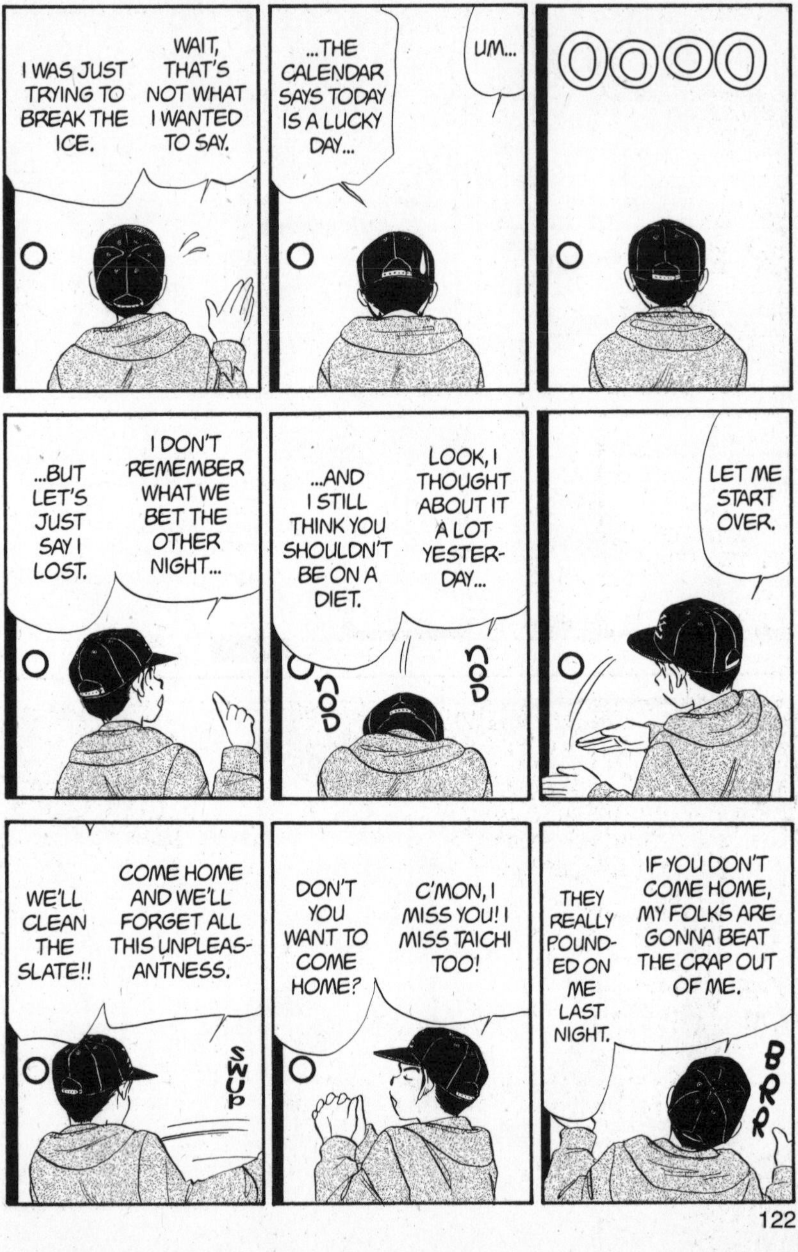
UM...
...THE CALENDAR SAYS TODAY IS A LUCKY DAY...
WAIT, THAT'S NOT WHAT I WANTED TO SAY.
I WAS JUST TRYING TO BREAK THE ICE.
LET ME START OVER.
LOOK, I THOUGHT ABOUT IT A LOT YESTER-DAY...
...AND I STILL THINK YOU SHOULDN'T BE ON A DIET.
NOD
NOD
I DON'T REMEMBER WHAT WE BET THE OTHER NIGHT...
...BUT LET'S JUST SAY I LOST.
IF YOU DON'T COME HOME, MY FOLKS ARE GONNA BEAT THE CRAP OUT OF ME.
THEY REALLY POUNDED ON ME LAST NIGHT.
BRRR
C'MON, I MISS YOU! I MISS TAICHI TOO!
DON'T YOU WANT TO COME HOME?
COME HOME AND WE'LL FORGET ALL THIS UNPLEAS-ANTNESS.
WE'LL CLEAN THE SLATE!!
SWUP

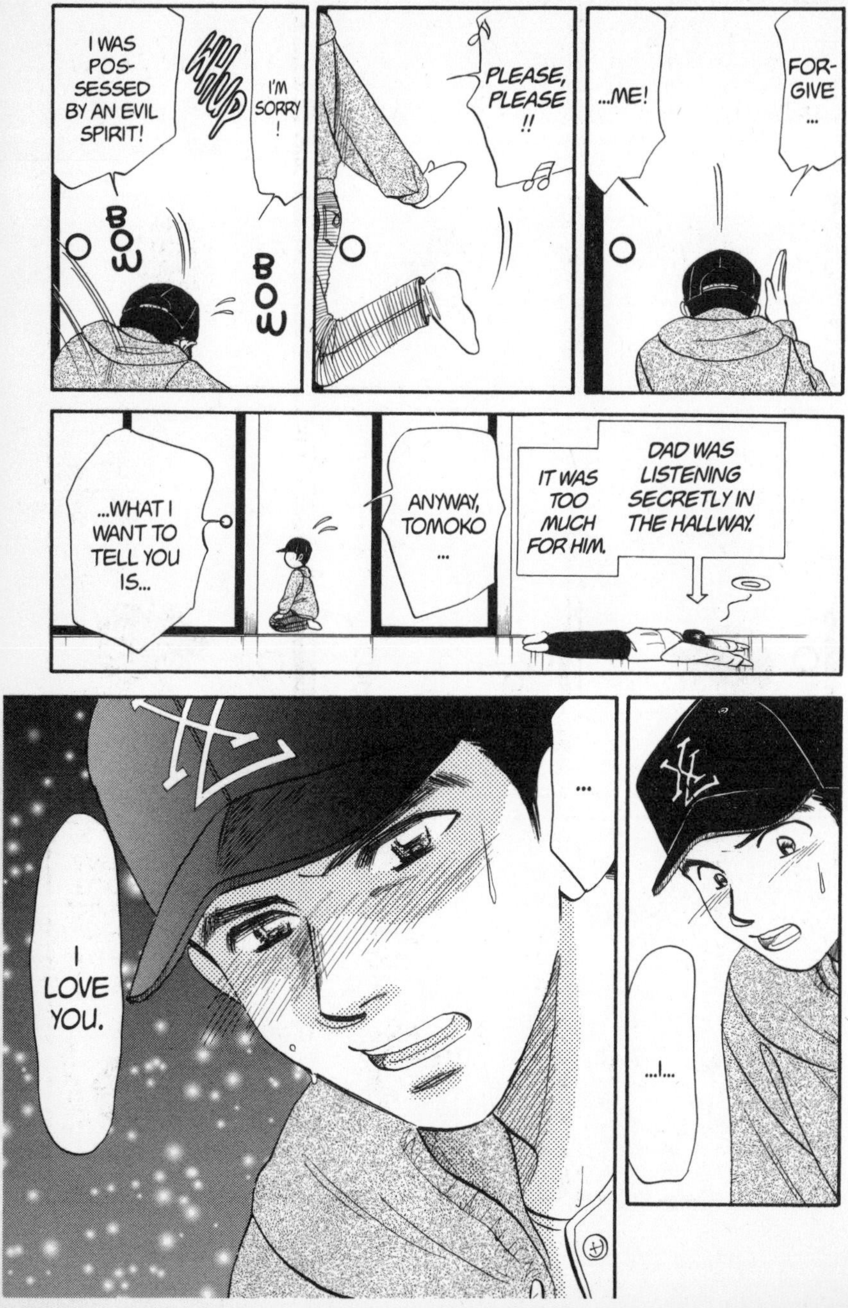
FOR-GIVE ...
...ME!
PLEASE, PLEASE !!
I'M SORRY !
WHUP
I WAS POS-SESSED BY AN EVIL SPIRIT!
BOW
BOW
DAD WAS LISTENING SECRETLY IN THE HALLWAY.
IT WAS TOO MUCH FOR HIM.
ANYWAY, TOMOKO ...
...WHAT I WANT TO TELL YOU IS...
...I...
...
I LOVE YOU.

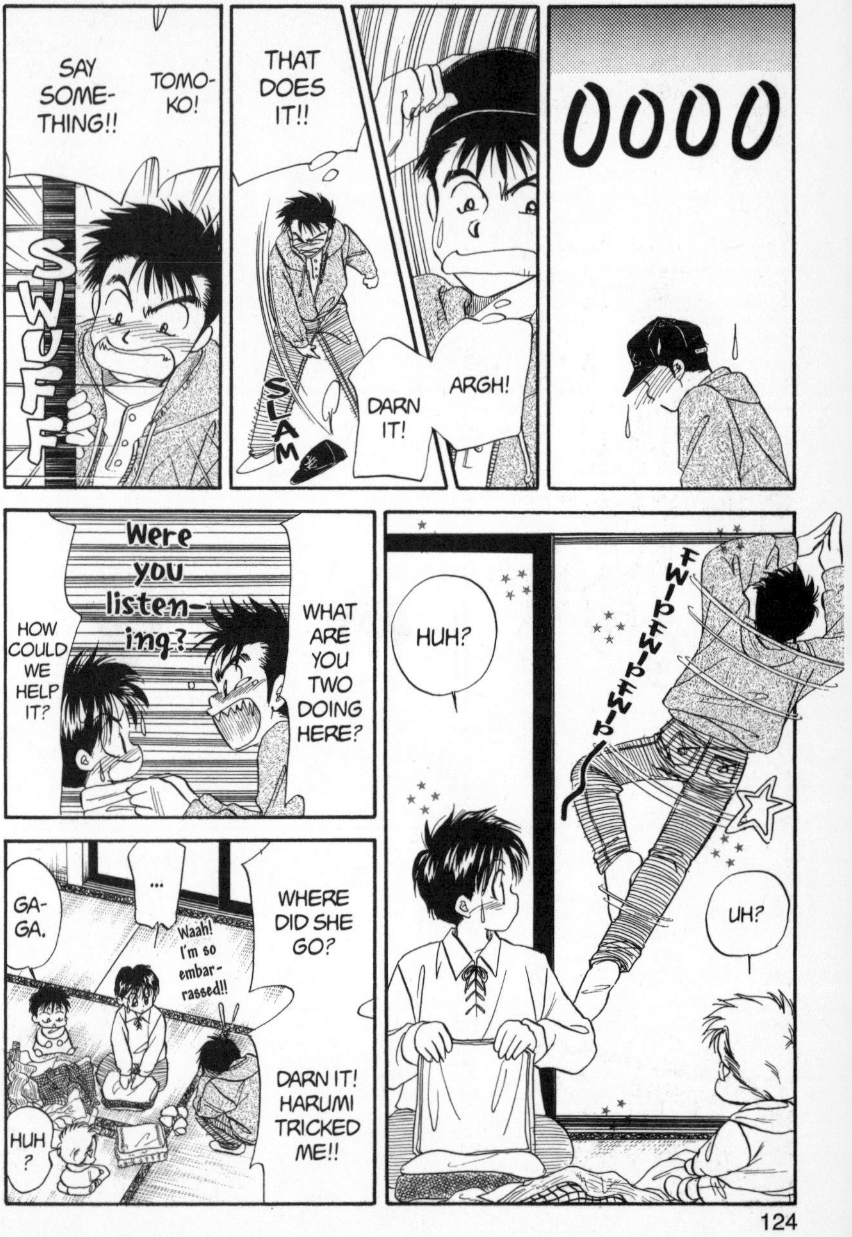
OOOO
ARGH!
DARN IT!
THAT DOES IT!!
SLAM
TOMOKO!
SAY SOMETHING!!
SWUFF
FWIPFWIPFWIP
HUH?
UH?
WHAT ARE YOU TWO DOING HERE?
Were you listening?
HOW COULD WE HELP IT?
WHERE DID SHE GO?
...
GA-GA.
Waah! I'm so embarrassed!!
DARN IT! HARUMI TRICKED ME!!
HUH?

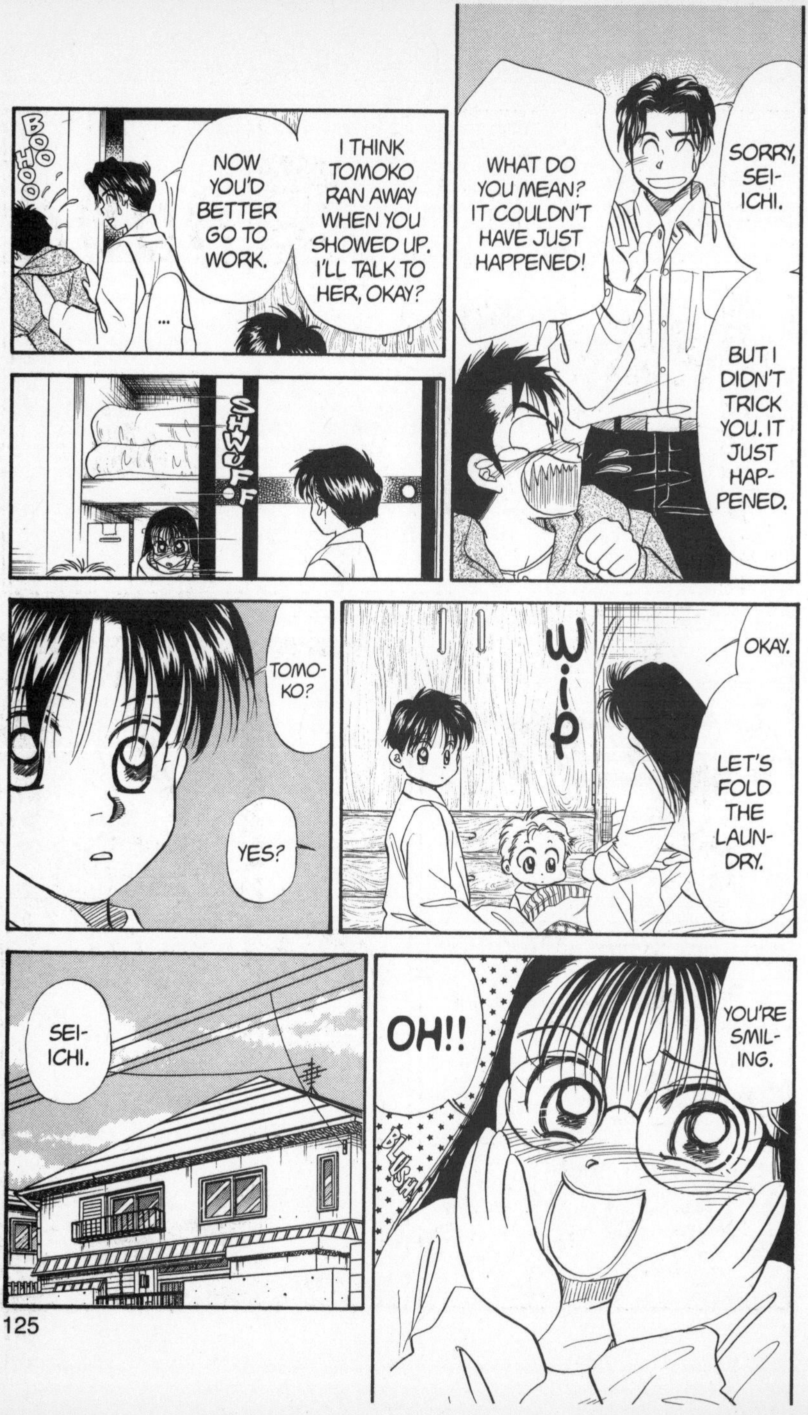
SORRY, SEI-ICHI.
WHAT DO YOU MEAN? IT COULDN'T HAVE JUST HAPPENED!
BUT I DIDN'T TRICK YOU. IT JUST HAP-PENED.
I THINK TOMOKO RAN AWAY WHEN YOU SHOWED UP. I'LL TALK TO HER, OKAY?
NOW YOU'D BETTER GO TO WORK.
...
BOO HOO
SHWOOFF
OKAY.
WIP
LET'S FOLD THE LAUN-DRY.
TOMO-KO?
YES?
YOU'RE SMIL-ING.
OH!!
BLUSH
SEI-ICHI.

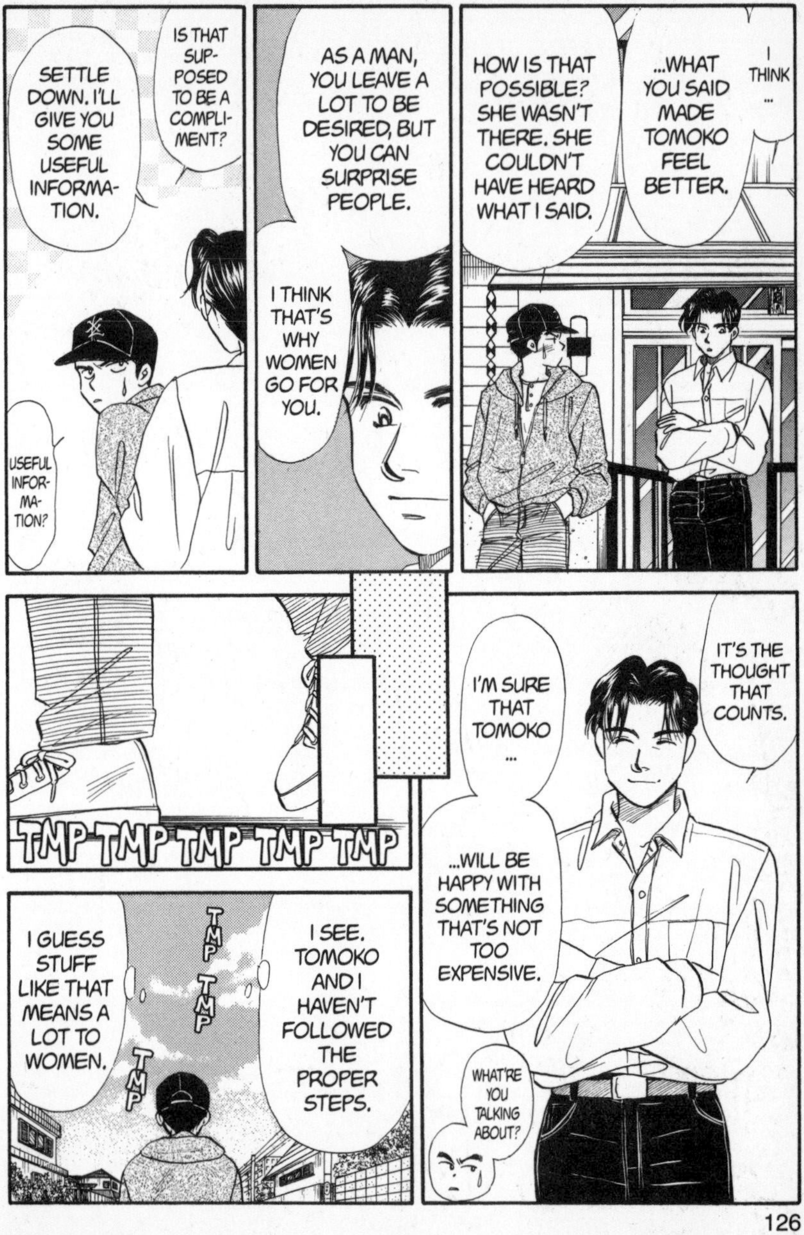
I THINK ...
...WHAT YOU SAID MADE TOMOKO FEEL BETTER.
HOW IS THAT POSSIBLE? SHE WASN'T THERE. SHE COULDN'T HAVE HEARD WHAT I SAID.
AS A MAN, YOU LEAVE A LOT TO BE DESIRED, BUT YOU CAN SURPRISE PEOPLE.
I THINK THAT'S WHY WOMEN GO FOR YOU.
IS THAT SUP-POSED TO BE A COMPLI-MENT?
SETTLE DOWN. I'LL GIVE YOU SOME USEFUL INFORMA-TION.
USEFUL INFOR-MA-TION?
IT'S THE THOUGHT THAT COUNTS.
I'M SURE THAT TOMOKO ...
...WILL BE HAPPY WITH SOMETHING THAT'S NOT TOO EXPENSIVE.
WHAT'RE YOU TALKING ABOUT?
TMP TMP TMP TMP TMP
I SEE. TOMOKO AND I HAVEN'T FOLLOWED THE PROPER STEPS.
I GUESS STUFF LIKE THAT MEANS A LOT TO WOMEN.
TMP TMP TMP

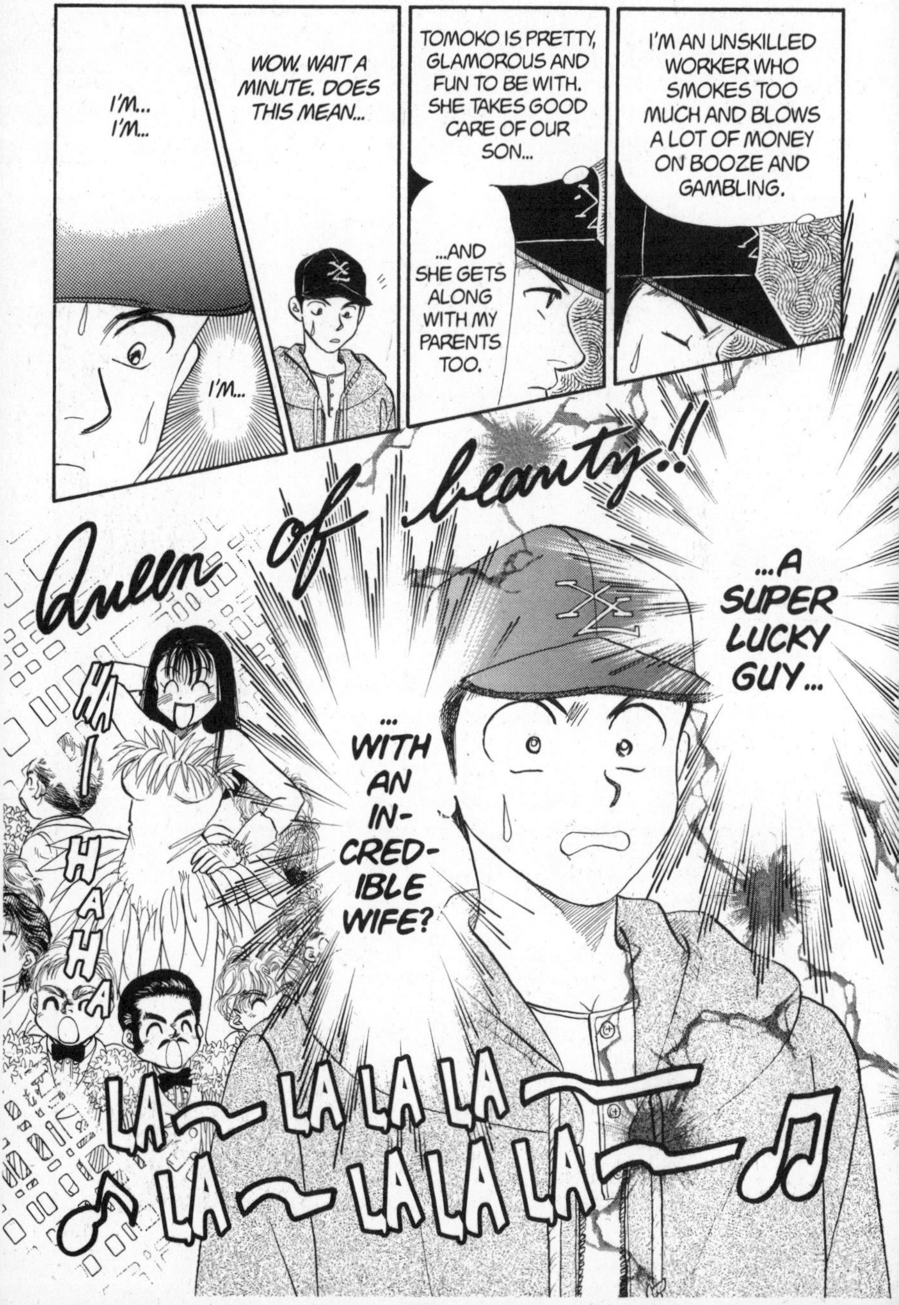
I'M AN UNSKILLED WORKER WHO SMOKES TOO MUCH AND BLOWS A LOT OF MONEY ON BOOZE AND GAMBLING.
TOMOKO IS PRETTY, GLAMOROUS AND FUN TO BE WITH. SHE TAKES GOOD CARE OF OUR SON...
...AND SHE GETS ALONG WITH MY PARENTS TOO.
WOW. WAIT A MINUTE. DOES THIS MEAN...
I'M... I'M...
I'M...
...A SUPER LUCKY GUY...
... WITH AN IN-CREDIBLE WIFE?
Queen of beauty!!
HA HA HA HA HA
LA~ LA LA LA—
LA~ LA LA LA—

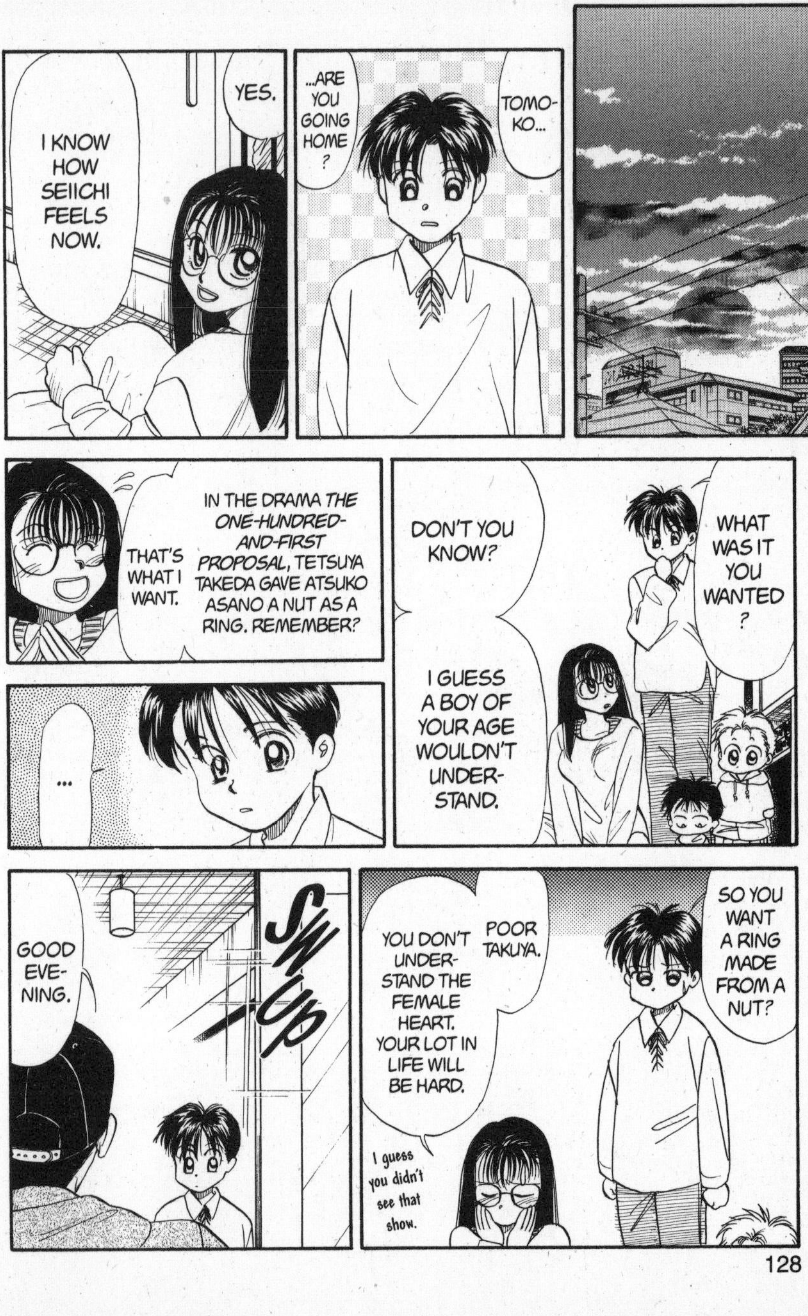

TOMO-KO...
...ARE YOU GOING HOME?
YES.
I KNOW HOW SEIICHI FEELS NOW.
WHAT WAS IT YOU WANTED?
DON'T YOU KNOW?
I GUESS A BOY OF YOUR AGE WOULDN'T UNDER-STAND.
IN THE DRAMA *THE ONE-HUNDRED-AND-FIRST PROPOSAL*, TETSUYA TAKEDA GAVE ATSUKO ASANO A NUT AS A RING. REMEMBER?
THAT'S WHAT I WANT.
...
SO YOU WANT A RING MADE FROM A NUT?
POOR TAKUYA.
YOU DON'T UNDER-STAND THE FEMALE HEART. YOUR LOT IN LIFE WILL BE HARD.
I guess you didn't see that show.
SWUP
GOOD EVE-NING.

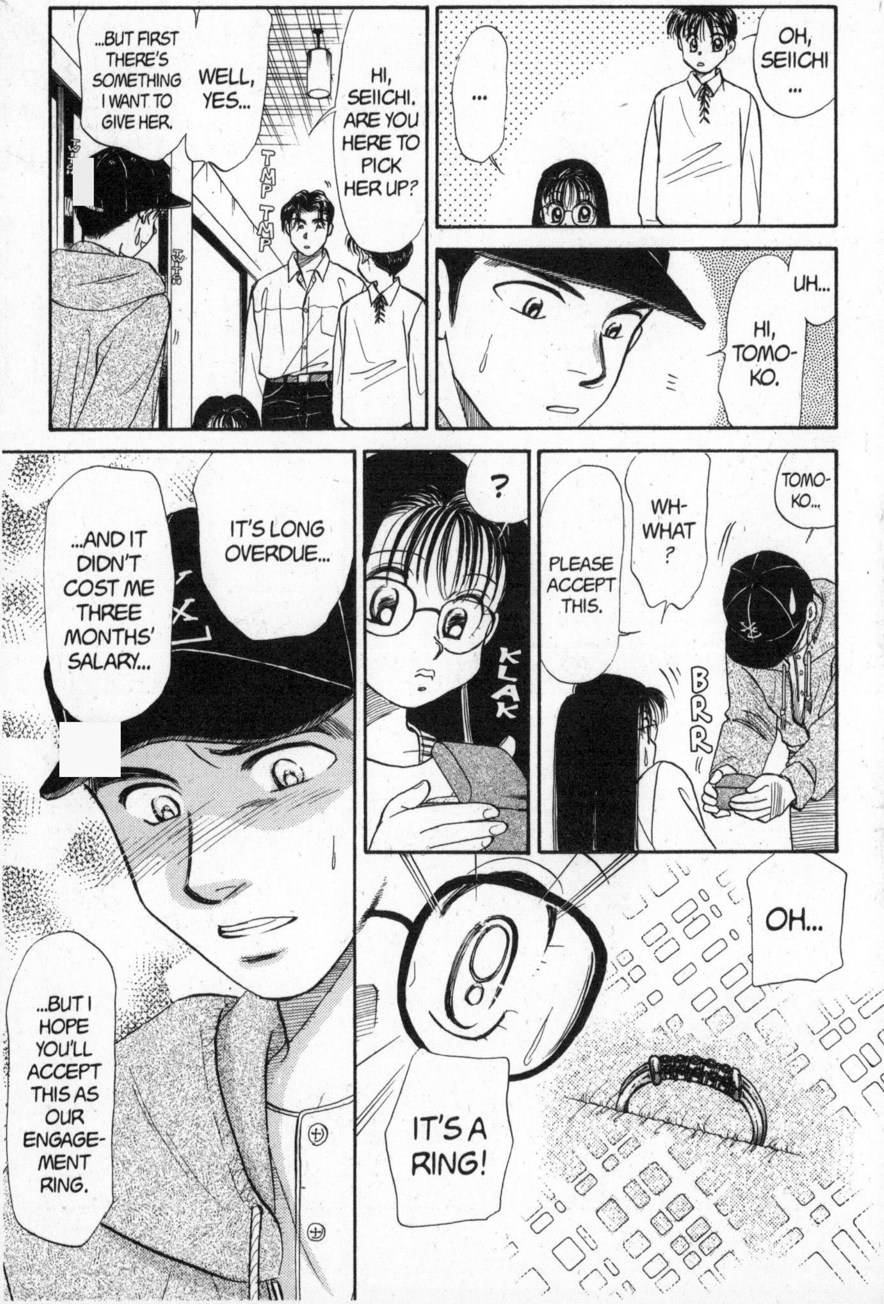
OH, SEIICHI...
...
UH...
HI, TOMOKO.
HI, SEIICHI. ARE YOU HERE TO PICK HER UP?
TMP TMP
WELL, YES...
...BUT FIRST THERE'S SOMETHING I WANT TO GIVE HER.
TWITCH
TWITCH
TOMOKO...
WH-WHAT?
PLEASE ACCEPT THIS.
BRR
?
KLAK
OH...
IT'S A RING!
IT'S LONG OVERDUE...
...AND IT DIDN'T COST ME THREE MONTHS' SALARY...
...BUT I HOPE YOU'LL ACCEPT THIS AS OUR ENGAGEMENT RING.

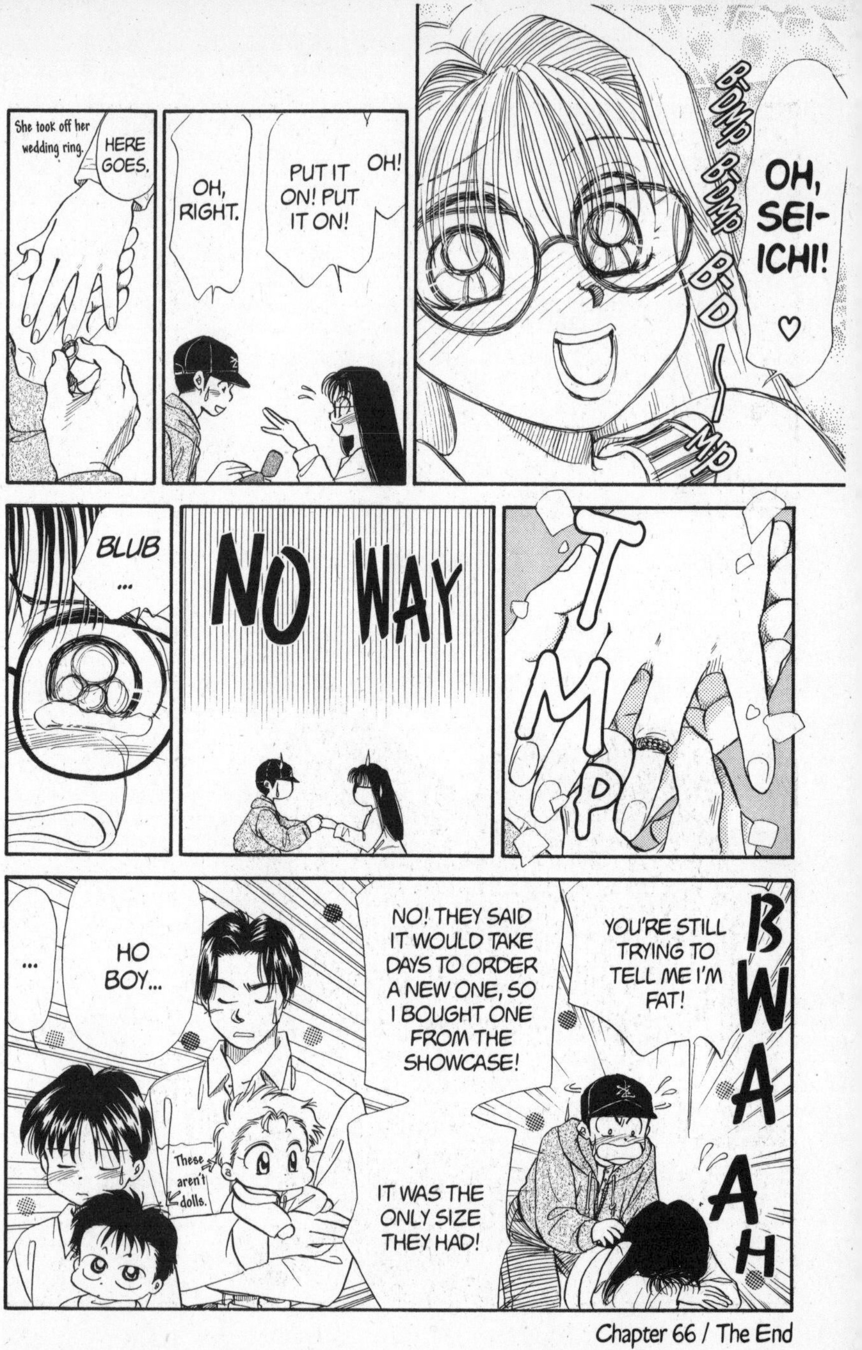
OH, SEI-ICHI! ♡
B'DMP B'DMP B'D—MP
OH!
PUT IT ON! PUT IT ON!
OH, RIGHT.
HERE GOES.
She took off her wedding ring.
TMP
NO WAY
BLUB ...
BWAAAH
YOU'RE STILL TRYING TO TELL ME I'M FAT!
NO! THEY SAID IT WOULD TAKE DAYS TO ORDER A NEW ONE, SO I BOUGHT ONE FROM THE SHOWCASE!
IT WAS THE ONLY SIZE THEY HAD!
HO BOY...
...
These aren't dolls.

Chapter 66 / The End

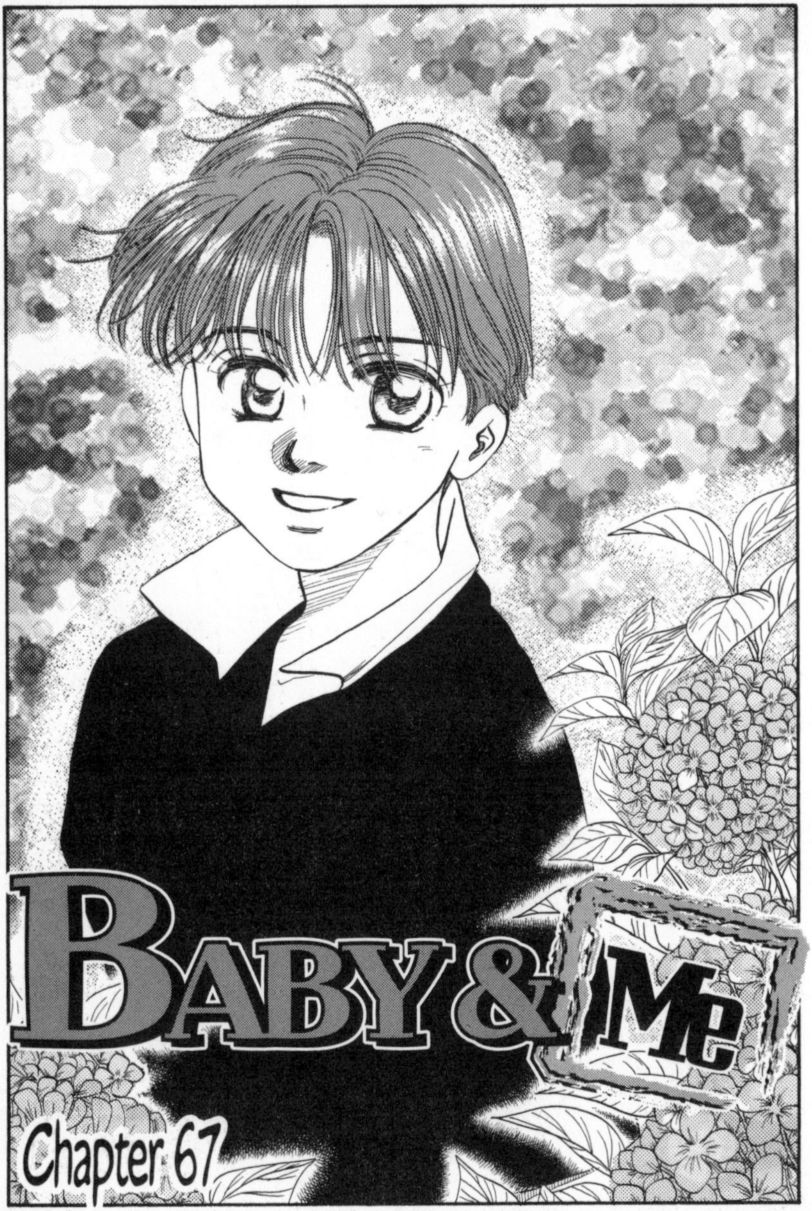
BABY & Me
Chapter 67

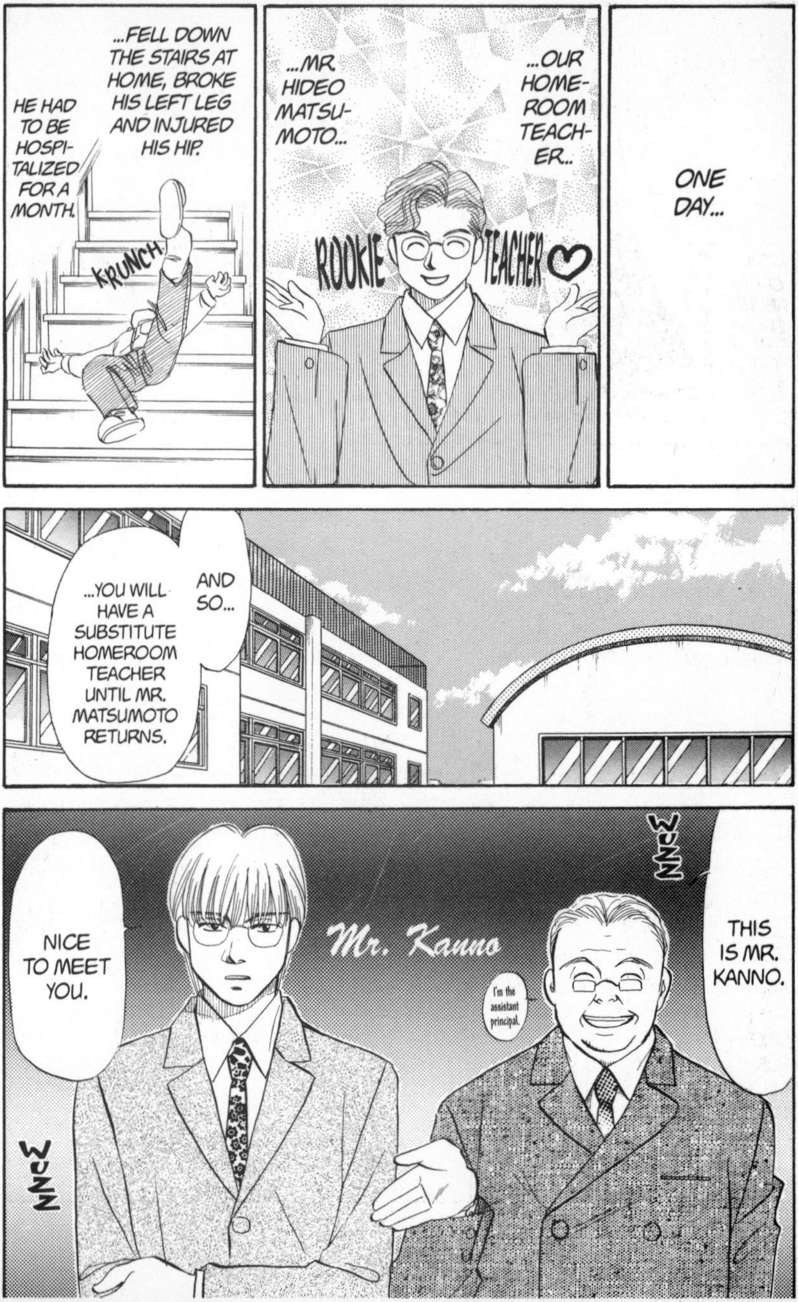
ONE DAY...
...OUR HOMEROOM TEACHER...
...MR. HIDEO MATSUMOTO...
ROOKIE TEACHER ♡
...FELL DOWN THE STAIRS AT HOME, BROKE HIS LEFT LEG AND INJURED HIS HIP.
HE HAD TO BE HOSPITALIZED FOR A MONTH.
KRUNCH
AND SO...
...YOU WILL HAVE A SUBSTITUTE HOMEROOM TEACHER UNTIL MR. MATSUMOTO RETURNS.
WUNN
THIS IS MR. KANNO.
I'm the assistant principal.
Mr. Kanno
NICE TO MEET YOU.
WUNN

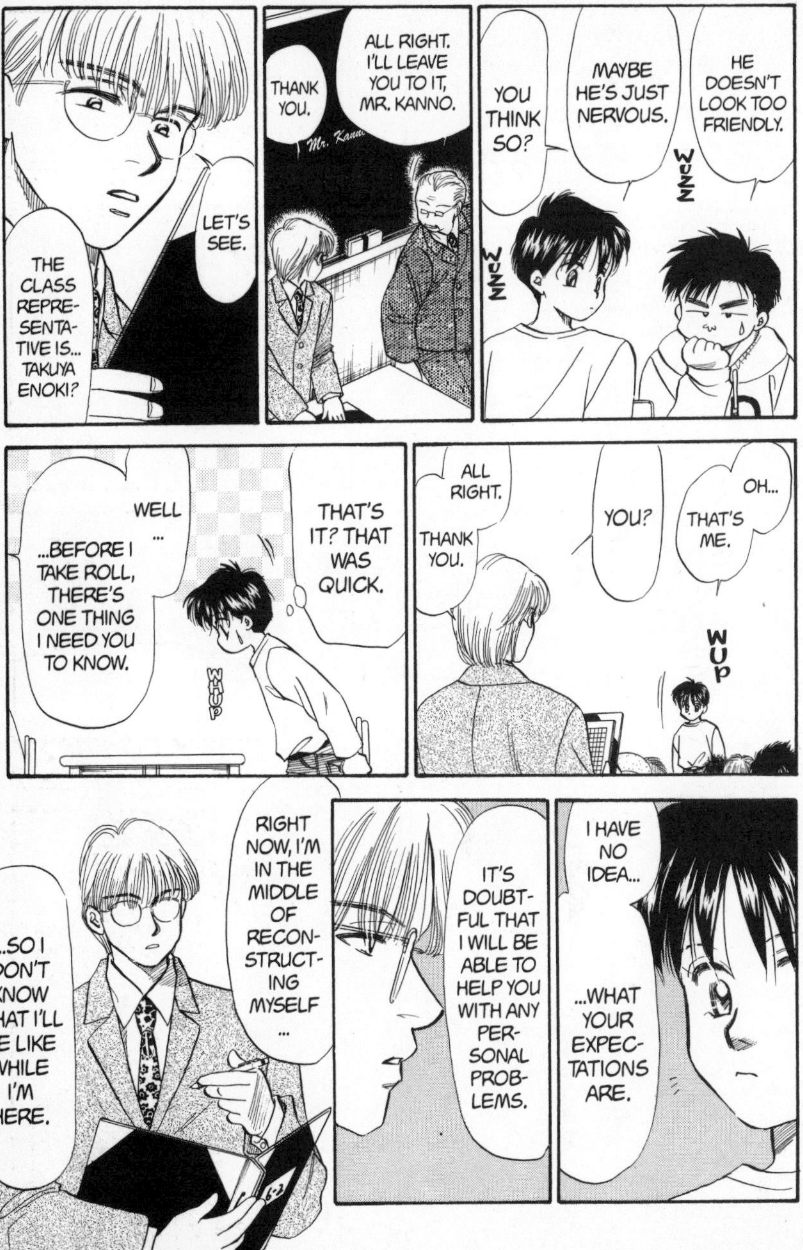
HE DOESN'T LOOK TOO FRIENDLY.
MAYBE HE'S JUST NERVOUS.
WUZZ
YOU THINK SO?
WUZZ
ALL RIGHT. I'LL LEAVE YOU TO IT, MR. KANNO.
THANK YOU.
LET'S SEE.
THE CLASS REPRESENTATIVE IS... TAKUYA ENOKI?
OH... THAT'S ME.
YOU?
WUP
ALL RIGHT.
THANK YOU.
THAT'S IT? THAT WAS QUICK.
WHUP
WELL ...
...BEFORE I TAKE ROLL, THERE'S ONE THING I NEED YOU TO KNOW.
I HAVE NO IDEA...
...WHAT YOUR EXPECTATIONS ARE.
IT'S DOUBTFUL THAT I WILL BE ABLE TO HELP YOU WITH ANY PERSONAL PROBLEMS.
RIGHT NOW, I'M IN THE MIDDLE OF RECONSTRUCTING MYSELF ...
...SO I DON'T KNOW WHAT I'LL BE LIKE WHILE I'M HERE.
6-2

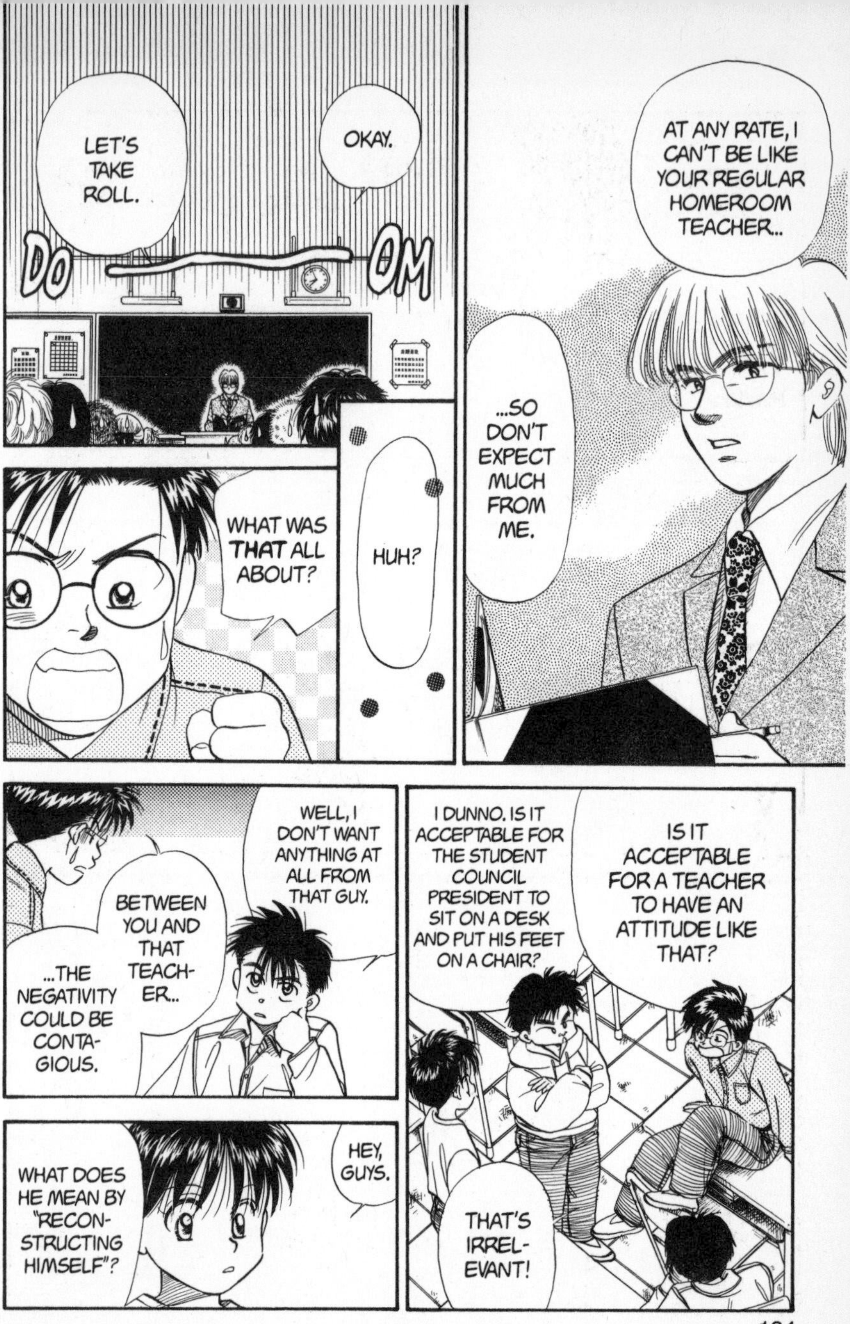
AT ANY RATE, I CAN'T BE LIKE YOUR REGULAR HOMEROOM TEACHER..
...SO DON'T EXPECT MUCH FROM ME.
LET'S TAKE ROLL.
OKAY.
DO—OM
HUH?
WHAT WAS THAT ALL ABOUT?
IS IT ACCEPTABLE FOR A TEACHER TO HAVE AN ATTITUDE LIKE THAT?
I DUNNO. IS IT ACCEPTABLE FOR THE STUDENT COUNCIL PRESIDENT TO SIT ON A DESK AND PUT HIS FEET ON A CHAIR?
THAT'S IRRELEVANT!
WELL, I DON'T WANT ANYTHING AT ALL FROM THAT GUY.
BETWEEN YOU AND THAT TEACHER...
...THE NEGATIVITY COULD BE CONTAGIOUS.
HEY, GUYS.
WHAT DOES HE MEAN BY "RECONSTRUCTING HIMSELF"?

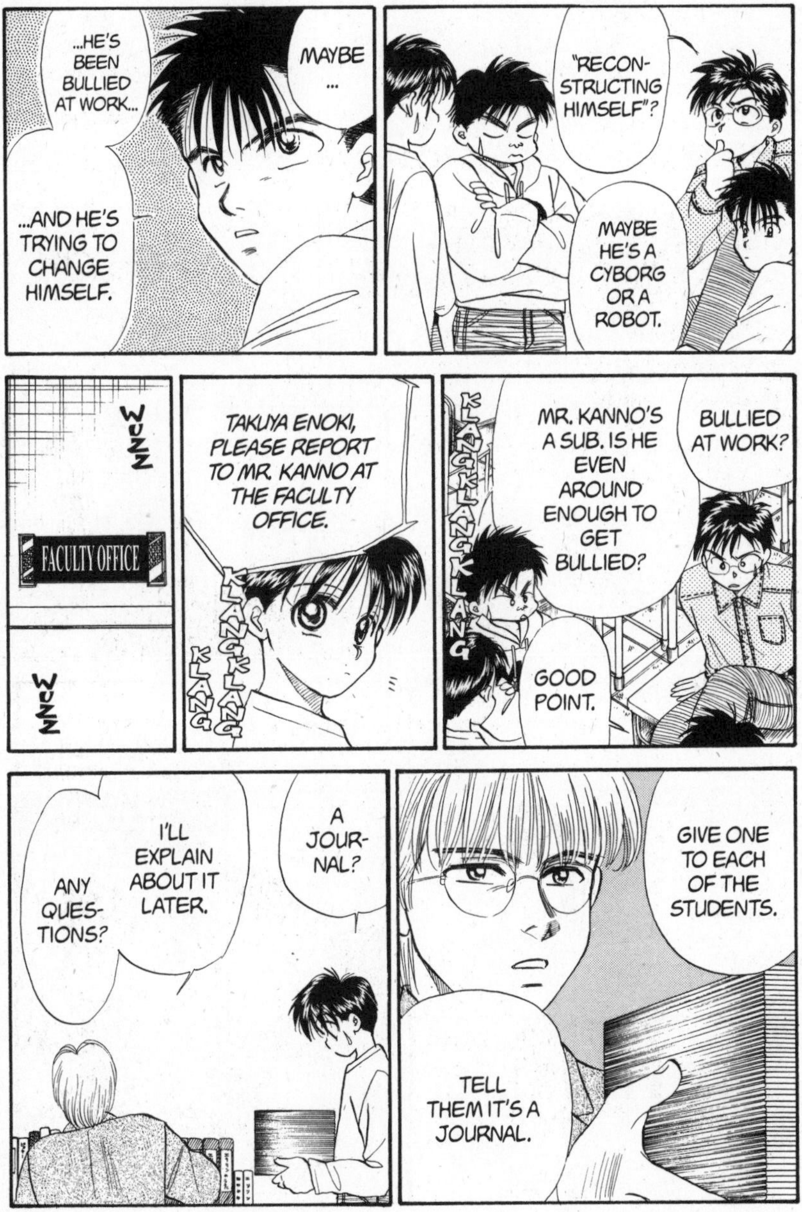
"RECON-STRUCTING HIMSELF"?
MAYBE HE'S A CYBORG OR A ROBOT.
MAYBE ...
...HE'S BEEN BULLIED AT WORK...
...AND HE'S TRYING TO CHANGE HIMSELF.
BULLIED AT WORK?
MR. KANNO'S A SUB. IS HE EVEN AROUND ENOUGH TO GET BULLIED?
KLANGKLANGKLANG
GOOD POINT.
TAKUYA ENOKI, PLEASE REPORT TO MR. KANNO AT THE FACULTY OFFICE.
KLANGKLANG
KLANG
WUZZ
FACULTY OFFICE
WUZZ
GIVE ONE TO EACH OF THE STUDENTS.
TELL THEM IT'S A JOURNAL.
A JOUR-NAL?
I'LL EXPLAIN ABOUT IT LATER.
ANY QUES-TIONS?

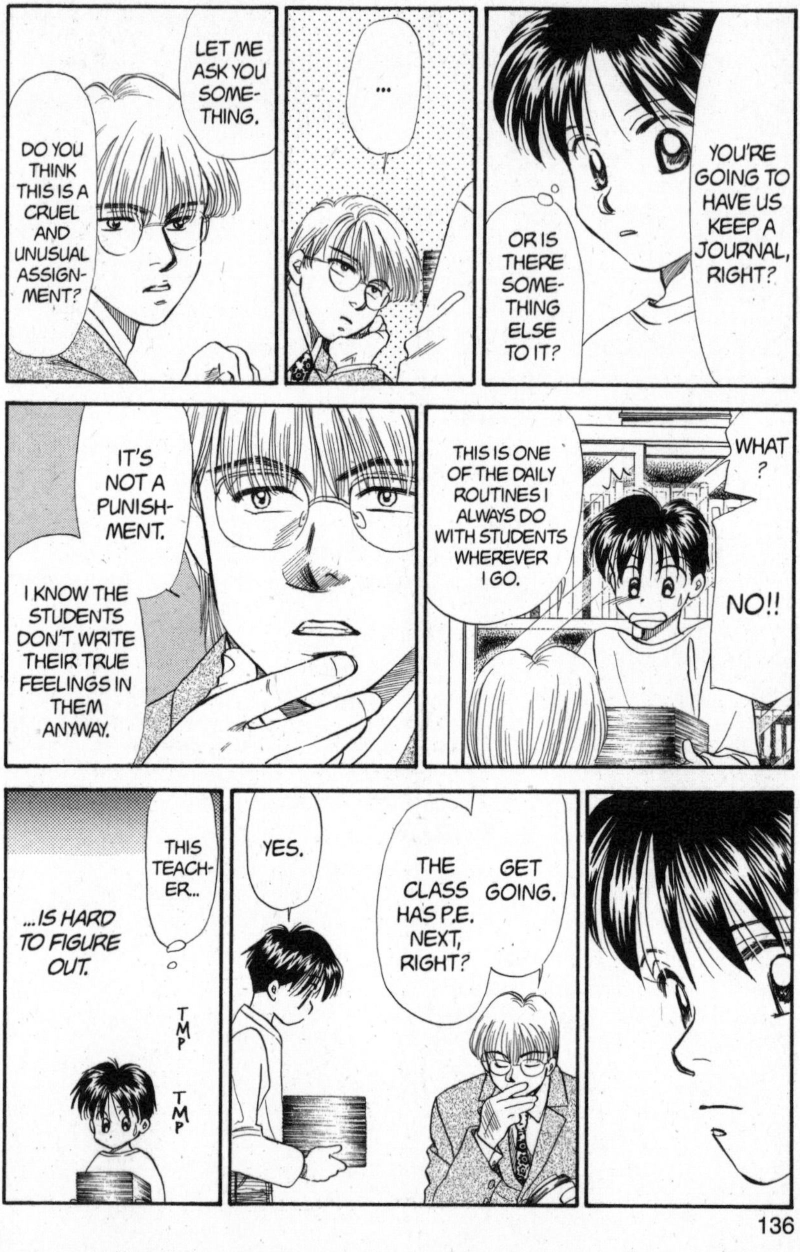
YOU'RE GOING TO HAVE US KEEP A JOURNAL, RIGHT?
OR IS THERE SOMETHING ELSE TO IT?
...
LET ME ASK YOU SOMETHING.
DO YOU THINK THIS IS A CRUEL AND UNUSUAL ASSIGNMENT?
WHAT?
NO!!
THIS IS ONE OF THE DAILY ROUTINES I ALWAYS DO WITH STUDENTS WHEREVER I GO.
IT'S NOT A PUNISHMENT.
I KNOW THE STUDENTS DON'T WRITE THEIR TRUE FEELINGS IN THEM ANYWAY.
GET GOING.
THE CLASS HAS P.E. NEXT, RIGHT?
YES.
THIS TEACHER...
...IS HARD TO FIGURE OUT.
TMP
TMP

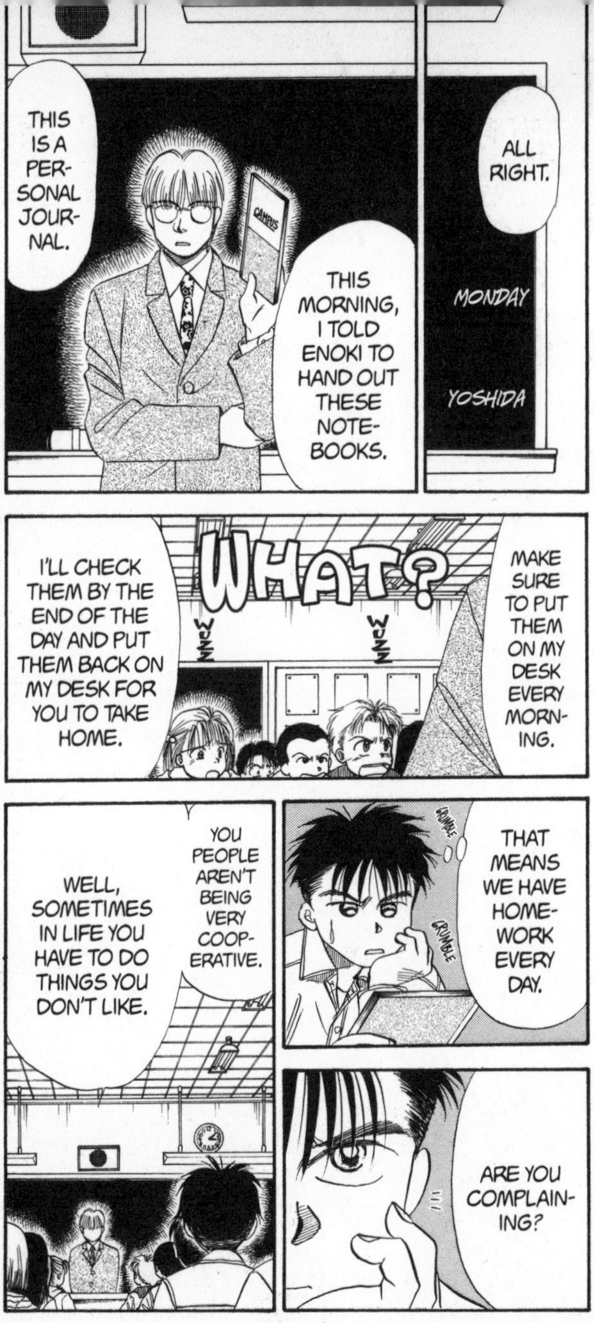
ALL RIGHT.
MONDAY
YOSHIDA
THIS MORNING, I TOLD ENOKI TO HAND OUT THESE NOTE-BOOKS.
THIS IS A PER-SONAL JOUR-NAL.
MAKE SURE TO PUT THEM ON MY DESK EVERY MORN-ING.
WHAT?
WUZZ
WUZZ
I'LL CHECK THEM BY THE END OF THE DAY AND PUT THEM BACK ON MY DESK FOR YOU TO TAKE HOME.
CRUMBLE
CRUMBLE
THAT MEANS WE HAVE HOME-WORK EVERY DAY.
ARE YOU COMPLAIN-ING?
YOU PEOPLE AREN'T BEING VERY COOP-ERATIVE.
WELL, SOMETIMES IN LIFE YOU HAVE TO DO THINGS YOU DON'T LIKE.

Author's Note Part 5

In June 1995, after I finished my scripts, my assistants and I went to play ping-pong. Eririn served incredibly well, but I kept serving the ball into the net. So I got serious and hit the ball as hard as I could.

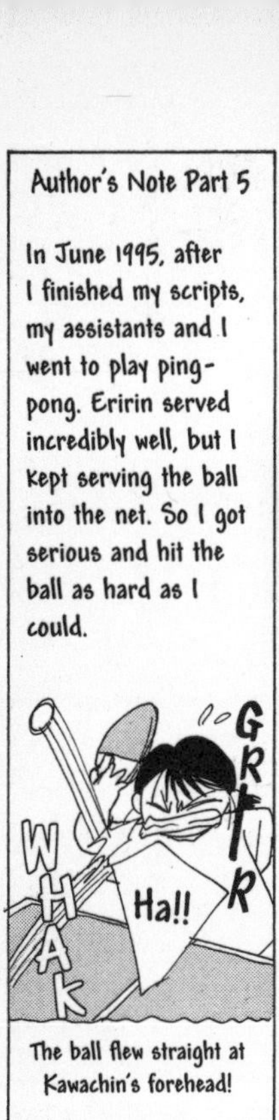
GRrR
WHAK
Ha!!

The ball flew straight at Kawachin's forehead!

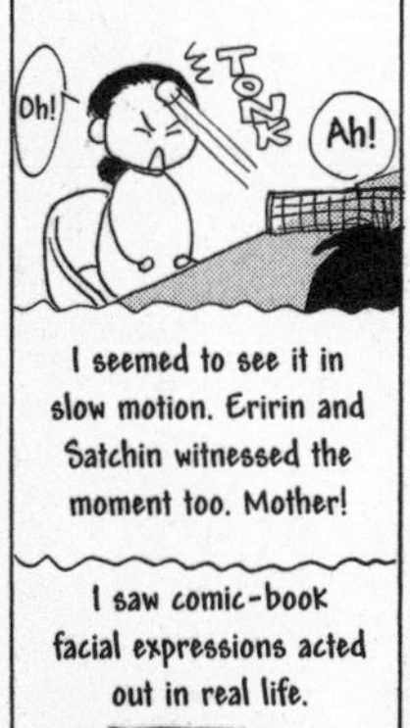
Oh!
TONK
Ah!

I seemed to see it in slow motion. Eririn and Satchin witnessed the moment too. Mother!

I saw comic-book facial expressions acted out in real life.

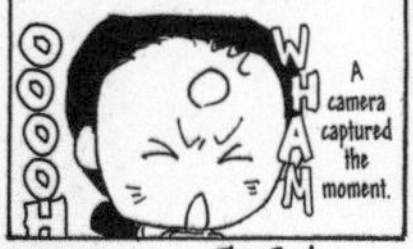
OOOOOOH
WHAM
A camera captured the moment.

The End

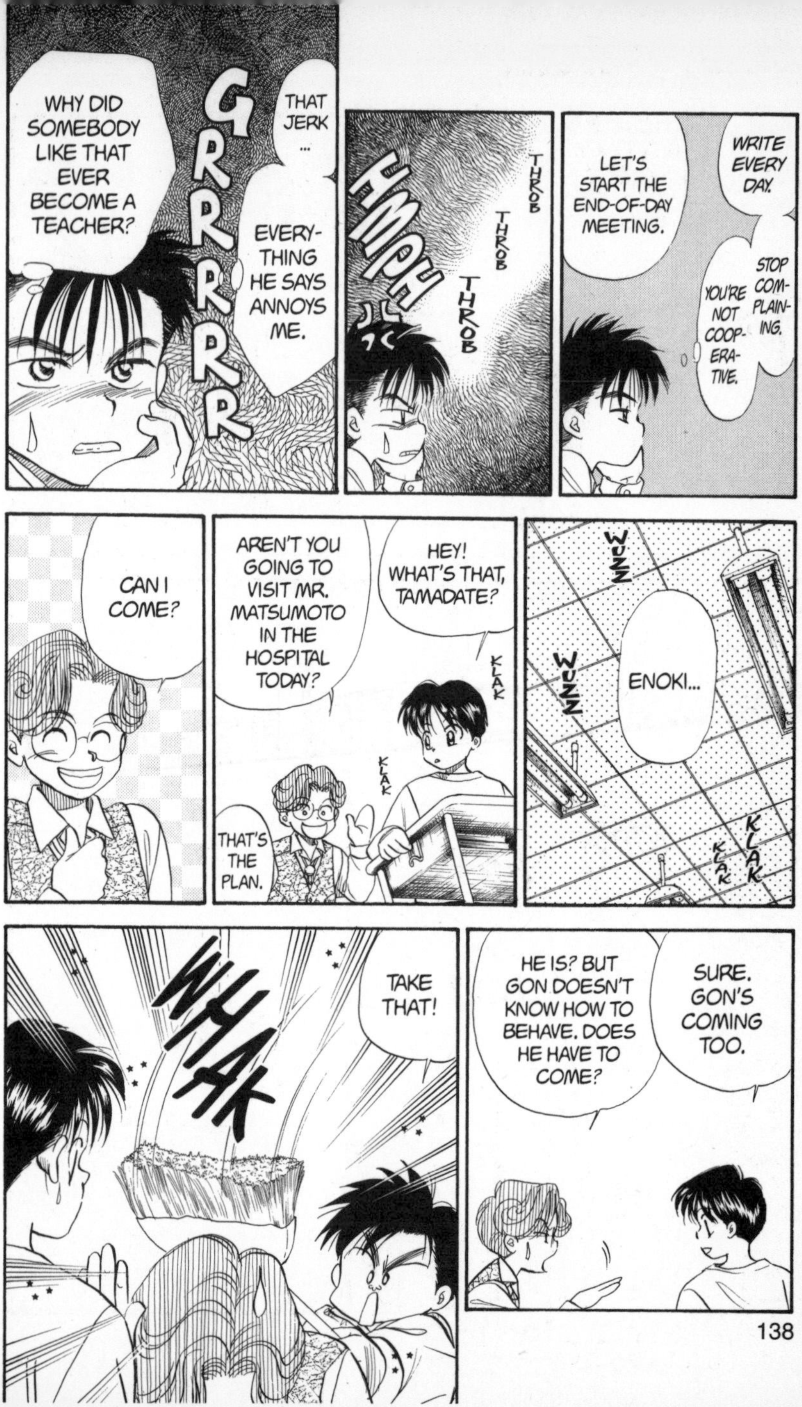
LET'S START THE END-OF-DAY MEETING.
WRITE EVERY DAY.
STOP COM-PLAIN-ING.
YOU'RE NOT COOP-ERA-TIVE.
HMPH
THROB
THROB
THROB
THAT JERK ...
EVERY-THING HE SAYS ANNOYS ME.
GRRRRR
WHY DID SOMEBODY LIKE THAT EVER BECOME A TEACHER?
WUZZ
WUZZ
ENOKI...
KLAK
KLAK
HEY! WHAT'S THAT, TAMADATE?
AREN'T YOU GOING TO VISIT MR. MATSUMOTO IN THE HOSPITAL TODAY?
KLAK
KLAK
THAT'S THE PLAN.
CAN I COME?
SURE. GON'S COMING TOO.
HE IS? BUT GON DOESN'T KNOW HOW TO BEHAVE. DOES HE HAVE TO COME?
TAKE THAT!
WHAK

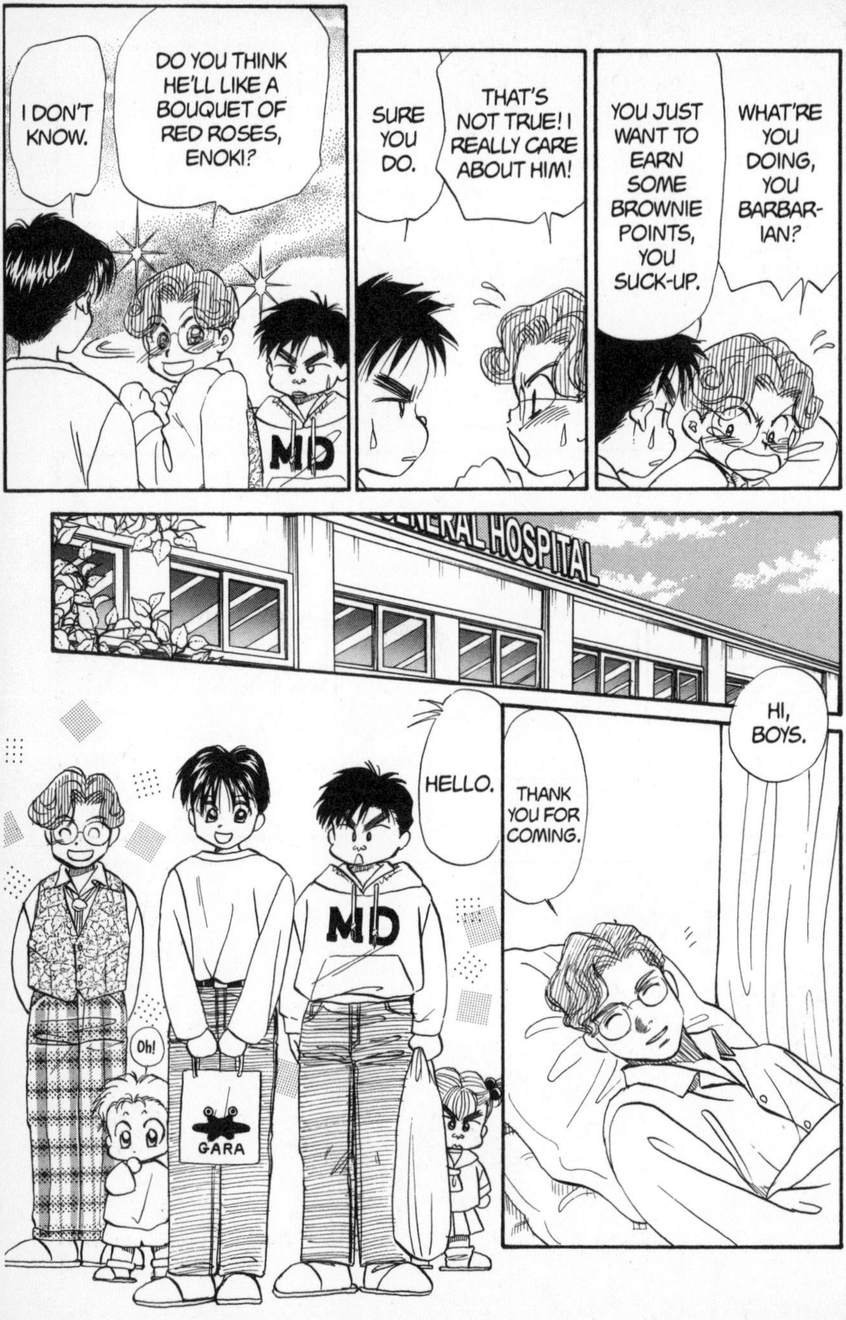
WHAT'RE YOU DOING, YOU BARBARIAN?
YOU JUST WANT TO EARN SOME BROWNIE POINTS, YOU SUCK-UP.
THAT'S NOT TRUE! I REALLY CARE ABOUT HIM!
SURE YOU DO.
DO YOU THINK HE'LL LIKE A BOUQUET OF RED ROSES, ENOKI?
I DON'T KNOW.
MD
HOSPITAL
HI, BOYS.
THANK YOU FOR COMING.
HELLO.
MD
Oh!
GARA

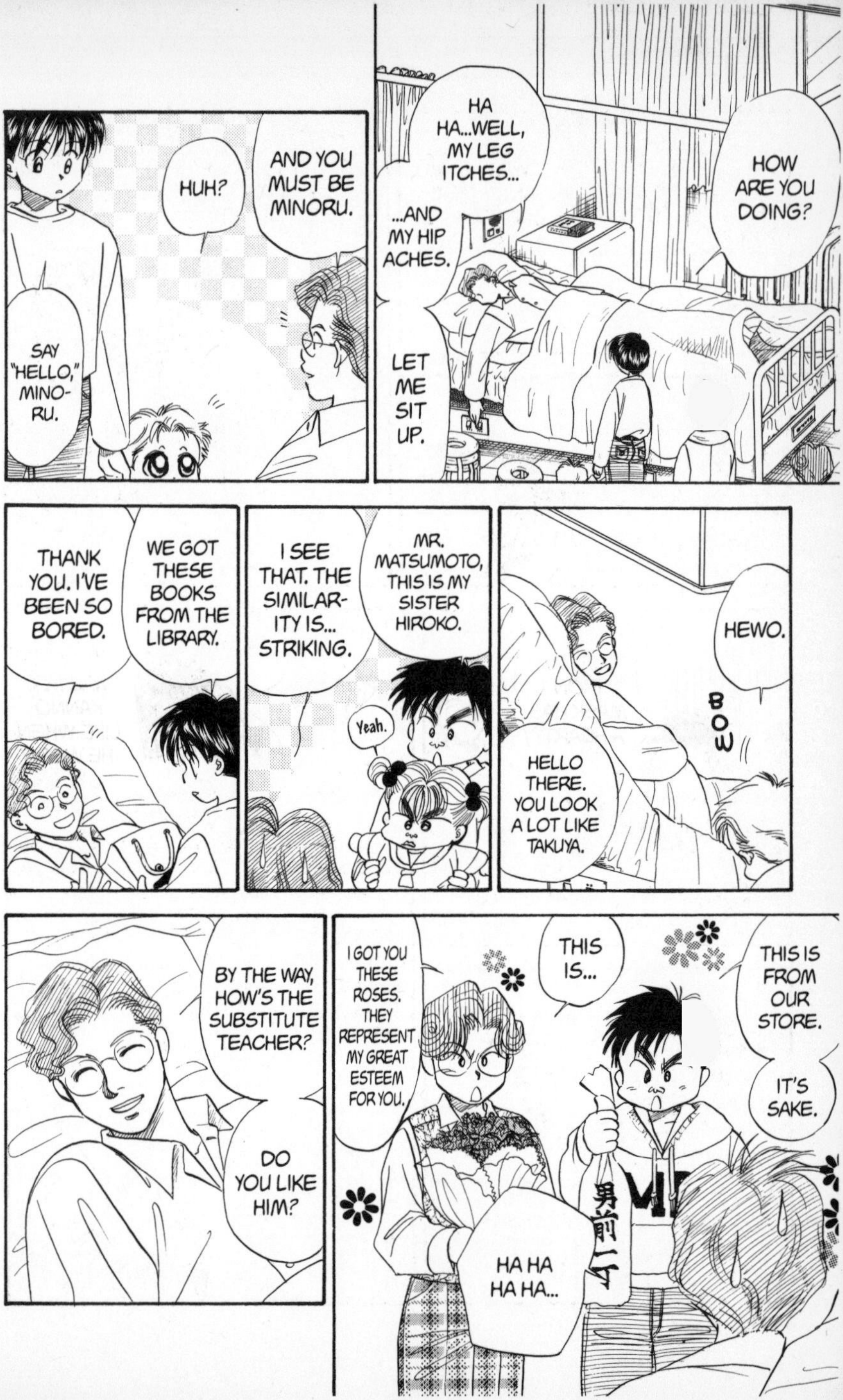
HOW ARE YOU DOING?
HA HA...WELL, MY LEG ITCHES...
...AND MY HIP ACHES.
LET ME SIT UP.
AND YOU MUST BE MINORU.
HUH?
SAY "HELLO," MINORU.
HEWO.
BOW
HELLO THERE. YOU LOOK A LOT LIKE TAKUYA.
MR. MATSUMOTO, THIS IS MY SISTER HIROKO.
Yeah.
I SEE THAT. THE SIMILARITY IS... STRIKING.
WE GOT THESE BOOKS FROM THE LIBRARY.
THANK YOU. I'VE BEEN SO BORED.
THIS IS FROM OUR STORE.
IT'S SAKE.
THIS IS...
I GOT YOU THESE ROSES. THEY REPRESENT MY GREAT ESTEEM FOR YOU.
男前一寸
HA HA HA HA...
BY THE WAY, HOW'S THE SUBSTITUTE TEACHER?
DO YOU LIKE HIM?

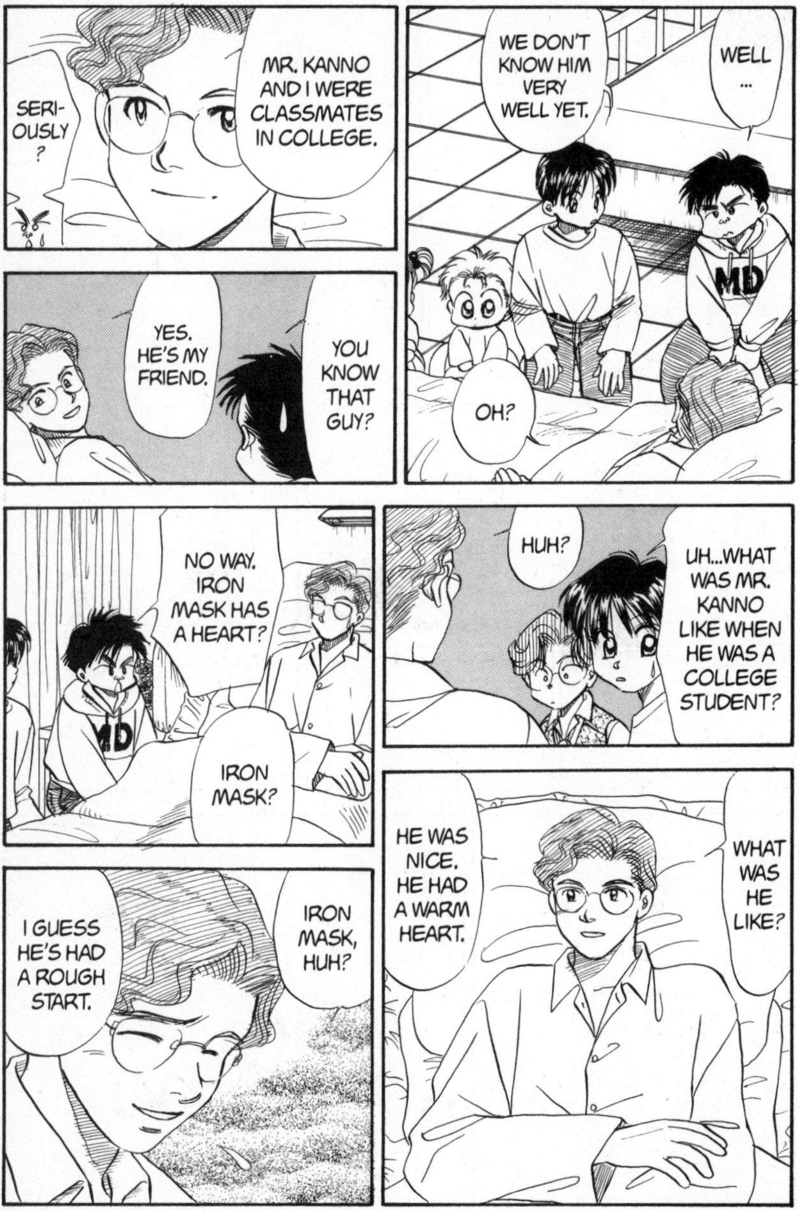
WELL ...
WE DON'T KNOW HIM VERY WELL YET.
OH?
MR. KANNO AND I WERE CLASSMATES IN COLLEGE.
SERIOUSLY?
YOU KNOW THAT GUY?
YES. HE'S MY FRIEND.
UH...WHAT WAS MR. KANNO LIKE WHEN HE WAS A COLLEGE STUDENT?
HUH?
NO WAY. IRON MASK HAS A HEART?
IRON MASK?
WHAT WAS HE LIKE?
HE WAS NICE. HE HAD A WARM HEART.
IRON MASK, HUH?
I GUESS HE'S HAD A ROUGH START.

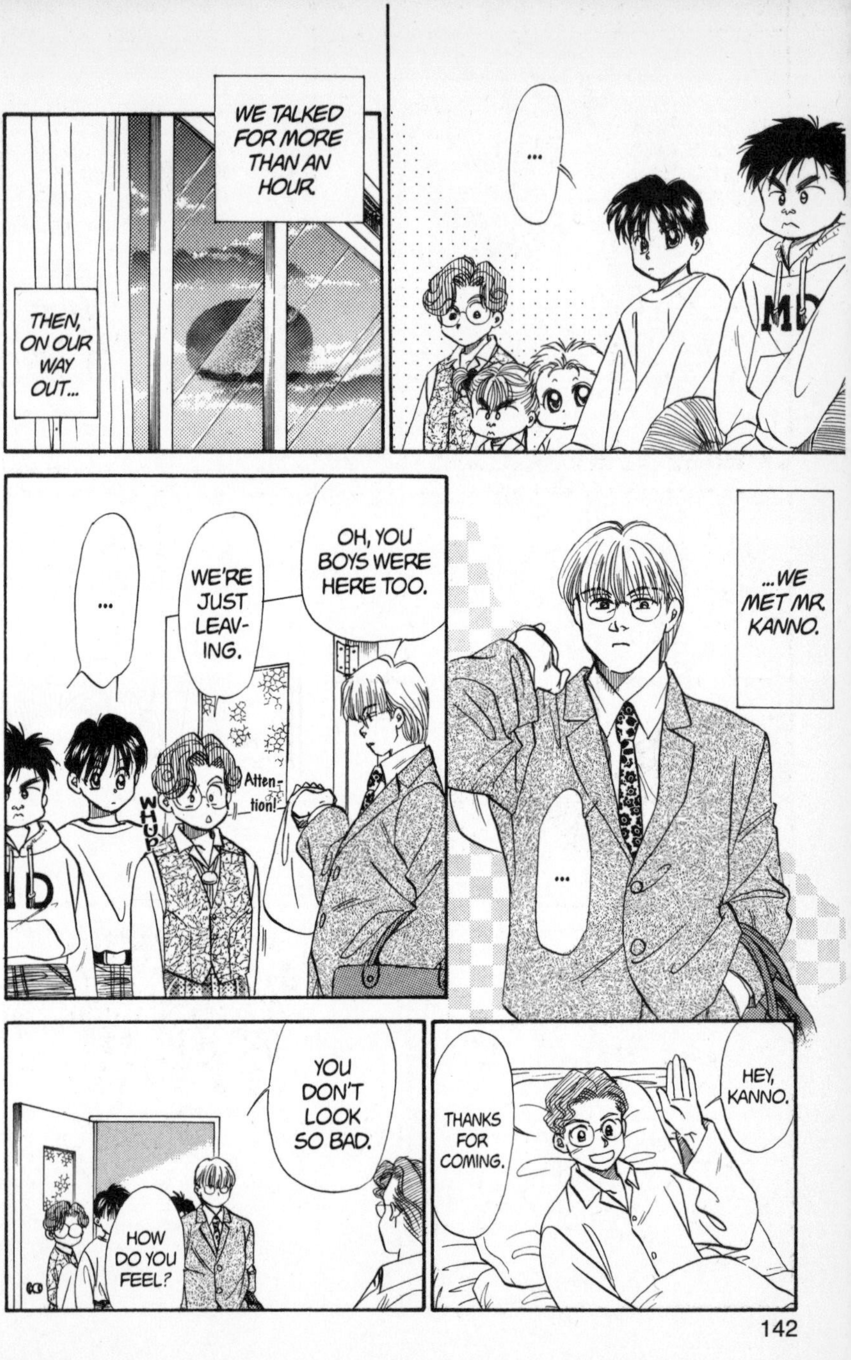
...
WE TALKED FOR MORE THAN AN HOUR.
THEN, ON OUR WAY OUT...
...WE MET MR. KANNO.
...
OH, YOU BOYS WERE HERE TOO.
WE'RE JUST LEAV-ING.
...
Atten-tion!
WHUP
HEY, KANNO.
THANKS FOR COMING.
YOU DON'T LOOK SO BAD.
HOW DO YOU FEEL?

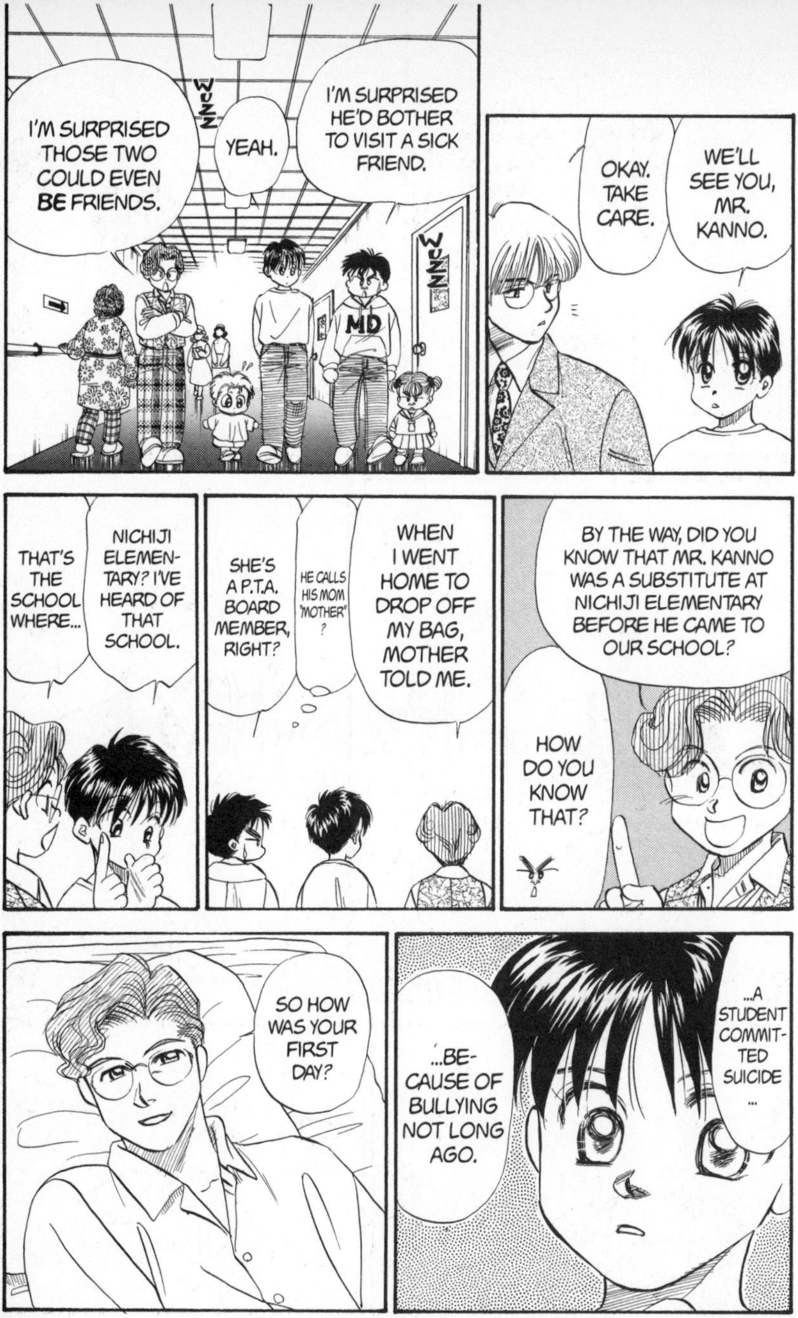
WE'LL SEE YOU, MR. KANNO.
OKAY. TAKE CARE.
WUZZ
I'M SURPRISED HE'D BOTHER TO VISIT A SICK FRIEND.
YEAH.
WUZZ
I'M SURPRISED THOSE TWO COULD EVEN BE FRIENDS.
BY THE WAY, DID YOU KNOW THAT MR. KANNO WAS A SUBSTITUTE AT NICHIJI ELEMENTARY BEFORE HE CAME TO OUR SCHOOL?
HOW DO YOU KNOW THAT?
WHEN I WENT HOME TO DROP OFF MY BAG, MOTHER TOLD ME.
HE CALLS HIS MOM "MOTHER"?
SHE'S A P.T.A. BOARD MEMBER, RIGHT?
NICHIJI ELEMENTARY? I'VE HEARD OF THAT SCHOOL.
THAT'S THE SCHOOL WHERE...
...A STUDENT COMMITTED SUICIDE...
...BECAUSE OF BULLYING NOT LONG AGO.
SO HOW WAS YOUR FIRST DAY?

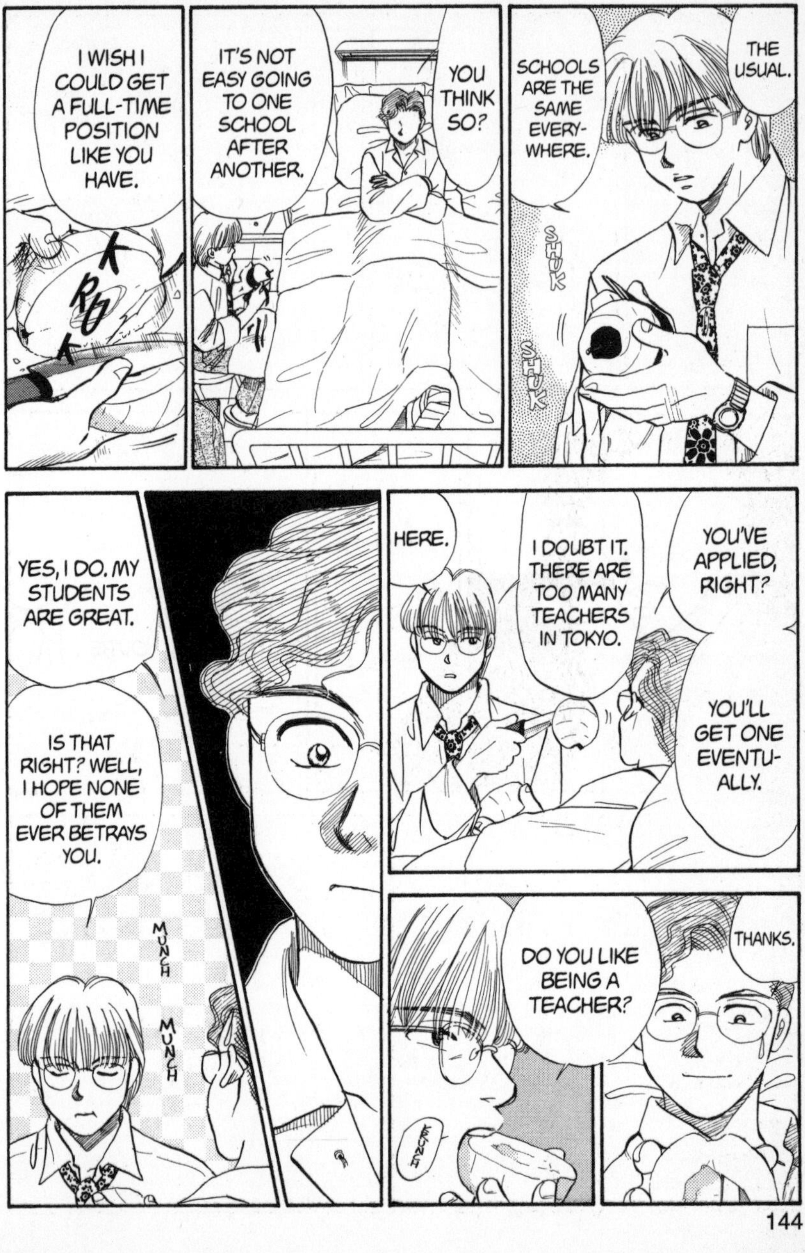
THE USUAL.
SCHOOLS ARE THE SAME EVERY-WHERE.
SHUK
SHUK
YOU THINK SO?
IT'S NOT EASY GOING TO ONE SCHOOL AFTER ANOTHER.
I WISH I COULD GET A FULL-TIME POSITION LIKE YOU HAVE.
YOU'VE APPLIED, RIGHT?
YOU'LL GET ONE EVENTU-ALLY.
I DOUBT IT. THERE ARE TOO MANY TEACHERS IN TOKYO.
HERE.
THANKS.
DO YOU LIKE BEING A TEACHER?
YES, I DO. MY STUDENTS ARE GREAT.
IS THAT RIGHT? WELL, I HOPE NONE OF THEM EVER BETRAYS YOU.
MUNCH
MUNCH

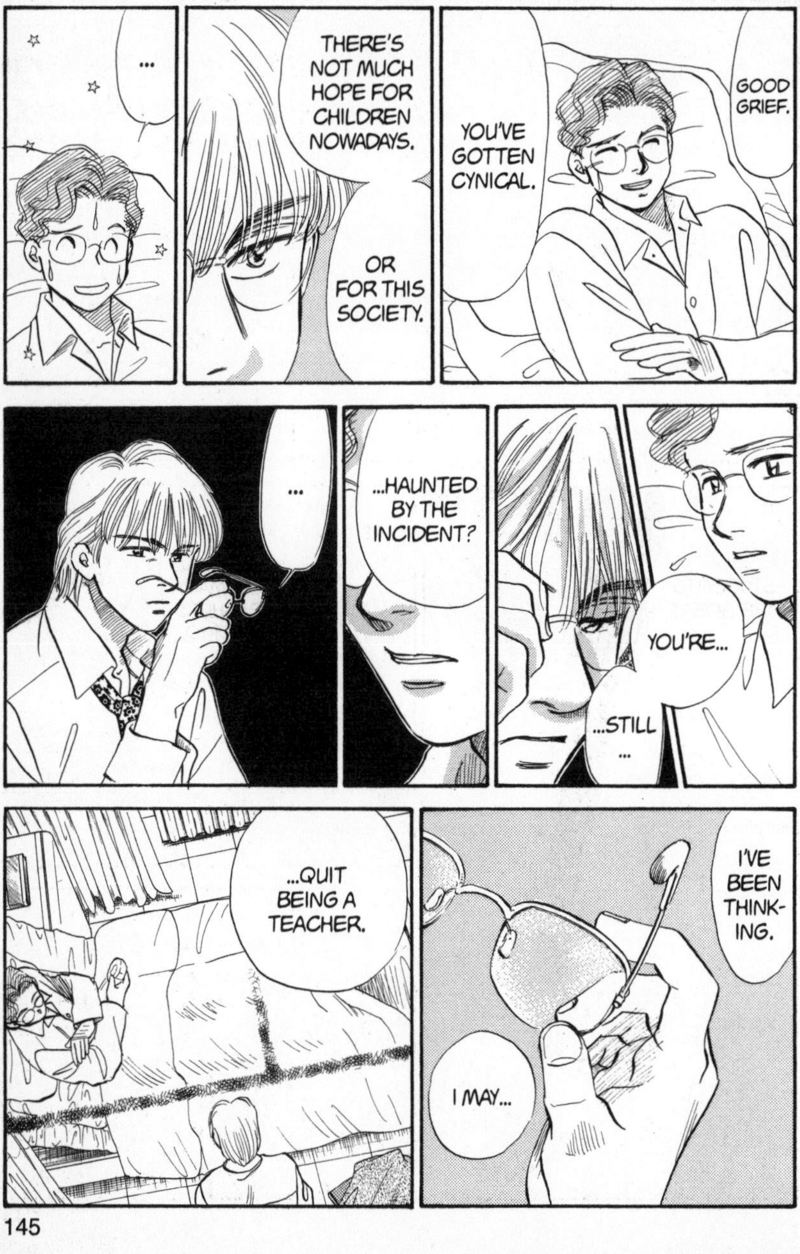
GOOD GRIEF.
YOU'VE GOTTEN CYNICAL.
THERE'S NOT MUCH HOPE FOR CHILDREN NOWADAYS.
OR FOR THIS SOCIETY.
...
YOU'RE...
...STILL ...
...HAUNTED BY THE INCIDENT?
...
I'VE BEEN THINKING.
I MAY...
...QUIT BEING A TEACHER.

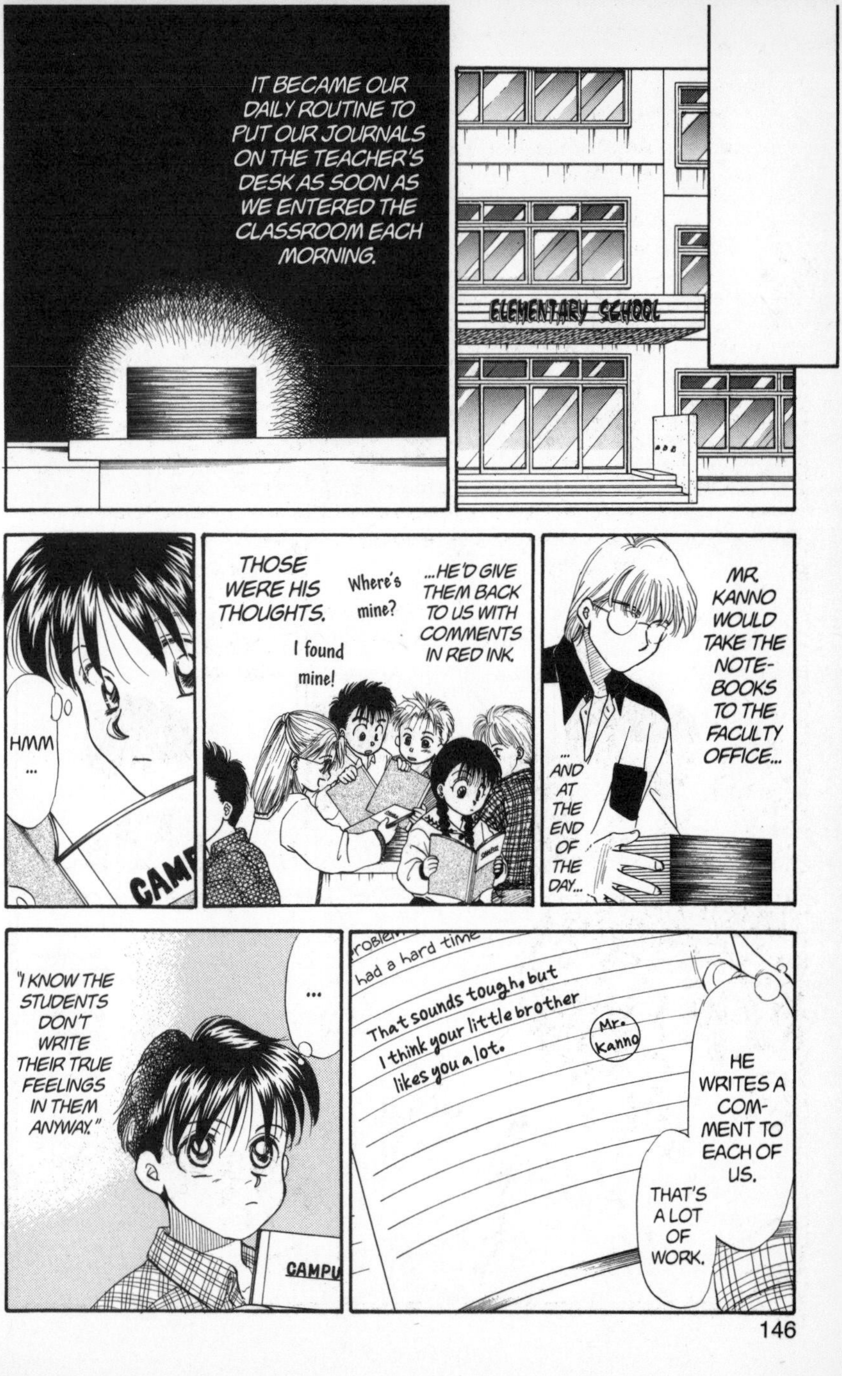
ELEMENTARY SCHOOL
IT BECAME OUR DAILY ROUTINE TO PUT OUR JOURNALS ON THE TEACHER'S DESK AS SOON AS WE ENTERED THE CLASSROOM EACH MORNING.
MR. KANNO WOULD TAKE THE NOTE-BOOKS TO THE FACULTY OFFICE...
...AND AT THE END OF THE DAY...
...HE'D GIVE THEM BACK TO US WITH COMMENTS IN RED INK.
Where's mine?
THOSE WERE HIS THOUGHTS.
I found mine!
HMM ...
had a hard time
That sounds tough, but I think your little brother likes you a lot.
Mr. Kanno
HE WRITES A COM-MENT TO EACH OF US.
THAT'S A LOT OF WORK.
...
"I KNOW THE STUDENTS DON'T WRITE THEIR TRUE FEELINGS IN THEM ANYWAY."
CAMPU

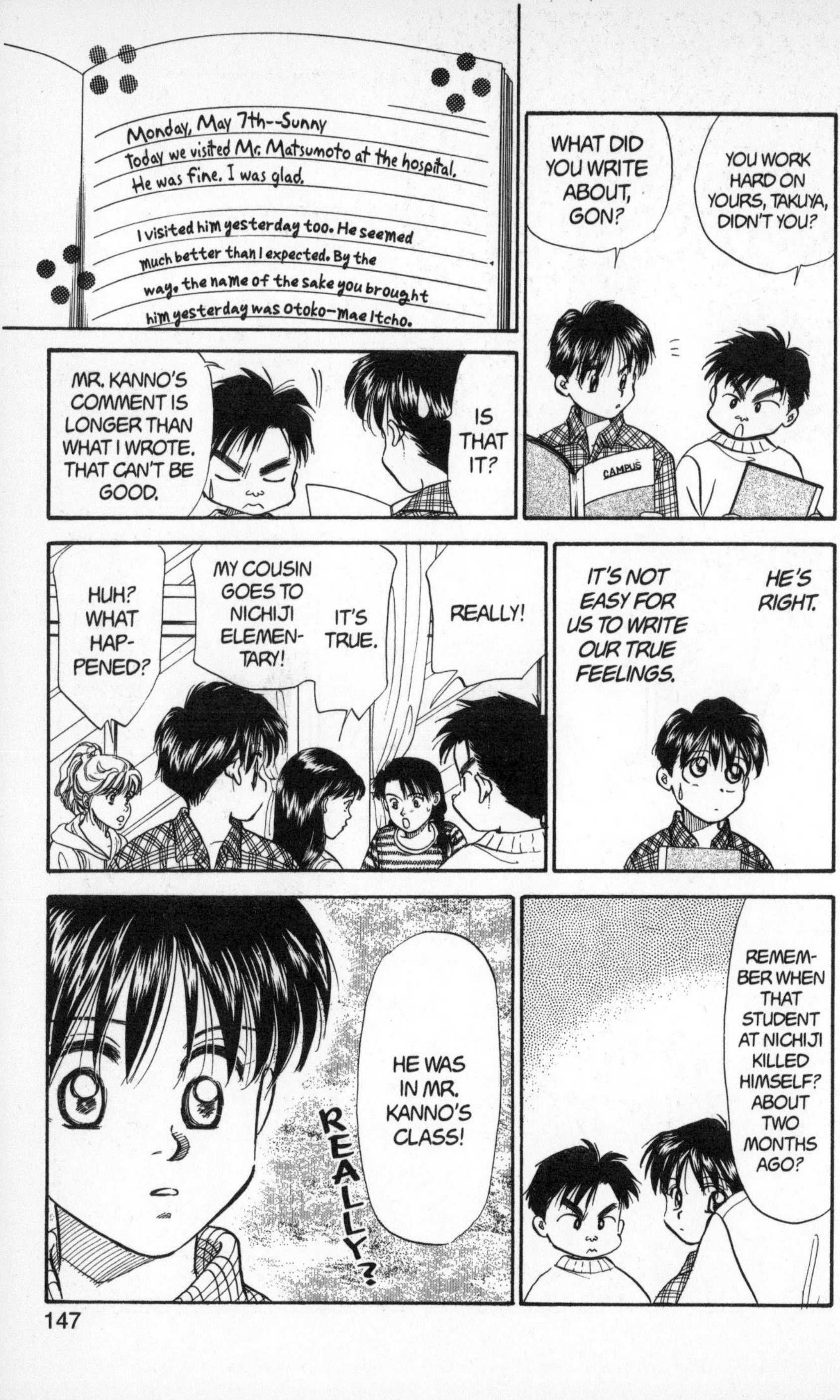
Monday, May 7th--Sunny
Today we visited Mr. Matsumoto at the hospital. He was fine. I was glad.
I visited him yesterday too. He seemed much better than I expected. By the way, the name of the sake you brought him yesterday was Otoko-Mae Itcho.
WHAT DID YOU WRITE ABOUT, GON?
YOU WORK HARD ON YOURS, TAKUYA, DIDN'T YOU?
CAMPUS
IS THAT IT?
MR. KANNO'S COMMENT IS LONGER THAN WHAT I WROTE. THAT CAN'T BE GOOD.
HE'S RIGHT.
IT'S NOT EASY FOR US TO WRITE OUR TRUE FEELINGS.
REALLY!
IT'S TRUE.
MY COUSIN GOES TO NICHIJI ELEMENTARY!
HUH? WHAT HAPPENED?
REMEMBER WHEN THAT STUDENT AT NICHIJI KILLED HIMSELF? ABOUT TWO MONTHS AGO?
HE WAS IN MR. KANNO'S CLASS!
REALLY?

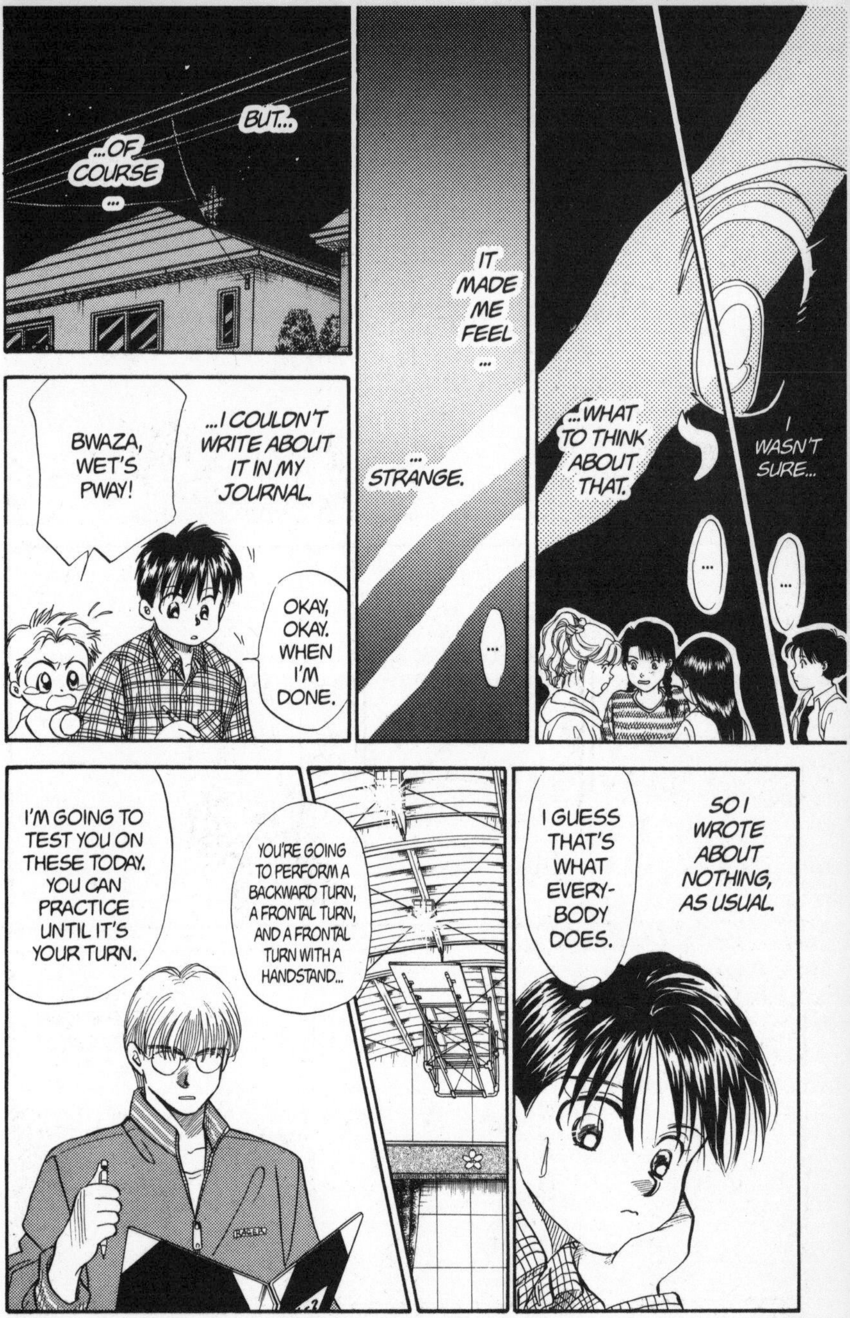
I WASN'T SURE...
...WHAT TO THINK ABOUT THAT.
...
...
IT MADE ME FEEL...
...STRANGE.
...
BUT...
...OF COURSE...
...I COULDN'T WRITE ABOUT IT IN MY JOURNAL.
BWAZA, WET'S PWAY!
OKAY, OKAY. WHEN I'M DONE.
SO I WROTE ABOUT NOTHING, AS USUAL.
I GUESS THAT'S WHAT EVERY-BODY DOES.
YOU'RE GOING TO PERFORM A BACKWARD TURN, A FRONTAL TURN, AND A FRONTAL TURN WITH A HANDSTAND...
I'M GOING TO TEST YOU ON THESE TODAY. YOU CAN PRACTICE UNTIL IT'S YOUR TURN.

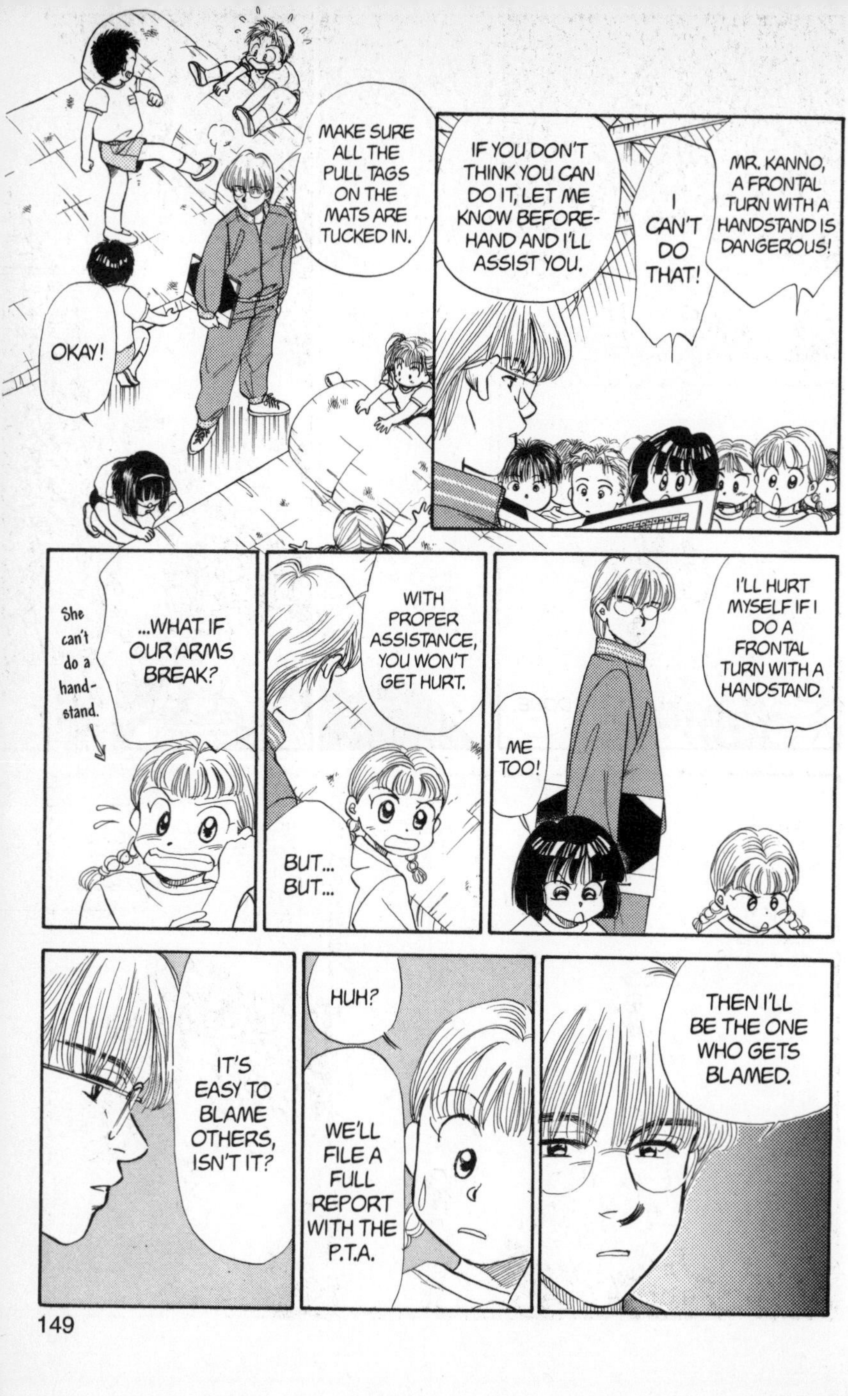
MR. KANNO, A FRONTAL TURN WITH A HANDSTAND IS DANGEROUS!
I CAN'T DO THAT!
IF YOU DON'T THINK YOU CAN DO IT, LET ME KNOW BEFORE-HAND AND I'LL ASSIST YOU.
MAKE SURE ALL THE PULL TAGS ON THE MATS ARE TUCKED IN.
OKAY!
I'LL HURT MYSELF IF I DO A FRONTAL TURN WITH A HANDSTAND.
ME TOO!
WITH PROPER ASSISTANCE, YOU WON'T GET HURT.
BUT... BUT...
...WHAT IF OUR ARMS BREAK?
She can't do a hand-stand.
THEN I'LL BE THE ONE WHO GETS BLAMED.
HUH?
WE'LL FILE A FULL REPORT WITH THE P.T.A.
IT'S EASY TO BLAME OTHERS, ISN'T IT?

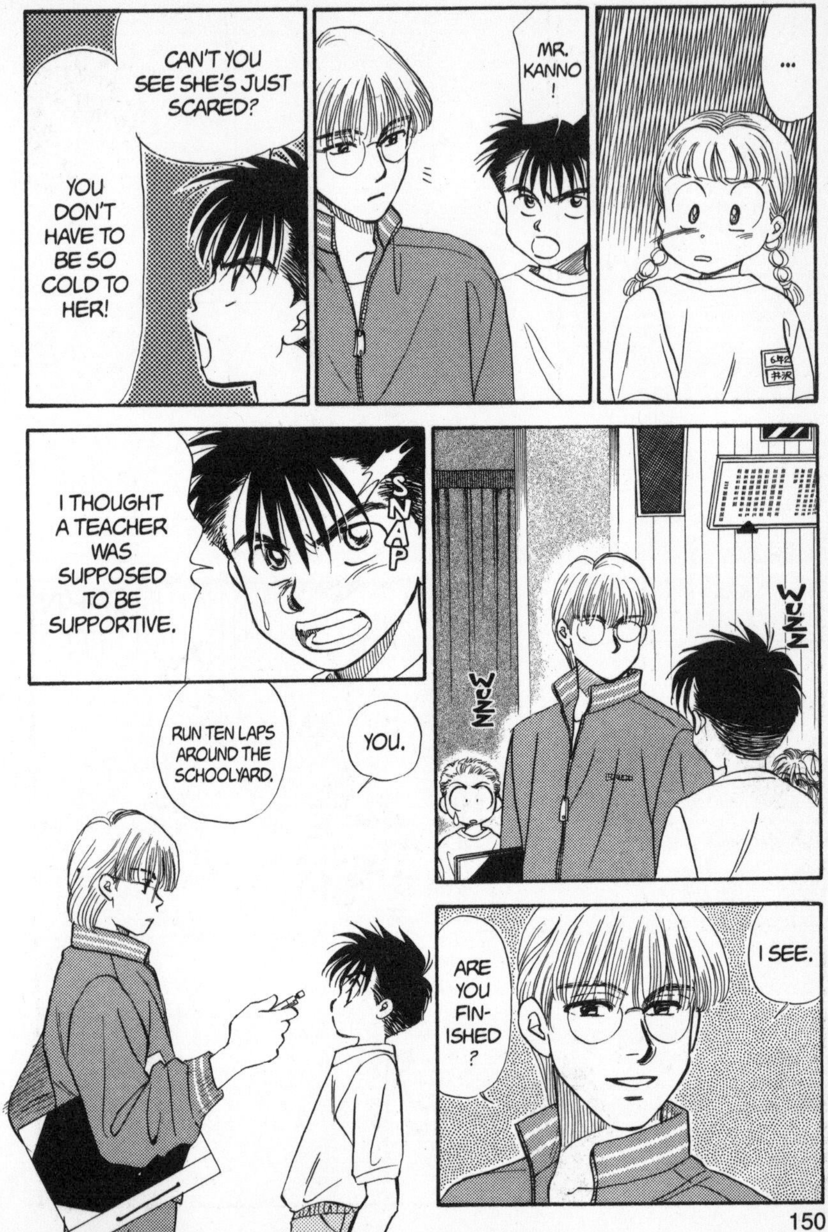
...
MR. KANNO!
CAN'T YOU SEE SHE'S JUST SCARED?
YOU DON'T HAVE TO BE SO COLD TO HER!
WUZZ
WUZZ
I THOUGHT A TEACHER WAS SUPPOSED TO BE SUPPORTIVE.
SNAP
I SEE.
ARE YOU FIN-ISHED?
YOU.
RUN TEN LAPS AROUND THE SCHOOLYARD.

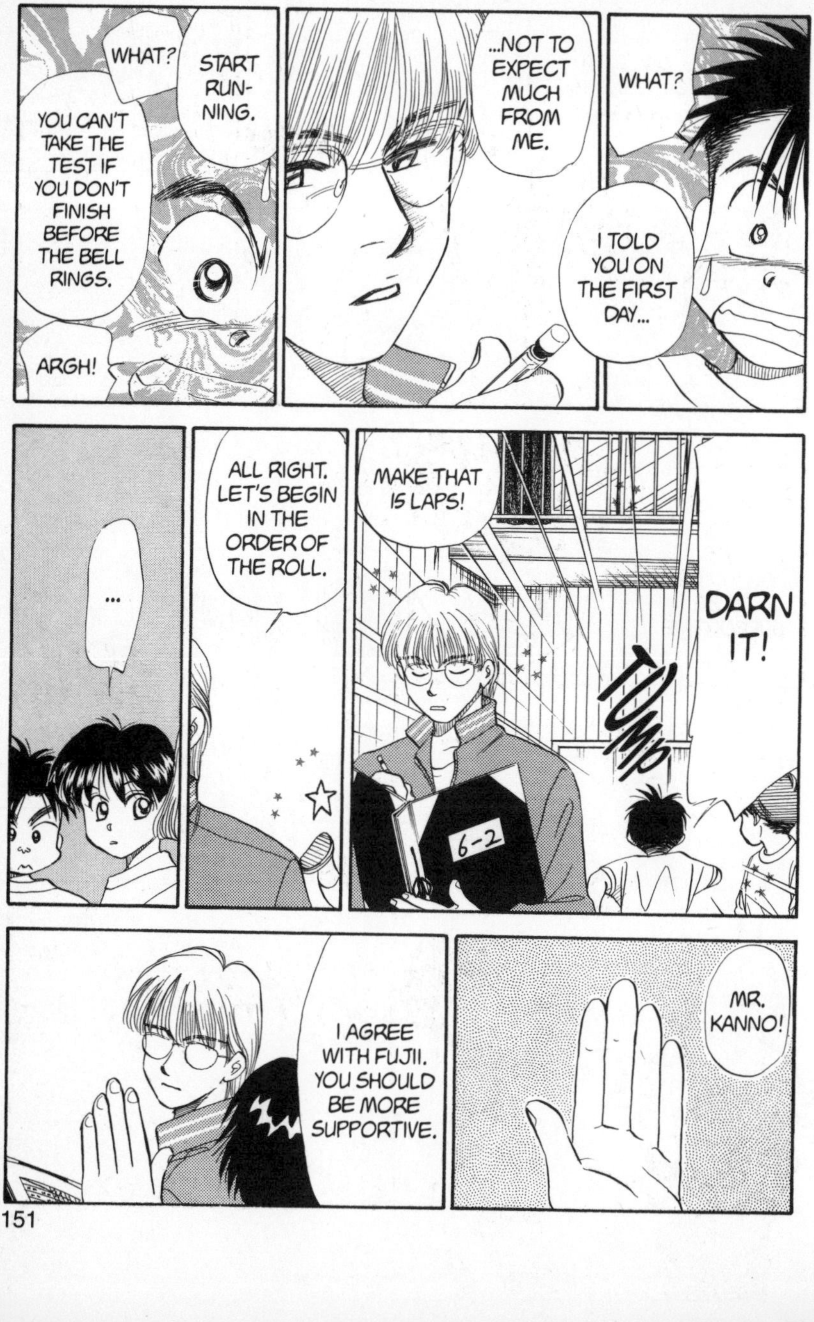
WHAT?
I TOLD YOU ON THE FIRST DAY...
...NOT TO EXPECT MUCH FROM ME.
START RUN-NING.
WHAT?
YOU CAN'T TAKE THE TEST IF YOU DON'T FINISH BEFORE THE BELL RINGS.
ARGH!
MAKE THAT 15 LAPS!
DARN IT!
TUMP
ALL RIGHT. LET'S BEGIN IN THE ORDER OF THE ROLL.
...
6-2
MR. KANNO!
I AGREE WITH FUJII. YOU SHOULD BE MORE SUPPORTIVE.

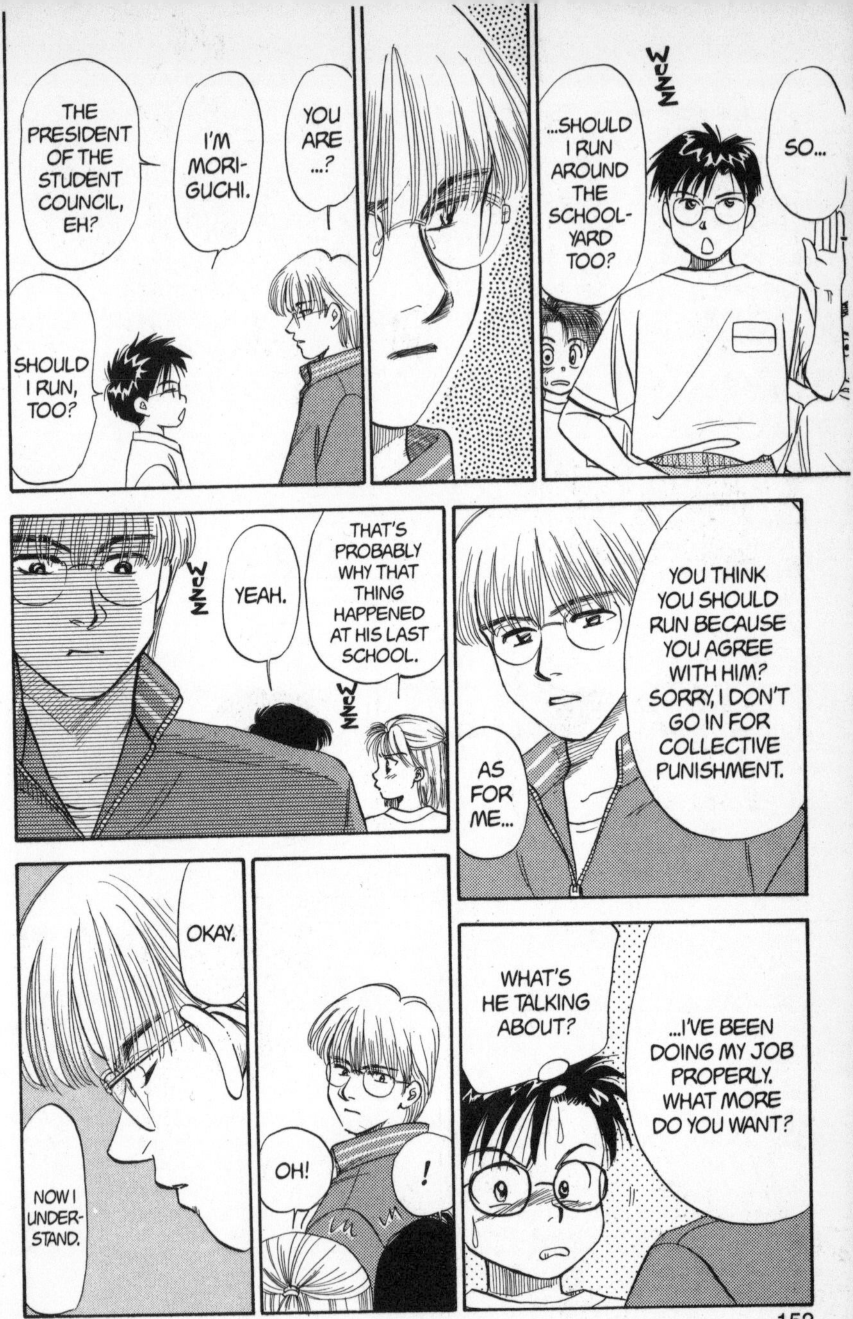
SO...
WUZZ
...SHOULD I RUN AROUND THE SCHOOL-YARD TOO?
YOU ARE ...?
I'M MORI-GUCHI.
THE PRESIDENT OF THE STUDENT COUNCIL, EH?
SHOULD I RUN, TOO?
YOU THINK YOU SHOULD RUN BECAUSE YOU AGREE WITH HIM? SORRY, I DON'T GO IN FOR COLLECTIVE PUNISHMENT.
AS FOR ME...
THAT'S PROBABLY WHY THAT THING HAPPENED AT HIS LAST SCHOOL.
WUZZ
YEAH.
WUZZ
...I'VE BEEN DOING MY JOB PROPERLY. WHAT MORE DO YOU WANT?
WHAT'S HE TALKING ABOUT?
!
OH!
OKAY.
NOW I UNDER-STAND.

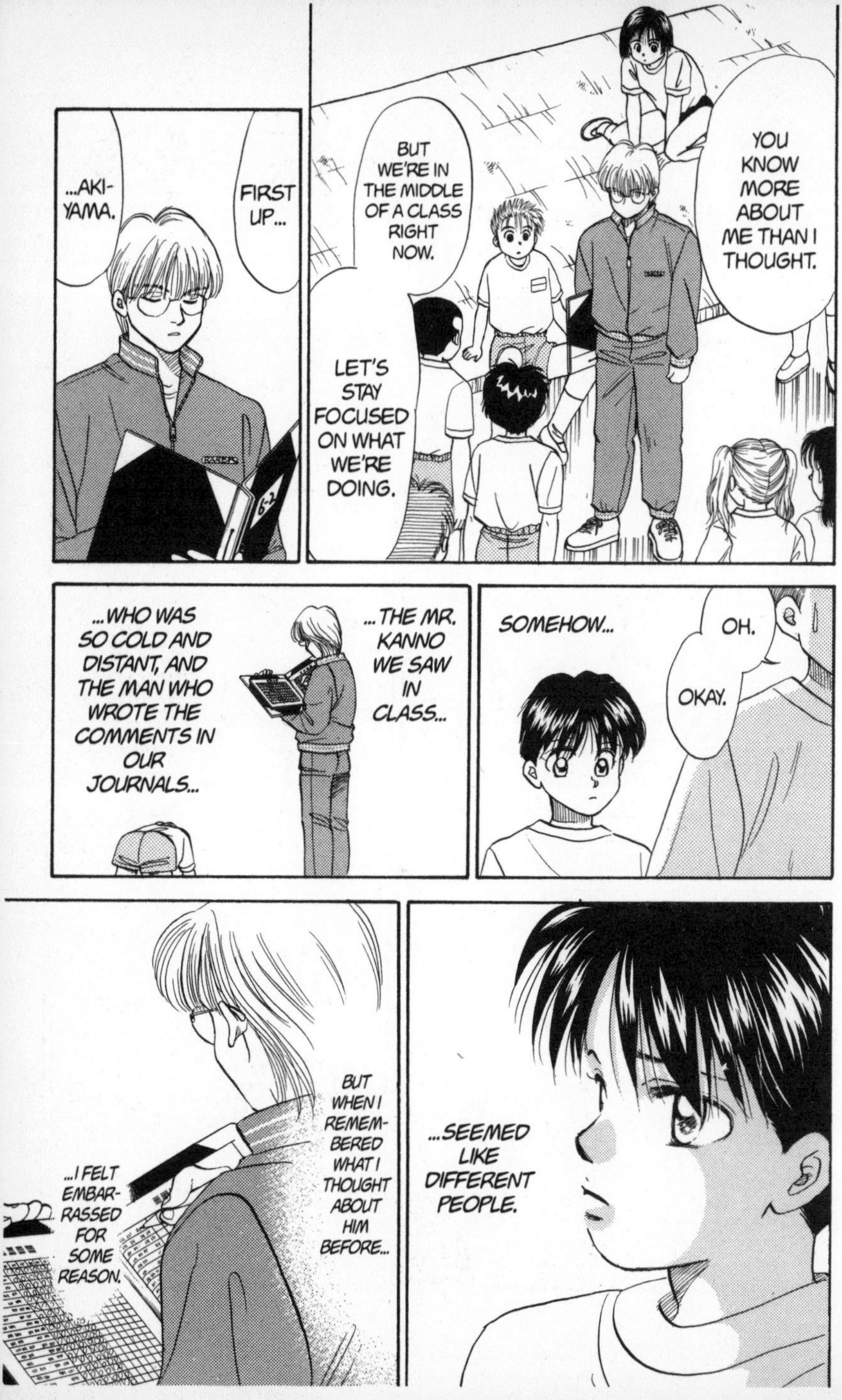
YOU KNOW MORE ABOUT ME THAN I THOUGHT.
BUT WE'RE IN THE MIDDLE OF A CLASS RIGHT NOW.
LET'S STAY FOCUSED ON WHAT WE'RE DOING.
FIRST UP...
...AKI-YAMA.
6-2
OH.
OKAY.
SOMEHOW...
...THE MR. KANNO WE SAW IN CLASS...
...WHO WAS SO COLD AND DISTANT, AND THE MAN WHO WROTE THE COMMENTS IN OUR JOURNALS...
...SEEMED LIKE DIFFERENT PEOPLE.
BUT WHEN I REMEM-BERED WHAT I THOUGHT ABOUT HIM BEFORE...
...I FELT EMBAR-RASSED FOR SOME REASON.

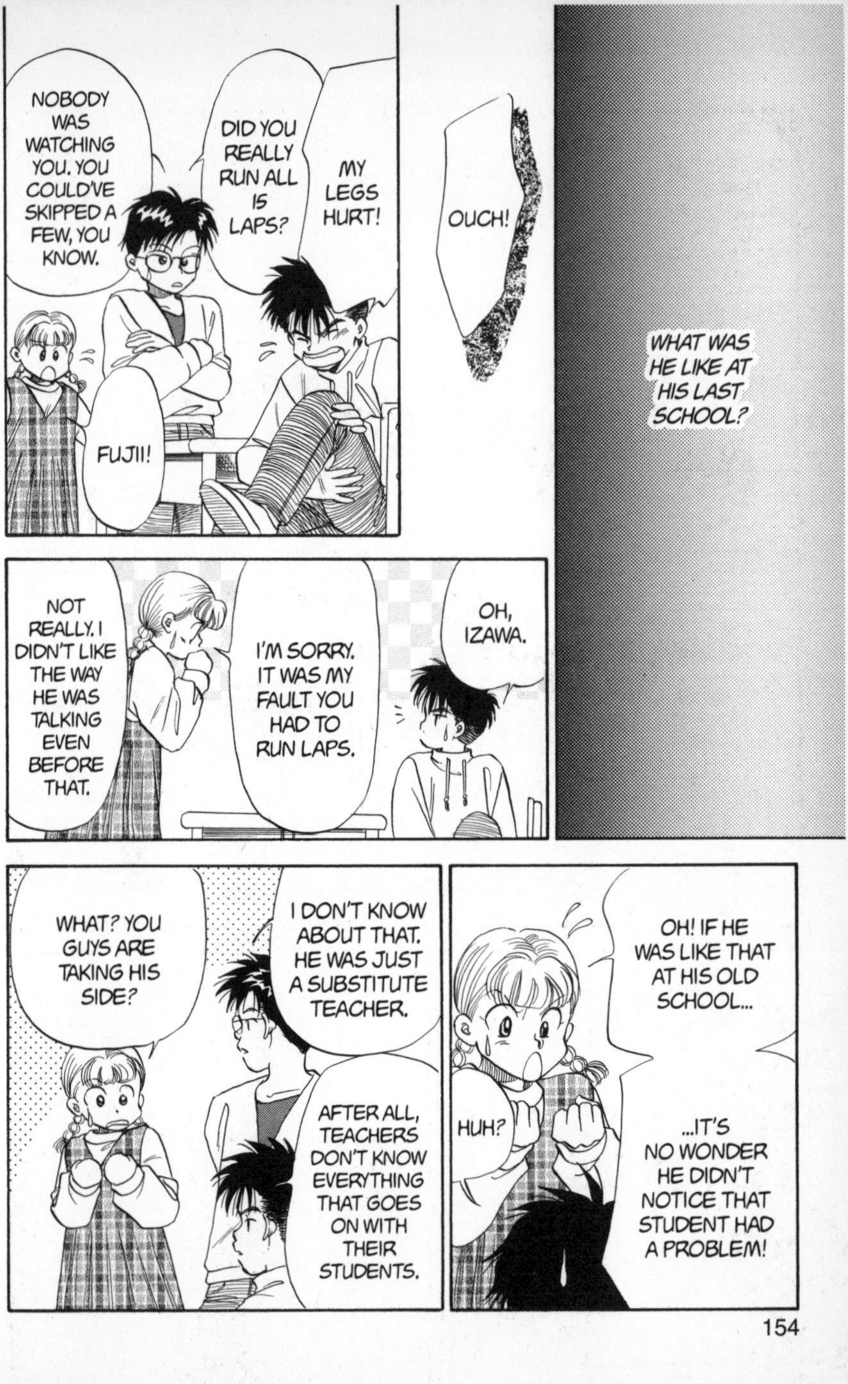
WHAT WAS HE LIKE AT HIS LAST SCHOOL?
OUCH!
MY LEGS HURT!
DID YOU REALLY RUN ALL IS LAPS?
NOBODY WAS WATCHING YOU. YOU COULD'VE SKIPPED A FEW, YOU KNOW.
FUJII!
OH, IZAWA.
I'M SORRY. IT WAS MY FAULT YOU HAD TO RUN LAPS.
NOT REALLY. I DIDN'T LIKE THE WAY HE WAS TALKING EVEN BEFORE THAT.
OH! IF HE WAS LIKE THAT AT HIS OLD SCHOOL...
...IT'S NO WONDER HE DIDN'T NOTICE THAT STUDENT HAD A PROBLEM!
HUH?
I DON'T KNOW ABOUT THAT. HE WAS JUST A SUBSTITUTE TEACHER.
WHAT? YOU GUYS ARE TAKING HIS SIDE?
AFTER ALL, TEACHERS DON'T KNOW EVERYTHING THAT GOES ON WITH THEIR STUDENTS.

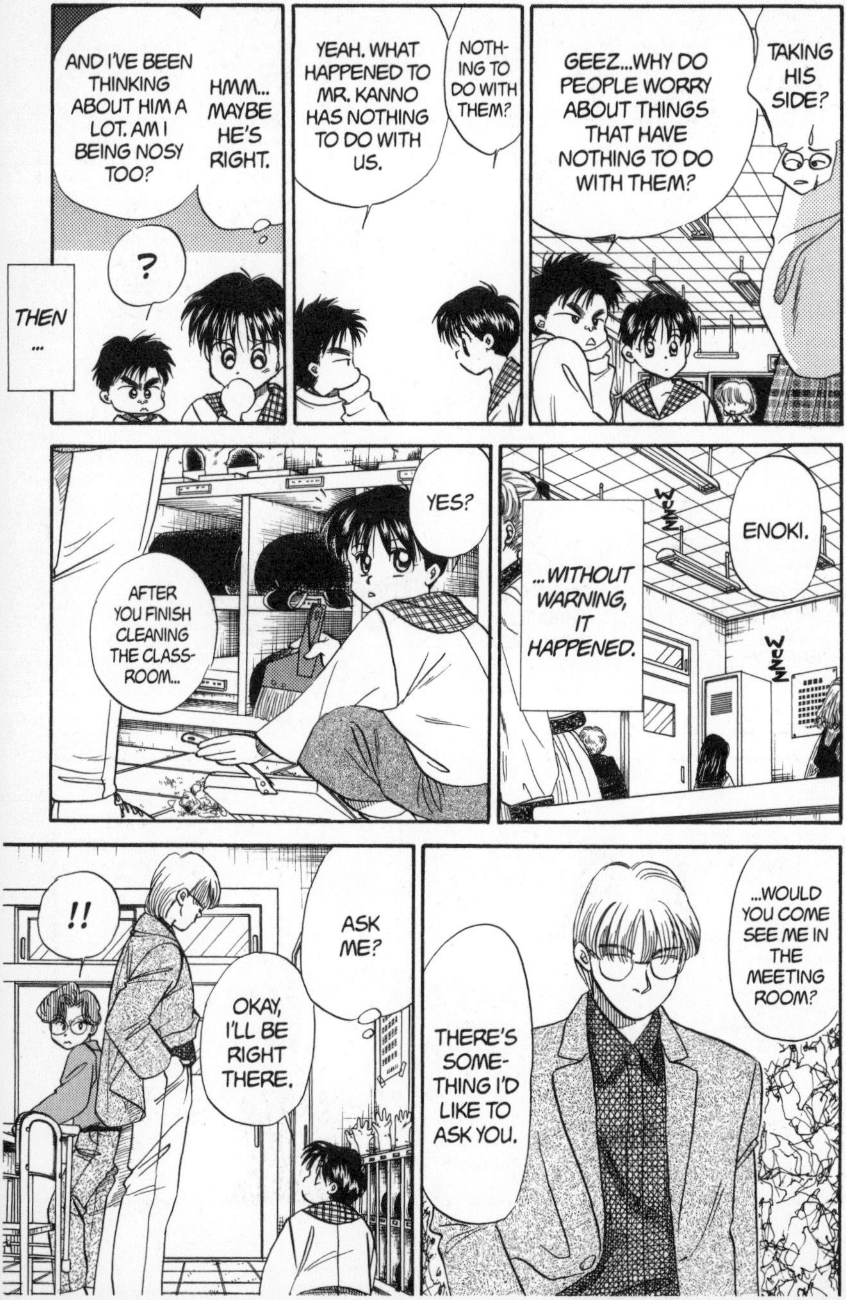
TAKING HIS SIDE?
GEEZ...WHY DO PEOPLE WORRY ABOUT THINGS THAT HAVE NOTHING TO DO WITH THEM?
NOTHING TO DO WITH THEM?
YEAH. WHAT HAPPENED TO MR. KANNO HAS NOTHING TO DO WITH US.
HMM... MAYBE HE'S RIGHT.
AND I'VE BEEN THINKING ABOUT HIM A LOT. AM I BEING NOSY TOO?
?
THEN ...
ENOKI.
WUZZ
...WITHOUT WARNING, IT HAPPENED.
WUZZ
YES?
AFTER YOU FINISH CLEANING THE CLASSROOM...
...WOULD YOU COME SEE ME IN THE MEETING ROOM?
THERE'S SOMETHING I'D LIKE TO ASK YOU.
ASK ME?
OKAY, I'LL BE RIGHT THERE.
!!

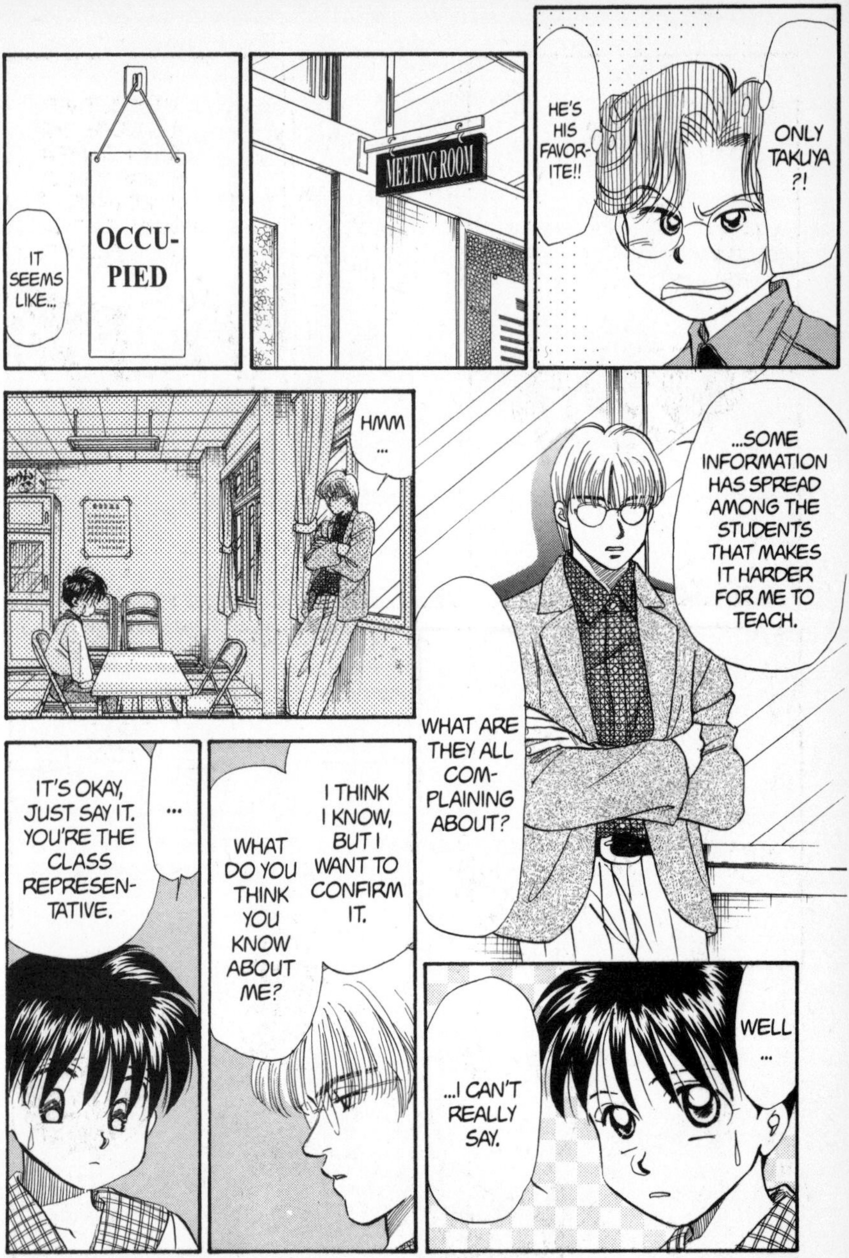
ONLY TAKUYA ?!
HE'S HIS FAVOR-ITE!!
MEETING ROOM
OCCU-PIED
IT SEEMS LIKE...
...SOME INFORMATION HAS SPREAD AMONG THE STUDENTS THAT MAKES IT HARDER FOR ME TO TEACH.
WHAT ARE THEY ALL COM-PLAINING ABOUT?
WELL ...
...I CAN'T REALLY SAY.
HMM ...
I THINK I KNOW, BUT I WANT TO CONFIRM IT.
WHAT DO YOU THINK YOU KNOW ABOUT ME?
...
IT'S OKAY, JUST SAY IT. YOU'RE THE CLASS REPRESEN-TATIVE.

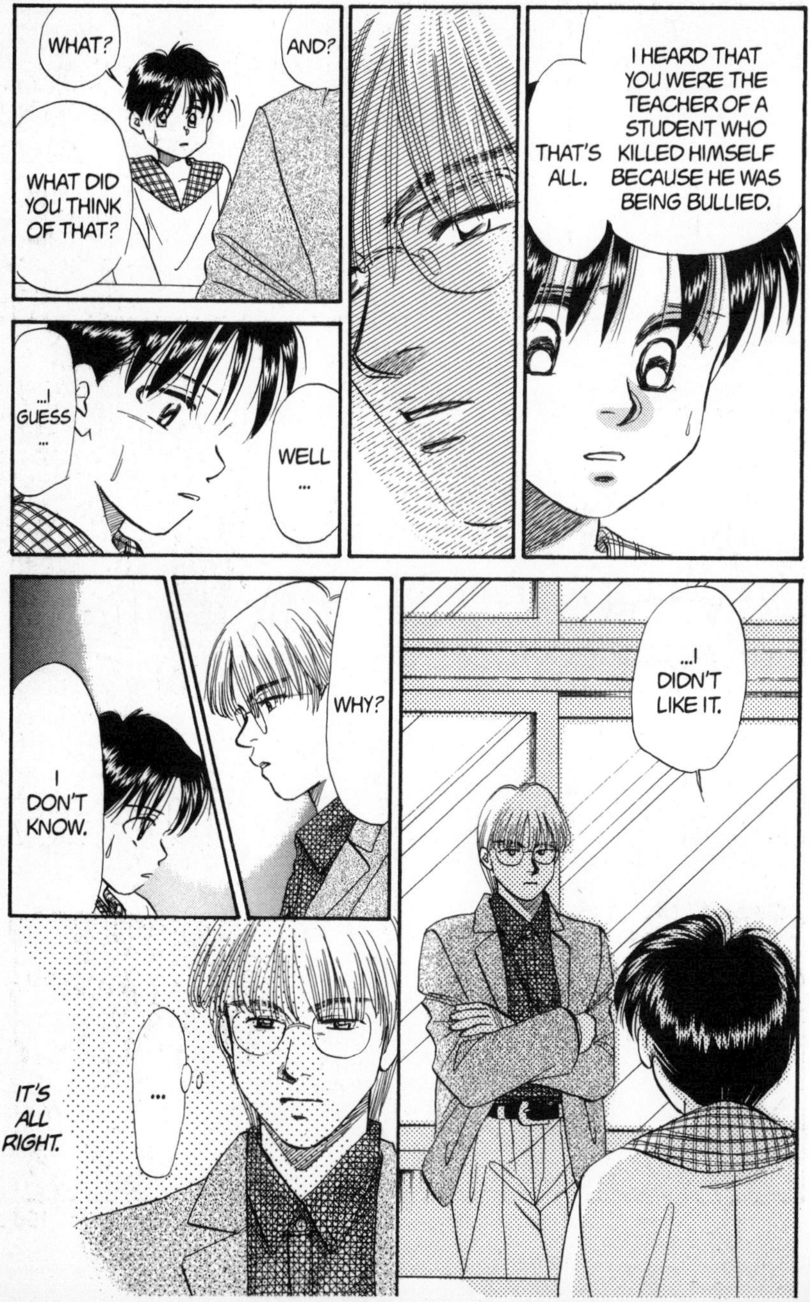
I HEARD THAT YOU WERE THE TEACHER OF A STUDENT WHO KILLED HIMSELF BECAUSE HE WAS BEING BULLIED.
THAT'S ALL.
AND?
WHAT?
WHAT DID YOU THINK OF THAT?
WELL ...
...I GUESS ...
...I DIDN'T LIKE IT.
WHY?
I DON'T KNOW.
...
IT'S ALL RIGHT.

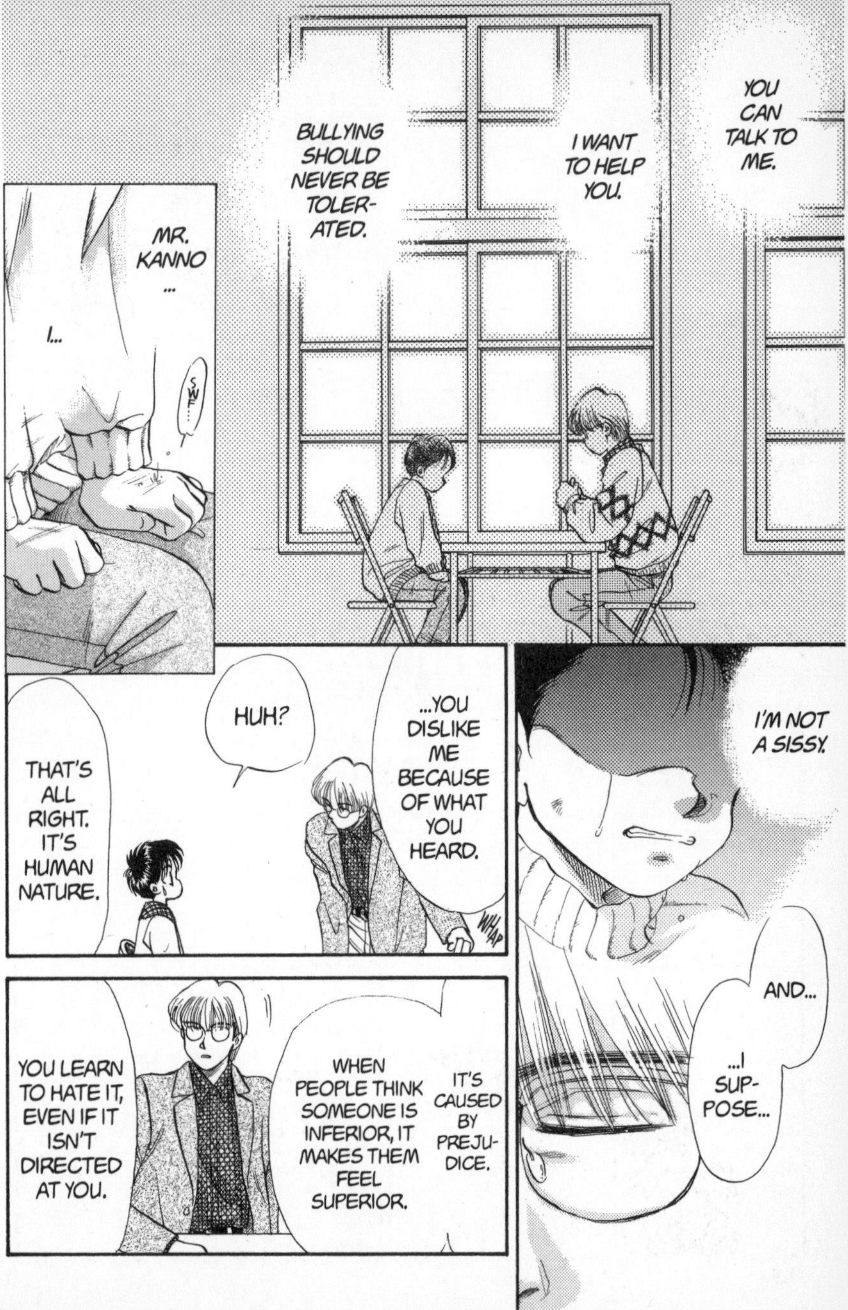
YOU CAN TALK TO ME.
I WANT TO HELP YOU.
BULLYING SHOULD NEVER BE TOLER-ATED.
MR. KANNO ...
I...
SWF...
I'M NOT A SISSY.
AND...
...I SUP-POSE...
...YOU DISLIKE ME BECAUSE OF WHAT YOU HEARD.
WHAP
HUH?
THAT'S ALL RIGHT. IT'S HUMAN NATURE.
IT'S CAUSED BY PREJU-DICE.
WHEN PEOPLE THINK SOMEONE IS INFERIOR, IT MAKES THEM FEEL SUPERIOR.
YOU LEARN TO HATE IT, EVEN IF IT ISN'T DIRECTED AT YOU.

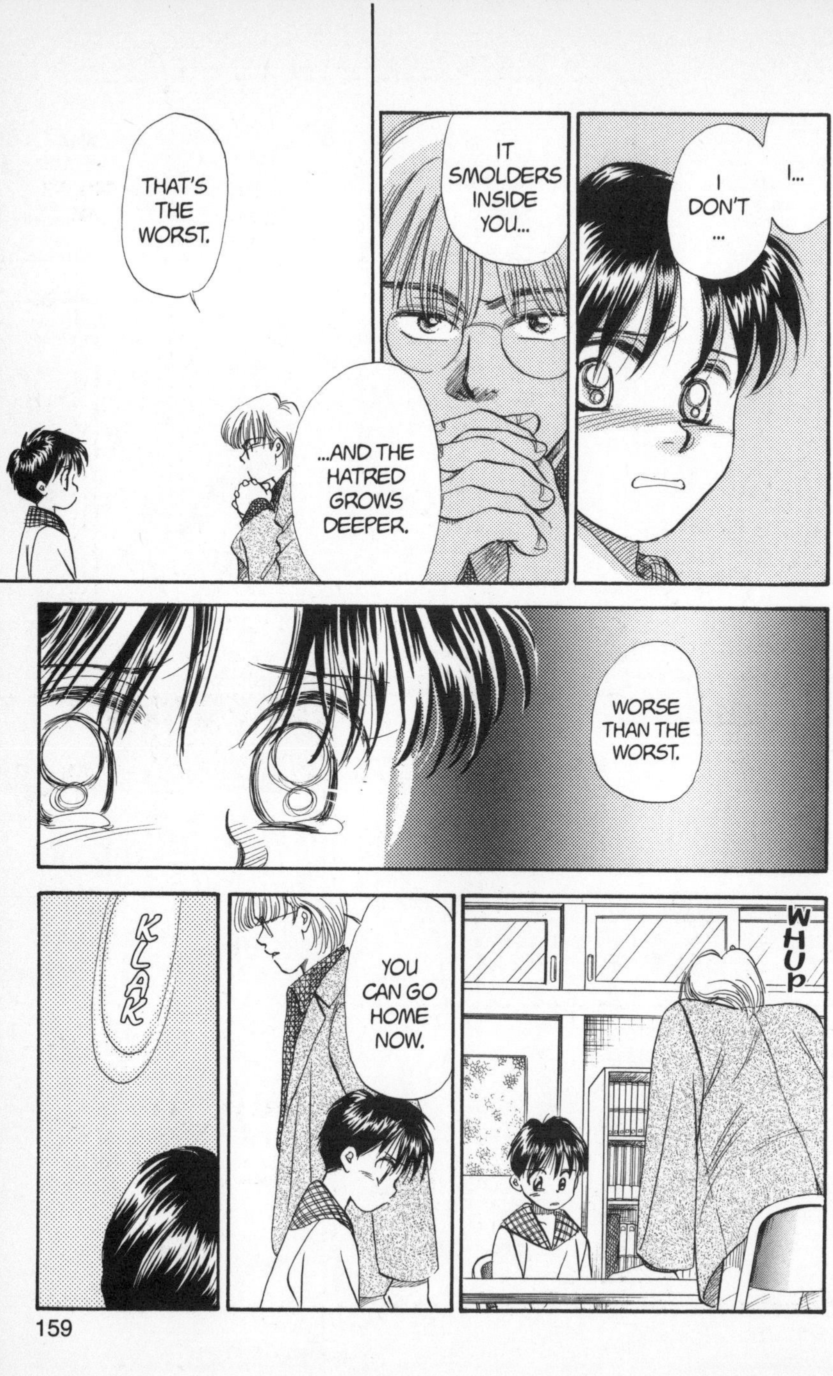
I...
I DON'T ...
IT SMOLDERS INSIDE YOU...
...AND THE HATRED GROWS DEEPER.
THAT'S THE WORST.
WORSE THAN THE WORST.
WHUP
YOU CAN GO HOME NOW.
KLAK

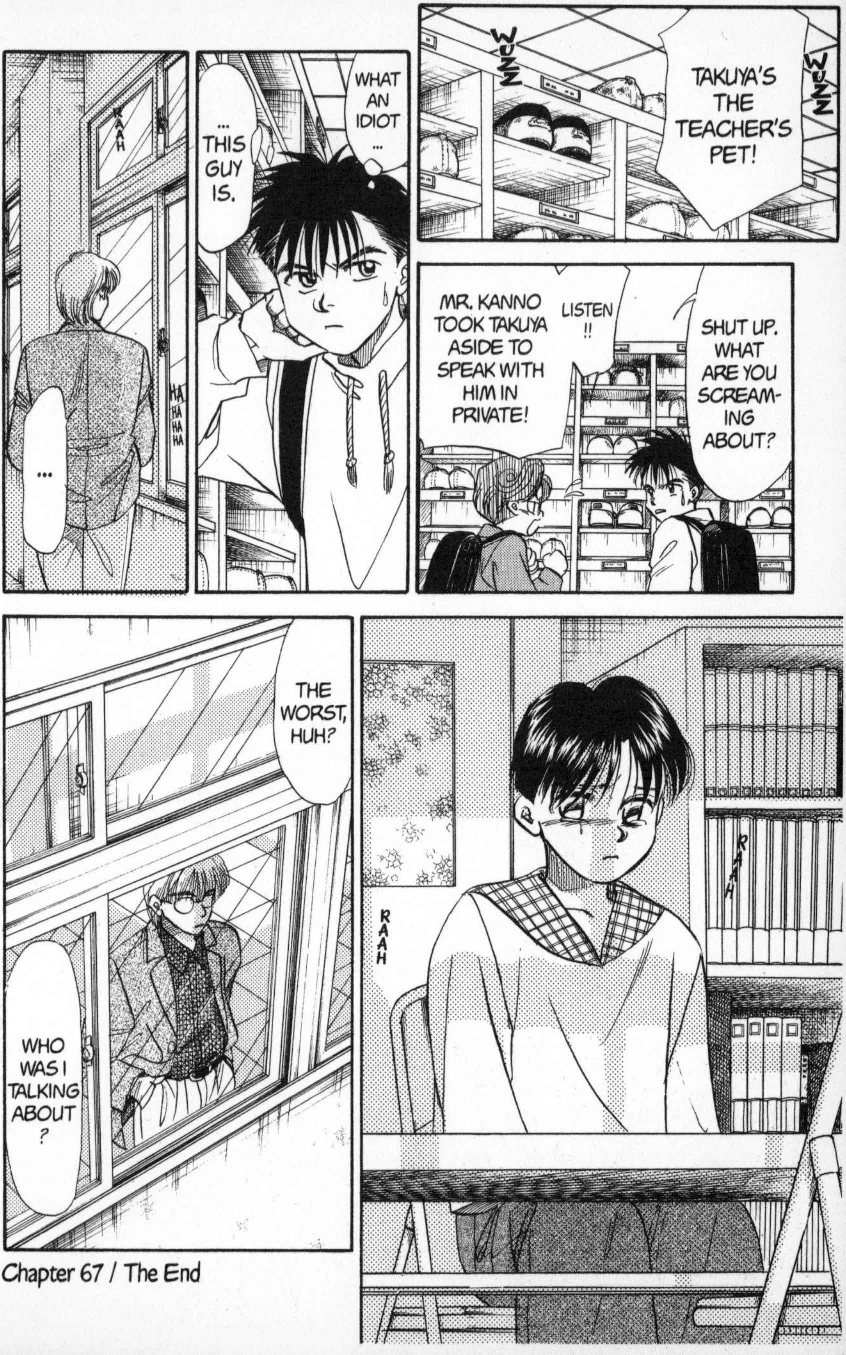
WUZZ
WUZZ
TAKUYA'S THE TEACHER'S PET!
SHUT UP. WHAT ARE YOU SCREAM-ING ABOUT?
LISTEN !!
MR. KANNO TOOK TAKUYA ASIDE TO SPEAK WITH HIM IN PRIVATE!
WHAT AN IDIOT ...
... THIS GUY IS.
RAAH
HA HA HA HA
...
RAAH
RAAH
THE WORST, HUH?
WHO WAS I TALKING ABOUT ?

Chapter 67 / The End

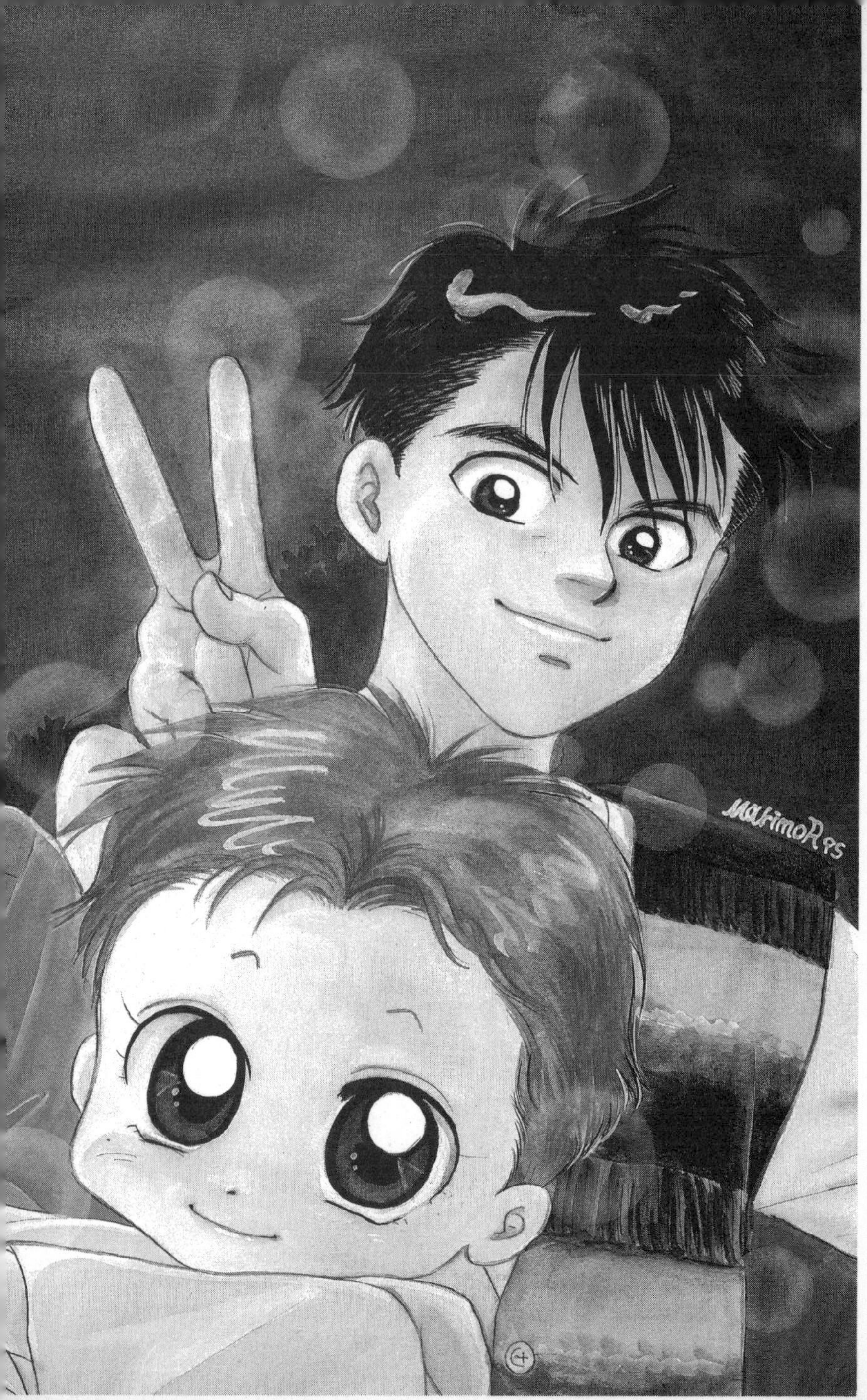

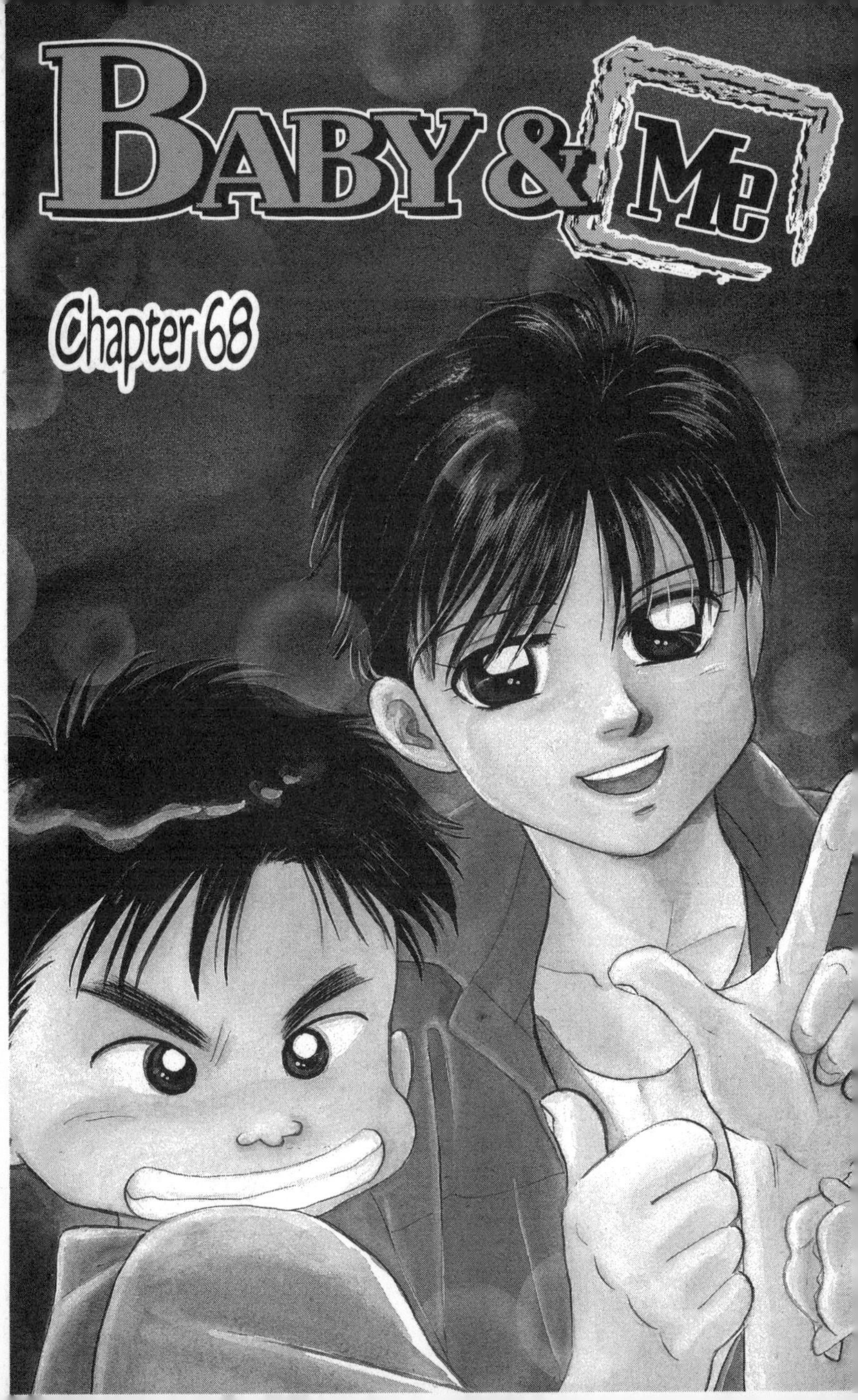
BABY & ME
Chapter 68

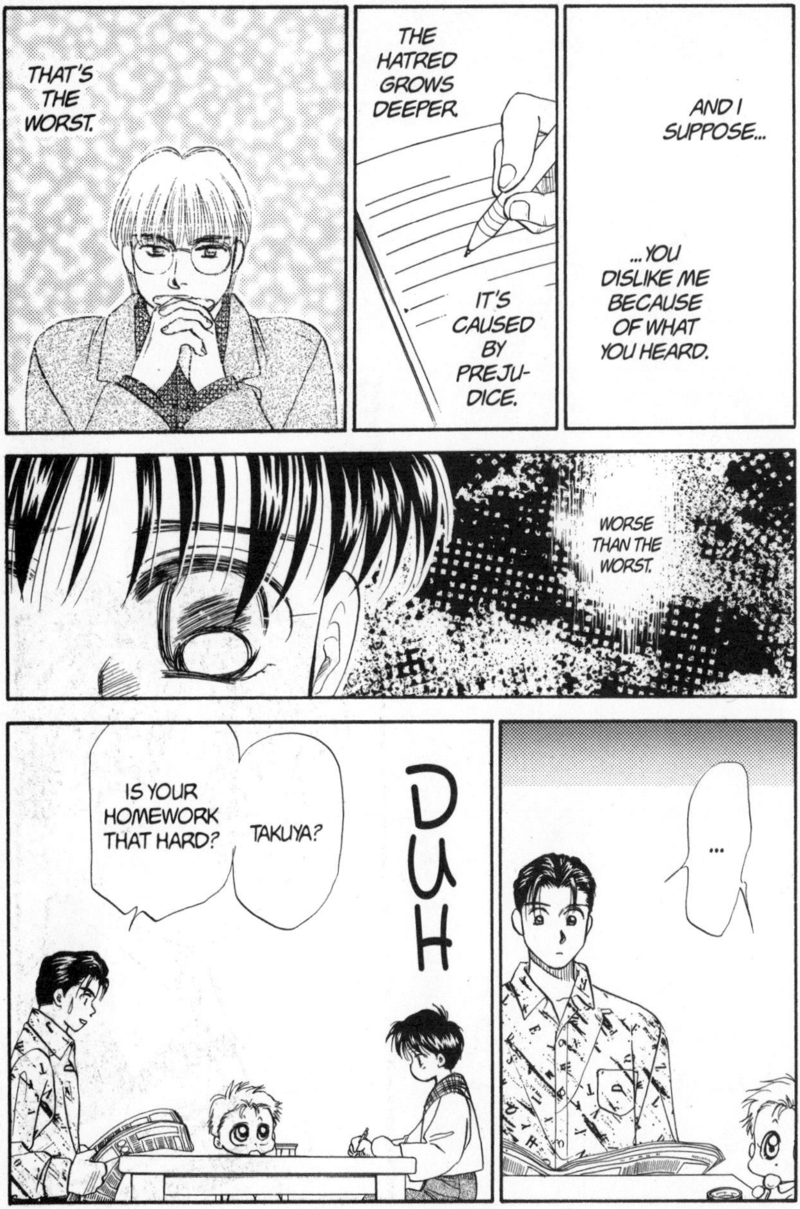
AND I SUPPOSE...
...YOU DISLIKE ME BECAUSE OF WHAT YOU HEARD.
THE HATRED GROWS DEEPER.
IT'S CAUSED BY PREJU-DICE.
THAT'S THE WORST.
WORSE THAN THE WORST.
...
DUH
TAKUYA?
IS YOUR HOMEWORK THAT HARD?

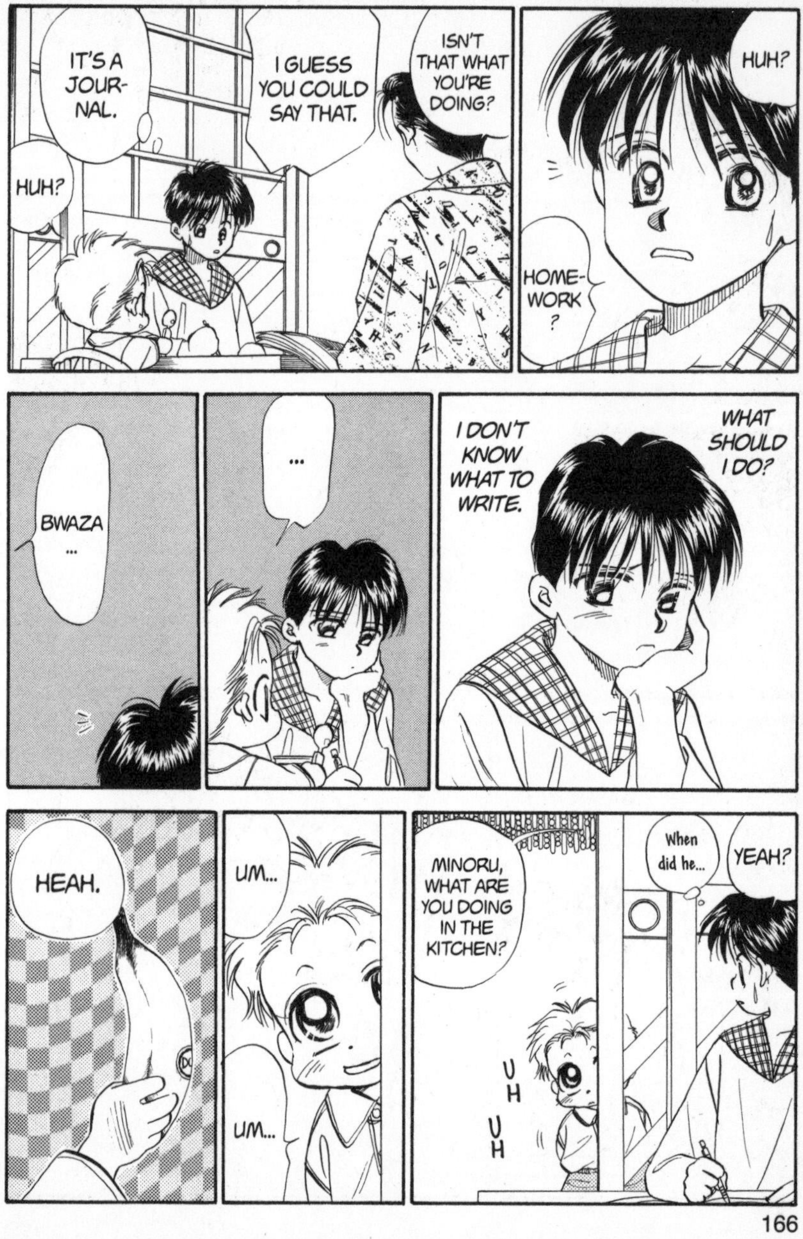
HUH?
HOME-WORK?
ISN'T THAT WHAT YOU'RE DOING?
I GUESS YOU COULD SAY THAT.
IT'S A JOUR-NAL.
HUH?
WHAT SHOULD I DO?
I DON'T KNOW WHAT TO WRITE.
...
BWAZA ...
YEAH?
When did he...
MINORU, WHAT ARE YOU DOING IN THE KITCHEN?
UH
UH
UM...
UM...
HEAH.

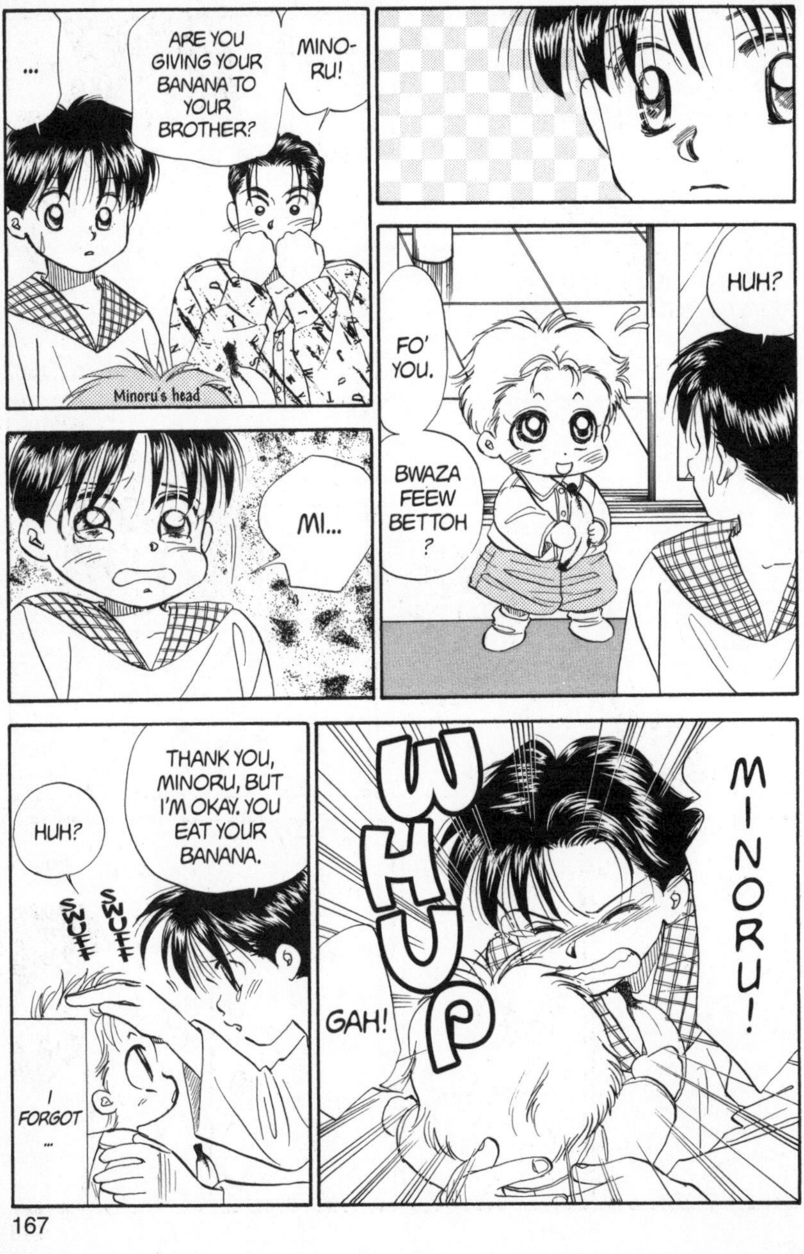
MINO-
RU!
ARE YOU GIVING YOUR BANANA TO YOUR BROTHER?
...
Minoru's head
HUH?
FO' YOU.
BWAZA FEEW BETTOH ?
MI...
MINORU!
WHUP
GAH!
THANK YOU, MINORU, BUT I'M OKAY. YOU EAT YOUR BANANA.
HUH?
SWUFF
SWUFF
I FORGOT ...

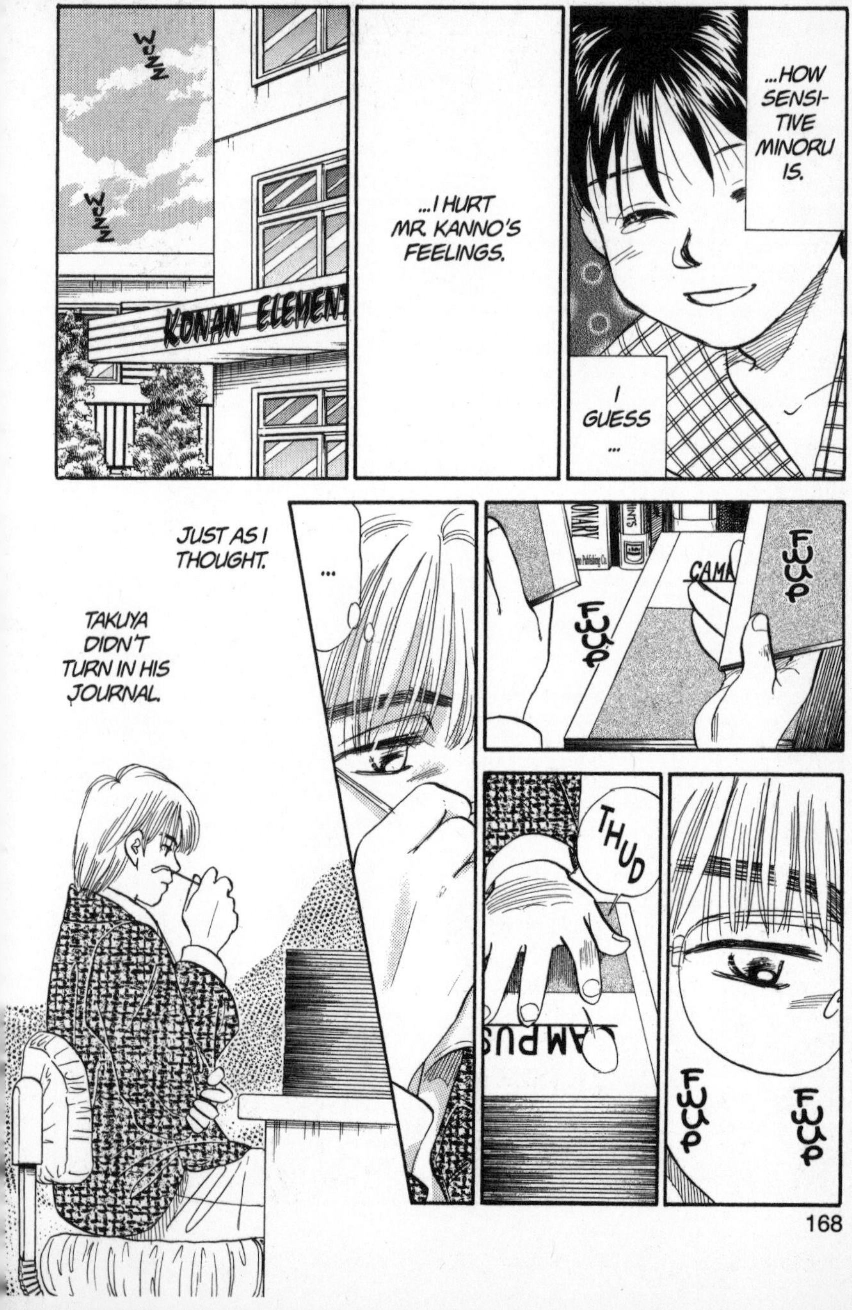

...HOW SENSITIVE MINORU IS.
I GUESS ...
...I HURT MR. KANNO'S FEELINGS.
WUZZ
WUZZ
KONAN ELEMENT
FWUP
FWUP
FWUP
FWUP
THUD
...
JUST AS I THOUGHT.
TAKUYA DIDN'T TURN IN HIS JOURNAL.

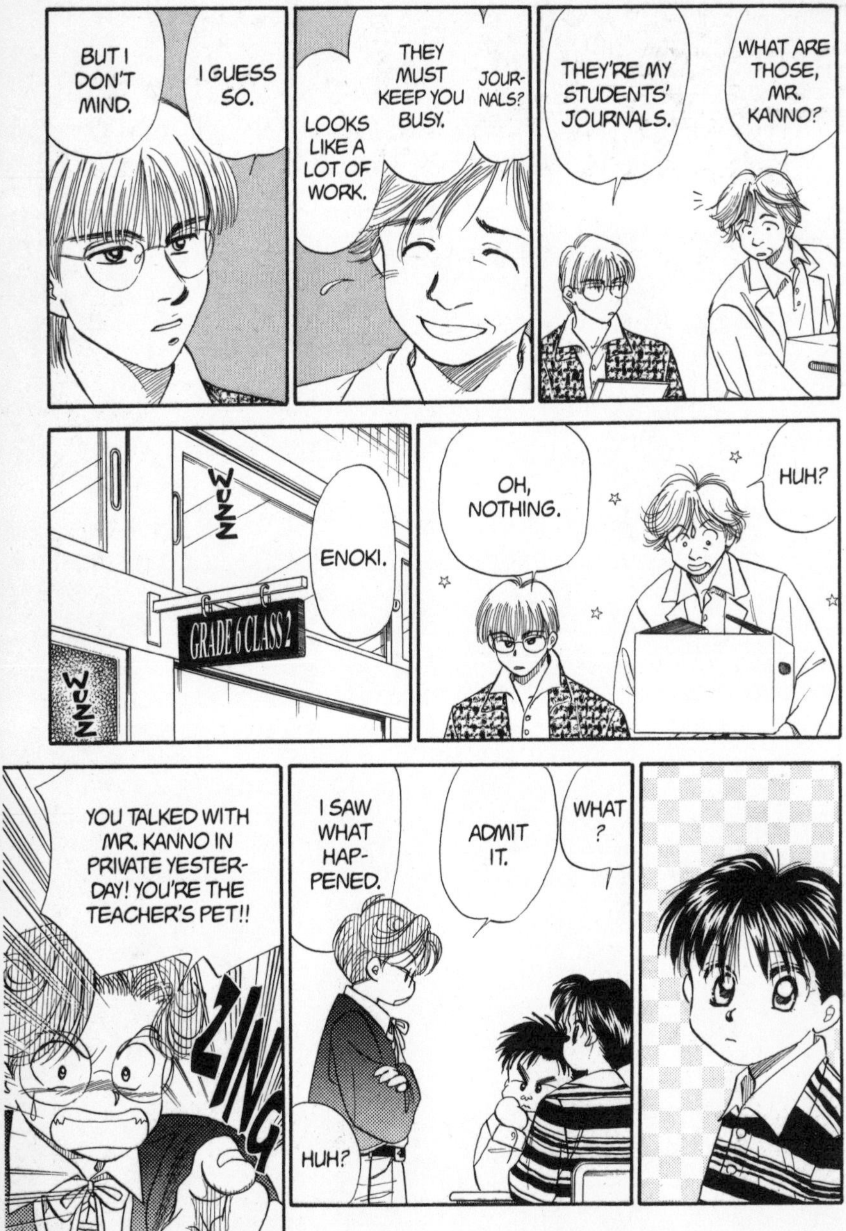
WHAT ARE THOSE, MR. KANNO?
THEY'RE MY STUDENTS' JOURNALS.
JOURNALS?
THEY MUST KEEP YOU BUSY.
LOOKS LIKE A LOT OF WORK.
I GUESS SO.
BUT I DON'T MIND.
HUH?
OH, NOTHING.
WUZZ
GRADE 6 CLASS 2
ENOKI.
WUZZ
WHAT ?
ADMIT IT.
I SAW WHAT HAPPENED.
HUH?
YOU TALKED WITH MR. KANNO IN PRIVATE YESTERDAY! YOU'RE THE TEACHER'S PET!!
ZING

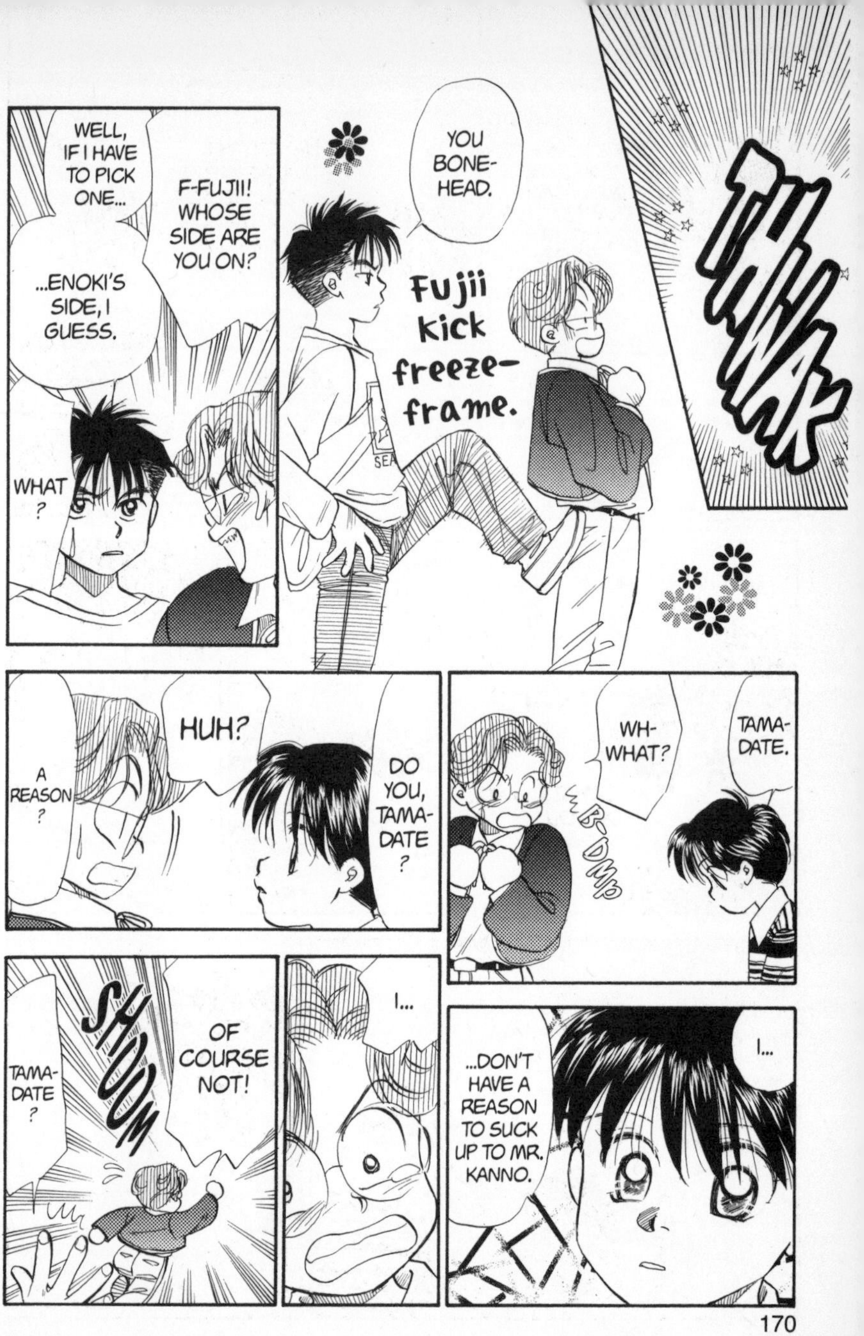
THWAK
YOU BONE-HEAD.
Fujii kick freeze-frame.
F-FUJII! WHOSE SIDE ARE YOU ON?
WELL, IF I HAVE TO PICK ONE...
...ENOKI'S SIDE, I GUESS.
WHAT?
TAMA-DATE.
WH-WHAT?
B-DMP
DO YOU, TAMA-DATE?
HUH?
A REASON?
I...
...DON'T HAVE A REASON TO SUCK UP TO MR. KANNO.
I...
OF COURSE NOT!
SHOOOM
TAMA-DATE?

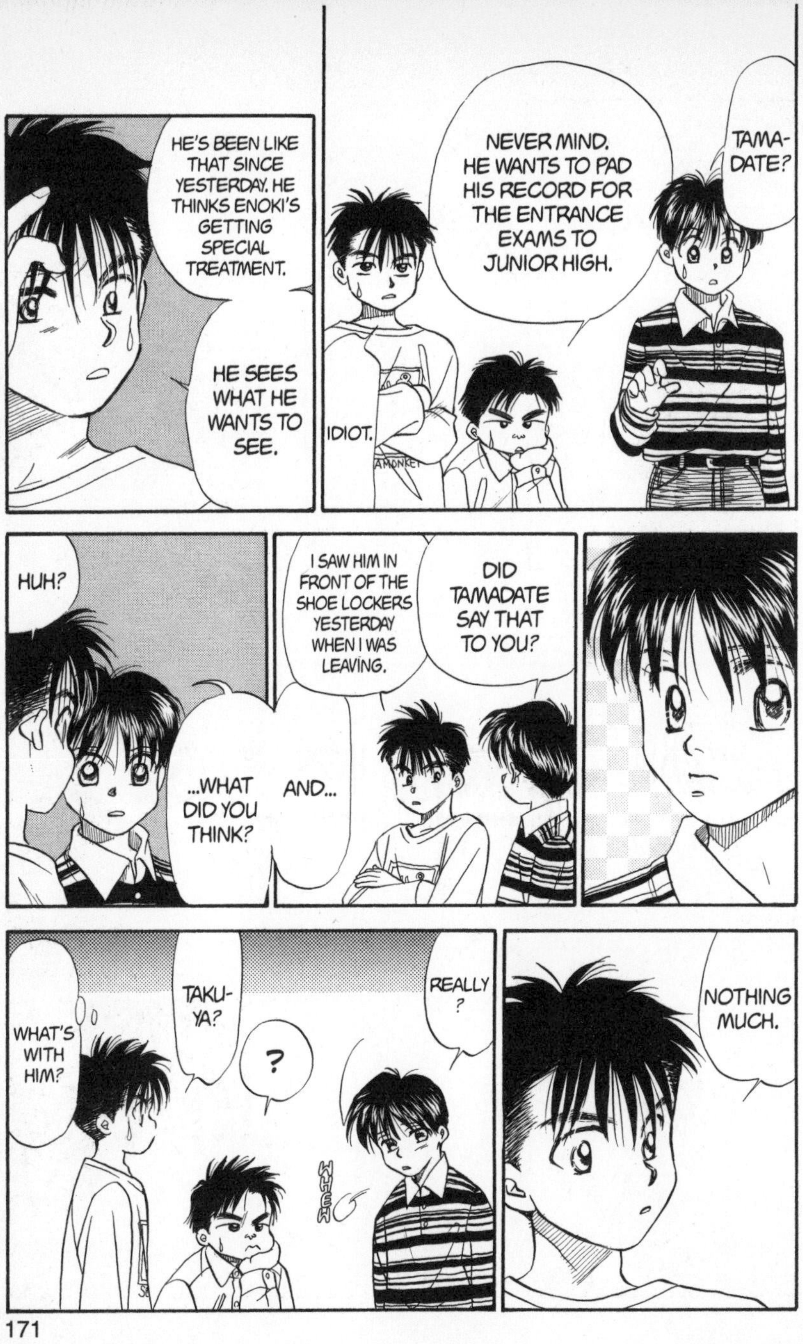

TAMA-DATE?
NEVER MIND. HE WANTS TO PAD HIS RECORD FOR THE ENTRANCE EXAMS TO JUNIOR HIGH.
IDIOT.
HE'S BEEN LIKE THAT SINCE YESTERDAY. HE THINKS ENOKI'S GETTING SPECIAL TREATMENT.
HE SEES WHAT HE WANTS TO SEE.
DID TAMADATE SAY THAT TO YOU?
I SAW HIM IN FRONT OF THE SHOE LOCKERS YESTERDAY WHEN I WAS LEAVING.
AND...
HUH?
...WHAT DID YOU THINK?
NOTHING MUCH.
REALLY?
WHEW
?
TAKU-YA?
WHAT'S WITH HIM?

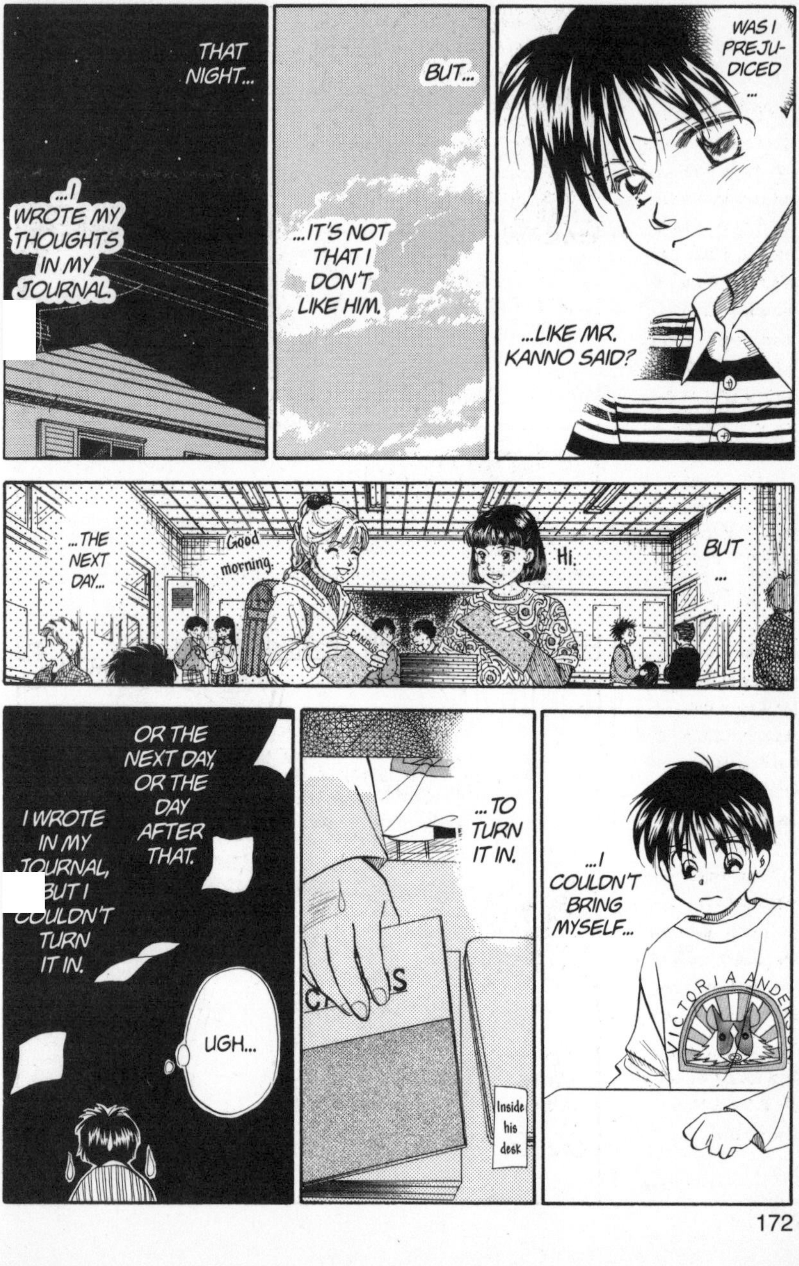
WAS I PREJU-DICED ...
...LIKE MR. KANNO SAID?
BUT...
...IT'S NOT THAT I DON'T LIKE HIM.
THAT NIGHT...
...I WROTE MY THOUGHTS IN MY JOURNAL.
BUT ...
Hi.
Good morning.
...THE NEXT DAY...
...I COULDN'T BRING MYSELF...
...TO TURN IT IN.
Inside his desk
OR THE NEXT DAY, OR THE DAY AFTER THAT.
I WROTE IN MY JOURNAL, BUT I COULDN'T TURN IT IN.
UGH...

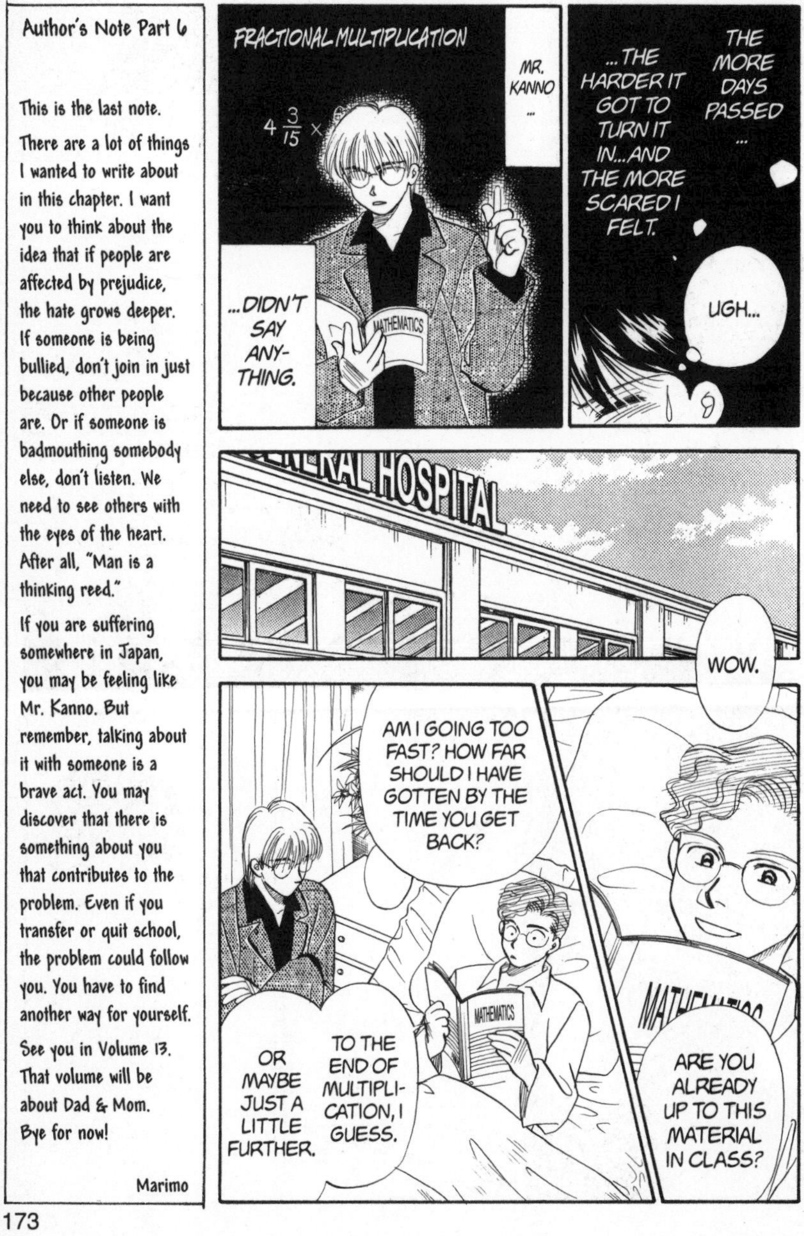
THE MORE DAYS PASSED...
...THE HARDER IT GOT TO TURN IT IN...AND THE MORE SCARED I FELT.
UGH...
FRACTIONAL MULTIPLICATION
MR. KANNO...
4 3/15 ×
MATHEMATICS
...DIDN'T SAY ANYTHING.
HOSPITAL
WOW.
MATHEMATICS
ARE YOU ALREADY UP TO THIS MATERIAL IN CLASS?
AM I GOING TOO FAST? HOW FAR SHOULD I HAVE GOTTEN BY THE TIME YOU GET BACK?
MATHEMATICS
TO THE END OF MULTIPLI-CATION, I GUESS.
OR MAYBE JUST A LITTLE FURTHER.

Author's Note Part 6

This is the last note.

There are a lot of things I wanted to write about in this chapter. I want you to think about the idea that if people are affected by prejudice, the hate grows deeper. If someone is being bullied, don't join in just because other people are. Or if someone is badmouthing somebody else, don't listen. We need to see others with the eyes of the heart. After all, "Man is a thinking reed."

If you are suffering somewhere in Japan, you may be feeling like Mr. Kanno. But remember, talking about it with someone is a brave act. You may discover that there is something about you that contributes to the problem. Even if you transfer or quit school, the problem could follow you. You have to find another way for yourself.

See you in Volume 13. That volume will be about Dad & Mom. Bye for now!

Marimo

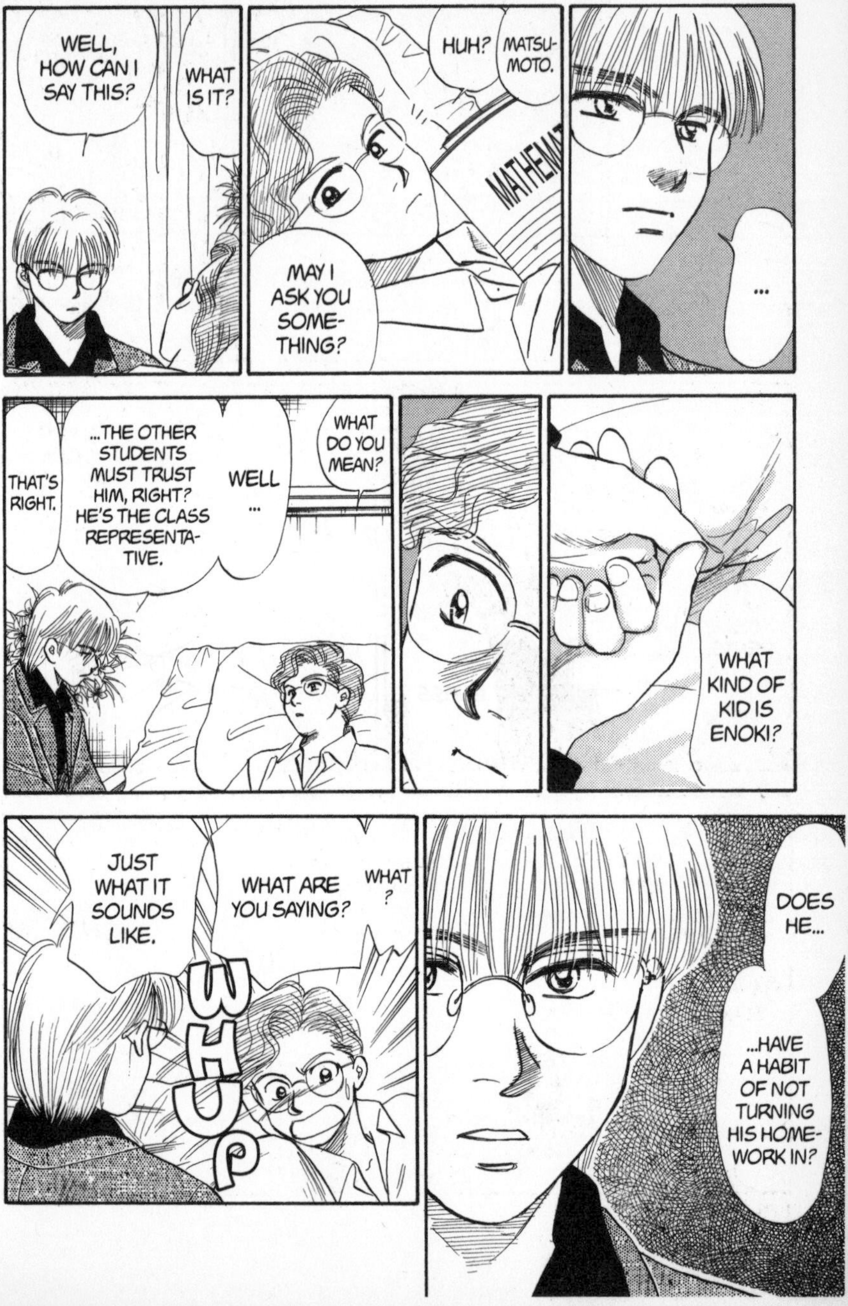
...
MATSU-MOTO.
HUH?
MATHEMAT
MAY I ASK YOU SOME-THING?
WHAT IS IT?
WELL, HOW CAN I SAY THIS?
WHAT KIND OF KID IS ENOKI?
WHAT DO YOU MEAN?
WELL ...
...THE OTHER STUDENTS MUST TRUST HIM, RIGHT? HE'S THE CLASS REPRESENTA-TIVE.
THAT'S RIGHT.
DOES HE...
...HAVE A HABIT OF NOT TURNING HIS HOME-WORK IN?
WHAT?
WHAT ARE YOU SAYING?
JUST WHAT IT SOUNDS LIKE.
WHUP

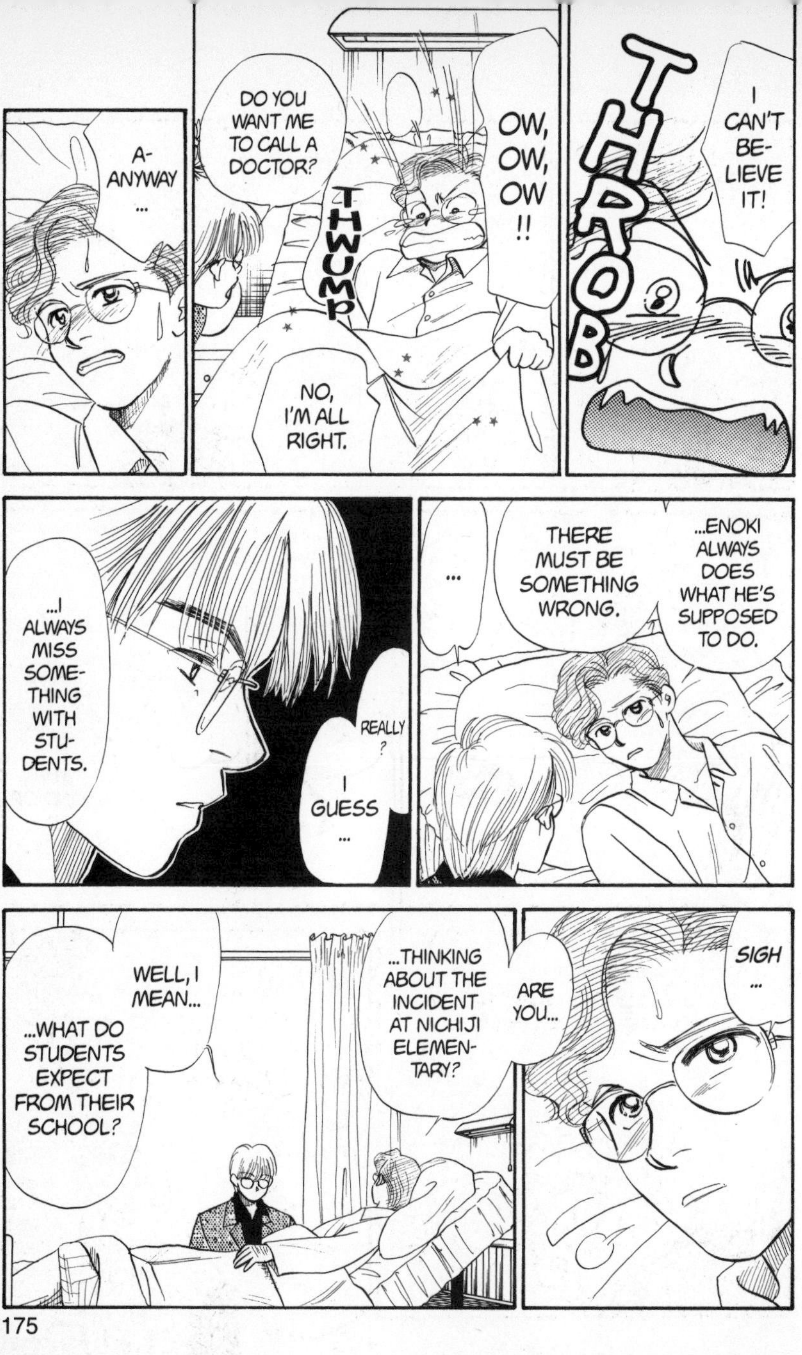
THROB
I CAN'T BE-LIEVE IT!
OW, OW, OW!!
THWUMP
DO YOU WANT ME TO CALL A DOCTOR?
NO, I'M ALL RIGHT.
A-ANYWAY...
...ENOKI ALWAYS DOES WHAT HE'S SUPPOSED TO DO.
THERE MUST BE SOMETHING WRONG.
...
REALLY?
I GUESS...
...I ALWAYS MISS SOME-THING WITH STU-DENTS.
SIGH...
ARE YOU...
...THINKING ABOUT THE INCIDENT AT NICHIJI ELEMEN-TARY?
WELL, I MEAN...
...WHAT DO STUDENTS EXPECT FROM THEIR SCHOOL?

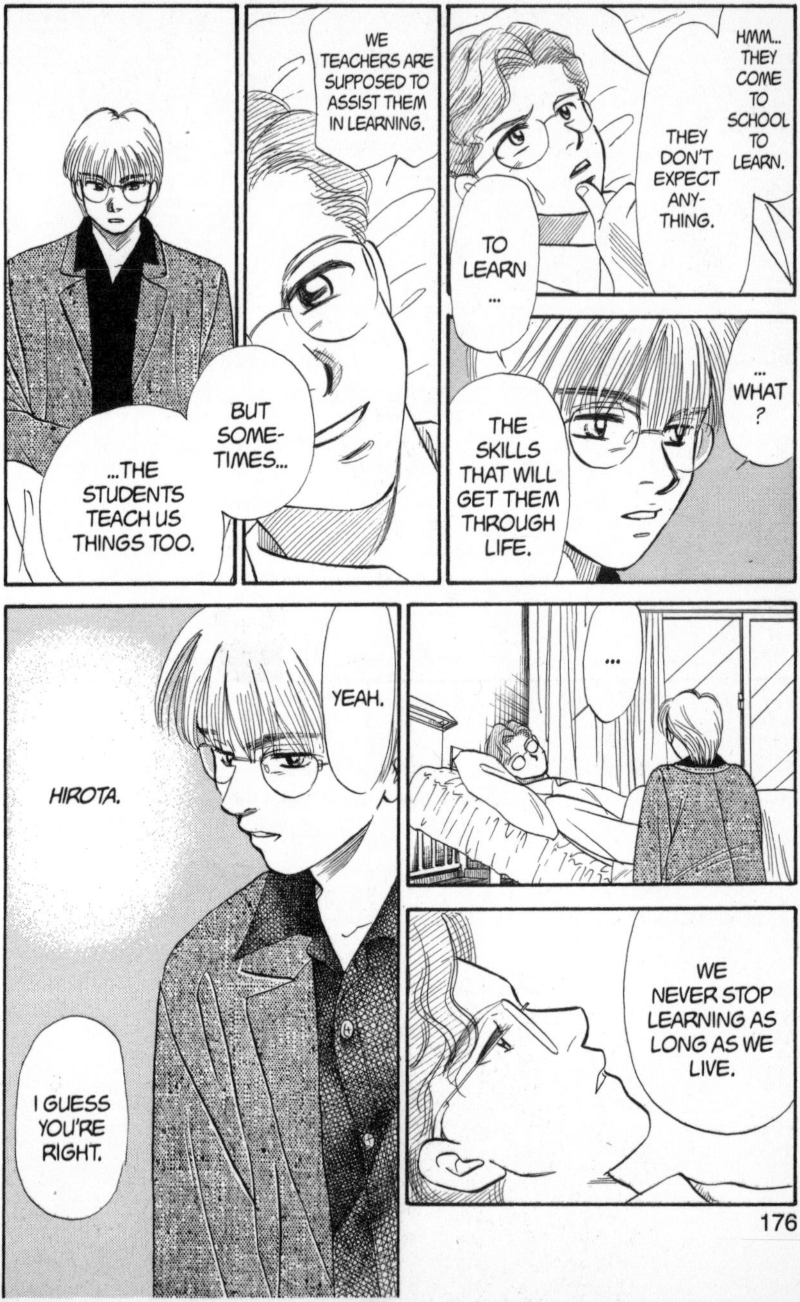
HMM... THEY COME TO SCHOOL TO LEARN.
THEY DON'T EXPECT ANY-THING.
TO LEARN ...
... WHAT ?
THE SKILLS THAT WILL GET THEM THROUGH LIFE.
WE TEACHERS ARE SUPPOSED TO ASSIST THEM IN LEARNING.
BUT SOME-TIMES...
...THE STUDENTS TEACH US THINGS TOO.
...
WE NEVER STOP LEARNING AS LONG AS WE LIVE.
YEAH.
HIROTA.
I GUESS YOU'RE RIGHT.

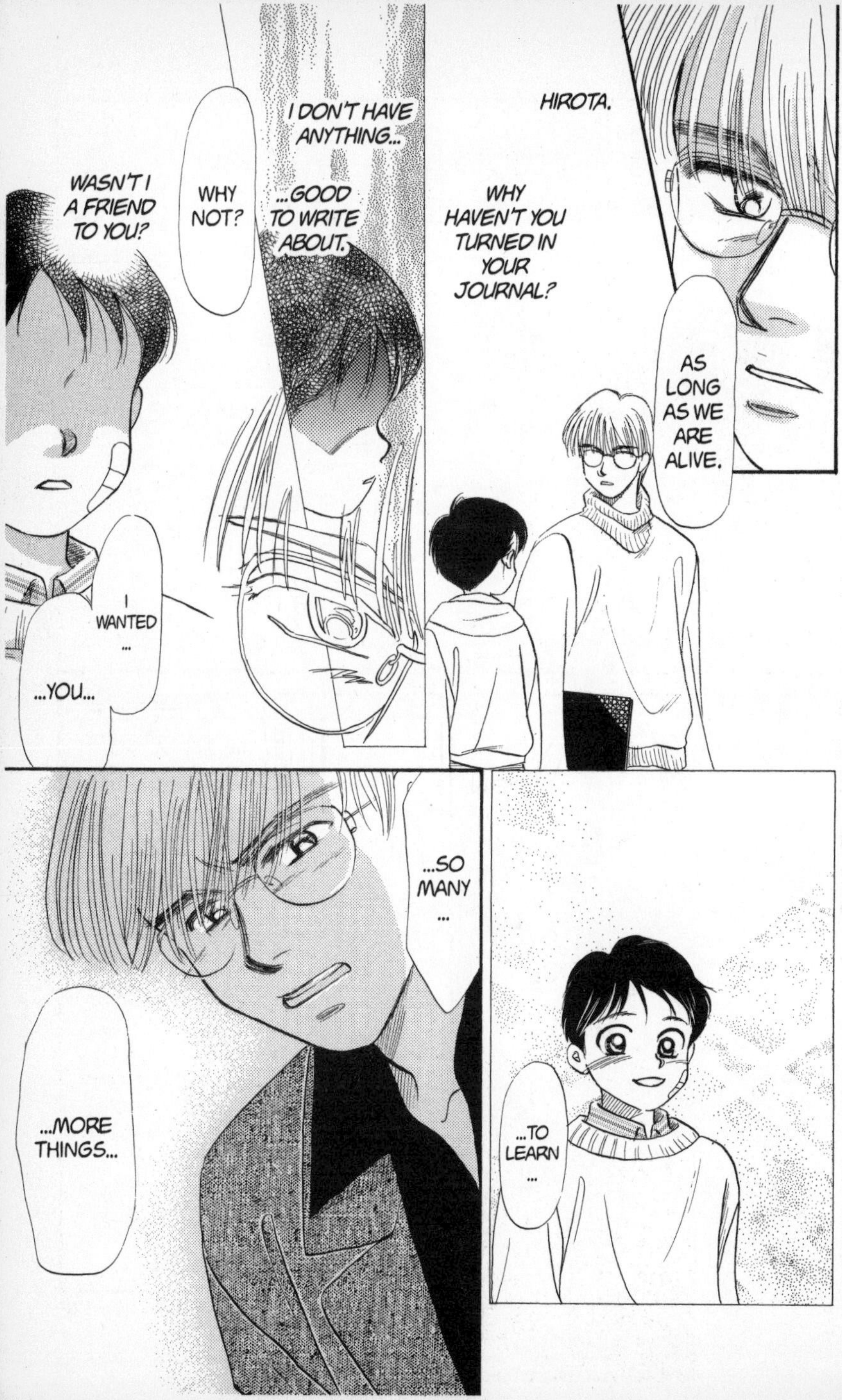
AS LONG AS WE ARE ALIVE.
HIROTA.
WHY HAVEN'T YOU TURNED IN YOUR JOURNAL?
I DON'T HAVE ANYTHING...
...GOOD TO WRITE ABOUT.
WHY NOT?
WASN'T I A FRIEND TO YOU?
I WANTED ...
...YOU...
...TO LEARN ...
...SO MANY ...
...MORE THINGS...

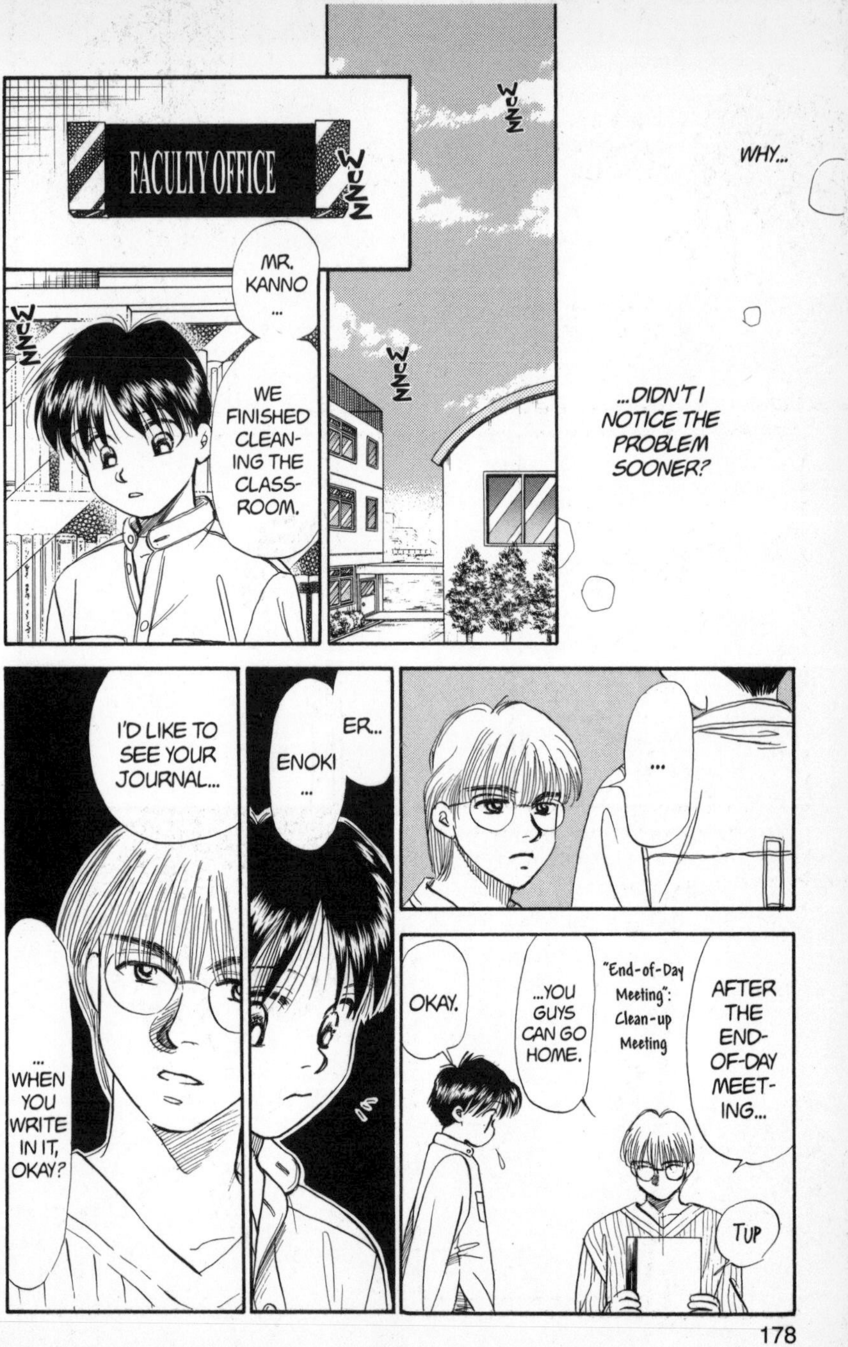
WHY...
...DIDN'T I NOTICE THE PROBLEM SOONER?
WUZZ
WUZZ
FACULTY OFFICE
WUZZ
MR. KANNO...
WE FINISHED CLEANING THE CLASSROOM.
WUZZ
...
AFTER THE END-OF-DAY MEETING...
"End-of-Day Meeting": Clean-up Meeting
...YOU GUYS CAN GO HOME.
OKAY.
TUP
ER...
ENOKI...
I'D LIKE TO SEE YOUR JOURNAL...
...WHEN YOU WRITE IN IT, OKAY?

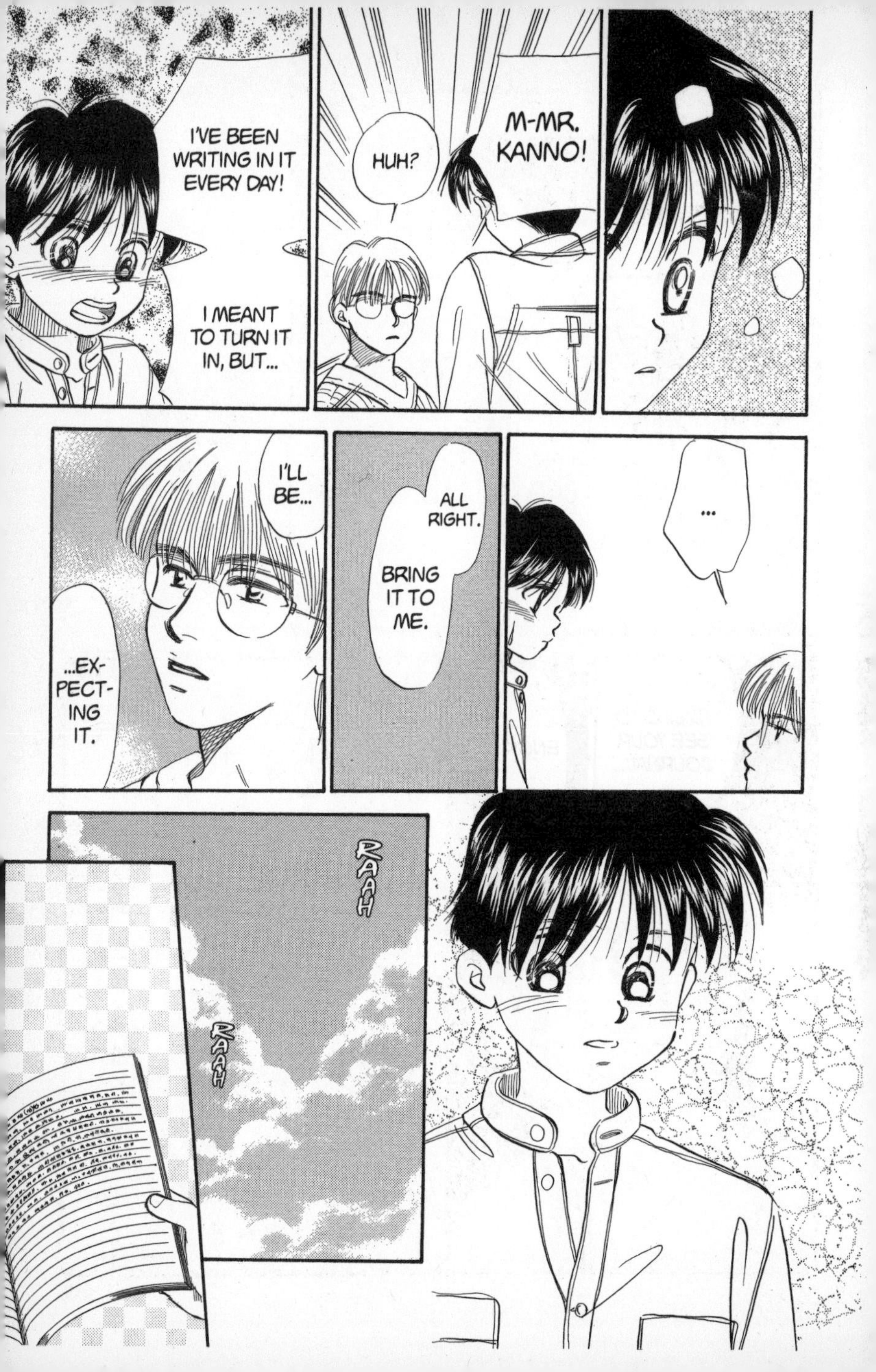
M-MR. KANNO!
HUH?
I'VE BEEN WRITING IN IT EVERY DAY!
I MEANT TO TURN IT IN, BUT...
...
ALL RIGHT.
BRING IT TO ME.
I'LL BE...
...EX-PECTING IT.
RAAAH
RAAAH

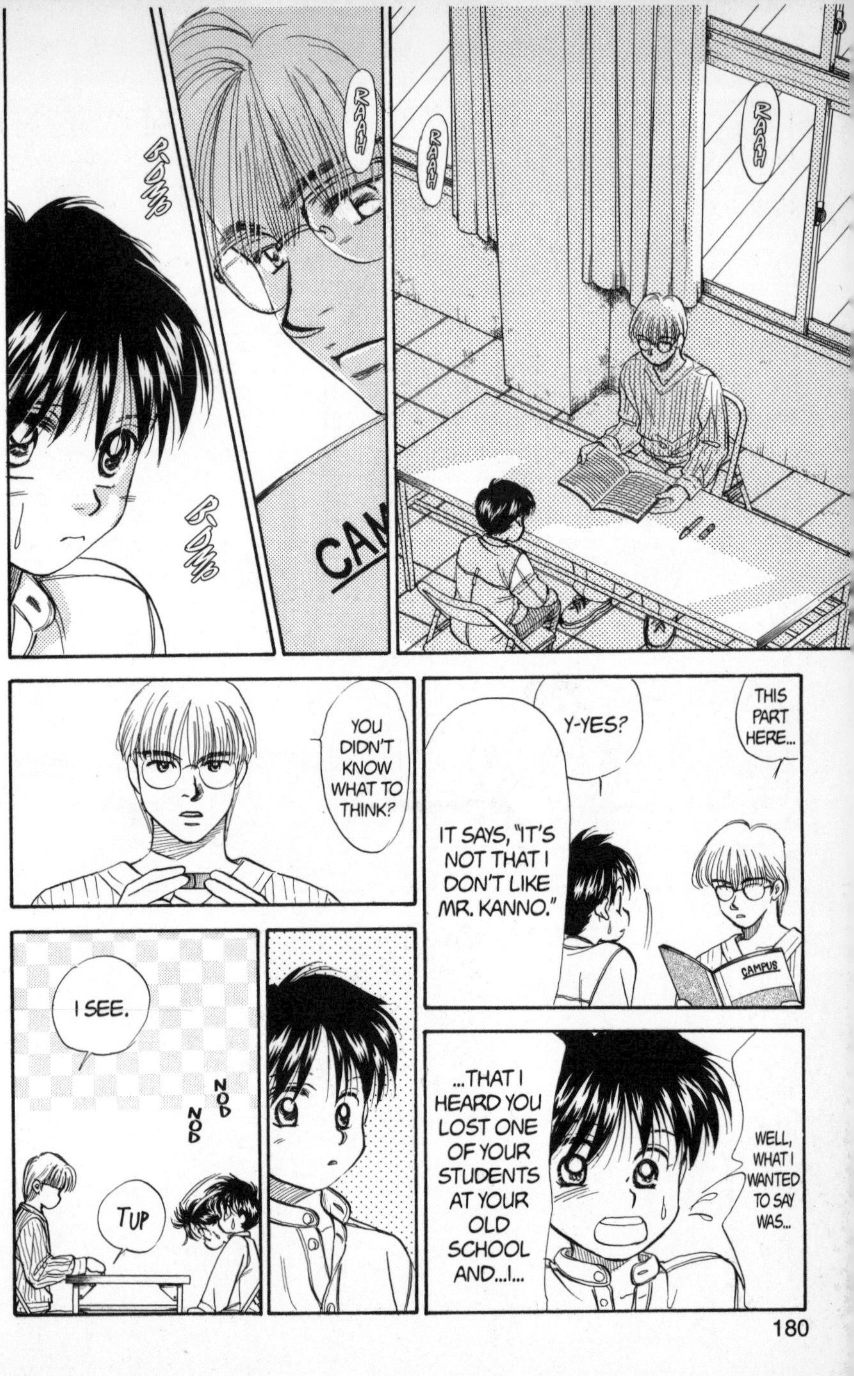
RAAAH
RAAAH
RAAAH
CAM
B-DMP
B-DMP
THIS PART HERE...
Y-YES?
IT SAYS, "IT'S NOT THAT I DON'T LIKE MR. KANNO."
YOU DIDN'T KNOW WHAT TO THINK?
WELL, WHAT I WANTED TO SAY WAS...
...THAT I HEARD YOU LOST ONE OF YOUR STUDENTS AT YOUR OLD SCHOOL AND...I...
I SEE.
NOD
NOD
TUP

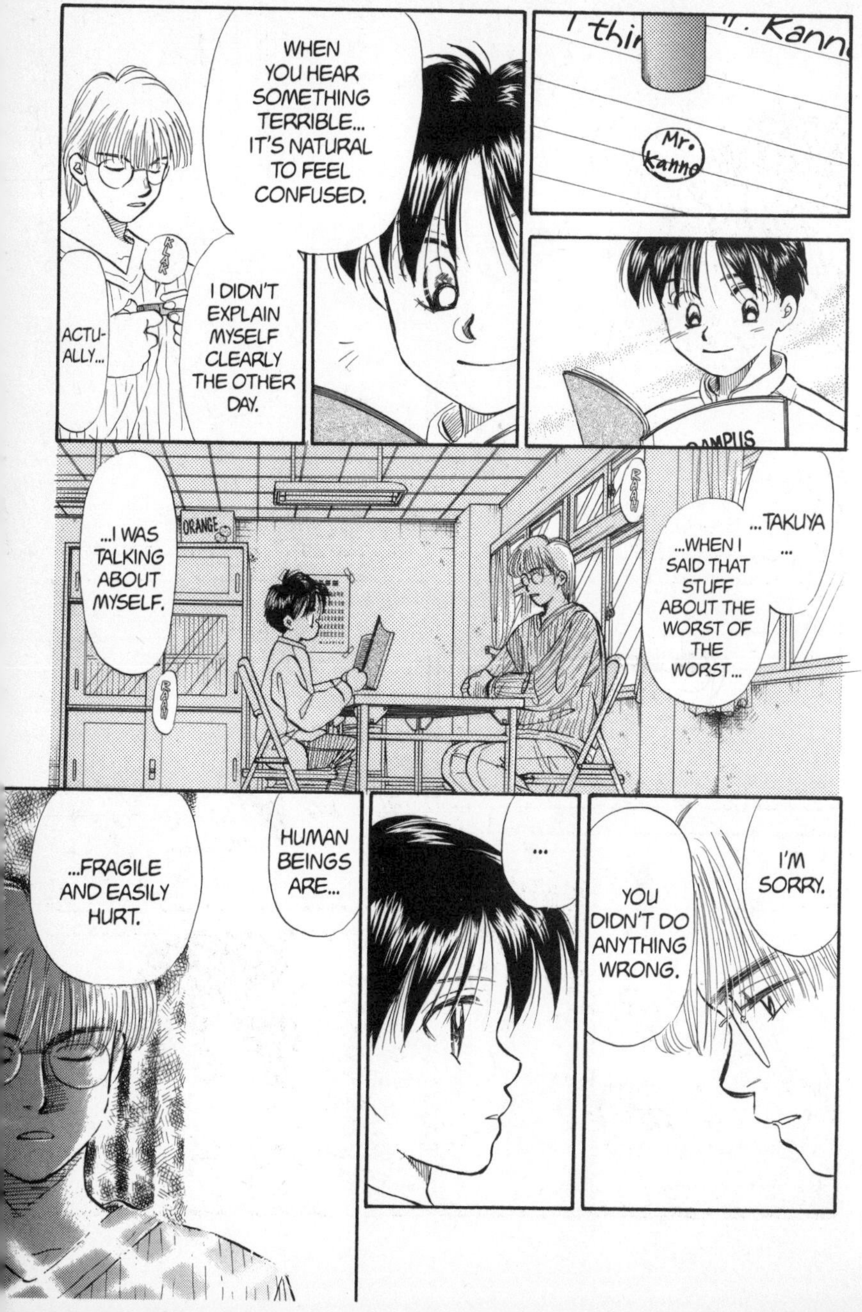

Mr. Kanno
WHEN YOU HEAR SOMETHING TERRIBLE... IT'S NATURAL TO FEEL CONFUSED.
I DIDN'T EXPLAIN MYSELF CLEARLY THE OTHER DAY.
KLAK
ACTUALLY...
...TAKUYA ...
...WHEN I SAID THAT STUFF ABOUT THE WORST OF THE WORST...
RAAH
...I WAS TALKING ABOUT MYSELF.
ORANGE
RAAH
I'M SORRY.
YOU DIDN'T DO ANYTHING WRONG.
...
HUMAN BEINGS ARE...
...FRAGILE AND EASILY HURT.

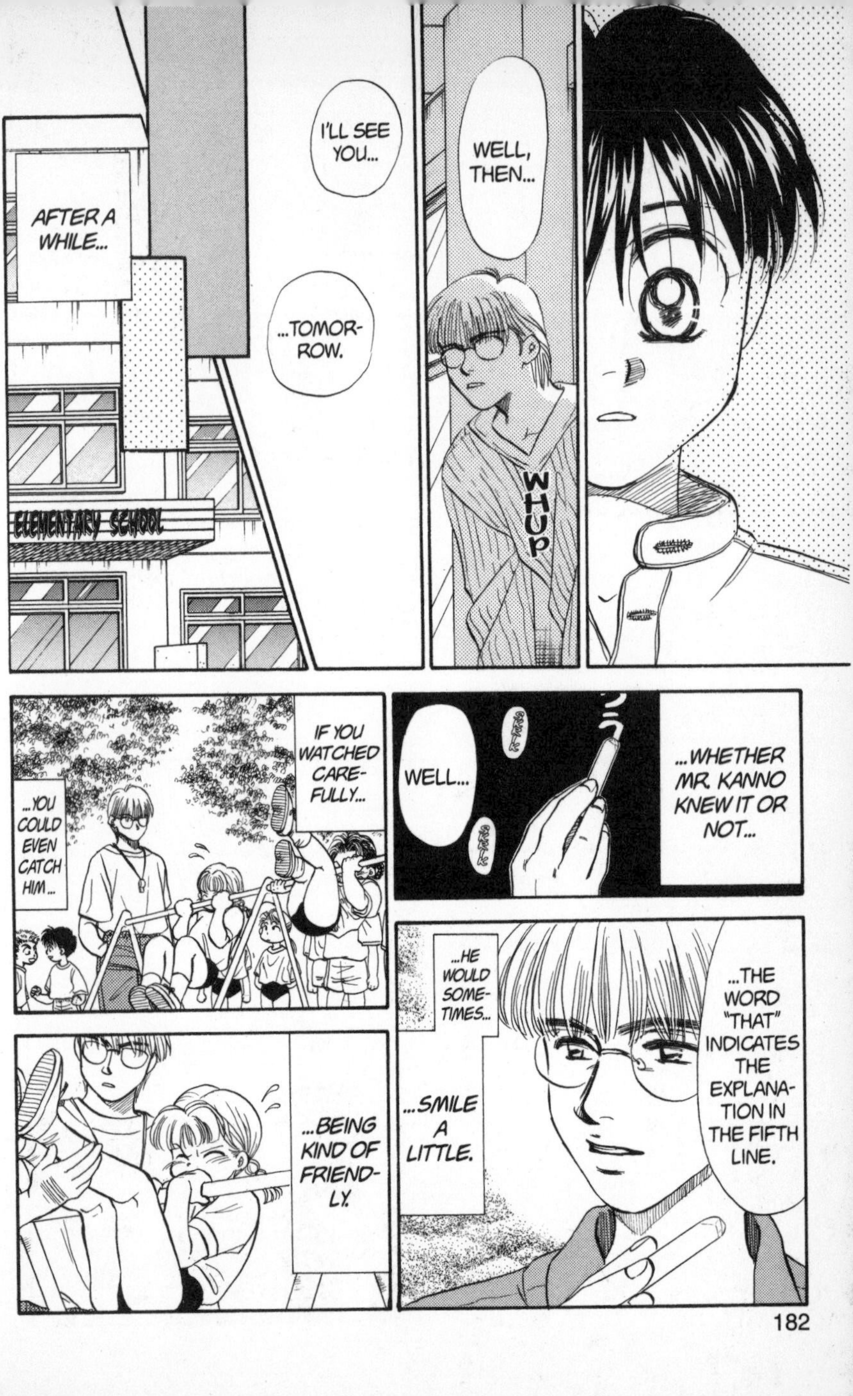
WELL, THEN...
WHUP
I'LL SEE YOU...
...TOMORROW.
AFTER A WHILE...
ELEMENTARY SCHOOL
...WHETHER MR. KANNO KNEW IT OR NOT...
WELL...
SKRIK
SKRIK
IF YOU WATCHED CAREFULLY...
...YOU COULD EVEN CATCH HIM...
...BEING KIND OF FRIENDLY.
...THE WORD "THAT" INDICATES THE EXPLANATION IN THE FIFTH LINE.
...HE WOULD SOMETIMES...
...SMILE A LITTLE.

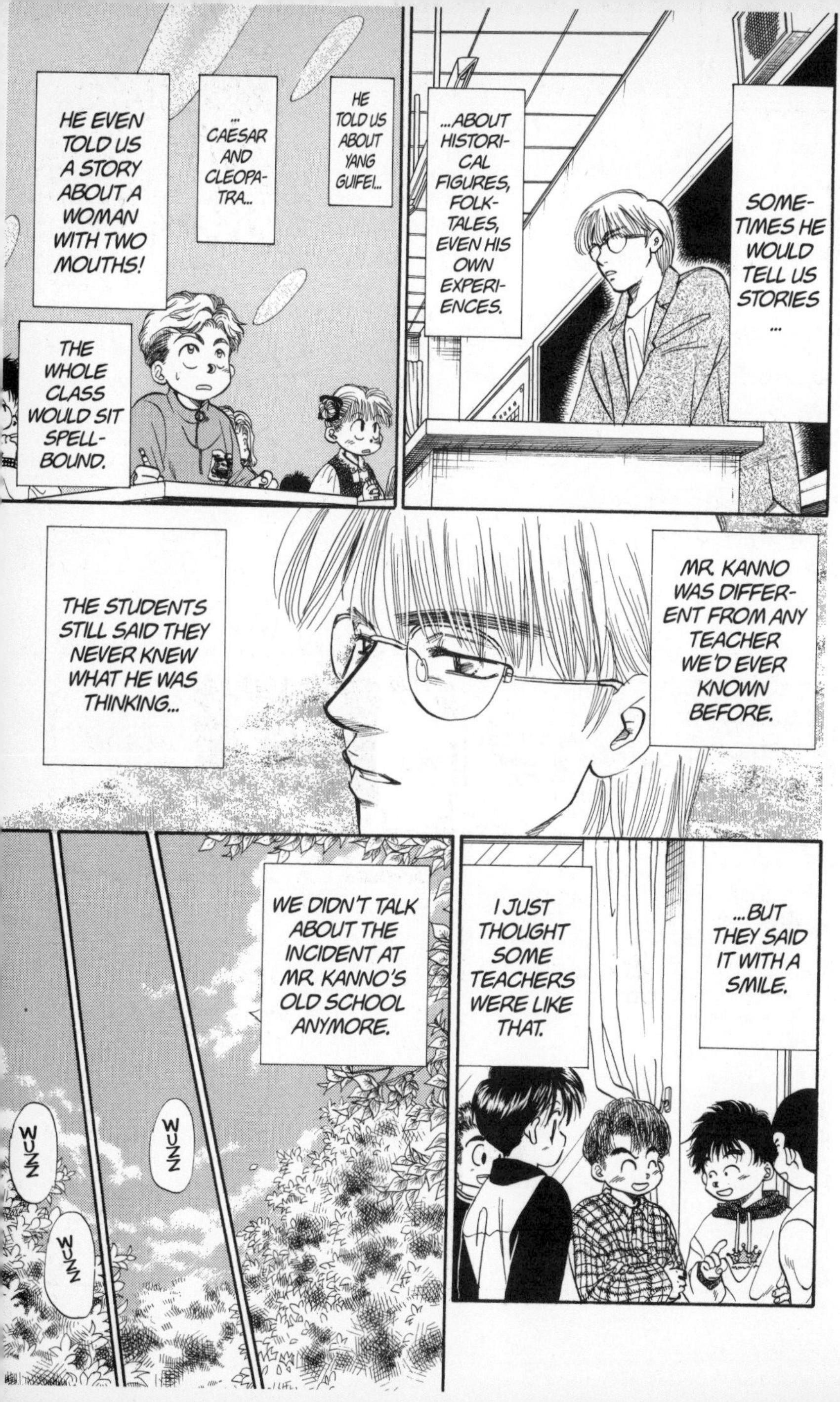
SOMETIMES HE WOULD TELL US STORIES...
...ABOUT HISTORICAL FIGURES, FOLKTALES, EVEN HIS OWN EXPERIENCES.
HE TOLD US ABOUT YANG GUIFEI...
...CAESAR AND CLEOPATRA...
HE EVEN TOLD US A STORY ABOUT A WOMAN WITH TWO MOUTHS!
THE WHOLE CLASS WOULD SIT SPELLBOUND.
MR. KANNO WAS DIFFERENT FROM ANY TEACHER WE'D EVER KNOWN BEFORE.
THE STUDENTS STILL SAID THEY NEVER KNEW WHAT HE WAS THINKING...
...BUT THEY SAID IT WITH A SMILE.
I JUST THOUGHT SOME TEACHERS WERE LIKE THAT.
WE DIDN'T TALK ABOUT THE INCIDENT AT MR. KANNO'S OLD SCHOOL ANYMORE.
WUZZ
WUZZ
WUZZ

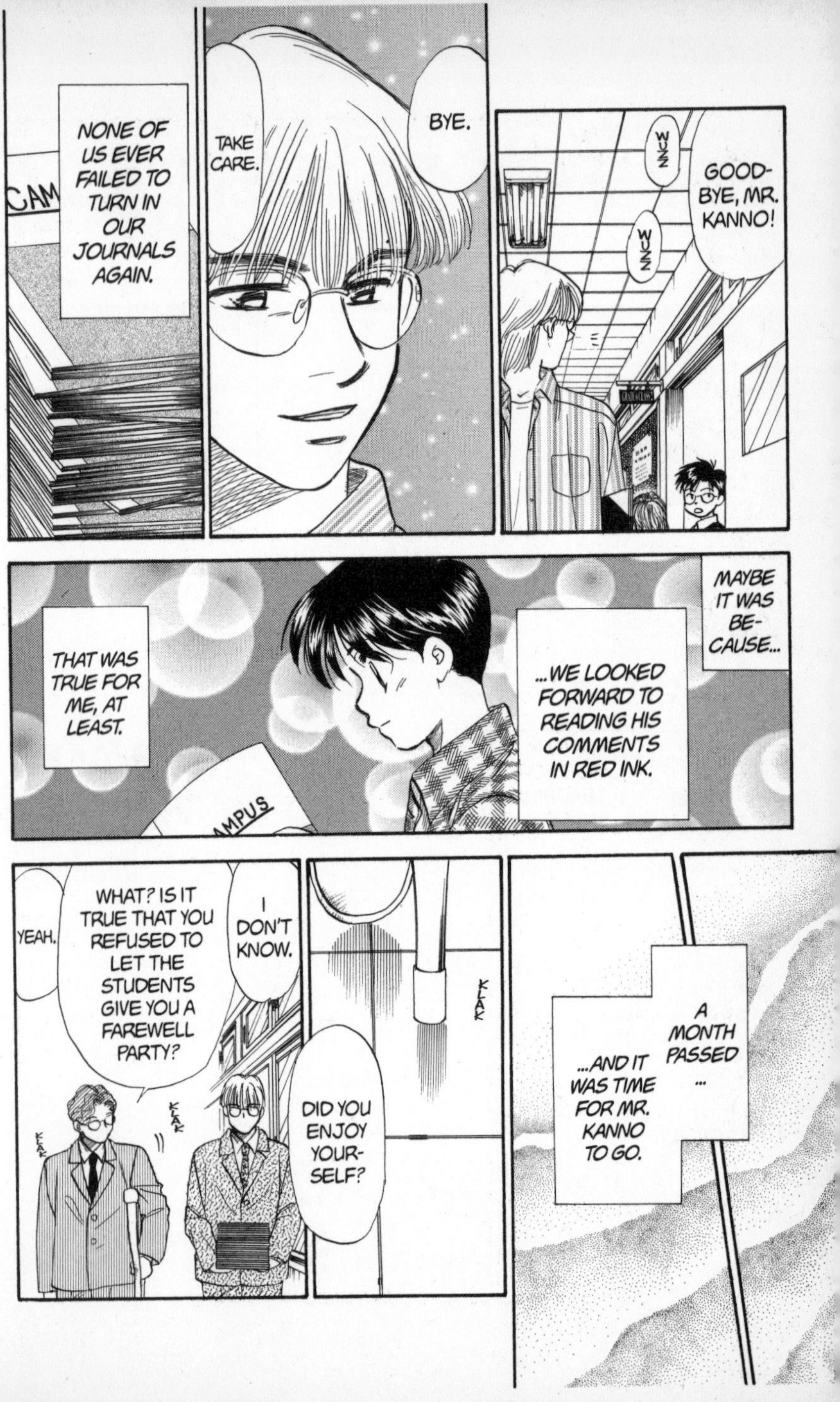
GOOD-BYE, MR. KANNO!
WUZZ
WUZZ
BYE.
TAKE CARE.
NONE OF US EVER FAILED TO TURN IN OUR JOURNALS AGAIN.
MAYBE IT WAS BE-CAUSE...
...WE LOOKED FORWARD TO READING HIS COMMENTS IN RED INK.
THAT WAS TRUE FOR ME, AT LEAST.
A MONTH PASSED ...
...AND IT WAS TIME FOR MR. KANNO TO GO.
KLAK
DID YOU ENJOY YOURSELF?
I DON'T KNOW.
WHAT? IS IT TRUE THAT YOU REFUSED TO LET THE STUDENTS GIVE YOU A FAREWELL PARTY?
YEAH.
KLAK
KLAK

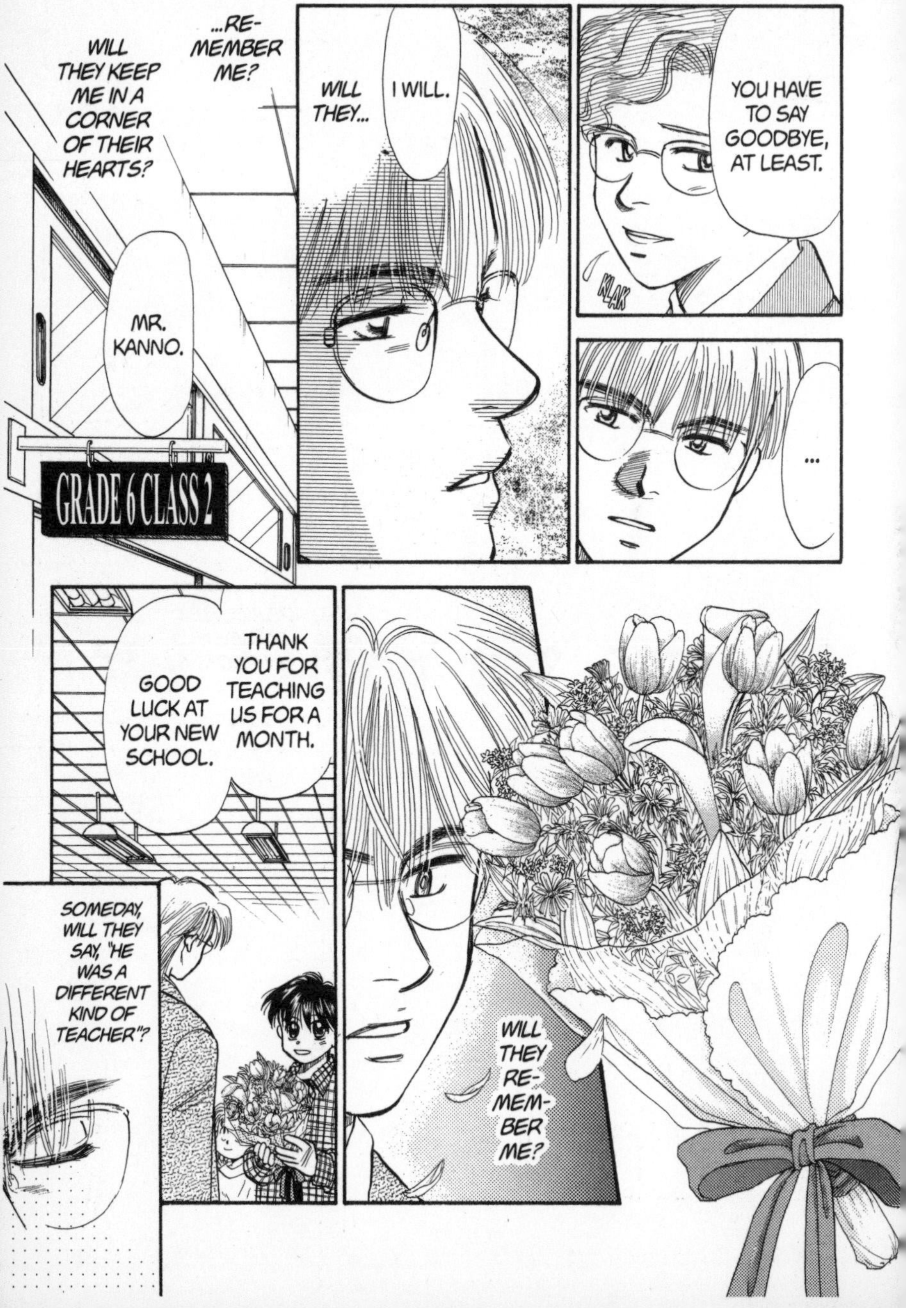
YOU HAVE TO SAY GOODBYE, AT LEAST.
KLAK
...
I WILL.
WILL THEY...
...RE-MEMBER ME?
WILL THEY KEEP ME IN A CORNER OF THEIR HEARTS?
MR. KANNO.
GRADE 6 CLASS 2
WILL THEY RE-MEM-BER ME?
THANK YOU FOR TEACHING US FOR A MONTH.
GOOD LUCK AT YOUR NEW SCHOOL.
SOMEDAY, WILL THEY SAY, "HE WAS A DIFFERENT KIND OF TEACHER"?

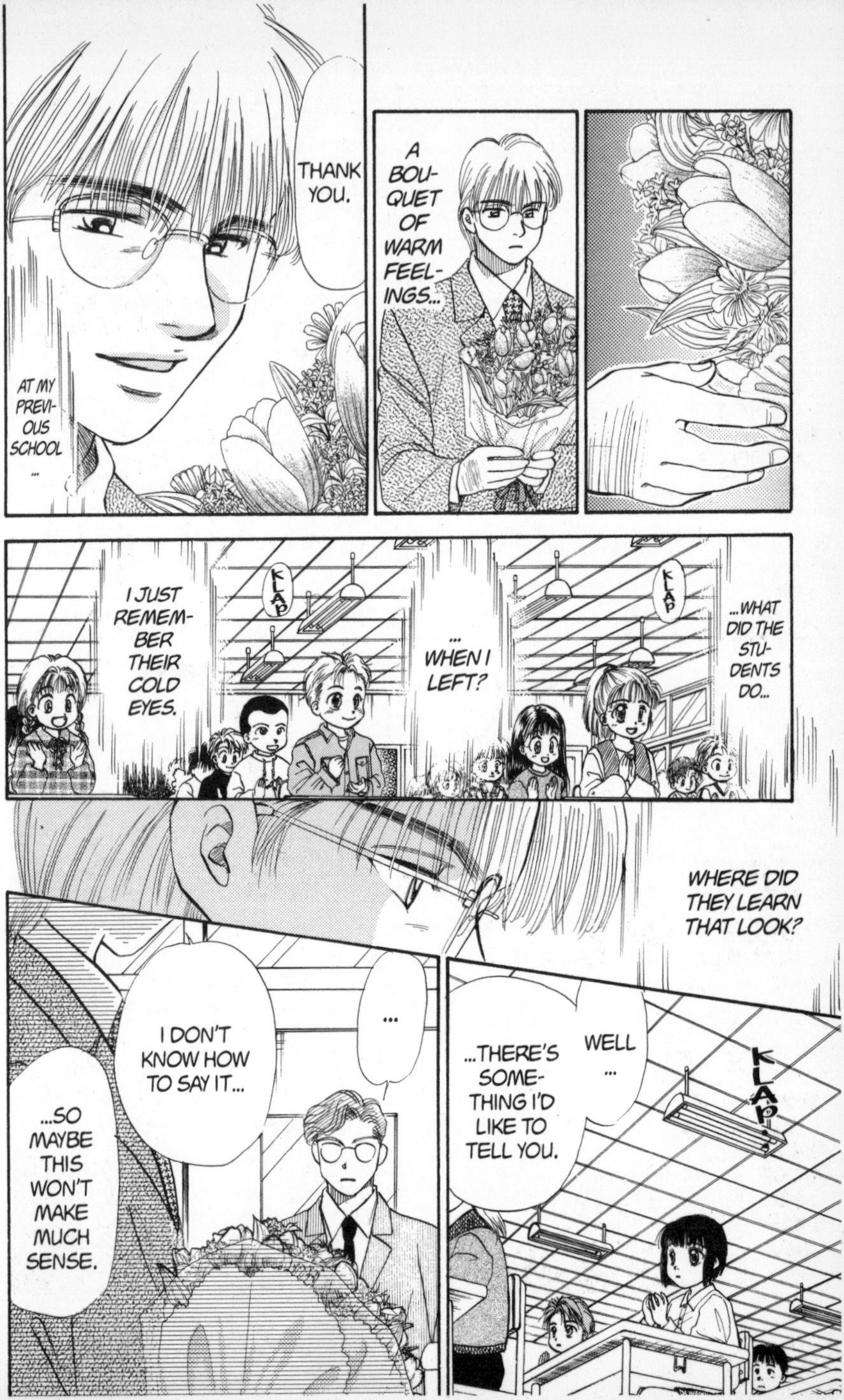
A BOUQUET OF WARM FEELINGS...
THANK YOU.
AT MY PREVIOUS SCHOOL ...
...WHAT DID THE STUDENTS DO...
KLAP
... WHEN I LEFT?
KLAP
I JUST REMEMBER THEIR COLD EYES.
WHERE DID THEY LEARN THAT LOOK?
KLAP
WELL ...
...THERE'S SOMETHING I'D LIKE TO TELL YOU.
...
I DON'T KNOW HOW TO SAY IT...
...SO MAYBE THIS WON'T MAKE MUCH SENSE.

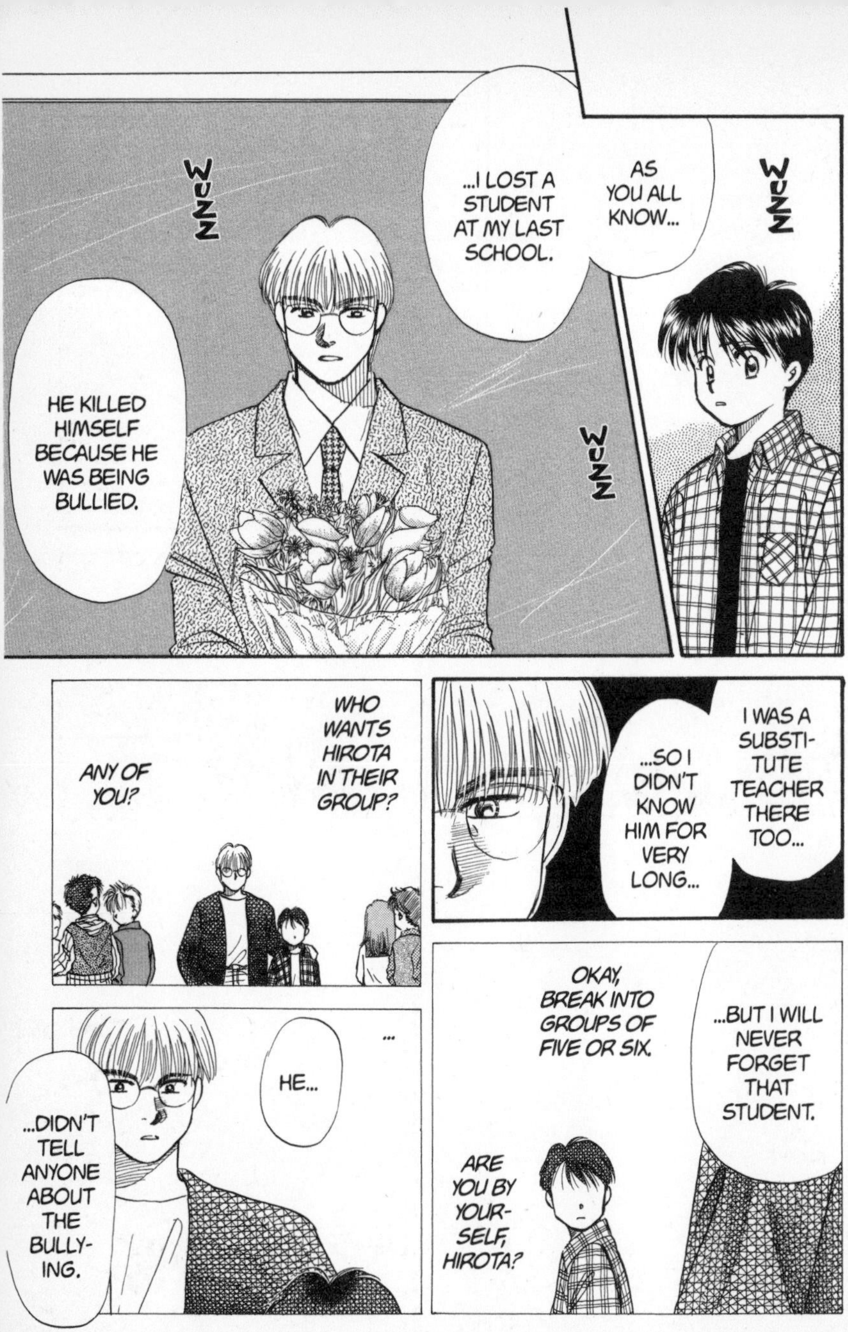
WUZZ
AS YOU ALL KNOW...
...I LOST A STUDENT AT MY LAST SCHOOL.
WUZZ
WUZZ
HE KILLED HIMSELF BECAUSE HE WAS BEING BULLIED.
I WAS A SUBSTITUTE TEACHER THERE TOO...
...SO I DIDN'T KNOW HIM FOR VERY LONG...
WHO WANTS HIROTA IN THEIR GROUP?
ANY OF YOU?
...BUT I WILL NEVER FORGET THAT STUDENT.
OKAY, BREAK INTO GROUPS OF FIVE OR SIX.
ARE YOU BY YOURSELF, HIROTA?
...
HE...
...DIDN'T TELL ANYONE ABOUT THE BULLYING.

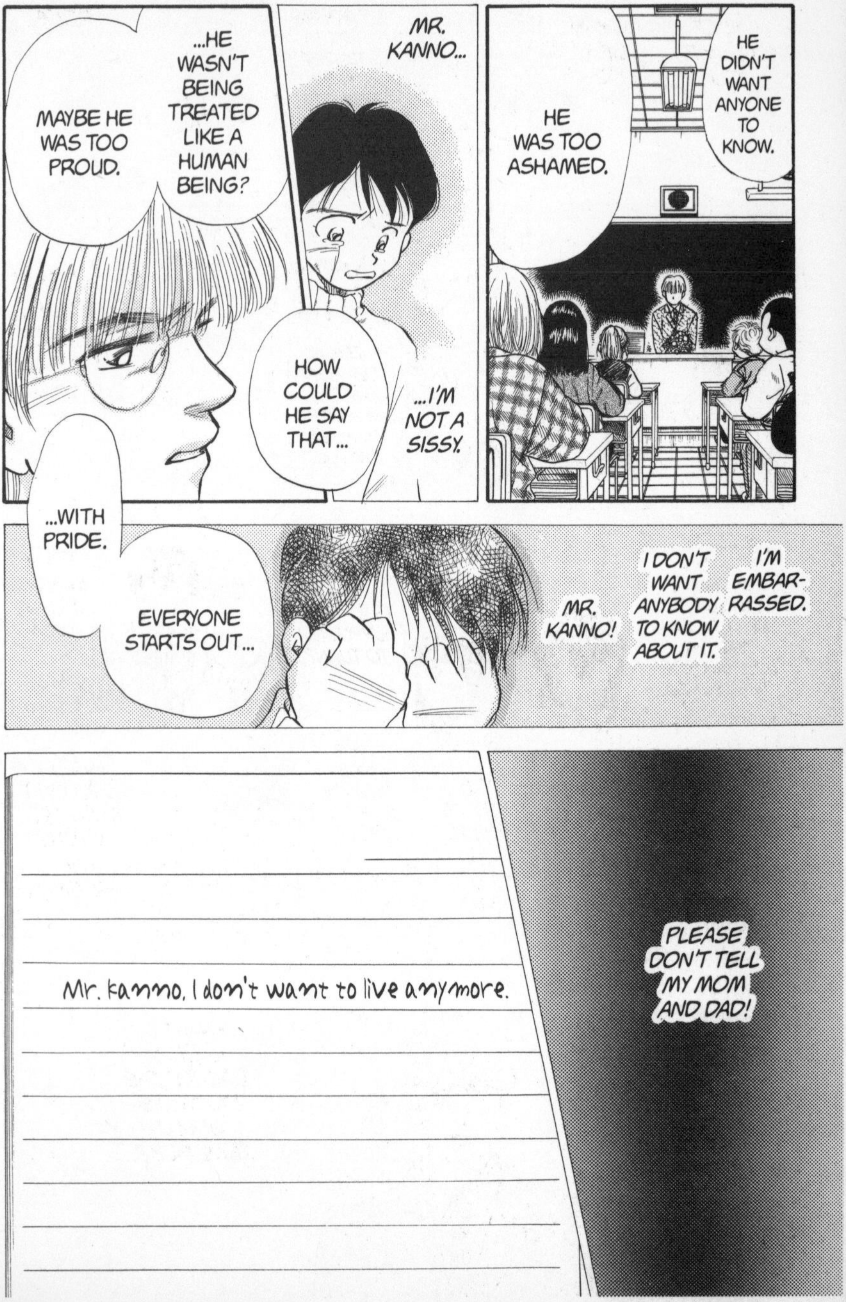
HE DIDN'T WANT ANYONE TO KNOW.
HE WAS TOO ASHAMED.
MR. KANNO...
...I'M NOT A SISSY.
HOW COULD HE SAY THAT...
...HE WASN'T BEING TREATED LIKE A HUMAN BEING?
MAYBE HE WAS TOO PROUD.
I'M EMBAR-RASSED.
I DON'T WANT ANYBODY TO KNOW ABOUT IT.
MR. KANNO!
EVERYONE STARTS OUT...
...WITH PRIDE.
PLEASE DON'T TELL MY MOM AND DAD!
Mr. kanno, I don't want to live anymore.

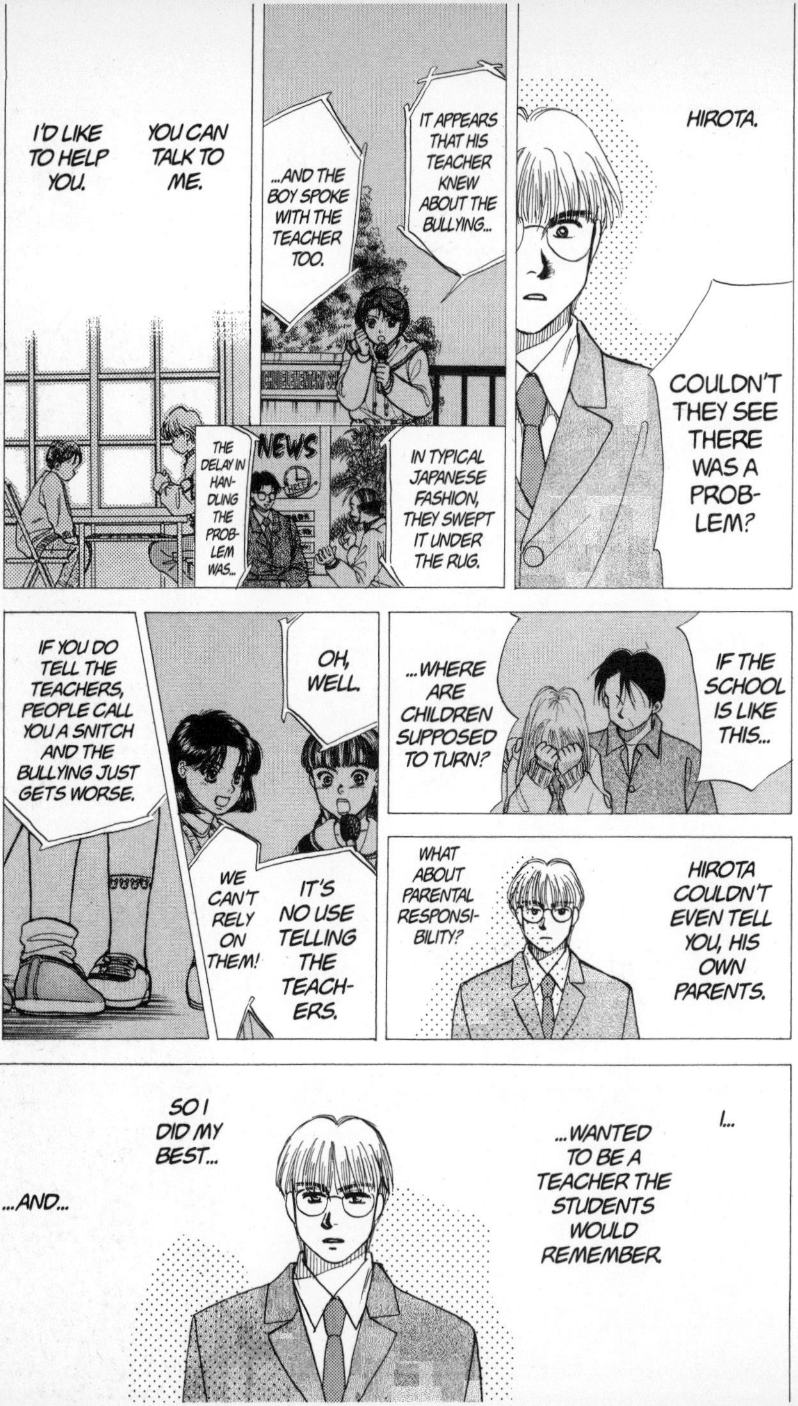
HIROTA.
COULDN'T THEY SEE THERE WAS A PROBLEM?
IT APPEARS THAT HIS TEACHER KNEW ABOUT THE BULLYING...
...AND THE BOY SPOKE WITH THE TEACHER TOO.
IN TYPICAL JAPANESE FASHION, THEY SWEPT IT UNDER THE RUG.
THE DELAY IN HAN-DLING THE PROB-LEM WAS...
NEWS
YOU CAN TALK TO ME.
I'D LIKE TO HELP YOU.
IF THE SCHOOL IS LIKE THIS...
...WHERE ARE CHILDREN SUPPOSED TO TURN?
HIROTA COULDN'T EVEN TELL YOU, HIS OWN PARENTS.
WHAT ABOUT PARENTAL RESPONSI-BILITY?
OH, WELL.
IT'S NO USE TELLING THE TEACH-ERS.
WE CAN'T RELY ON THEM!
IF YOU DO TELL THE TEACHERS, PEOPLE CALL YOU A SNITCH AND THE BULLYING JUST GETS WORSE.
I...
...WANTED TO BE A TEACHER THE STUDENTS WOULD REMEMBER.
SO I DID MY BEST...
...AND...

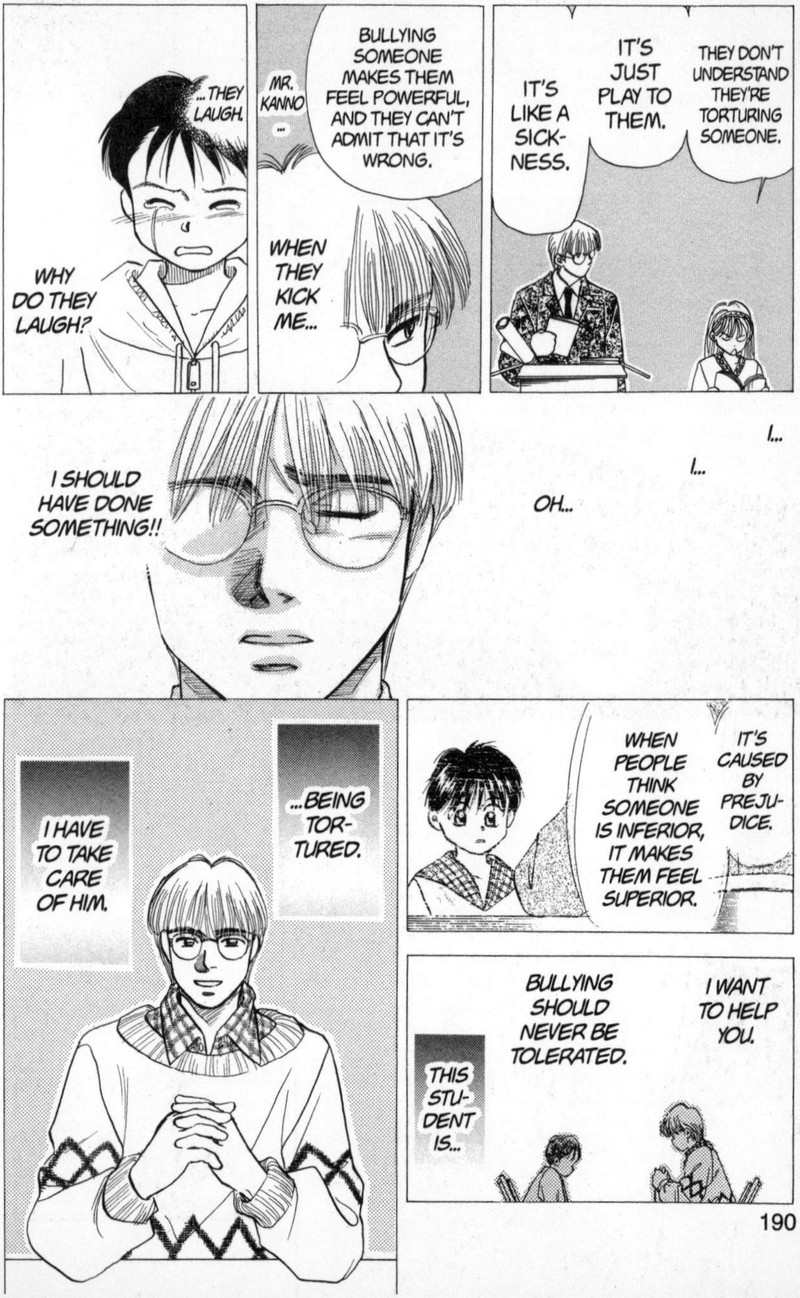
THEY DON'T UNDERSTAND THEY'RE TORTURING SOMEONE.
IT'S JUST PLAY TO THEM.
IT'S LIKE A SICK-NESS.
BULLYING SOMEONE MAKES THEM FEEL POWERFUL, AND THEY CAN'T ADMIT THAT IT'S WRONG.
MR. KANNO ...
WHEN THEY KICK ME...
...THEY LAUGH.
WHY DO THEY LAUGH?
I...
I...
OH...
I SHOULD HAVE DONE SOMETHING!!
IT'S CAUSED BY PREJU-DICE.
WHEN PEOPLE THINK SOMEONE IS INFERIOR, IT MAKES THEM FEEL SUPERIOR.
I WANT TO HELP YOU.
BULLYING SHOULD NEVER BE TOLERATED.
THIS STU-DENT IS...
...BEING TOR-TURED.
I HAVE TO TAKE CARE OF HIM.

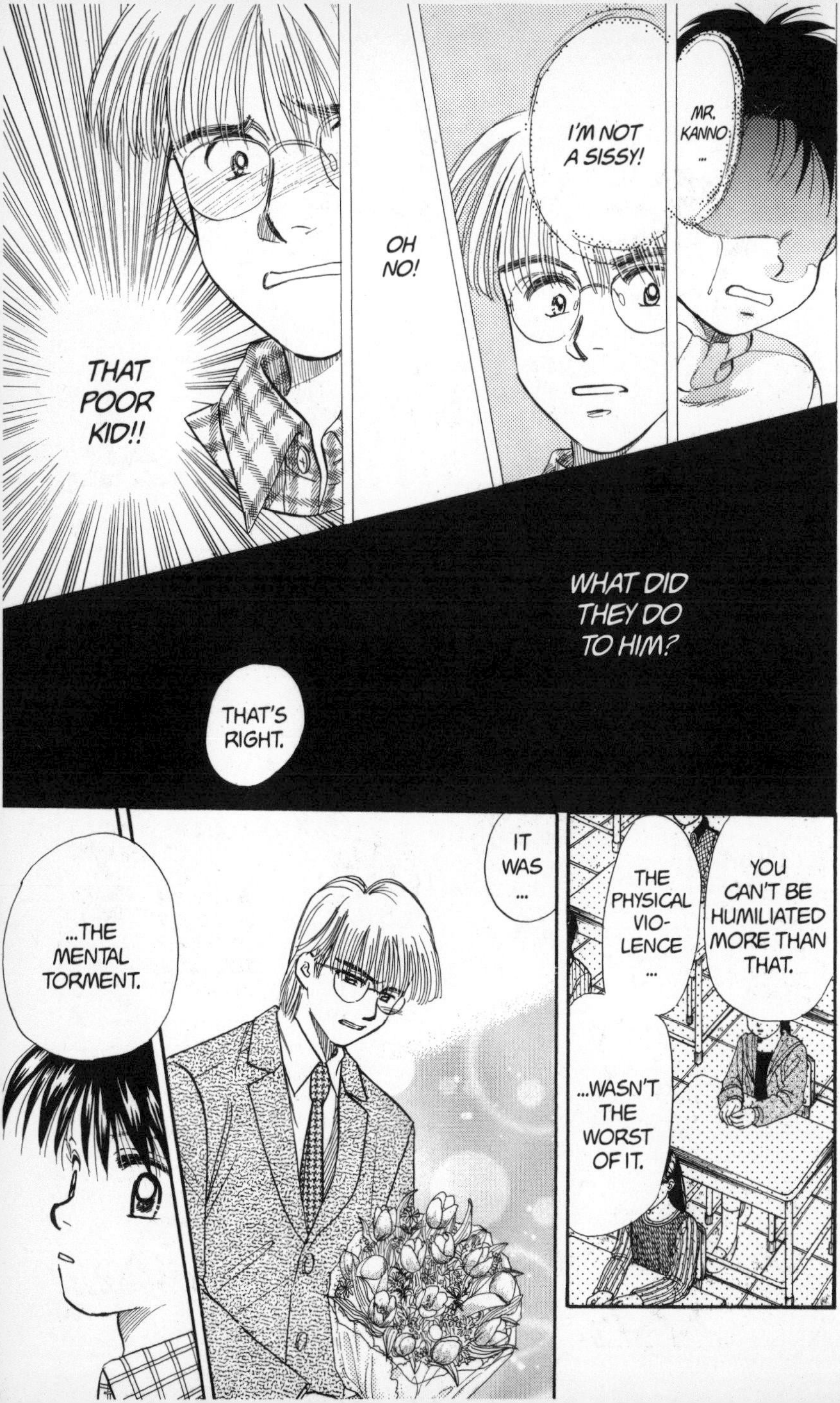
MR. KANNO ...
I'M NOT A SISSY!
OH NO!
THAT POOR KID!!
WHAT DID THEY DO TO HIM?
THAT'S RIGHT.
YOU CAN'T BE HUMILIATED MORE THAN THAT.
THE PHYSICAL VIO-LENCE ...
...WASN'T THE WORST OF IT.
IT WAS ...
...THE MENTAL TORMENT.

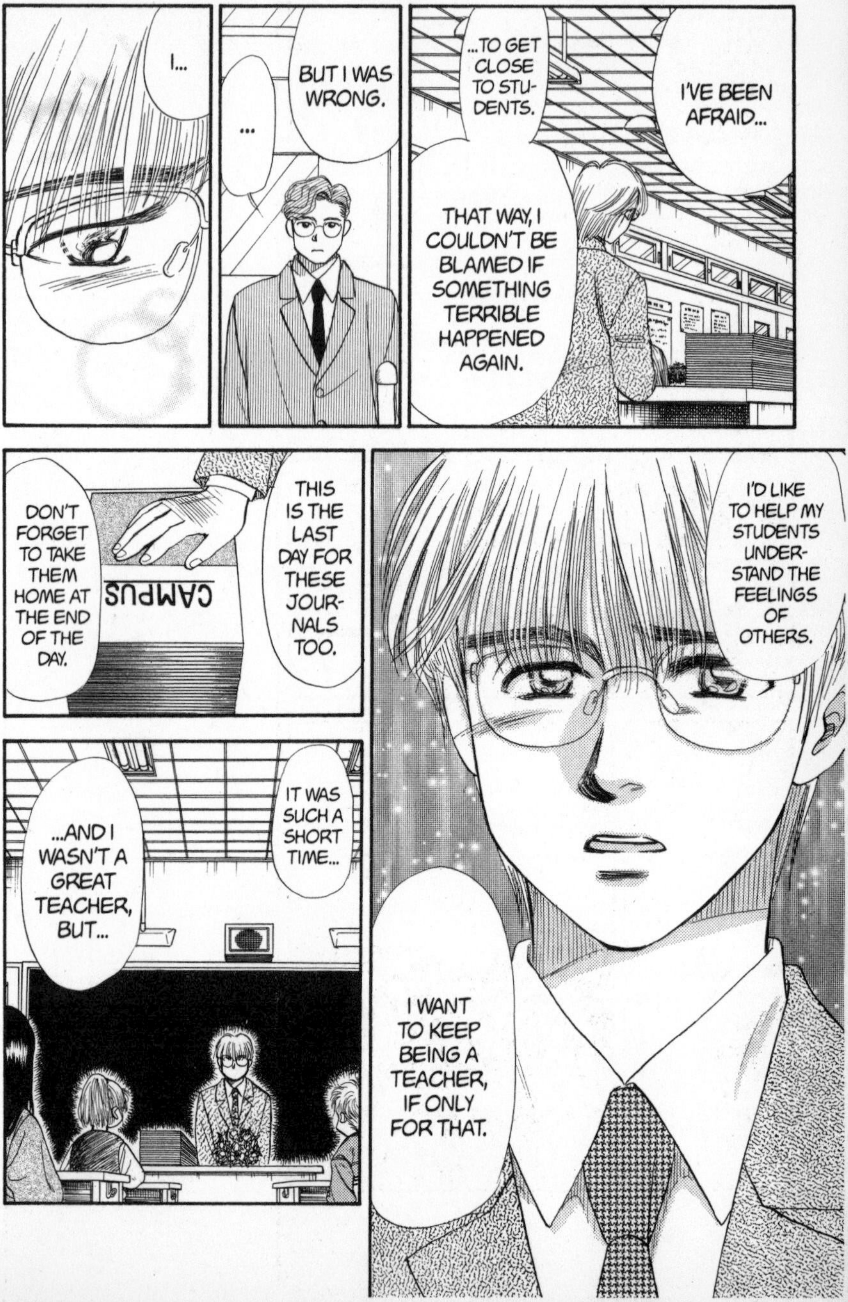
I'VE BEEN AFRAID...
...TO GET CLOSE TO STU-DENTS.
THAT WAY, I COULDN'T BE BLAMED IF SOMETHING TERRIBLE HAPPENED AGAIN.
BUT I WAS WRONG.
...
I...
I'D LIKE TO HELP MY STUDENTS UNDER-STAND THE FEELINGS OF OTHERS.
I WANT TO KEEP BEING A TEACHER, IF ONLY FOR THAT.
THIS IS THE LAST DAY FOR THESE JOUR-NALS TOO.
DON'T FORGET TO TAKE THEM HOME AT THE END OF THE DAY.
CAMPUS
IT WAS SUCH A SHORT TIME...
...AND I WASN'T A GREAT TEACHER, BUT...

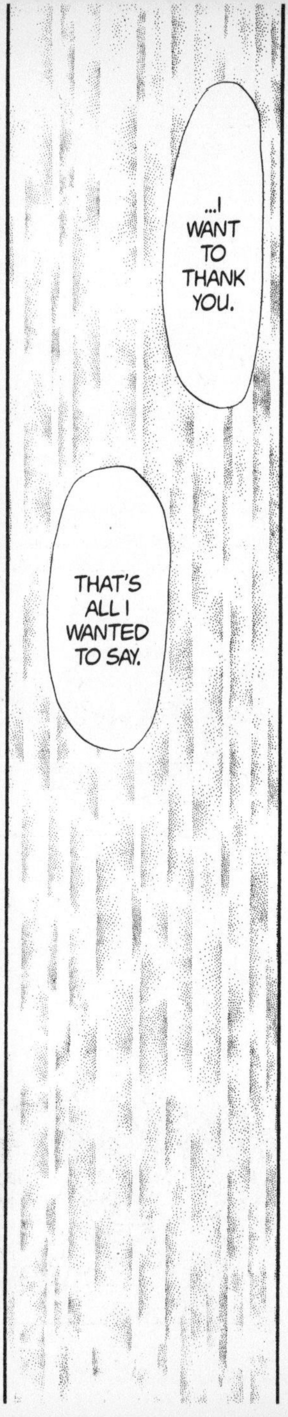
...I WANT TO THANK YOU.
THAT'S ALL I WANTED TO SAY.

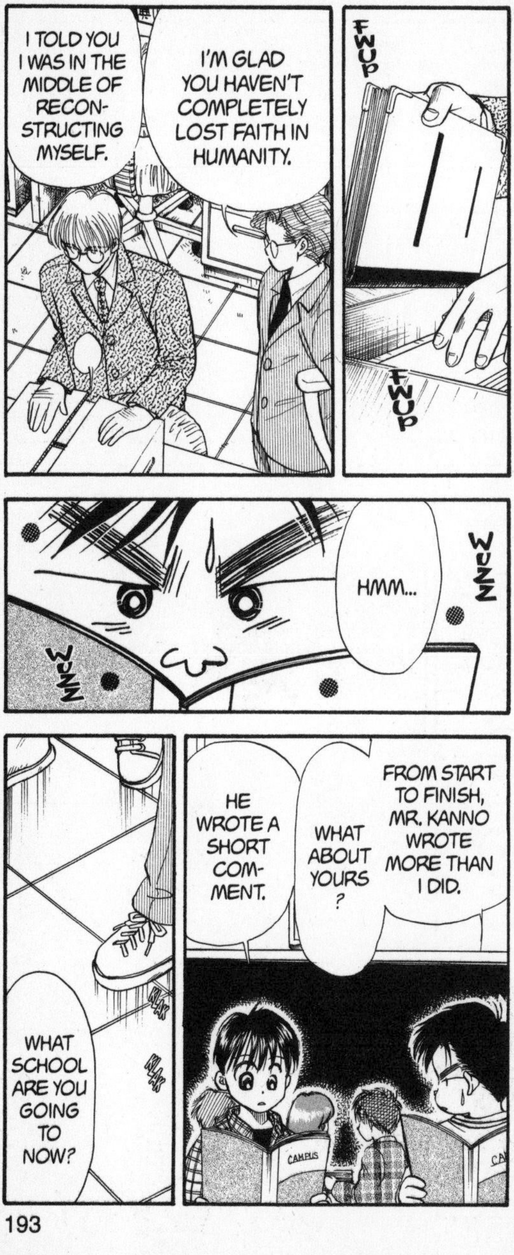
FWUP
FWUP
I'M GLAD YOU HAVEN'T COMPLETELY LOST FAITH IN HUMANITY.
I TOLD YOU I WAS IN THE MIDDLE OF RECON-STRUCTING MYSELF.
WUZZ
HMM...
WUZZ
FROM START TO FINISH, MR. KANNO WROTE MORE THAN I DID.
WHAT ABOUT YOURS?
HE WROTE A SHORT COM-MENT.
CAMPUS
KLAK
KLAK
WHAT SCHOOL ARE YOU GOING TO NOW?

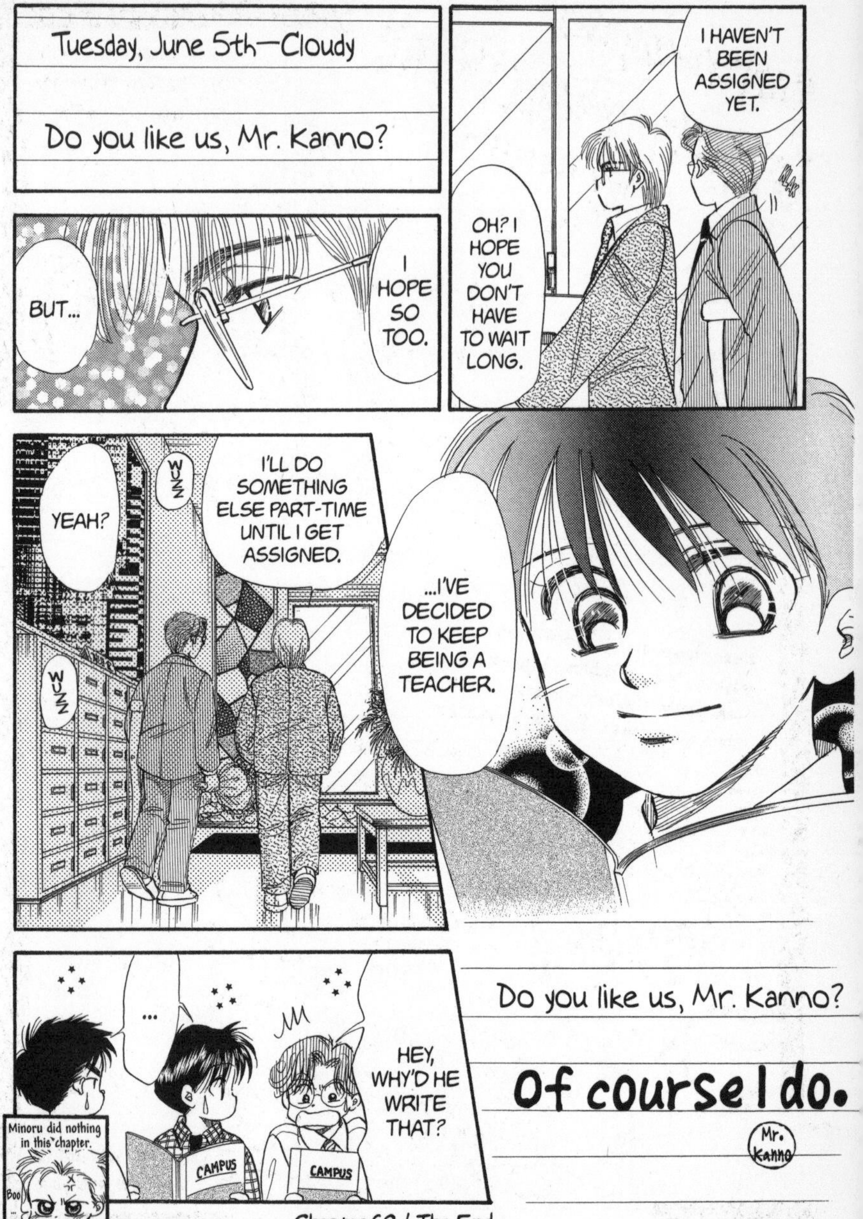
I HAVEN'T BEEN ASSIGNED YET.
KLAK
OH? I HOPE YOU DON'T HAVE TO WAIT LONG.
Tuesday, June 5th—Cloudy
Do you like us, Mr. Kanno?
I HOPE SO TOO.
BUT...
...I'VE DECIDED TO KEEP BEING A TEACHER.
WUZZ
I'LL DO SOMETHING ELSE PART-TIME UNTIL I GET ASSIGNED.
YEAH?
WUZZ
Do you like us, Mr. Kanno?
Of course I do.
Mr. Kanno
HEY, WHY'D HE WRITE THAT?
CAMPUS
...
CAMPUS
Minoru did nothing in this chapter.
Boo...

Chapter 68 / The End

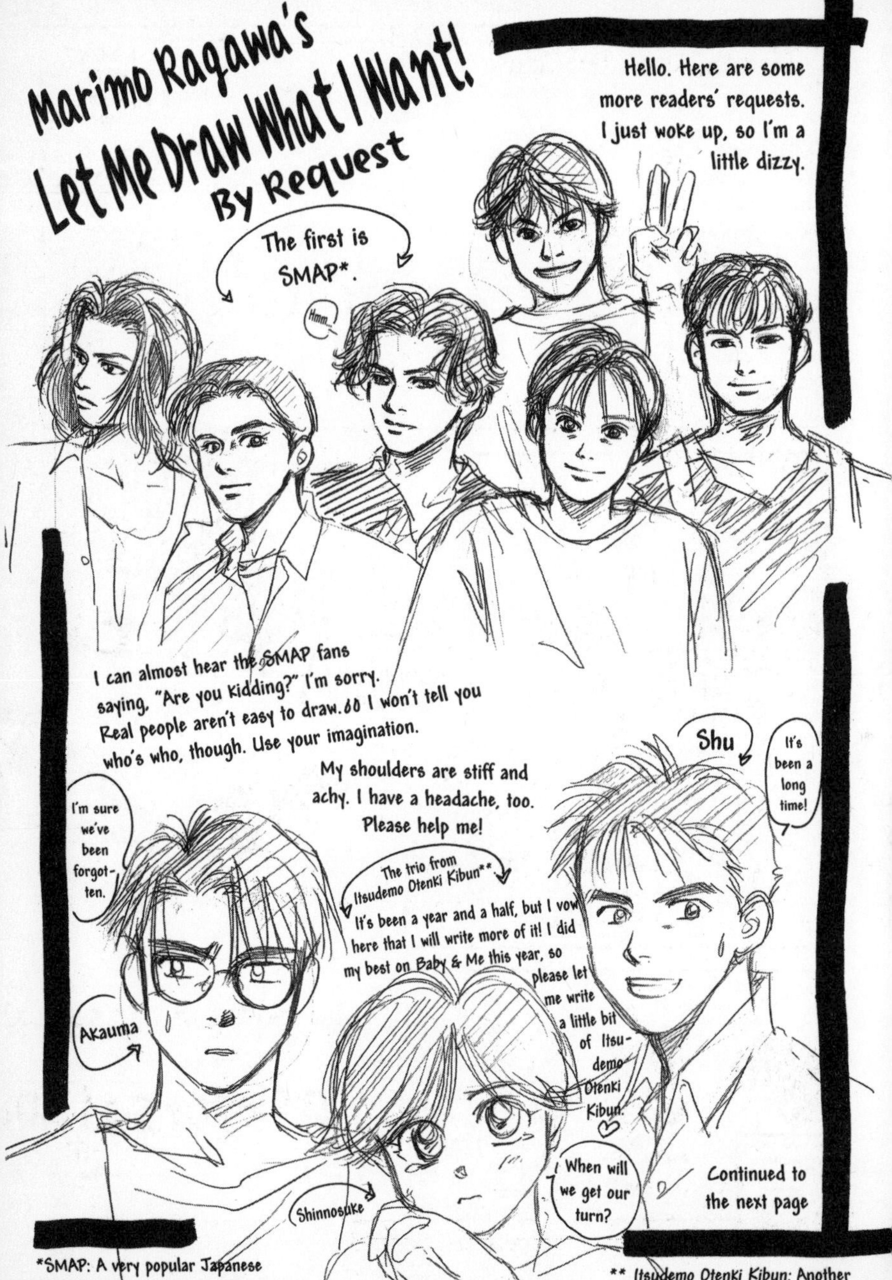
Marimo Ragawa's
Let Me Draw What I Want!
By Request
Hello. Here are some more readers' requests. I just woke up, so I'm a little dizzy.
The first is SMAP*.
Hmm...
I can almost hear the SMAP fans saying, "Are you kidding?" I'm sorry. Real people aren't easy to draw. So I won't tell you who's who, though. Use your imagination.
My shoulders are stiff and achy. I have a headache, too. Please help me!
Shu
It's been a long time!
I'm sure we've been forgot-ten.
The trio from Itsudemo Otenki Kibun**
It's been a year and a half, but I vow here that I will write more of it! I did my best on Baby & Me this year, so please let me write a little bit of Itsudemo Otenki Kibun.
Akauma
Shinnosuke
When will we get our turn?
Continued to the next page

*SMAP: A very popular Japanese idol group. The name stands for "Sports and Music Assemble People."

** *Itsudemo Otenki Kibun*: Another manga by Marimo Ragawa.

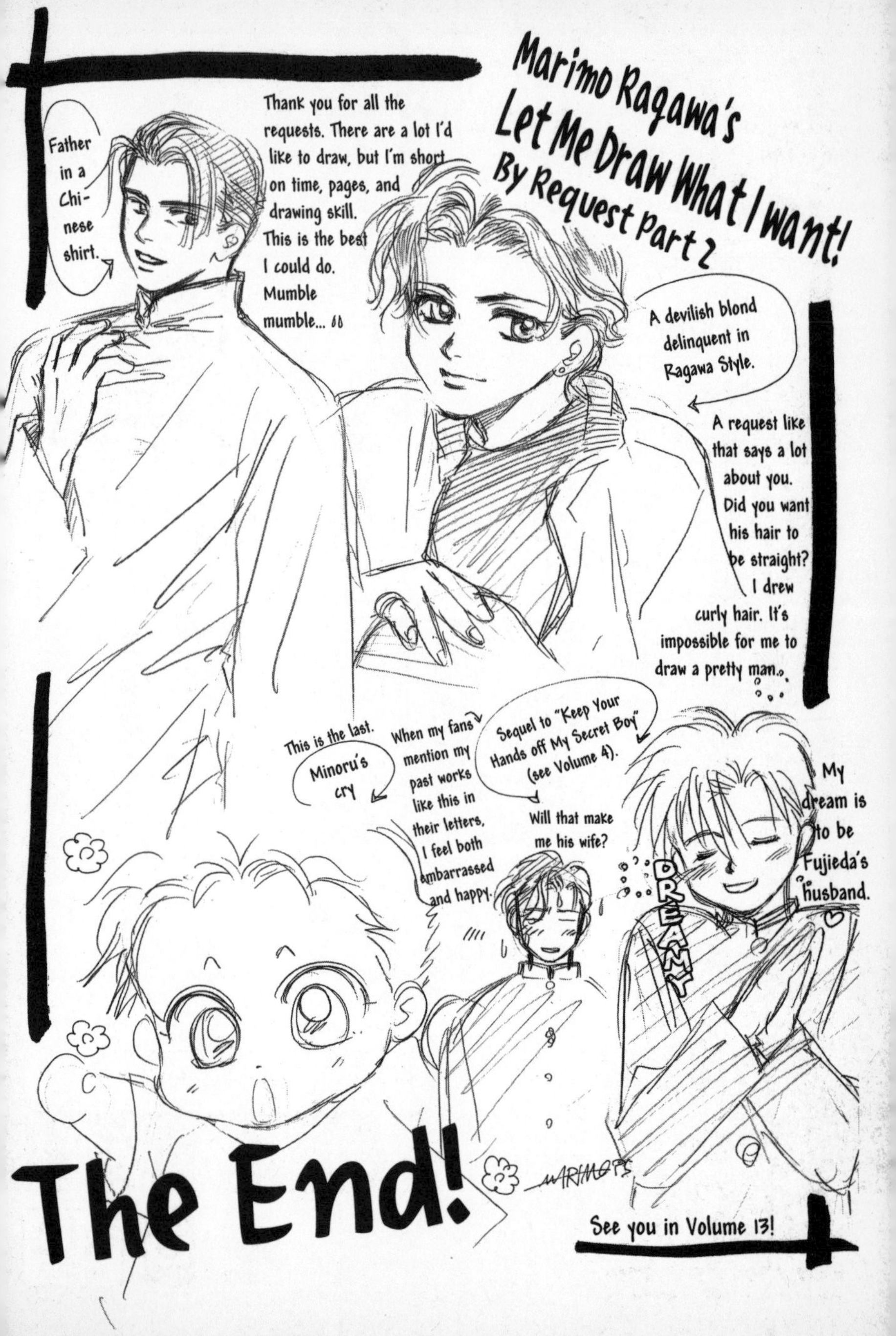

Marimo Ragawa's
Let Me Draw What I want!
By Request part 2
A devilish blond delinquent in Ragawa Style.
A request like that says a lot about you. Did you want his hair to be straight? I drew curly hair. It's impossible for me to draw a pretty man.
Thank you for all the requests. There are a lot I'd like to draw, but I'm short on time, pages, and drawing skill. This is the best I could do. Mumble mumble...
Father in a Chi-nese shirt.
My dream is to be Fujieda's husband.
DREAMY
Will that make me his wife?
Sequel to "Keep Your Hands off My Secret Boy" (see Volume 4).
When my fans mention my past works like this in their letters, I feel both embarrassed and happy.
This is the last.
Minoru's cry
The End!
MARIMO
See you in Volume 13!

Tell us what you think about Shojo Beat Manga!

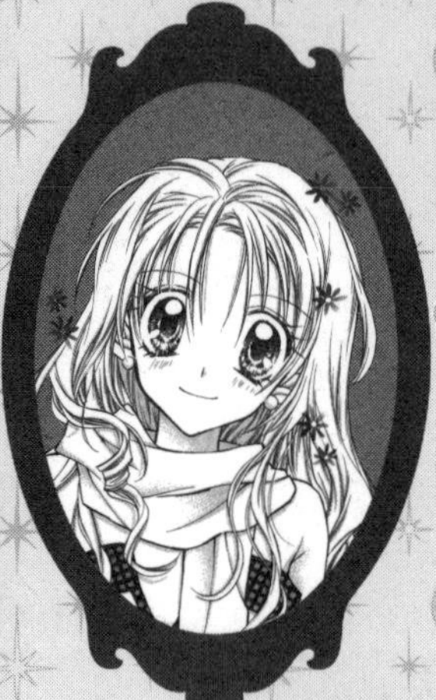

Our survey is now available online. Go to:

shojobeat.com/mangasurvey

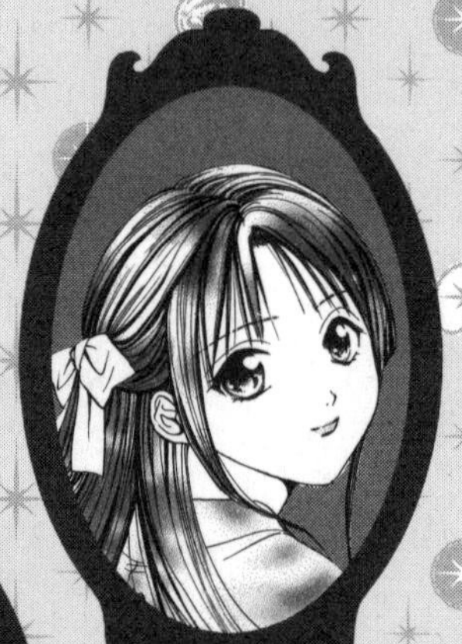

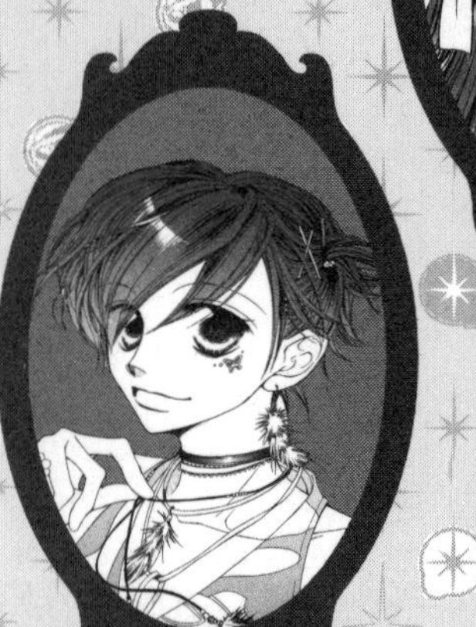

Help us make our product offerings better!

THE REAL DRAMA BEGINS IN...

Shojo Beat

MANGA from the HEART

viz media